Edible and
Useful Plants
of
TEXAS
and the
SOUTHWEST

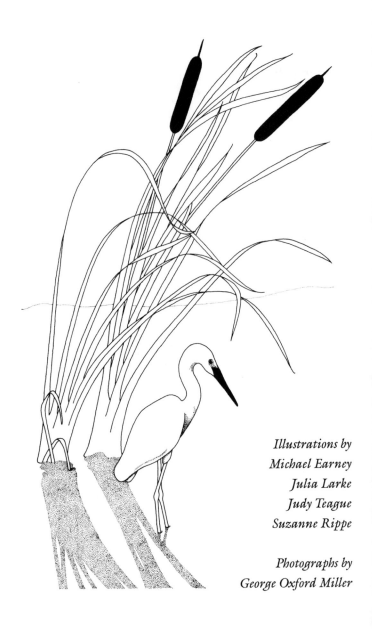

Illustrations by
Michael Earney
Julia Larke
Judy Teague
Suzanne Rippe

Photographs by
George Oxford Miller

Edible and Useful Plants of TEXAS and the SOUTHWEST

Including Recipes, Harmful Plants, Natural Dyes, and Textile Fibers

by Delena Tull

A Practical Guide

UNIVERSITY OF TEXAS PRESS, AUSTIN

LIBRARY OF CONGRESS CATALOGING-IN-PUBLICATION DATA

Tull, Delena, 1950–
   [Practical guide to edible & useful plants]
   Edible & useful plants of Texas & the southwest : a practical guide /
by Delena Tull ; illustrations by Michael Earney . . . [et al.] ; photography
by George Oxford Miller.
      p.   cm.
   Originally published: Practical guide to edible & useful plants. Austin,
Tex. : Texas Monthly Press, © 1987.
   Includes bibliographical references (p.   ) and index.
   ISBN 0-292-78164-4 (pbk.)
   1. Wild plants, Edible—Texas. 2. Plants, Useful—Texas. 3. Poi-
sonous plants—Texas. 4. Cookery (Wild foods) I. Title.
QK98.5.U6T85   1999
581.6′3′09764—dc21   98-41330

This is the Day wherein
the earth hath told out her tidings
and hath laid bare her treasures;
when the oceans have brought forth their pearls
and the divine Lote-Tree its fruit . . .

Bahá' u' lláh
Bahá' í Sacred Writings

Contents

viii

2. TEAS AND SPICES   155

Teas   156

List of Photographs

List of
Illustrations

Preface
To the Paperback Edition

A lot of changes have occurred in my life since I first wrote *Edible and Useful Plants of Texas and the Southwest.*

One significant change is that I am living in Alaska, the only state claiming to be bigger and better than Texas. Don't worry, folks, it may be bigger, but Alaska will never compete with Texas and Texans for the warmth of the people. People in Alaska tend to get a bit crabby by the end of the long, dark winter. However, while I sorely miss Texas' beautiful array of wildflowers in the spring, I must admit that I do not miss Texas summers!

Life in Alaska is fascinating and challenging. My best friend in Texas warned me not to go. "You'll get cold," she said. But north I went, armed with the Swiss army knife and the flashlight my brother Jack told me to always carry (so I can dig out of avalanches, he said).

In my recent trips back to Texas, I have delighted in going to classrooms to answer the questions of children and adults about Alaska: Yes, we have grizzly bears. No, we don't live in igloos. Yes, the dark winters are difficult to adjust to, but we do have daylight hours in my area in winter. And, yes, it does get cold, but it was colder in my mother's hometown in Michigan last winter than in southwest Alaska. Beyond the spectacular landscape, one of the most fascinating aspects of my life in Alaska has been discovering that many people here still rely on native plants for food.

Alaska is home to an astoundingly diverse population. Twenty different languages are indigenous to Alaska. I live in Dillingham, Alaska, about 350 air miles southwest of Anchorage. Dillingham, with 2,000 people, is the largest town in this region of the state. About twenty smaller villages surround us, and their inhabitants consider Dillingham a major metropolitan area. The villages to the west of Dillingham are almost exclusively populated by Yup'ik-speaking Alaska Natives. This is one of several groups of people that Anglo-Americans call Eskimos.

The Yup'ik people in my area of the state still rely heavily on subsistence harvest of native plants and animals. Imported foods are extremely expensive and far less nutritious than native foods. Wild game is much lower in fat than commercial meats. In fall and winter, moose and caribou are harvested. Virtually everyone spends virtually all of the summer catching and preserving fish (King salmon, red salmon, and silver salmon are the main catches). A wide variety of wild plants are harvested for medicinal and food purposes, including fiddleheads, wormwood, and plantains. In some coastal areas, a wide variety of kelps and other algae are harvested.

A number of women in southwest Alaska weave exquisite grass baskets. In late summer, the women harvest berries—blueberries, cranberries, salmonberries (similar to a raspberry), and crowberries. All these berries grow in the tundra, and all within two inches of the ground. The berry harvest is back-breaking work, but essential to life in bush Alaska. The berries and greens that are harvested and preserved are an essential source of vitamins A and C, among other nutrients.

While I miss the Texas bluebonnet trail in spring, several species of lupines grow in Alaska, and the one I see in my yard is blue. The other wildflower that is most common in this area is called fireweed. I have made a delicious pink jelly from its flowers. But nothing can match the diverse array of wildflowers that bloom throughout Texas in the spring, summer, fall, and even in winter. I love the snow in Alaska, but when March and April come around, I always long for the brightly colored roadsides of Texas.

Acknowledgments

Writing a book on uses of wild plants necessitates much personal investigation. I spent a summer with dozens of dye pots brewing on my back porch. I spent the fall, winter, spring, and summer searching the back alleys, woodlots, and fields of Texas for edible plants. But compiling the information for this book involved much more than my own simple experiments. I also relied on the experiments of dozens, if not hundreds, of other individuals. Only through countless hours of library research was I able to discover which plants I could safely sample, which plants have caused poisoning, and which plants have value in industry. And so, in acknowledging those who assisted in this book, I must first thank the many who conducted their own investigations and then saw fit to publish their findings. I have tried to give each one of them credit by listing bibliographical information throughout the book.

A few of these authors deserve a more personal acknowledgment. I would like to offer my deepest gratitude to two men whom I will never be able to thank in person: Euell Gibbons, whose sense of adventure and sense of humor have inspired me since I first read one of his books and listened to him lecture one spring at Michigan State University, and Carroll Abbott, another man with an inimitable sense of humor, who gave his all to make Texans aware of our great natural heritage, our native plants.

I also wish to acknowledge the generous assistance of my friends in the Weavers and Spinners Society of Austin, particularly Dona Price, Pat Crow, and Dorothy Matheson, whose own results with native dyes are incorporated into this book. Elizabeth Coulter's dye research also furnished much useful information. And I thank Sue Smith for teaching me how to weave a basket and for her invaluable knowledge on native fibers.

I thank Lynn Marshall and Scooter Cheatham for so generously sharing their dye results and knowledge about edible plants. Along with Dr. Marshall Johnston, Scooter has been laboring for more than a decade on an upcoming monumental work on useful Texas plants. The botanical reference *Manual of the Vascular Plants of Texas,* by Drs. Correll and Johnston, has not left my side for the past two years. I relied heavily on that text for details of species descriptions.

I thank Michael Ellis of the Galveston Poison Control Center for reviewing the sections on poisonous plants. And I thank my longtime friends Eve and John Williams—John, for introducing me to Texas' native plants and reviewing my manuscript, and Eve, for giving me my first list of Texas dye plants.

Much thanks to my former husband, George Oxford Miller, for the many hours he spent taking the photographs that grace this book. And I can never thank him enough for helping me get through the three years that it took to write it.

Four illustrators created the fine drawings for the book. I thank them greatly for their labors of love. Michael Earney, Julia Larke, and Judy Teague drew the illustrations found throughout the book. My childhood friend, Suzanne Rippe, created the beautiful cattails drawing for the frontispiece.

And finally, I thank my mother, whose curiosity about wildflowers and all things natural sparked my own, and whose arts, crafts, and writing filled my childhood.

Introduction
What's in This Book

This book covers a wide range of topics related to the uses of Texas plants, both wild and ornamental. The term "wild" of course refers to plants native to Texas. But the term also includes naturalized plants, those plants that were brought to the United States from other countries and other continents and that flourish so well in our environment that they now grow "like weeds." These nonnative plants may have been introduced to our country as ornamentals, as agricultural crops, or by accident.

The information on edible and poisonous wild plants includes plant characteristics (description, habitat, and range in Texas) to assist you in identifying the plants. These short descriptions can be supplemented by referring to other books on Texas plants. Botanists at local colleges often are more than willing to help identify plants, and the Native Plant Society of Texas (P.O. Box 891, Georgetown, Texas, 78627) holds regional meetings and field trips that will help you in learning more about your local flora.

The following books all provide excellent illustrated references to Texas plants: Delena Tull and George Oxford Miller's *A Field Guide to Wildflowers, Trees and Shrubs of Texas*, Del Weniger's *Cacti of Texas and Neighboring States*, and Robert Vines' *Trees, Shrubs, and Woody Vines of the Southwest*. See Susan and Van Metzler's *Texas Mushrooms* for excellent photographs and detailed information on edible fungi, including recipes. Donovan Correll and Marshall Johnston's *Manual of the Vascular Plants of Texas*, the bible for plant identification, is useful only to those with a background in botany.

The first two chapters of this book cover edible plants and teas and spices, with recipes and instructions for their preparation. The next chapter, on edible and poisonous berries and other fleshy fruits, groups the fruits by color. Jelly and jam recipes are scattered throughout the section on edible fruits.

In addition to giving details on toxic wild plants, the chapter on poisonous and harmful plants provides information on toxic ornamentals as well as plants in our vegetable gardens and on our spice racks that can cause us harm. A section on dermatitis, with special reference to poison ivy, and a section on hay fever plants also are included in the chapter.

The chapter on plant dyes provides detailed instructions on dyeing wool and other fibers. A list at the end of that chapter includes more than 120 dye plants with recipes for their use. The chapter on fibers explains how to prepare plant materials for use in weaving baskets or textiles, how

2

to use natural dyes on plant fibers, and how to make paper. Plants with industrial value are reviewed in the final chapter.

A glossary at the back of the book furnishes definitions of the botanical terms used in the plant descriptions. Other terms can be found in a standard dictionary. Bibliographical references, noted throughout the text, are compiled in the back of the book. A single index includes both scientific and common plant names. Some allegedly edible plants can cause poisoning, so if you are interested in using a plant, be sure to check all pages listed in the index, to find out its potentially harmful qualities.

Vegetation Regions in the State

Variations in climate, elevation, geology, and soil across the state enable a remarkable diversity of plant life to grow in Texas. The state has a little bit of everything, from a subtropical climate in far South Texas to frequent winter snows in the Panhandle, from 60 inches of rain per year in the Big Thicket to less than 8 inches in the Chihuahuan Desert, from sea level along the Gulf Coast to altitudes of more than 8700 feet in the mountains. Because of the wide range of physical conditions, most plants are restricted to specific areas of the state. I have relied on a few general terms to define the regions that each plant inhabits. For a more detailed description of the various vegetational regions of the state, refer either to Ajilvsgi's or Correll and Johnston's books (listed above).

Briefly, regional terms I have chosen to rely on are the following:

East Texas—A very broad term, basically designating everything east of Austin. This flat to hilly region has a relatively high annual rainfall (30–60 inches). Southeast Texas refers to the Big Thicket, an area of dense pine and hardwood forests and swamps. The Coast includes the flat, humid area from Beaumont to Houston to Brownsville and slightly inland.

South Texas—Another broad term, referring to everything roughly south of San Antonio. Flat to hilly, the area not adjacent to the Coast experiences periodic drought. The western half may have as little as 16 inches annual rainfall, with close to 30 inches in the east. Far South Texas consists of the area around Brownsville. Known as the Rio Grande Valley, this zone has a subtropical climate and rarely experiences freezing temperatures. The Rio Grande, from Brownsville to El Paso, flows through some of the driest areas of Texas and provides moisture to the alluvial bottomland flanking it, yielding some distinctive vegetation.

North Central Texas—The region centered around Dallas, with extreme summer and winter temperatures, rolling hills, and moderate annual rainfall (25–40 inches).

Edwards Plateau—A specific geographical region, 1000 to 3000 feet in elevation, extending west of Austin roughly to the Pecos River, and from Del Rio north about to Abilene. Also known as the Hill Country, the area has moderate annual rainfall (30 inches) in the east and is semiarid (15 inches) in the west. Summer temperatures can be extreme, with frequent drought, but winters are generally mild.

Panhandle—An area including the High Plains and the Rolling Plains, roughly north of San Angelo and west of Wichita Falls. Encompassing a high (3000–4500 feet), flat plateau in the west and hilly to rough terrain (800–3000 feet) in the east, the Panhandle has extreme summer and winter temperatures and experiences frequent drought (15–21 inches annual rainfall).

Trans-Pecos—Roughly everything west of the Pecos River, ranging from mountains as high as 8700 feet to the Chihuahuan Desert, with an elevation above 2000 feet. The area experiences extreme summers and can have mild or very cold winters. Annual rainfall averages 8 to 12 inches in the desert and 16 inches in the mountains.

Why Use Botanical Terminology?

When you first learn to recognize wild plants, you probably will rely mainly on common names. However, if you move to a different area of the state or the country, you may find that people in that area use a different name for the same plant. Even in the same region a single plant may have several common names. In addition, two different plants may share the same name. For example, "pigweed" may refer to a member of either the genus *Amaranthus* or the genus *Chenopodium*. Because of the confusion that often arises from the use of common names, learning the scientific name of a plant becomes more and more important as you become more familiar with wild plants. Nonetheless, common names are also useful handles for plants. Ideally, you should become familiar with both the common and scientific names of the plants you know. In this book I have provided the common names that appear to be the most widespread. I have attempted to include both an English and a Spanish common name for the plants.

International Congresses decide on the rules that determine validity of scientific names, and those names are recognized worldwide. Unfortunately for the amateur botanist, scientific names occasionally change, as new data on plant identity are provided through field research. Some of the scientific names used in this book differ from those found in previous publications because of name changes that have occurred in recent years. For example, the agave family, Agavaceae, is a newly created family and consists of several plants that formerly were located in the lily and amaryllis families. Scientific names are based on a Latin word, or as in the case of plants named after botanists, the non-Latin word is given a Latin ending.

Botanists classify plants into groups based on genetic relationships and structural similarities, predominantly of flower and fruit. Other physical characteristics, such as those of root and leaf, also are noted but are not as reliable. The concept of species is complex, but generally a species can be defined as a more or less genetically isolated population of plants that share the same basic characteristics. By the way, "species" is used as both a singular and a plural noun. Species considered genetically and structurally similar are classified in the same genus (plural: genera). Groups of genera with similar characteristics are classified in the same family. Botanists also use larger classification groups, but only species, genera, and families are relevant to this book.

The scientific name of each plant consists of two parts, the generic name, which is first, and the specific epithet, the second part of the name. For example, the scientific name of the potato is *Solanum tuberosum*. The potato belongs to the nightshade family, Solanaceae. More than a thousand different species are included in the genus *Solanum*, but the specific epithet "tuberosum" immediately distinguishes the potato from its many cousins. However, there may be plants in another genus with the specific epithet "tuberosum." The generic name "Solanum" is necessary to distinguish this "tuberosum" from all others in the world (*Phlox drummondii* and *Hedeoma drummondii* provide an example of two unrelated plants with the same specific epithet).

A species may be subdivided into subspecies (abbreviated "subsp.") and varieties (abbreviated "var.") when botanists discover distinctive local variations. Many generic names and specific epithets have as their root the name of a botanist, such as Drummond, Engelmann, and Maximilian. Often, the botanist named is the one who first discovered the species. In some cases the classifying botanist names a plant in honor of another botanist.

With these basic tips in hand, you are ready to begin your adventure into the world of wild plants.

Plants as Medicine: A Commentary

For thousands of years the science of botany has been closely aligned with the study of the healing properties of plants. In fact, the botanist and the healer often were one and the same. The importance of being able to recognize the healing herbs formed the basis for the earliest systems of plant classification. Often plant relationships were based on the

Yarrow—*Achillea millefolium*

active principles of plants, as demonstrated by their therapeutic actions.

In spite of this long history of association, botany and medicine today are viewed as quite distinct professions. In fact, most individuals would be surprised to learn that many of the pills they take are formed from plant extracts, use plants as the basis of synthesis, or are manufactured from synthetic imitations of plant constituents. In a country in which synthetic chemicals seem to have taken over the pharmaceutical industry, roughly 35 percent of the prescriptions written in the United States still include a plant product as at least one of the major ingredients.

And yet the superstition that often surrounds the use of folk remedies has caused a certain distrust and disdain on the part of the medical community toward the idea of using plants in medicine. Such early medical practices as the doctrine of signatures (the theory that each medicinal plant resembled in appearance the bodily organ it was meant to heal) hindered medical progress for centuries. The modern medical profession, in attempts to disassociate itself from superstition and charlatanism, has labeled folk medicine too frequently as quackery and has tried to discredit herbal remedies as useless and even harmful. It is true that a number of herbs are ineffectual in curing the diseases for which such claims have been made (for example, people the world over have used innumerable species of plants in vain attempts to treat syphilis). In addition, many herbal remedies can cause poisoning if misused. But the attempt to discredit the value of herbal medicine has in its turn held back valuable medical knowledge. In spite of the rituals and myths that often shroud traditional herbal medicine, our modern medicinal knowledge emerged from that source and has the potential to gain much more information from herbal medical practice (Swain 1972; Kreig 1964).

Without careful documentation of the effects plants have had on the people who have used them, it is difficult to separate the potentially valuable plant medicines from the bunk. Many medicinal plants, however, have been in common usage for centuries, and their effects are well known. The United States Pharmacopeial Convention has been selecting, naming, and standardizing drugs since 1820. Early editions of the convention publication, *The United States Pharmacopeia,* list many plants that have long been recognized healers.

If you look in your own bathroom cabinet, you will probably find some herbal medicines that you didn't know were there. Witch hazel is a multipurpose remedy made from the distilled extract of the twigs of a small tree called *Hamamelis virginiana,* which grows in East and Central Texas. Among other effects, its astringency makes it useful as a skin freshener and as an external treatment for minor cuts, bruises, burns, and insect bites. You may find a cough syrup that contains slippery elm. The inner bark of *Ulmus rubra,* a large East Texas elm tree, is the source of this long-valued herbal remedy.

Today, for the first time in history, we have the tools for distinguishing myth from fact. Indeed, modern biochemical techniques have brought about a revolution in our understanding of the chemical constituents in plants and their values in medicine. Besides the drugs obtained from microorganisms, such as penicillin and other antibiotics, researchers are finding that the flowering plants have an enormous potential for providing us with new medicines. In the past few decades, as a result of some major discoveries of plant-derived drugs (particularly the discovery of reserpine, a treatment for hypertension and mental illness, from the herb *Rauwolfia*), universities and medical research centers around the world have taken a renewed interest in investigation of plants. To mention but one example, the Cancer Chemotherapy National Service Center already has examined more than 26,000 chemical constituents from more than 6500 plant species.

Through biochemical analysis, researchers have discovered thousands of plant alkaloids that we never knew existed before this century. In the 1940s, scientists were aware of only 1000 alkaloids, but by 1969, 3350 new ones had been isolated. In addition, many glycosides, saponins, flavonoids, and more than 2000 other organic plant substances are now known. Any or all of these may have value in medicine. Many chemicals from plants will never be put into commercial use because their synthetic equivalents can be more easily derived in the laboratory. But a number of useful chemicals are more readily and cheaply extracted from Mother Nature's laboratory.

For example, the leaves of the foxglove, *Digitalis,* contain cardiac glycosides, digoxin, and digitoxin among others, highly toxic substances that have become invaluable aids in the treatment of heart disease. Because a therapeutic dose may be as high as 70 percent of a toxic dose, drug manufacturers and doctors must take great care in preparing and using the drugs. Drugs derived from the periwinkle, *Vinca rosea,* have become important in the treatment of childhood leukemia and Hodgkin's disease (Lewis and Elvin-Lewis 1977). And recent studies have shown that cortisone and some sex hormones, already synthesized from some plants, are available in a number of other plants, such as in the toxic saponins found in *Agave lecheguilla.*

In spite of the work that already has been done, we have just touched the surface of this vast body of knowledge. Only a small percentage of the world's plants have been analyzed so far. We have much more to learn. And the storehouse of material for study is exceedingly large. A single plant may contain several dozen compounds, each capable of producing a different effect on the human body. The opium poppy, *Papaver somniferum,* for example, contains at least 22 alkaloids (Kingsbury 1964; LeStrange 1977). Only through extensive research can we discover exactly which compounds or combination of compounds are responsible for producing the healing effects observed in folk medicine and in what new ways we can employ them.

A few medicinals have been included in the chapter on teas and spices, such as recipes for preparing soothing remedies for sore throats and coughs from horehound, *Marrubium vulgare,* and mullein, *Verbascum thapsus* (both illustrated). Refer to books by Euell Gibbons, especially *Stalking the Healthful Herbs,* for details of some of the many uses of these valuable herbs. Yarrow, *Achillea millefolium* (illustrated), and its relatives have been used medicinally throughout the world for thousands of years. During the Trojan War, about 1200 B.C., Achilles is said to have applied bruised yarrow leaves to the wounds of his soldiers to stop bleeding. Yarrow was used in a similar manner to treat battle wounds in the Civil War. Native Americans have used the plant to treat a variety of complaints, including fever, pain, burns, earache, indigestion, toothache, and sore throat. Yarrow gained a listing in *The United States Pharmacopeia* from 1836 to 1882 as a stimulant and an agent to promote menstrual flow. Chemical analysis of yarrow has uncovered more than 120 compounds! It's not surprising that the plant should have been employed in such a wide range of uses. While it may seem contradictory that the same plant should be used both to stop bleeding and to cause it, that anomaly was readily explained once the chemical constituents were known. The plant contains achilleine, an alkaloid that has been found to be a hemostatic agent, which stops the flow of blood. But yarrow also contains coumarin, which promotes blood flow and can cause hemorrhage. Yarrow demonstrates quite graphically the variety of pharmaceuticals that can be extracted from a single species. And it serves as a warning of the potential hazards of misuse of herbal remedies (Chandler, Hooper, and Harvey 1982).

A thorough review of the medicinal uses of wild Texas plants is beyond the scope of this book. I have not attempted to include extensive information on herbal medicines for several reasons. First, a full documentation of the uses of plants in the traditional medicine of native Americans and early American pioneers would easily fill a large volume of text. Practically every edible and poisonous plant mentioned here has been used by someone somewhere as a medicinal, along with many other native plants. Second, many plant uses remain in the realm of hearsay, with few, if any, valid records of how the plants actually affect the body. Third, *most* of the plants used as medicines can have harmful effects if served up in the wrong dosages. Just as with the druggists' pharmaceuticals, herbal medicines must be treated with great caution.

In the chapters on poisonous plants, you will find scattered, brief references to the past and present uses of certain plants in medicine. It seems one of the wonderful ironies of nature that the same alkaloids, glycosides, saponins, and other plant chemicals that can cause human deaths can also save lives. But plants cannot be regulated like manufactured drugs. They come with no warning labels. They do not contain a carefully measured dose of medicine per teaspoon of root, leaf, or flower. Indeed, one of the difficulties in using plant remedies is the unpredictable nature of the chemical composition. In a plant, the concentrations of compounds may differ considerably with variations in climate, soil, stage of growth, amount of water, and method of collecting and preserving the plant. A plant growing in the hot, dry soils of West Texas cannot be expected to contain the same levels of alkaloids as the same species growing in the moist, rich soils of the east. In addition, different plant parts have different chemical compositions.

Besides the alkaloids and toxic substances found in plants, a number of edible plants have medicinal value owing to their vitamin, mineral, or protein content. For example, long before we knew what a vitamin was, chickweed was used to prevent and treat scurvy, a disease caused by vitamin C deficiency. You will find occasional brief notes on these nutritive healers in the chapter on edible plants.

Though folk medicine lacks a scientific basis of evaluation, it can lead us to those plants with the greatest potential for use in modern pharmaceuticals. The Chinese may well be the world leaders in restoring and validating herbal medicine. More than five thousand medicinal plants have been used in China's past, with over a thousand of them remaining in common usage after millennia. In recent times the Chinese have increasingly emphasized the study of plant chemistry. Chinese scientists are in the process of isolating many new compounds from plants and evaluating their effects (National Academy of Sciences 1975).

Folk medicine is plagued with several limitations, notably the superstitions of its practitioners, the lack of careful documentation and analysis of the short-term and long-term effects of plant remedies, and the unpredictable nature of plant chemistry. And yet, herbal remedies still form the basis of medicine in the developing nations. The World Health Organization has concluded that only by using traditional herbal medicine can we meet the minimum health needs of the developing nations by the year 2000 (Croom 1983). Clearly, we cannot ignore the influence that folk medicine still has on a major portion of the world. So perhaps rather than disclaim its validity, we can explore ways of overcoming the limitations of folk practices and encourage the documentation that is so important for guiding us to more and better uses of plants in medicine.

Mushrooms: To Eat or Not to Eat

Mushroom hunting has become a popular sport in recent decades among a growing group of people. Edible wild mushrooms provide an astounding variety of delicious foods. Along with the delightful flavors of wild mushrooms, the thrill of the hunt—exploring forests, fields, and back yards—adds much to the excitement of eating wild fungi. But because of the fear of confusing edible species with poisonous ones, wild mushrooms remain a taste sensation enjoyed by few.

More than five thousand species of mushrooms grow in the United States. Along with many edible species, about a hundred species are known to contain toxic substances. The edible or toxic qualities of many more have never been documented. "Toadstool" is a folk term used to refer to mushrooms that should not be eaten. But as with the flowering plants, no generalities can assist you in distinguishing toxic from edible mushrooms. In fact, some edible mushrooms can cause poisoning if you pick them at the wrong stage or eat the wrong part, while some so-called toadstools can be eaten if properly cooked. So much for folk terminology.

Several good field guides are available to assist you in learning to identify mushrooms. I have listed some at the end of this section. Though an essential resource, a field guide alone cannot ensure safe foraging, however. No book can substitute for time spent in the field with someone who has years of experience in identifying and eating wild mushrooms. A number of clubs for mushroom enthusiasts now exist around the country. In Texas, look up the Texas Mycological Society (7445 Dillon Street, Houston, Texas 77061). The society conducts field trips and has monthly meetings, a newsletter, and a list of the species of mushrooms found in Texas. You can also join the North American Mycological Association through the Texas group. Participation in these organizations puts you in contact with local and national experts on mushroom identification and use.

Before you take off for the woods or the cow pasture in search of wild fungi, heed the following warnings. About one hundred cases of mushroom poisoning are officially reported each year in the United States, and probably many cases go unreported. While deaths rarely occur in the United States from eating any wild plants, more than 50 percent of those deaths in recent decades were caused by mushrooms. In 1984 a Houston teenager died after eating a wild mushroom (Michael Ellis, letter to the author, August 1986).

Fortunately for the mushroom aficionado, deaths in healthy adults are attributed to only a few species. Thus, the first goal of the mushroom hunter should be to learn the identity of those species. Members of the following genera contain the most highly toxic fungi in the U.S.: *Amanita, Galerina, Gyromitra, Clitocybe, Omphalotus,* and *Inocybe.* Members of the genus *Amanita*—which includes death cup (*Amanita phalloides*) and fly agaric (*Amanita muscaria,* illustrated)—the false morel (*Gyromitra esculenta*), and some members of the genus *Galerina* are responsible for the highest numbers of mushroom fatalities. The chance of death from

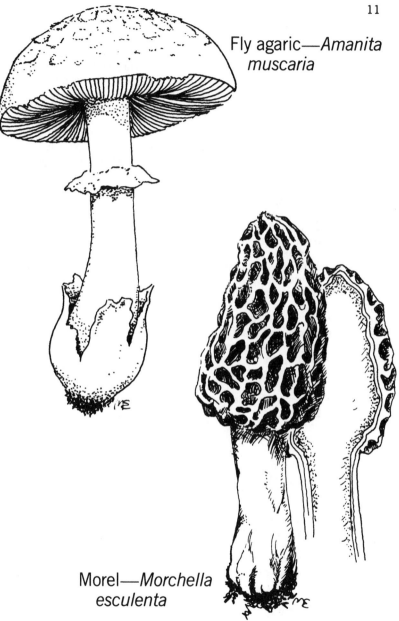

Fly agaric—*Amanita muscaria*

Morel—*Morchella esculenta*

ingestion of members of the genera *Amanita* and *Galerina* is 50 to 90 percent. Though some members of the genus *Cortinarius* are considered edible, in rare instances they have caused permanent kidney failure. Children and elderly people in poor health are more likely to become ill from eating toxic mushrooms than are healthy adults. The mortality rate among children and the elderly also is much higher (DiPalma 1981; Keeler, Van Kampen, and James 1978; Kinghorn 1979).

While the above groups of mushrooms have caused extreme illness and death, a number of others can cause less severe poisoning. Individuals react in different ways to edible mushrooms. What one person considers a delicacy may make another very ill. Allergic reactions to certain species are common. Inky cap (*Coprinus atramentarius*), an allegedly edible mushroom that resembles the delicious shaggy mane (*Coprinus comatus*), can be toxic if alcohol is consumed at the same meal or even four or five days later (DiPalma 1981; Kinghorn 1979). People seek out the psilocybin mushrooms for their hallucinogenic effects, but a number of those mushrooms can also cause mild to severe poisoning. In addition, some nontoxic mushrooms are considered inedible, so never experiment with unknown mushrooms.

Most fatal mushroom poisonings occur when foragers mistake an *Amanita* for an *Agaricus*. The genus *Agaricus* contains a number of edible species, including the domestic mushrooms found in groceries. The gills and shredded collar of members of the genus *Agaricus* make it impossible to distinguish these succulent edibles from the deadly members of *Amanita* without looking at the color of the spores.

Even edible mushrooms that are more easily recognized, such as the puffballs (*Calvatia gigantea, Bovista pila,* and others), morels (*Morchella,* illustrated), and shaggy mane have inedible or poisonous look-alikes. To ensure safe foraging, the mushroom hunter must become familiar with the characteristics that distinguish each edible fungus from mushrooms that it may resemble.

For example, always slice puffballs in half and examine them for any signs of gills, which indicate that the plant is not a puffball at all but may be the button stage of one of the *Amanita* species. In addition, throw out any puffballs with pinholes (indicating worms) or a yellow tinge on the interior, signs that the mushroom is past its prime.

One clue for distinguishing the true morels from the deadly poisonous *Gyromitra esculenta* is that true morels have hollow interiors while the interior of this false morel is chambered. But other false morels also exist (for example, *Verpa bohemica*), so familiarize yourself with all of the identifying characteristics of the true morels before sampling (Rodriguez 1985).

If you develop an interest in eating wild mushrooms, start by learning to identify just one or two of the edible species. And remember, even edible mushrooms can cause digestive distress or more severe poisoning if picked at the wrong stage or improperly prepared. Too often a field guide tells you little more than that the mushroom is edible. But you need further information before you bite into the fungus. You must find out what parts of the mushroom you can eat. You need to know whether you must cook the mushrooms before eating them. Some "edible" mushrooms are actually toxic when raw. Also you need to learn to recognize an overripe mushroom, another possible source of toxicity or digestive discomfort. You should eat or preserve most wild mushrooms the same day you pick them. Some species, such as the shaggy mane and inky cap, deliquesce; that is, they become a slimy mass within a day of being collected. Most mushrooms can be preserved by drying and freezing. Refer to the resources listed below for information on identifying and using wild mushrooms.

Recommended Reading

Lincoff, Gary H., and D. H. Mitchell, M.D. 1977. *Toxic and Hallucinogenic Mushroom Poisoning: A Handbook for Physicians and Mushroom Hunters.* New York: Van Nostrant Reinhold Co. (Excellent information for physicians. Fairly technical for the layperson, but comprehensive.)

Metzler, Susan and Van Metzler. 1992. *Texas Mushrooms: A Field Guide.* Austin: University of Texas Press. (Excellent photographs; details on edible and poisonous fungi; also includes recipes.)

Miller, Orson K., Jr. 1978. *Mushrooms of North America.* New York: E. P. Dutton. (Provides valuable information on toxic mushrooms and how to prepare edible mushrooms.)

Rice, Miriam C., and Dorothy Beebee. 1980. *Mushrooms for Color.* Eureka, Calif.: Mad River Press. (This interesting and unusual book tells you how to use mushrooms to dye wool beautiful colors.)

PERIODICAL

Mushrooms: The Journal of Wild Mushrooming. (Box 3156 University Station, Moscow, Idaho 83843.)

Dandelion—*Taraxacum officinale*

1 Edible and Useful Wild Plants

Cautions and Notes on Using Wild Edibles

Why Bother With Wild Foods?

When you come right down to it, living off wild edibles involves a lot of hard work. Finding, collecting, and preparing wild plants consumes a great deal of time and often results in a meager amount of food for the table. The task gives one a greater appreciation for the daily toil of early peoples who relied on wild plants for much of their food. Once you've tried a few of these wild delectables, you may find that the satisfaction of creating a meal from wild foods is well worth the effort. Besides, who knows when you might get stranded in the Chihuahuan Desert or lost in the Big Thicket and need to know what plants to rely on for food? (Do you have your pocketknife, matches, and first aid kit?)

Cultivated vegetables often have larger leaves, fruits, and tubers, but the flavor of wild plants often makes up for what they lack in size. Experimenting with wild edibles adds a variety of good-tasting foods to your diet. And many wild plants are highly nutritious. Euell Gibbons, author of *Stalking the Healthful Herbs,* had the nutritional value of a number of plants analyzed. The results were astounding. For example, half a cup of violet leaves (*Viola papilionacea*) supplies 8200 international units of vitamin A, well above the minimum daily requirement and equivalent to the amount found in carrots. Violet leaves supply as much vitamin C as four oranges, about 210 milligrams. Stinging nettle (*Urtica dioica*) leaves also are rich in vitamins and contain 42 percent protein by dry weight, an uncommon level of protein for a leafy vegetable. It seems unlikely that Americans will replace their hamburgers with nettle leaves anytime soon, but these data certainly give us "food" for thought.

The *American Heritage Dictionary* defines "edible" as "capable of being eaten; nonpoisonous." To qualify as "capable of being eaten," however, a food must be more than simply nonpoisonous. It must be both palatable and digestible. Surprisingly, the definition of "edible" does not include the term "nutritious." Some would say that many foods consumed by Americans are not nutritious. Nonetheless, those foods are edible.

While many wild plants are nonpoisonous, some are far too bitter to eat, and some are too woody or fibrous to digest. Of those wild plants that truly are edible, however, many provide more nutrition than the foods we normally eat, even the foods that we consider "good for us." In vitamins, minerals, and protein, wild foods can match and even surpass the nutritional content of our common foods. Amaranth grain furnishes a better source of protein than corn, rice, or wheat. Dandelion greens are more nutritious than spinach. Have we sacrificed nutrition and flavor to a larger strawberry and a bigger ear of corn? The emphasis on producing larger, more attractive fruits and vegetables for the market seems to have taken precedence over valuable nutritional qualities.

Native Plants for Agriculture

Of the more than 500,000 plant species in the world, only about 1000 are commonly used for human food, though many more are edible. Anthropological studies in the Sonoran Desert of Arizona revealed that of the 2500 species of flowering plants in the area, nearly 450 were utilized as foods by the local native American tribes. In the United States today, we use only 30 plant species for 95 percent of our vegetables, fruits, and grains.

It is no longer practicable or even desirable that Americans harvest all their meals from the wild. But by putting the more desirable wild plants into cultivation, we have the potential to expand the variety of foods vastly and to improve the nutritional quality of our diet. An abundance of useful plants grow in the Chihuahuan Desert of West Texas, for instance. Those suitable for cultivation would be better adapted to drought and extremes of heat and cold than most of the plants we currently grow for food in Texas.

By testing wild plants from all over the world for parameters such as resistance to disease, drought, and temperature extremes, we can open the door to innumerable alternatives to the delicate species that we have become so dependent upon for our daily bread. Some varieties of amaranth are highly resistant to drought and disease, making them desirable for use in drought-prone areas of the world. Further studies of the way indigenous peoples use wild plants can provide us with valuable information on plants for the agriculture of the future.

Incorporating native plants into the agricultural structure has the potential for providing more-nutritious foods to poverty-stricken areas of the world. Native species are better adapted to local climate and soil conditions than the imported species on which we lavish water, pesticides, and soil conditioners. In some cases, such as in developing African nations, a number of native plants already are a part of the indigenous diet, thus making their use in agriculture much more readily acceptable to the local people.

Disastrous events in our history point out the danger of becoming over-dependent on a limited variety of food crops. For example, in 1845, a fungus destroyed the potato crop in Europe. For the poverty-stricken people of Ireland, that meant the loss of their number-one food staple. More than one million people died of hunger in that country, and another million emigrated, mostly to the United States. In spite of such catastrophes, a number of countries, particularly in the developing world, count on one or a few crops to buoy up their entire economy. Seven crops—wheat, rice, maize (corn), barley, soybeans, common beans, and potatoes—are the major sources of nutrition for the majority of the world's people.

The famines that have occurred recently in northern Africa should force us to reevaluate both our outdated methods of crop growing, which have resulted in disastrous losses of topsoil on a worldwide scale, and our choices of crops. We have already put ourselves in a dangerous position. By increasing the diversity of crops and using crops better adapted to the local environment, we may avert future agricultural tragedies such as the famine caused by the potato blight.

The same concern about overreliance on a limited number of food crops applies to plants valued in industry. During both world wars the United States was faced with critical shortages of imported raw materials, such as rubber and certain fibers. In several cases Americans were forced to rely on native wild plants to make up the deficit. For example, industries obtained rubber from guayule, a plant that grows in the Chihuahuan Desert of West Texas and Mexico, and the Navy used yucca fibers for paper and rope. When the wars ended, we went back to importing sources of these materials.

Today we rely even more heavily on imported materials such as rubber than before World War II. And many products manufactured from plants are now more cheaply synthesized from petroleum. Substitutes for fibers, rubber, medicinals, chemicals, fuel, and building materials come from oil. During the seventies, we got a taste of what can happen if our imported supplies of petroleum are curtailed. The rapid depletion of Texas' vast oil reserves, which currently supply a third of the oil used in the United States, is a reality that we cannot afford to ignore much longer.

Petroleum products became substitutes for plant products in just the past 40 years. Now is the time to start looking to plants for substitutes for products made from oil. A number of potential industrial uses of native plants, such as guayule, are reviewed in the chapter "Rubber, Wax, Oil, and Soap." Cultivation of native plants with industrial value has tremendous potential for stimulating local economies.

Harvesting plants from the wild served our ancestors well, but we no longer can depend on wild harvests to supply us with the vast quantity of food and industrial products required in our modern society. In a heavily populated world we have driven many plants to extinction, with many more on the way. Deforestation is a major problem in many developing nations that rely on firewood as their main fuel. If native plants are to play a major part in our industrial future, they must be put into widespread cultivation. Developing alternative crops for industry, building construction, and fuel may become a necessity rather than a choice in the not so distant future.

Grazing From the Wild: Tips and Precautions

While some wild plants are in danger of extinction, many others grow in abundance. Some people consider nonnative naturalized plants to be noxious weeds—I consider some of these our best wild foods, plentiful and free for the taking. You can safely harvest plants from the wild for your personal use as long as you keep in mind the following guidelines.

State, federal, and local laws protect wild plants on public lands so you'll need to restrict your harvest to privately owned property. Most of the plants included in the edible plants section grow commonly in Texas. Use plants that are uncommon, such as yuccas, agaves, and sotols, only if you have a large local population, and harvest them in a manner that minimizes damage to the population and the individual plant.

Collect only as much as you need. When gathering flowers and fruit, collect a small percentage of the total crop, leaving enough to produce a good crop next year. If gathering perennial herbs, clip the plant off above ground, leaving the roots intact for next year's growth. With many wild-flowers and herbs, you can collect seeds and grow your own crop at home. Digging up roots and tubers, of course, kills the whole plant, so harvest them sparingly unless the plants grow in abundance. With the permission of the landowner, you can pick and dig to your heart's content on urban and rural lots about to go under the bulldozer.

In the paragraphs below, I present a number of cautions to guide you in your experiments with wild plants. I include these warnings with the hope of encouraging a cautious approach to harvesting wild foods. But at the same time, I wholeheartedly encourge you to try the wild edibles included in this book. While not all of them will appeal to your senses, chances are high that you will discover some delightfully delicious new foods to enhance your menu.

MODERATION IS THE KEY

Before indulging in a large meal of wild foods, every prospective eater needs to keep in mind Ben Franklin's admonition "moderation in all things." Some wild foods cause unpleasant side effects with overindulgence. Prickly pear cacti are among the best-tasting wild edibles in Texas. While many people eat the pads or fruit with no ill effects, however, an overconsumption of the raw fruits causes constipation. For some people, eating a few small pads can cause diarrhea. How much is too much? is a question that only your body can answer.

Some families of plants contain a high percentage of species that frequently cause allergic reactions. For instance, the members of Anacardiaceae, the cashews and mangoes, cause contact dermatitis in some people (poison ivy is another member of the family). If you are allergic to cashews or mangoes, stay away from the sumacs.

You don't have a lifetime of experience with wild foods to tell you which ones may not be right for you. Anyone can develop food allergies at any age. When experimenting with any wild foods, eat moderate amounts until you find out how your system reacts.

TOXIC IN QUANTITY

Certain wild foods can cause severe toxicity if they are eaten in large amounts. That type of toxicity occasionally affects livestock. Only when those plants become a major part of the diet do they cause problems for humans. For example, in times of famine, people in northern Africa have relied on the beans of *Lathyrus sativus*, a livestock forage crop, as their main or sole source of protein. Though apparently harmless if eaten occasionally, the beans eventually cause paralysis and death when consumed as the main food over a period of several weeks. A number of our common food crops such as spinach can also cause problems when eaten in quantity (see the section "Poisons in the Garden" in Chapter 4). I have included warnings on potential toxicity throughout this chapter, "Edible and Useful Wild Plants." Unfortunately, some wild plants have not been used as foods often enough to determine whether they can cause problems when eaten in quantity. Again, the key to good health is moderation.

WHAT PART CAN I EAT?

One of the most important warnings to heed, and one that you'll find repeated throughout this book, is that many edible plants have poisonous parts. A number of the plants that we commonly grow as vegetables—rhubarb, for example—also have toxic parts (see the section "Poisons in the Garden" in Chapter 4). A long tradition of how to prepare and eat garden vegetables and fruits prevents poisoning, even though most of us are not aware of the potential for poisoning.

In using wild plants for food, we need to be extra cautious. We can't look back to "how my mother did it" to give us guidance on what parts to eat or how to cook the plant properly. Warnings included with the descriptions of edible plants furnish information on toxic parts. Though pokeweed is considered a premier vegetable by those who have a family tradition of its use, I have included it in the chapter on poisonous plants because of the high toxicity of all the plant parts, even the greens.

Carefully consider all warnings included in the information on each plant. And keep in mind that, for most wild plants, there is a sad lack of valid research on chemical makeup and potential toxicity. **Do not experiment with eating any plant part that is not specifically mentioned for use in the book.**

In other publications, I have seen instructions for sampling wild plants to determine whether or not they are safe to eat. Allegedly, the bad taste will warn you of toxicity. If the plant tastes all right, those authors advocate that you swallow a small amount and wait a few hours. They say that if you experience no ill effects, you can eat the plants. Those instructions show ignorance of several facts about wild plants: (1) a number of highly toxic plants actually taste good; (2) eating even a small amount of some plants can be deadly; (3) with some toxic plants, symptoms of toxicity may not appear for several days or weeks. For all of the above reasons, **never** experiment with unknown plants as foods. For further details on toxic wild plants, refer to Chapter 4.

Edible and Useful Wild Plants By Family, Including Recipes

The following plants are arranged in family groups. The groups occur in alphabetical order by the scientific family name. The plant characteristics section provides useful information to assist you in recognizing them. For additional listings of edible plants, see Chapter 3, "Edible and Poisonous Berries and Other Fleshy Fruits." Chapter 2 includes information on wild teas and spices.

AGAVACEAE—AGAVE FAMILY

The Spanish who first encountered Texas west of the Pecos called the area the *despoblado*—the uninhabited land. But in spite of its foreboding appearance, the Chihuahuan Desert has provided food, fiber, medicine, and shelter for humans for thousands of years. Taking advantage of seasonal wild harvests, nomadic groups, such as the Mescalero and Lipan Apaches, found food and made a living in the desert. Among the plants those peoples relied on were agaves, sotols, and yuccas—spiny shrubs of the family Agavaceae.

Agaves, sotols, and yuccas bear long, swordlike leaves and are often mistakenly thought to be cacti. Texas hosts 9 species of agaves, 4 species of sotols, and 20 species of yuccas. The earliest Americans probably had uses for them all.

AGAVE—*AGAVE* SPECIES

All of the more than two hundred species of agaves originated in the Americas. By the time the Spanish invaded the highlands of Mexico, indigenous Americans had used wild agaves for food and fiber for at least nine thousand years, and the Aztecs had cultivated agaves for food, fiber, paper, and beverages for several centuries.

Today agaves hold economic importance in the warm regions of both hemispheres as ornamentals and as sources of fiber. Sisal and henequen provide 80 percent of the world's hard fibers, which are used for rope and twine. Agave fibers furnish a major source of income in various regions of Mexico today. Residue from fiber production yields a commercially valuable wax (Schery 1972). And Mexican markets still occasionally offer the cooked agave heart (Gentry 1982).

Agave, Maguey, Century Plant—*AGAVE AMERICANA* and Other Species
(See photograph, plate 3.)

Perhaps the most widely recognized century plant is *Agave americana*. One of the largest agaves, this magnificent sword-bearer stands 3–6 feet tall (1–2 m) and sends up a flower stalk more than 20 feet (7 m) tall. Used as an ornamental in warm dry regions throughout the world, the gray-green shrub is a native of Mexico and South Texas.

Rather than using maguey as a food, Mexican villagers rely on the shrub as a source of a refreshing beverage. If the large leaf bud emerging from the center of a living plant is cut out, a basin is formed. The sap pools into the basin and can be drawn off daily for a cool, nutritious drink called aguamiel. The sweet drink contains calcium, phosphorous, vitamins, and amino acids. Aguamiel can be obtained from a number of other large agaves. In Texas these are *Agave scabra,* found in South Texas, and *Agave weberi,* used in landscaping in the Lower Rio Grande Valley. For *mexicanos* living in isolated areas where potable water is scarce or nonexistent, aguamiel remains a valued source of water and nutrition.

Slightly fermented, agave juice furnishes a mild intoxicant called pulque, which held an important place in the culture of the Aztecs. Its use evolved with the religious rituals of the theocracy and was strictly regulated. The Aztecs invoked severe penalties for illegal drunkenness, including death for a repeat offender. It was not until the Spanish introduced the indigenous people to the distillation process that the highly intoxicating agave beverages, mescal and tequila, were developed. Today huge farms near Tequila, in the state of Jalisco, grow *Agave tequilana* for the distilleries (Gentry 1982).

The Mexican people use the flowering stalks of the large agaves as building materials for roofing and walls and as fishing poles. In addition to making excellent rope and twine from agave fibers, *mexicanos* use the fibers for saddle blankets, ornamental braiding, nets, bags, cloth, and paper. The juice of the leaf is used as an insecticide (Watt and Breyer-Brandwijk 1962). Most agaves, and particularly *Agave americana,* have caustic leaves, so scraping out the fibers by hand results in painful burning and blistering (Mitchell and Rook 1979). To minimize this problem, soak the leaves in water for several days until most of the pulp has dissolved from the fibers, a process known as retting. In cutting and handling the leaves, protect your skin and eyes from the blister-causing juice. Commercially, the flesh of the leaf is scraped from the fibers by machine.

Lechuguilla, Tula Ixtle—*AGAVE LECHEGUILLA*
(See photograph, plate 3.)

Warning_____

Lechuguilla hearts are not safe to eat. Lechuguilla contains dangerously high concentrations of saponins and other toxic compounds. Cattle, goats, and sheep, which eat lechuguilla as a last resort, have died from consuming the leaves. Saponins provide soap, medicine, and arrow poison used by Indians, and cortisone and sex hormones for modern medicinal use have been synthesized from the saponins in lechuguilla and a number of other agaves. Agave lophantha, *another small narrow-leaved agave, also is too toxic for use as a food. That species, rare in Texas, is found only in Starr and Zapata counties.*

If you have ever hiked anywhere in the Chihuahuan Desert of West Texas, you have probably cursed the lechuguilla. This smallest yet most abundant Texas agave covers the floor of the Chihuahuan Desert. The nasty spines make travel by foot or horse difficult. But lechuguilla acts as an important soil stabilizer in the West Texas desert, an area that has been heavily grazed by livestock for one hundred years.

Native Americans living in the desert held the plant in great esteem. They used the toxic juice pounded from the leaves as an arrow poison, a fish stupefier, a medicine, and a soap. They extracted the leaf fibers for cordage for bowstrings and wove them into nets, baskets, mats, sandals, blankets, and cloth.

Rural Mexicans in north central Mexico still harvest lechuguilla for fiber. The stiff, resilient fibers of lechuguilla and *Yucca carnerosana* are known as ixtle, and the harvesters as *ixtleros*. The fibers provide a major source of income for several hundred thousand *mexicanos* in the area locally known as the Zona Ixtlera. The *ixtleros* collect the lechuguilla leaves from the wild and scrape out the fibers by hand. Apparently, lechuguilla leaves are not as caustic as the leaves of other agaves. I have successfully extracted the leaf fibers with a knife bare-handed and had no skin irritation. The fiber is sold for making rope, twine, carpet pads, rugs, and saddle blankets. Imported into the United States as Tampico fiber, lechuguilla provides high-quality bristles for industrial and household brushes (Gentry 1982; Schery 1972; Sheldon 1980).

The *ixtleros* use the leaf pulp and spines that remain after extracting the fibers as an abrasive soap. They also pound out the roots and soak them in water for laundry soap and shampoo.

MESCAL—*AGAVE NEOMEXICANA, AGAVE HAVARDIANA, AGAVE GRACILIPES,* AND *AGAVE PARRYI*

Warning

Do not eat raw agave heart—the caustic juice will burn your mouth. Use only the food species mentioned here because the saponin levels in some other species make them unsafe for food. The root, fruit, and green parts of the leaves of all the Texas agaves contain saponins and thus are toxic.

The significance of the mescal in the life of the Apaches of the Southwest cannot be exaggerated. The Spanish named the Mescalero Apaches for the food on which they depended so heavily for survival. In 1869 Lt. Howard Cushing led a Cavalry raid on a Mescalero Apache village in the

Guadalupe Mountains. While the Apaches fled into the mountains for refuge, the soldiers destroyed 20,000 pounds of prepared mescal. With the Indians' winter food stores gone, the soldiers soon starved the Apaches into submission.

Mescal was such an important source of food, fiber, and drink that for nearly six hundred years the home ranges of the Apaches coincided with those of various species of agave. The Lipan Apaches relied on *Agave havardiana* in the mountains of the Big Bend region, and the Mescaleros depended on *Agave neomexicana* and *Agave gracilipes* from the Guadalupe Mountains and on *Agave parryi* into southern New Mexico. These medium-sized shrubs all stand about 1−2 feet (4−6 dm) tall, notably smaller than *Agave americana.*

The Apaches used the heart and the flower stalk of the mescals for food. The women harvested the flowering plants in the spring or late summer. They simply charred the young flower stalks on an open fire, but the bitter white heart of the plant, at the base of the leaves, required lengthy preparation. The workers dug a baking pit and lined it with stones. Then they built a fire in the pit and burned it down to coals. After placing the agave hearts into the pit, they covered the hearts with leaves and earth and left them to bake for one to three days.

When brown and soft, the hearts were ready for eating. The Apaches scooped the soft pulp out of the center and chewed the fibrous sections to extract the sweet nutritious juice, spitting out the fibers. They often pressed the juice out of the pulp to form dry cakes for storage and used the sweet juice for making syrups, candies, and cough medicine. Slightly fermented, the juice made a mildly intoxicating beverage (Struever 1971). The Apaches also used the liquid as a brown face paint and a waterproofing material for baskets.

The huge harvests of wild agaves must have drastically reduced the populations of those plants over time. Knowing that the older plants were sweeter, however, the Apaches generally collected only the mature plants as the flowering stalk emerged (Howard Gentry, letter to the author, 25 November 1985). The younger plants were left to generate suckers for new plant growth. None of the wild agaves occur in abundance in Texas today. Besides the wild harvests, more-recent human activities in West Texas, such as ranching and farming, have taken their toll on agave populations. Since the edible agaves mostly grow on mountain slopes of the Trans-Pecos, I have not had the opportunity to try this staple of the desert. But if you get a chance to rescue one from a bulldozer, you might try the following recipe for baked agave using a modern oven.

Protect your skin and eyes from the caustic juice of the leaves as you collect the hearts. Use a hatchet to chop off the leaves and root so that only the white heart and white leaf bases remain. Do not use the green part of the leaves or the root, because they contain toxic saponins. Cover the heart with aluminum foil and place it in a roasting pan to catch the sweet juice. Bake at 350°F for 10 hours or until the pulp is soft and brown. Considering the time required for baking agave hearts, the underground oven may still be the best method (Niethammer 1974; Scooter Cheatham, interview, September 1984).

Plant Characteristics

An agave blooms only once, in the final year of its life. The common name, century plant, reflects the belief that the plants bloom once in one hundred years. The life span of the species ranges from about 8 to 30 years, however. Perhaps "decade plant" is a more appropriate name, though I doubt that it will ever catch on.

The agaves have a sharp spine on the tips of the leaves, and all of the Texas species but one (Agave weberi) have wicked spines along the leaf margins. From spring to fall, the different species send up their flowering stalks, some shooting up well over 20 feet. After the large clusters of yellow, green, or red flowers go to seed, the plant dies, having expended all of its energy on this one attempt at sexual reproduction. Most plants leave behind a small colony of offspring, however, from suckers sent out over the years.

Distinguishing one species from another is difficult even for a botanist. The lanceolate leaves of Agave americana may be more than 5 feet (1.7 m) long, typically seven to nine times longer than broad. The surface of the leaf is grayish, and the margins are heavily armed with large teeth. The tall summer flowering stalk produces a huge panicle of yellow flowers.

Agave weberi, though similar to A. americana in size, either lacks spines on the leaf margin or has only a few small spines. Agave scabra, another large agave similar to A. americana, has large spines and more roughly textured leaves.

The short, triangular leaves of Agave havardiana are about 16–30 inches (40–75 cm) long, about three to four times longer than broad. The leaves of Agave neomexicana and Agave gracilipes may be about 1 foot long (30 cm) and about 2–4 inches (5–10 cm) wide at the base. All three species grow in the mountains of the Trans-Pecos. Agave neomexicana blooms from spring to summer, and Agave gracilipes from summer to fall. Agave parryi does not occur in Texas.

Agave lecheguilla, the smallest agave in the Trans-Pecos, hardly looks like an agave. The linear leaves are about 1 inch wide (2–3 cm) and 1–1¾ feet (30–50 cm) long. The upcurved, yellowish green leaves may be streaked dark green or reddish. The yellow to reddish flowers grow in a dense spike.

SOTOL—*DASYLIRION* SPECIES
(See photograph, plate 3.)

Warning

The similar-looking beargrasses (Nolina species, photographed) are toxic plants. Another member of the agave family, beargrass has long, narrow, grasslike leaves with finely toothed or smooth margins. The flower stalks of beargrasses are short in comparison with those of sotol. (Beargrass leaves also furnish excellent materials for basket weaving.)

For thousands of years the early inhabitants of West Texas relied on sotol as a major source of food. Archeologists working in Seminole Canyon, west of Del Rio, have discovered the remains of sotol roasting pits, several thousand years old, in sheltered rock overhangs. Near the roasting pits they found sandals, mats, and rope manufactured from the fiber of sotol leaves.

To prepare sotols for eating, native Americans dug up the shrubs and removed the slender leaves, using the heart and the meat at the base of the leaves for food. The Indians dug a roasting pit, lined it with rocks, and built a fire in it. When the fire had burned down to coals, they placed the sotol hearts inside the pit and covered them with leaves and earth. After about 48 hours the pulp was soft and sweet. They scooped out and chewed the soft fibrous pulp in the center to extract the sweet nutritious juice, spitting out the fiber.

During droughts, modern-day West Texas ranchers burn off the leaves and split open the sotol heart to enable cattle to feed on the nutritious starch. Unfortunately, this practice has resulted in the decimation of many wild populations of sotols. If you want to try baking sotol hearts, keep in mind that you must kill the shrubs to collect the hearts. Collect sotols only if you have a number of them on your property. In many areas of West Texas the shrubs no longer grow in abundance. The underground roasting pit may still be the most efficient method of cooking the hearts. If you want to bake them in your oven, wrap the hearts in aluminum foil, set them in a roasting pan, and bake them at 350°F until they are soft, mushy, and brown. Baking may take 10 hours or longer.

Sotol leaves, with spines removed, provide excellent materials for weaving baskets and sandals and for thatching. You can soak the leaves in water for several days to loosen the fibers to use as threads for sewing and weaving textiles. The leaf fiber can also be used for papermaking. Early Mexican settlers in West Texas used the woody flowering stalk in building construction and for fuel. They also distilled an alcoholic drink from the juice of the roasted hearts. During World War II, alcohol was produced commercially from sotol in Val Verde County (Maxwell 1968; Vines 1960; Scooter Cheatham, interview, September 1984).

Plant Characteristics

Four species of *Dasylirion* grow in Texas, predominantly on the Edwards Plateau and on rocky slopes in the Trans-Pecos. The shrub consists of many long, narrow, swordlike leaves emerging from the base. The leaves may be 3 feet (1 m) long. Sotols resemble yuccas, which do not have edible hearts, but the edges of sotol leaves are armed with short spines. A flowering stalk 6–15 feet (2–5 m) tall rises from the center of the leaves each year.

YUCCA, IZOTE, SOYATE—*YUCCA* SPECIES
(See photograph, plate 4.)

Warning

Though the flowers and fleshy fruits of yuccas are edible, the leaves, roots, heart, and trunk of the plants are not—they may contain toxic levels of saponin. The flower stalk of some species also may be toxic. The seeds may be purgative and should not be eaten.

As have the agaves and sotols, yuccas have provided food, fiber, and shelter for humans for thousands of years. The Mescalero Apaches cooked the young flowering stalks of *Yucca elata,* the soap-tree yucca, over an open fire. The Indians peeled off the outer skin of the stalk and ate the soft interior. Other species may not have edible flower stalks, however.

The Apaches also relished the fruit of datil, *Yucca baccata.* When ripe, the fleshy brown outer layer of the banana-shaped fruit resembles a date in flavor. The women roasted large numbers of the ripe fruit on the coals of a wood fire, peeled off the charred outer layer, split the fruit open, removed the seeds, and sun-dried the flesh. About half of the two dozen Texas species of yucca produce a fleshy edible fruit; the others bear inedible woody fruits. Use the fruit raw, dried, or baked (Basehart 1974).

You can eat the creamy-white flowers of yuccas raw or cooked. They add an interesting touch to a salad and are high in vitamin C (Tate 1972). Try them pickled, fried, or sautéed with onions and tomatoes. Some are definitely more palatable than others, so sample a few different species before you pass judgment on this delicacy. Use only the white petals, as the green center of the flower tends to be bitter.

In addition to providing food, yuccas furnish wood and fiber. Early Mexican settlers in West Texas used the woody trunks of the tree yuccas and the flowering stalks of all yuccas for building material, fencing, and fuel. You can use the leaves of yuccas for weaving baskets, mats, and thatch. Split the leaves to the desired width and dry them. Then wet the strips before weaving. You can extract the leaf fibers by soaking them in water for several days. Use the needle tip of the leaf with the fibers as needle and thread. The fibers can be woven into rough cloth (Vines 1960).

During World War I, when imported supplies of jute were unavailable, U.S. industries substituted yucca fibers in making burlap bags. Thousands of rural *mexicanos* still rely on the income from the harvest of ixtle fibers from the leaves of *Yucca carnerosana, palma samandoca* (Sheldon 1980). In World War II, the U.S. Navy manufactured rope, twine, and a heavy paper from yucca fibers.

The saponins in the yucca root yield a good soap. Navaho weavers use yucca root soap to wash their wool before weaving their beautiful rugs (Bryan 1978). If you want to try out this interesting soap, remember that to do so, you must kill the whole plant. I have salvaged several yuccas for soap and basket making materials, however, by retrieving ornamental varieties that neighbors had removed from their yards. Also be on the lookout for vacant lots that are about to go under the bulldozer. With the permission of the owner, you can often find dozens of useful plants.

YUCCA LAUNDRY SOAP OR SHAMPOO

Dig up the roots at any time of the year. Scrub off loose dirt, and chop the root into small pieces. Peel off the tough outer covering. Pound the root to a pulp (a hammer will do the trick). You can store the pulp by freezing it, or dry it in the sun and store it in a cool place.

When you are ready to use your soap, add a handful of the pulp to a quart of cold water and slosh it around till it makes a lather. I've read that if your hands are greasy, you will not have a good lather.

Once you stir up a lather, strain out the fibers and add as much warm water as you need to do your washing. If you use the soap on your skin, test a small area of skin for allergic reaction first.

The soap was used for thousands of years by Southwestern Indian tribes to wash clothing and hair and as a ceremonial bath. Besides producing a lather, saponins have medicinal value. Medicine made from a yucca extract has been used in the treatment of some forms of arthritis (Bingham, Bellew, and Bellew 1975).

Yuccas provide many valuable products. Unfortunately, the shrubs have always been harvested from the wild for human use. The popularity of the unusual plants as ornamentals has resulted in the decimation of many populations of yuccas in the Southwest. Greedy individuals remove them from the deserts by the truckload and ship them around the world for use as ornamentals.

The Apaches and other southwestern tribes harvested wild yuccas, agaves, and sotols for food and shelter for thousands of years, but the small numbers of Indians and their nomadic lifestyle prevented wholesale destruction of the plants. These desert plants have many gifts to offer the modern world. But if we wish to use those gifts, we must recognize that the day of the wild harvest is over. The Mexicans already cultivate some species of agaves. To take advantage of the fibers and medicines that yuccas offer, we need to cultivate them as well. Meanwhile, let's leave the wild plants where they are, standing tall and majestic in the deserts of West Texas and the sandy soils of East Texas.

Plant Characteristics

Two basic forms of yucca grow in Texas. The tree yuccas, with spine-tipped leaves radiating out of a tall trunk, are 5–30 feet (1.5–9 m) tall. The low-growing species produce a rosette of spine-tipped leaves joined at ground level. Unlike agaves, yuccas bloom yearly and do not die after flowering. Yuccas produce a flowering stalk topped with a cluster of large creamy-white flowers. Yuccas have a needle point on the swordlike leaves, but they do not have the marginal spines of agave and sotol leaves.

We tend to associate yuccas with the harsh environment of West Texas, but yuccas also grow in the sandy lands of East Texas and the eastern United States. An interesting ecological side note: Yuccas depend on certain moths to pollinate their flowers. In return for her services, the female moth lays her eggs in the ovary of the flower. The larvae live on the seeds inside the developing fruit, leaving enough seeds for future generations of yuccas.

ALISMATACEAE—WATER-PLANTAIN FAMILY

ARROWHEAD, WAPATO—*SAGITTARIA* SPECIES

In times past, arrowhead tubers provided an important source of carbohydrates for native American tribes across the continent. For some tribes, arrowhead, or wapato, was the main vegetable. The Lewis and Clark Expedition relied on the tubers for survival while exploring the Columbia River.

The small tubers that cling to the ends of the long underwater roots are what you are after. Collecting them is a messy job. If you are careful, you can remove the tubers without pulling up the whole plant. Follow the root underwater with your hands until you find the round lumps. The tubers are best in the late fall, when the flower stalk is dying back, and they vary in size. You may find some as large as a new potato or as small as a peanut. Boil them or bake them like a potato, then peel and eat them.

I have never seen arrowheads growing in abundance in Texas. Use them only if you find a large supply. The Chinese cultivate arrowheads for food. The plants may be deserving of cultivation in this country (Fernald, Kinsey, and Rollins 1958; Crowhurst 1972; Harrington 1972; Gibbons 1962; Medsger 1966).

Plant Characteristics

Arrowheads are aquatic plants, growing in a variety of shallow wetland habitats, such as streams, ponds, marshes, and roadside ditches. Nine species occur in Texas. These wildflowers may be 1–4 feet (3–12 dm) tall. In several species the large leaf blade is shaped like an arrowhead. Leaves clasp the base of the flower stalk, and the sap of the plant is milky. The delicate white flowers have three showy petals and are attached to the flower stalk in whorls of three.

AMARANTHACEAE—AMARANTH FAMILY

AMARANTH, PIGWEED, ALEGRÍA—*AMARANTHUS* SPECIES
(See illustration.)

Warning

Amaranth leaves contain some oxalic acid, which tends to bind calcium and thus restrict its absorption by the body. As long as your diet contains plenty of calcium from other sources, eating amaranth and other vegetables that contain oxalic acid should cause no problems. See "spinach" in the index for details on problems with oxalic acid in spinach.

Amaranths can accumulate excess nitrates in their leaves (not in the grain). While that does not pose a problem for humans eating a normal-sized meal of amaranth greens, it has caused some livestock losses. Researchers have found that nitrate accumulations occur only under special circumstances, such as when amaranths have been treated with the herbicide 2,4-D, which causes an imbalance in nitrogen metabolism. In Hawaii 39 dairy cows died in 1973 after being fed a green sorghum that was found to consist of nearly one-third Amaranthus spinosus, a spiny-stemmed pigweed, and the pigweed contained nitrates. That kind of poisoning is rare because cattle normally would not eat such a large quantity

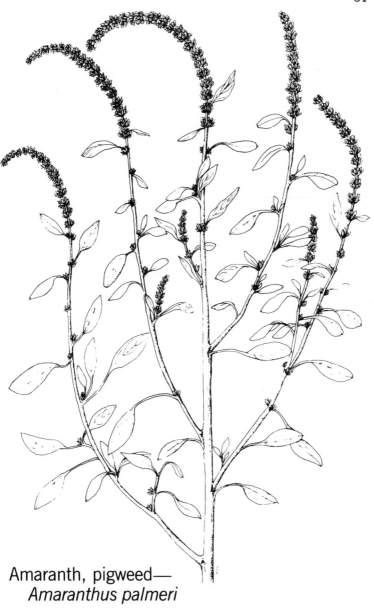

Amaranth, pigweed—
Amaranthus palmeri

of pigweed on the open range (Kingsbury 1964; Ritchie 1979; Sperry et al. 1964).

"What kind of dressing would you like on your pigweed salad, madam?" Though not an appetizing suggestion today, pigweed may someday become a regular dinner item. In the more exclusive restaurants, however, waiters will probably refer to it by its more exotic-sounding name, "amaranth."

Easily ignored by passing motorists, wild pigweeds appear on practically every street corner and in every open field in Texas. Some of the homely annuals grow in such abundance that worldwide they are considered some of the most damaging weeds to crops such as corn, soybeans, and cotton. Despite those problems, members of the genus *Amaranthus* deserve better press.

Pigweeds furnish nutritious greens that are commonly eaten by native peoples in South Africa, India, and Australia (Holm et al. 1977; Watt and Breyer-Brandwijk 1962). Several vegetable species are cultivated in India, China, and the Caribbean. All species found wild in Texas are considered edible, though one species, *Amaranthus albus,* may be too bitter for use. You can harvest your own salad and cooking greens from back alleys, mowed fields, and vacant lots, practically year-round. In mowed areas new plants emerge from late winter to late fall. Collect the young, tender plants when they are less than a foot tall. The stems and leaves become fibrous and bitter as the plant ages. Use the leaves and succulent stems raw in salads, or boil them for 10 to 15 minutes and serve with pepper sauce or lemon.

The tiny dark seeds, produced on slender spikes from summer to late fall, are an excellent source of protein. For thousands of years before the arrival of the Spanish, native Americans cultivated amaranths for the nutritious seeds. As early as 8700 years ago, amaranths were cultivated in the Tehuacán Valley of Mexico (MacNeish 1971). For the Aztecs, amaranths rivaled maize as the most valued crop. When Hernando Cortés invaded Mexico in 1519, his men reportedly found eighteen imperial granaries filled with the seeds of *Amaranthus hypochondriacus* (Schery 1972). The Aztecs used the red flower spikes of a second grain amaranth, *A. cruentus,* as a ceremonial red dye. Amaranth was a symbol of immortality for ancient Americans. The generic name *"Amaranthus"* is derived from a Greek word meaning "unfading."

Recognizing the importance of amaranths in the diet and the religion of the Aztecs, Cortés ordered the destruction of the amaranth fields and made growing the crop a crime punishable by death. The grain quickly disappeared as a major food source, though it has remained in quiet cultivation in isolated areas of Central and South America to the present day.

In recent times amaranth grain has become popular in east Africa and in India and other parts of Asia (Harlan 1975; Simmonds 1976; Struever 1971). Experiments at the Organic Gardening Research Center near Maxatawny, Pennsylvania, have found amaranths to be highly productive and nutritious. The seeds contain 15 grams of protein per 100 grams, more than that found in rice and corn and equivalent to, if not surpassing, that in wheat. Amaranth is particularly rich in lysine, an amino acid deficient in the true cereal grains, and thus it provides a more balanced source of protein. Amaranth also contains more fiber and calcium than cereal grains. The leaves are high in fiber, vitamins C and A, and the minerals calcium, magnesium, and iron. The greens have been valued in the past in the prevention of scurvy, which is caused by vitamin C deficiency, and they provide some protein as well (Ritchie 1979).

Amaranths have the potential to become an important world food crop. Cultivation of drought-resistant crops such as the amaranths could play an important part in the prevention of famine in drought-prone areas of the world. Studies in Africa have revealed the importance of wild amaranth greens in the diet of a number of tribes. The protein, mineral, and vitamin content of the wild vegetable provides a better source of nutrition than a number of the plants currently in cultivation in Africa.

Research and publicity by the group in Maxatawny has brought about a revival for amaranth use in the United States. Amaranth seeds, flour, flakes, and granolas are appearing in health food stores around the country. Seed companies now offer amaranth seed, both vegetable and grain varieties, for home gardens.

To make your own wild amaranth flour, clip the ripe seed spikes from the plants in the summer or fall. Lay the stalks out in the sun to dry, and then rub them between your hands to release the tiny dark seeds. Winnow out the chaff by tossing the seeds in a basket in a slight breeze, and toast the seeds in the oven. You can use the whole seeds as a cooked cereal or grind them up for flour. Amaranth flour has a distinctive flavor and is a bit strong when used alone. Mix it with other flours for breads and pancakes. Here's a recipe for a sweet bread using jujubes, a datelike fruit from a small tree, *Ziziphus jujuba,* occasionally found escaped from cultivation in Texas (see the index for information on jujubes).

AMARANTH-JUJUBE BREAD

1 cup chopped jujubes or dates	½ cup sugar
1 cup boiling water	¼ cup honey

Combine the above ingredients in a small bowl.

2 cups whole wheat flour	½ teaspoon cinnamon
¾ cup amaranth flour	1 egg
3 teaspoons baking powder	

Combine the dry ingredients in a separate bowl and mix well. Stir in the egg. Now add the jujube mixture and blend well. Pour the dough into a greased and floured loaf pan. Place in a preheated oven at 350° F for about an hour.

The characteristics that cause amaranths to become problem weeds are the same characteristics that make them so attractive as crops. The plants grow quickly and produce seeds prolifically. A number of species are drought-tolerant and grow in a variety of soil and lighting conditions. The fast-growing plants, which can be started from seed or transplanted as seedlings, are large enough for use as a green vegetable in four to six weeks. In Texas the greens can be harvested several times in one season (Hackett and Carolane 1982).

Plant Characteristics

Many species of amaranths occur throughout the world. Texas has more than 20. Most species hybridize with other members of the genus and, therefore, are difficult to distinguish from each other. These annual plants are, for the most part, unattractive weedy herbs, not the sort of plant you would find in a book on wildflowers. The purple amaranth (*Amaranthus cruentus*) and prince's-feather (*Amaranthus hypochondriacus*), both grain amaranths, grow as ornamentals in Texas, and sometimes they grow wild. The closely related water hemps, *Acnida* species, also are edible. A few species of amaranths are too prickly to use for food.

Amaranths vary from small prostrate herbs to large plants several feet tall. Oval to lance-shaped leaves alternate on the stem, and the midribs and veins protrude noticeably from the bottoms of the leaves. The margins are entire or undulating. Leaves and stems vary from hairy to smooth in texture. The inconspicuous flowers grow clustered together in dense spikes that protrude from the axils of the leaves and may droop rather sadly from the top of the plant. Though most plants are green, some may have a red or purple tinge on the flower petals, bracts, and branches.

ANACARDIACEAE—SUMAC FAMILY

SUMAC—*RHUS* SPECIES
(See illustration.)

*Warning*_____

Some people have an allergic reaction to contact with sumacs, particularly the oily surface of the fruit. If you come down with a skin rash from handling cashews or mangoes, there is a strong possibility you also are allergic to their cousins the sumacs. Poison sumac (Toxicodendron vernix), another member of this family, has white berries, making it easy to distinguish from the nonpoisonous sumacs (see the index for further information on poison ivy and poison sumac).

In autumn the leaves and the fruit of the sumacs add brilliant shades of orange and red to the countryside across the state. Seven species of sumacs find a home in Texas, all with value as ornamental shrubs. Southwestern Indians used various species in basketry, as dyes and medicines, and for making a cool, refreshing drink.

Malic acid, which gives apples their tartness, also flavors the sour fruits of the sumacs. To make sumac-ade from the hard, red fruits, refer to the recipe on page 226. When making the drink, use warm water rather than boiling water to prevent the extraction of an excess of tannic acid.

Tannic acid, present in all parts of the shrubs, furnishes a number of useful industrial products. The leather industry relies on the astringent tannins to transform skins into leather. Oil-well drillers use it to control the viscosity of mud. The leaves and finely ground twigs of several Texas *Rhus* species are considered among the best sources of vegetable tannins in the world. *Rhus copallina, Rhus aromatica,* and *Rhus glabra* contain from 10 to 33 percent tannic acid.

The leaves, branches, and fruits of sumacs provide colorfast dyes for wool. Tannic acid acts as a natural mordant, so the fiber does not need to be treated with other chemicals to assist it in absorbing the dyes. The dye colors range from tan to a rich reddish brown.

The limber branches of aromatic sumac, *Rhus aromatica,* work well in basketmaking and were used for that purpose by several southwestern native American groups. The slender, flexible branches of other species may be tried for baskets. Native Americans also used the sumacs medicinally (Bryan 1978; Schery 1972; Vines 1960; Scooter Cheatham, interview, September 1984).

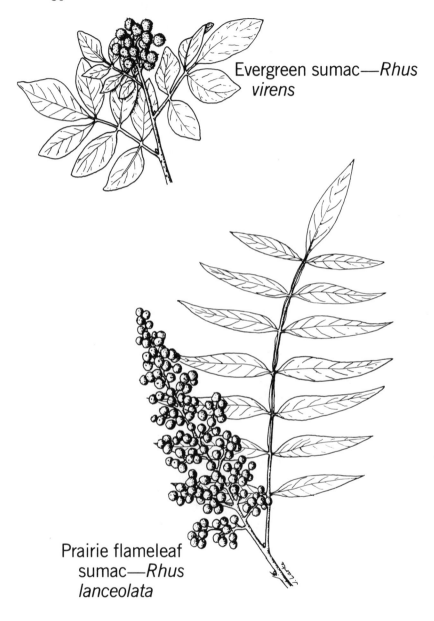

Evergreen sumac—*Rhus virens*

Prairie flameleaf sumac—*Rhus lanceolata*

Plant Characteristics

The six Texas species of sumacs vary considerably in appearance. All are shrubs with compound leaves having a lemony aroma. Clusters of tiny white to greenish or yellowish flowers are followed by the hard, red fruits.

Prairie flameleaf sumac (*Rhus lanceolata*), smooth sumac (*Rhus glabra*), and winged sumac (*Rhus copallina*) all have large clusters of fruit. These tall slender shrubs bear large pinnately compound leaves. The numerous leaflets (as many as 31 on *Rhus glabra*) are several times longer than broad, having entire or serrated margins. Leaves turn bright scarlet in the fall.

Several varieties of aromatic sumac, *Rhus aromatica,* occur across the state. The small shrub has three leaflets per leaf, causing the leaves to resemble those of its cousin poison ivy. The margins of the leaflets are toothed, and the yellowish flowers produce few fruits per cluster. Small-leaved sumac, *Rhus microphylla,* usually a little, somewhat spiny shrub, has five to nine miniature leaflets per leaf and small clusters of fruits. It grows in the western three fourths of the state, including the southern Gulf Coast.

The evergreen sumacs *Rhus virens* and *Rhus virens* subsp. *choriophylla* differ markedly from the deciduous sumacs. They form large, beautifully rounded shrubs. The compound leaves have three to nine rounded leaflets that are smooth, shiny, and leathery, with entire margins. *Rhus virens* occurs in the western half of the state.

ASTERACEAE—COMPOSITE FAMILY, SUNFLOWER FAMILY (FORMERLY COMPOSITAE)

*Warning*_____

Refer to "Asteraceae" in the index for information about toxic members of the family. The pollen of the composites is highly allergenic. The section "Hay Fever Plants" in Chapter 4 describes those plants that cause the most hay fever problems in Texas. Many composites also cause allergic dermatitis reactions in sensitive individuals. If you develop skin rashes from handling chrysanthemums or lettuce, you may also have trouble with the wild Texas composites. For more information on this topic, see the section "Contact Dermatitis" in Chapter 4.

From early spring to late fall, brightly colored wildflowers cover the roadsides, streamsides, fields, and deserts of Texas. As the seasons progress through the year, fields change color from the vivid yellows of Engelmann's daisy to the reds and golds of Indian blankets to the purples of the fall-blooming asters and gay feathers. Many of Texas' most spectacular wildflowers have something in common. They belong to the composite family, the largest family of flowering plants in the world.

The composite family has yielded a number of economically important agricultural crops, including sunflowers, lettuce, artichokes, and Jerusalem artichokes. Besides growing sunflowers, native Americans of what is now the United States probably cultivated the composites ragweed (*Ambrosia trifida*) and pelocote (*Iva annua* and *Iva xanthifolia*) for their nutritious seeds before the introduction of maize, beans, and squash from the south.

Quite a few wild edible composites grow in abundance across the state. Numerous salad greens and potherbs mature in the fall. The colorful flowers of many composites produce lovely yellow and orange dyes for wool. You'll see a number of them in the chapter on dye plants.

In Texas, Asteraceae is represented by close to six hundred species. Except for a few shrubs, all Texas species are herbaceous. Besides those mentioned above, other Texas wildflowers include *Coreopsis,* greenthreads, goldenrods, and Texas star. Many garden flowers come from this family as well: daisies, dandelions, chrysanthemums, and marigolds, to name but a few.

Family Characteristics

You can easily recognize members of the composite family once you become familiar with the flower type. Pick a sunflower, marigold, or chrysanthemum, and examine the flowers closely. Gently pull on the petals, opening the cluster carefully. What you may have thought was a single flower with numerous petals is actually a cluster of many flowers. Each miniature flower has its own set of petals and reproductive parts. The flowers group together in such close quarters that they appear to be a single blossom.

The dense flower cluster is known as a head. A group of tiny leaflike bracts, collectively known as an involucre, holds the head together. The heads vary in shape from the flattened sunflower to the globe-shaped thistle. The inner flowers of the sunflower are shaped differently from the outer ones. The petals of the inner flowers, called disk flowers, form a tiny tube or funnel. The petals of the outer flowers, called ray flowers, are elongated and open out into a flat strap. On the sunflower the infertile rays provide a showy blossom that attracts insects toward the central disk for pollination. On the thistle the flowers all are the disk type. The common family name "composite" refers to this diagnostic flower head, which may consist of rays alone, disks alone, or rays and disks together.

The fruits of composites are called achenes. An achene consists of a small capsule containing a single seed. The sunflower seed exemplifies a typical achene. On a number of species you will find feathery bristles attached to the achenes. The bristles enable the achenes to float in the wind—an effective means of dispersing the seeds of herbs such as the dandelion.

Once you become familiar with the peculiar flower type of the family, you should be able to recognize composites throughout the world. Though plants in some other families, such as the legume family, also may have flowers arranged in heads, the individual flowers aren't differentiated into rays and disks. When in doubt, look for the developing achenes at the bases of the flowers.

CHICORY—*CICHORIUM INTYBUS*

Warning

The raw plant can cause dermatitis in sensitive persons.

During World War II, soldiers in Europe used roasted chicory root as a substitute for coffee. Southern soldiers also used it during the Civil War (Elliott 1976). Though it doesn't make a very satisfactory substitute by itself, coffee producers sometimes use chicory as a coffee additive. To make your own, dig up chicory roots anytime from fall to spring. Scrub them, slice large roots in half, and roast them at a low oven temperature (250° F) for 2 to 4 hours, until they become dark brown and brittle. Break up the roots, and grind them in a coffee grinder. Add 1 part chicory to 4 parts coffee, and brew yourself a cup (Silverman 1977).

The young basal leaves and the flower buds hidden at the base of the leaves are edible and may also be collected from fall to spring (Elias and Dykeman 1982). You will probably need to boil the plant in one to three changes of water to reduce the bitterness. If collected when very young, the buds and leaves may be mild enough to eat raw. In Europe the buds are pickled and canned (Hackett and Carolane 1982). Endive, the bitter salad green, is a relative of chicory.

Plant Characteristics

The perennial herb grows to more than 3 feet (1 m) tall, on slender, rigid, angular, sparsely leafed stems. The pinnately lobed basal leaves resemble dandelion leaves. Unstalked flower heads are scattered along, and sometimes clasp, the stems. Others emerge at the tips of leafless branches. The attractive blue flower heads appear from spring to fall. On some plants, pink or white flowers are found. About 2 inches (5 cm) in diameter, the heads consist of about 15 to 20 ray flowers. The square tips of the spreading strap-shaped flowers have five tiny teeth. The fleshy taproot is branched and difficult to pull out. The sap is milky.

Introduced from Europe as a garden flower, the perennial now grows wild throughout the United States. Chicory occasionally occurs wild in Texas, mostly along roadsides and the edges of fields in North Texas and the Panhandle. Finding it before the flower stalk emerges is difficult—you may need to grow your own supply.

DANDELION—*TARAXACUM OFFICINALE*
(See illustration, page 14.)

The common dandelion provides one of the best-tasting and most nutritious wild vegetables in Texas. Europeans and Chinese have used dandelions for food and medicine for centuries. Farmers in New Jersey grow them for markets in New York. Health food stores sell teas containing dandelion roots. Throughout the United States in the early part of this century, particularly during the Depression, dandelions were harvested regularly for food and wine making. In spite of its many uses, most Americans consider dandelions mere weeds. We spend much time and money trying to eradicate the herbs from lawns and gardens. Perhaps after reading this, instead of despising the common dandelion, you will look forward to the bright splashes of yellow that color your lawn from fall to summer (Fleming 1975).

Just about every part of the plant is edible. Dig up the whole plant before the flowers emerge. You can use the root, the leaves, and the flower buds tucked away at the crown of the root. Though available year-round, the plants are best from late fall to spring. If you collect the leaves and buds when they are very young, you can use them raw in salads. I have rarely found greens that were not already too bitter to eat raw. Use bitter greens and scrubbed roots as a potherb, and reduce the bitterness by boiling the plant in a small amount of water for about five minutes. Pour off the water, add more boiling water to the pot, and cook again for a couple of minutes. The procedure can be repeated if necessary. But even in the middle of summer you should be able to produce a pleasant-tasting dish after boiling the plant no more than three times. Serve it with butter and lemon. A few slivered almonds on top adds a special touch (Elliott 1976).

According to research initiated by Euell Gibbons (1966), dandelion greens are an excellent source of vitamin A, iron, calcium, phosphorus, and potassium. They outrank just about any garden vegetable in nutrition. So the next time you weed your lawn and garden, dig up the dandelions, but don't throw them out. Serve them for supper instead.

Dandelion flowers may be fermented for dandelion wine. And the thick taproot and whitish root crown provide a reasonable coffee substitute, with no caffeine. It's easy to see why this plant was put to so much use during the Depression. Collect the roots at any season, though they are best from late fall to early spring. Scrub them, and cut large roots in half.

Cook them for 2 to 4 hours at a low oven temperature (250° F) until they are brittle and brown inside. Break up the roots, grind them in a coffee grinder, then brew the powder just like coffee—alone or added to your regular coffee (Scooter Cheatham, interview September 1984).

The United States Pharmacopeia listed the dandelion as a medicinal plant from 1831 through 1926, and the *National Formulary* until 1965. The Latin name "Taraxacum officinale" roughly translates as "the official remedy for illnesses." The Chinese used an extract of the root as a diuretic, an antibacterial, and an antifungal agent, among other uses. I have seen no report of the chemical constituents in the plant that might explain its many uses. Its nutritional content would make it useful in the prevention and treatment of diseases caused by vitamin and mineral deficiencies. Thought to be a native of the Old World, the dandelion has been widespread in North America for so long that several native American tribes have used it for food and medicine (Gibbons 1962; Silverman 1977).

Older dye books report that dandelions yield purple dyes for wool, but I have gotten nothing better than a pale yellow out of the flowers and a light tan from the roots. From interviews with other dyers and recent articles on dyeing, it would appear that the purple dandelion dye information is erroneous.

Plant Characteristics

The common dandelion, probably a native of Europe, grows throughout much of the Northern Hemisphere and most of Texas. A taprooted annual or perennial, *Taraxacum officinale* sprouts in lawns and gardens and along roadsides. The medieval Latin name for the plant, "dens leonis," or lion's-tooth, refers to the jagged-toothed pinnately lobed leaves, which form a basal rosette. The solitary yellow flower head emerges from the center of the rosette on a leafless hollow stem several inches tall. About 1–1.5 inches (2.5–4 cm) across, the rounded heads consist solely of ray flowers. The plant has white milky sap. Tiny achenes are attached to miniature parachutes. Children love to pick the round seed heads and blow on them to watch the parachutes float on the breeze.

GOLDENROD, SWEET GOLDENROD, PLUMERO—*SOLIDAGO ODORA*
(See photograph, plate 4.)

The fresh green leaves and flowers of the fall-blooming sweet goldenrod smell and taste much like licorice or anise. After the colonists dumped the British tea into Boston Harbor in 1773, they used *Solidago odora* as an ingredient in what came to be known as liberty tea. Even the Chinese imported sweet goldenrod tea. Today one of America's best and most unusual herb teas is all but forgotten (Silverman 1977; Gibbons and Tucker 1979).

Though you can store the dried herb for year-round use as tea, I find the flavor of the fresh plant far superior. Collect sweet goldenrod only when you find the plants growing in fairly large numbers. Goldenrods are perennials, so don't pull them up by the roots. You can minimize damage to the plants by stripping the leaves and flowers from a single branch of a few plants. Better yet, grow your own from wild seeds.

SWEET GOLDENROD TEA

Collect and rinse several cups of leaves and flowers (if you are allergic to pollen, don't use the flowers in the tea). Measure the volume of plants, place the fresh herbs in a pot, and pour boiling water over them. For 2 cups of fresh plant parts, use 4 cups of water. (Dry and store any leaves and flowers that are not used right away. If making your tea from dried herbs, use a smaller volume of the herb.) Let the tea steep for 10 to 30 minutes, then strain it. Drink it hot, with sweetening and lemon if you like. Or refrigerate the sweetened juice for a licorice-flavored cold drink.

SWEET GOLDENROD JELLY

1 cup goldenrod tea,   2 tablespoons pectin
   made as above with   ¾ cup sugar
   fresh leaves and flowers

Add the pectin to the tea and heat to a rolling boil, stirring continuously. Add the sugar all at once, and heat to a rolling boil again. Stir and boil 1 to 3 minutes until the concoction passes the jelly test (see the index). Pour into jelly jars. If you like licorice, you'll go nuts over sweet goldenrod jelly!

The oil extracted from the surface of sweet goldenrod leaves has been used in perfumes. Besides producing a delightful beverage and aroma, the yellow flowers yield a bright yellow dye for wool (see Chapter 5 for recipes). In fact, all species of goldenrod can be used as dyes. Thomas Edison promoted the use of the latex of several goldenrods for rubber production. At least one Texas species, *Solidago altissima,* contains enough hydrocarbons to have commercial potential.

The fall-blooming goldenrods have an undeserved bad reputation. Hay fever sufferers frequently blame goldenrods for their misery. Though the pollen is allergenic, insect-pollinated flowers, such as goldenrods, do not usually produce large quantities of airborne pollen (Wodehouse 1971). Ragweeds and molds cause most of the fall hay fever problems, but people overlook the weedy-looking ragweeds and shake their fingers at the neighboring colorful blooms of the goldenrods. Let's give goldenrods their due. They have a number of valuable uses. And at the end of a long, hot summer, these gorgeous wildflowers brighten up the autumn roadsides, giving one the false sense that spring, not winter, is on its way.

Plant Characteristics

Solidago odora, a perennial herb, produces beautiful flowers in early fall. The herb consists of a single slender stem, 2−3 feet (6−10 dm) tall, that branches near the top. Numerous narrowly lanceolate leaves crowd the stem, alternating and spiraling around it. Several times longer than broad, the leaves gradually become smaller on the upper portion of the stem, and the margins are entire or finely toothed. Bright yellow flowers occur in tiny heads that are clustered on the upper branching tips of the stem. Solidago odora occurs in open sandy soil in East and Southeast Texas. It grows throughout the eastern United States. The licorice aroma of the leaves and flowers clearly distinguishes it from other goldenrods.

More than a score of goldenrod species find a home in Texas. Several have become extremely rare, so if you are looking for dye plants, use goldenrods only when they are found in abundance.

LETTUCE—LACTUCA SPECIES
(See illustration.)

Warning

Because of the presence of the latex, the raw greens of the wild lettuces can cause stomach upset if eaten in quantity. The latex also causes dermatitis in sensitive persons (Lampe and Fagerström 1968; Elias and Dykeman 1982).

If you did not plant lettuce in a fall garden this year, head for the open fields to harvest wild lettuce. The various species of wild Lactuca that grow throughout Texas are first cousins to garden lettuce. The wild greens contain more vitamin A than spinach and a good quantity of vitamin C (Zennie and Ogzewella 1977).

Collect wild lettuce from late fall to early spring. The young basal leaves of the blue lettuce Lactuca floridana may be mild enough to use raw in salads. But unfortunately, even the earliest leaves of the more common prickly lettuce, Lactuca serriola, taste quite bitter. Boil them for a few minutes in two or three changes of water to reduce the bitterness.

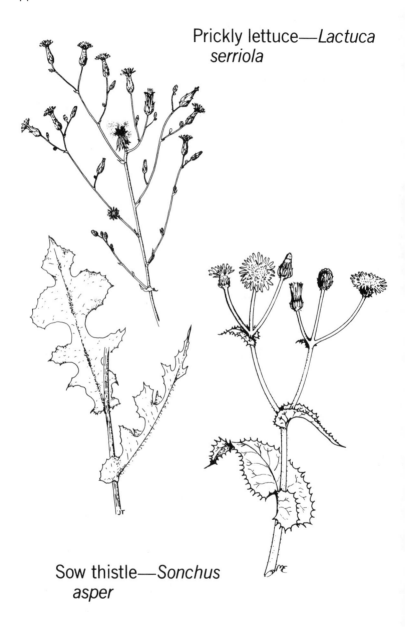

Prickly lettuce—*Lactuca serriola*

Sow thistle—*Sonchus asper*

You can also use the early shoots and stem leaves of both species. The basal rosettes emerge in late fall, and the plants begin flowering in late spring. The earlier you collect the leaves, the better the flavor (Fleming 1975; Gibbons 1966; Silverman 1977).

An extract of the sticky white sap of two European species of *Lactuca* has been used to replace opium in cough remedies. The extract, called lactucarium, is reported to be a mild sedative (Emboden 1979; Lewis and Elvin-Lewis 1977).

Plant Characteristics

Of the seven species of wild lettuce in Texas, prickly lettuce (*L. serriola*) and blue lettuce (*L. floridana*) are the common species. Prickly lettuce, an annual herb, produces a basal rosette of pinnately lobed leaves before sending up the leafy flowering stalk. The alternate leaves clasp the stem. Fine flexible prickles tip the teeth of the leaves, and the midrib on the back of the leaf bears a row of soft spines. The single stalk, sometimes as tall as 6 feet (2 m), branches near its summit. Small heads of yellow flowers emerge at the tips of these upper branches. When garden lettuce bolts, it produces flower heads that look just like those of the wild prickly lettuce, which grows along roadsides and as a weed in fields and yards throughout much of the northern two thirds of the state. A native of Europe, the species now grows wild in much of the United States. The garden lettuce, *L. sativa,* in cultivation as early as 4500 B.C. in Egypt, may be a derivative of prickly lettuce.

Blue lettuce, a native of the eastern United States, grows in East, Central, and North Central Texas. You can distinguish it from prickly lettuce by its blue flowers and lack of prickles on the leaves.

RAGWEED, GIANT RAGWEED—*AMBROSIA TRIFIDA*
(See illustration, page 302.)

Giant ragweed and its cousins win the prize as the most despised weeds in America. Every fall, millions of innocent civilians are struck down by an army of pollen. Ragweeds produce pollen in prodigious quantities. To be fair, the plants do not intentionally do us harm. Their only interest is in the propagation of the species. But when we unwittingly come into the path of the floating masses of pollen, oh, how we suffer. Hidden under the guise of a plain green weed, ragweeds go unnoticed, and yet they grow in abundance throughout Texas along roadsides, in fields, and in stream bottoms. Before the introduction of agriculture and ranching, the ragweeds were limited in their distribution. Ironically, the disturbance of the soils caused by human actions enables the herbs to spread rapidly, following us wherever we go across the continent. Ragweed is an important soil binder, but it is cursed by humans, who wage a never-ending battle with hay fever.

Archeological studies in Kentucky have uncovered evidence that ancient native American peoples in the central Mississippi Valley cultivated *Ambrosia trifida* for its nutritious seeds. Along with sunflowers and pelocote (*Iva annua*), this early cultivar may have formed an agricultural complex that predates the introduction of maize into the region. The Indians used the seeds as a grain, the stem fibers for making rope, and the plant for treating a variety of ailments (Struever 1971; Silverman 1977).

Although I sneeze and sniffle throughout the fall, I have come to consider the giant ragweed a welcome friend in other seasons. As a light green dye for wool, giant ragweed leaves are one of my favorites. The red sap of the plant was used as a stain by the Omaha Indians. And if you want some thread for sewing or weaving, the stems of this ragweed yield a good fiber. Cut down the tall stalks after the pollen has finished its work in the late fall. Loosen the fibers from the outer layer of the stalks by soaking the stalks in water for a few days.

Another attribute that has won giant ragweed to my heart forever is its value as a treatment for the rash of poison ivy. Make an infusion by pouring boiling water over a bowl full of ragweed leaves. Fresh aromatic leaves work best. **Don't drink the tea!** Instead, let it steep till it cools. Then throw away the leaves, and dab the tea on the itchy pimples produced by poison ivy. The astringent tea relieves the itch temporarily, so dab more on as needed. The wash also seems to help dry up the rash. Ragweed tea loses its potency in a couple of days. This astringent wash is good for bathing your skin anytime you venture into areas infested with poison ivy. By washing off the poison ivy sap right away, you can limit the extent of the dermatitis.

Warning

Though I have had good success with ragweed tea as a treatment for poison ivy when it is applied during the early stages of the rash, the wash is not strong enough for advanced cases of poison ivy rash. Don't use any nonsterile substance on oozing sores. (For details on alternative treatments for poison ivy rash, see Chapter 4.) Some individuals get a skin rash from ragweed as well as poison ivy, though giant ragweed causes dermatitis much less frequently than the small ragweed species Ambrosia artemisiifolia and A. bidentata. Ragweed pollen also can cause dermatitis (Mitchell and Rook 1979).

Plant Characteristics

The annual *Ambrosia trifida* rapidly grows to a height of 15 feet (5 m) or taller by late summer. The rough angular stem has red sap. When crushed, the sandpaper-textured leaves emit a fragrant odor, similar to that of menthol. Most of the leaves occur in pairs. Those on the upper stem are unlobed, and the larger lower leaves usually have three to five fingerlike lobes with serrated margins. The flowers have no petals and form clusters of stamens or pistils in a tiny green cup. The cups form bunches in the leaf axils and at the top of the stem. Giant ragweed grows across the eastern two thirds of the state and across much of the country.

Seven other annual and perennial ragweeds grow in Texas, most less than 5 feet (1.8 m) and often less than 3 feet (1 m) in height. The leaves alternate either throughout the stem or at least on the upper stem, and they vary from unlobed to greatly dissected. The flower clusters are similar to those of giant ragweed.

SOW THISTLE, ACHICORIA DULCE—*SONCHUS OLERACEUS,*
SONCHUS ASPER
(See illustration, page 44.)

Sow thistles grow as weeds in gardens and yards. The next time you pull them out of your lawn, try cooking them instead of tossing them into the garbage. Sow thistle provides a reasonable, though bitter, potherb. While our cultivated greens wither in the heat, sow thistle keeps on sprouting in our lawns, along roadsides, and in open fields practically year-round.

Collect the young basal leaves from fall to spring. If you get them early enough, they might be mild enough for use in a salad. But it's more likely that you'll want to boil them briefly in one to three changes of water to reduce the bitterness. You can mix them with other greens, such as dandelions and wild lettuce. Serve them with butter and lemon or with pepper sauce. Harvest the young shoots when they are only a few inches tall for a cooked vegetable. Boil leaves and peeled shoots at least twice. After buds form, the plants become too bitter to eat. In mowed lawns young plants pop up and can be harvested any time of year (Scooter Cheatham, interview, March 1985; Elias and Dykeman 1982).

Around the turn of the century the Chinese in the San Francisco area used an evaporated extract of the white milky sap of *Sonchus oleraceus* as an antinarcotic to help break opium addiction (Emboden 1979). The extract yields a powerful cathartic. In Tanganyika the root is eaten raw to eliminate worms (Watt and Breyer-Brandwijk 1962). I have found no details on the chemical constituents of this species.

Plant Characteristics

Both species are slender annuals, natives of Europe that now grow wild throughout Texas and the rest of the United States. The alternate leaves clasp the stem, thickly covering it. Flexible prickles tip the teeth of the pinnately lobed leaves. Flower heads top a leafy stalk that is usually less than 2 feet (6 dm) tall but may reach 6 feet (2 m). The yellow flowers and the ball of seeds attached to feathery parachutes resemble the flowers and seeds of dandelions, but sow thistle flower heads are smaller, usually less than 1 inch (25 mm) across. Although the two species of *Sonchus* are quite similar to each other, *Sonchus asper* has slightly rougher, spinier foliage.

SUNFLOWER—*HELIANTHUS* SPECIES

COMMON SUNFLOWER, MIRASOL, GIRASOL—*HELIANTHUS ANNUUS*

While large fields of cultivated sunflowers with flower heads a foot in diameter grow across Texas, unplanted fields covered with smaller wild sunflowers brighten the roadsides in summer and fall. The abundant wildflowers bind the soil and restore lost nutrients to fallow fields. Much smaller in size than the seeds of cultivated varieties, wild sunflower seeds are no less nutritious—eat them raw or roasted. The tiny unopened flower buds, available in summer, also provide a tasty morsel with a flavor reminiscent of artichokes. The buds become bitter quickly, so you may need to boil them in two or three changes of water. Serve them with lemon and melted butter.

Native Americans have cultivated the sunflower for several thousand years. The Hopis and Havasupais of Arizona and several other tribes still grow the cultivated strains they developed centuries ago. In the United States, cultivation of the sunflower may predate the introduction of maize from the south. Native Americans developed giant sunflowers, as large as those later developed in Russia. Many crops of importance today came from the Americas, but the sunflower is the only major crop that originated in what is now the United States.

The sunflower was one of the first New World crops introduced to Europe in the late 1500s. Today the USSR produces more sunflower seeds than any other nation. In fact, the Russians developed most of the cultivars now grown in the United States.

Sunflower seeds yield good protein, vitamins, minerals, and a high-quality oil. Raw or roasted sunflower seeds and 100 percent sunflower oil are familiar items in groceries these days. Besides being useful in cooking, the oil is used in soaps, paints, and varnishes. Birds relish the nutritious seeds, so birdwatchers often fill their bird feeders with the seeds. The whole plant and oil cakes (the pulp that remains after oil is extracted) provide food for livestock.

Sunflowers figured in the religious ceremonies and creation myths of the Onondagas of New York. American Indians ground the seeds into meal, used the oil as food and as a base for paint pigments, and used various parts of the plant medicinally. They made cordage with the stem fibers and used the seeds and flowers for dyes (Heiser 1976; Struever 1971).

The stalks yield fibers that the Chinese reportedly have used in fabrics, and the pulp shows promise for paper production. The Russians have used the pith of the stalks as a buoyant material for life preservers (Fleming 1975; Hill 1952; Schery 1972).

Large fields of sunflowers can produce enough allergenic pollen to cause problems for those who live nearby. Fortunately, the heavy pollen does not become airborne as readily as that of ragweeds, also members of the sunflower family.

Plant Characteristics

The common sunflower, a branching annual up to 8 feet (2.5 m) tall, bears bright yellow flat flower heads at the tips of the branches. Its large ovate leaves occur on long petioles, and most leaves alternate on the stem. Stiff, harsh hairs cover leaves and stem, and leaf margins are coarsely toothed. Flower heads, 2–5 inches (5–12 cm) across, consist of 20 to 25 yellow ray flowers circling the central disk. The flat seeds develop from the disk flowers, which may be purplish or red.

Helianthus annuus grows throughout Texas and the United States. It is particularly abundant in the eastern and southern halves of the state in abandoned fields and along roadsides and railroad tracks. Several varieties occur in Texas.

Maximilian Sunflower—*HELIANTHUS MAXIMILIANI*

(See photograph, plate 5.)

Though not nearly as well known as its cousin the common sunflower, *Helianthus maximiliani* also provides nutritious seeds. Scooter Cheatham (interview, September 1984) reports that Maximilian sunflower bears a thickened root that produces white succulent rootlets. Resembling small potatoes, the rootlets can be eaten raw, boiled, or roasted. Closely related to the Jerusalem artichoke (*Helianthus tuberosus*), they have a similar slightly nutty flavor (Heiser 1976). The tall stately Maximilian sunflower produces a spectacular array of wildflowers in mid-fall. The rootlets can be dug up anytime after flowering to late winter. I have had no success in retrieving the rootlets so far. The rocky or clay-rich soils in which I usually find the plants growing make it difficult to dig up anything but the woody main root. Growing your own plants from wild seeds in loose soil may yield good results, however.

Considering the quality of the seeds and oil and the added bonus of edible rootlets, it's surprising that improved varieties of Maximilian sunflower have never been cultivated. The Soil Conservation Service has put Maximilian sunflower to use as food and cover for birds, deer, and other wildlife, as a forage for livestock, and as a soil stabilizer (Fleming 1975; Elliott 1976; Gibbons 1962).

Use the wild Maximilian sunflower seeds, buds, and fiber in the same manner as those of the common sunflower. Both the beautiful bright yellow flowers and the taproot produce good dyes for wool.

Plant Characteristics

Helianthus maximiliani, a perennial wildflower, was named for German naturalist Prince Maximilian of Wied-Neuwied, who explored the West in the early 1800s. Several flat heads of yellow flowers bloom in a spike at the top of the slender stalks, to 10 feet (3 m) tall. Heads also occur in the leaf axils along the upper half of the stalk. Rough hairs cover the stem and simple leaves. Numerous long, slender lanceolate leaves alternate along the usually unbranched stem. The leaves may be 4 – 12 inches long (1 – 3 dm) and generally have no petiole. Leaf margins usually are entire. The heads, 2 – 3 inches (5 – 7.5 cm) across, consist of bright yellow ray flowers circling the yellow central disk.

Maximilian sunflower grows in colonies along roadsides, in ditches, and in open fields throughout much of the state but is particularly common on the Edwards Plateau and North Central and Southeast Texas. It is also found from southern Canada across the central United States to the southeastern states.

THISTLE—*CIRSIUM* SPECIES

Bull Thistle—*CIRSIUM HORRIDULUM*
Texas Thistle—*CIRSIUM TEXANUM*

(See illustration.)

In spite of their spines, thistles provide one of the best wild salad greens and cooked vegetables in the state. Take along thick gloves, a knife, and a shovel to harvest this succulent delight. Sensitive persons can develop dermatitis from the prickles and hairs. From fall to early spring, gather the fleshy taproot and the large basal leaves. Scrub the roots and clip the spines from the leaves. Add both leaves and roots raw to salads, or steam them for a few minutes and serve with lemon and melted butter. Cooked, the leaf blades are a bit tough, but the thickened central vein is juicy and tender. The flavor of the cooked root resembles that of its relative the artichoke.

The thick young flower stalk also provides a tasty vegetable, if gathered in the early spring before the flowers bloom. Older stalks become dry, fibrous, and extremely bitter. Grasp the young stem with a gloved hand, and cut it off at the base. Trim off the spines, and peel off the outer fibers of the stem. You will be left with a tender vegetable, similar in texture and flavor to celery. This vegetable is excellent raw, or it can be boiled or steamed for a few minutes and then dipped in lemon butter. The bottom

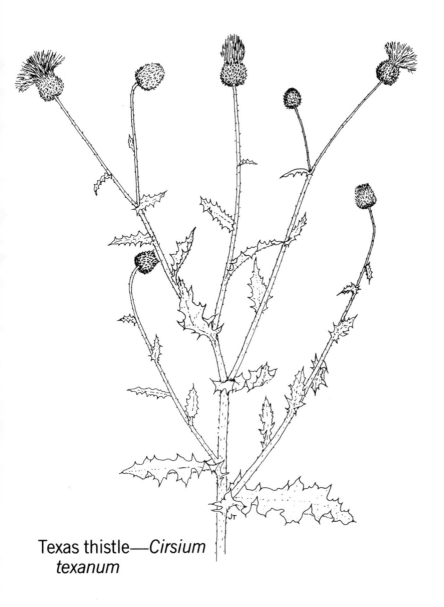

Texas thistle—*Cirsium texanum*

of the large flower buds of *Cirsium horridulum* also can be cooked and eaten (Stahl 1974; Scooter Cheatham, interview, March 1985).

Of the nine species of *Cirsium* in Texas, these two probably provide the best food. The stems and roots of other species tend to be more fibrous.

The stem fibers of any thistle species can be used for thread or cordage. Soak the stalks in water for several days to loosen the fibers from the outer layer of the stalks. In summer, collect the white fluff that clings to the seeds and use it as tinder for starting fires or as a stuffing for pillows.

Plant Characteristics

A biennial or perennial herb, Texas thistle grows 3−5 feet (1−1.5 m) tall. The basal and stem leaves are pinnately lobed. Lower leaves may be 4−9 inches (1−2 dm) long. Needles tip the lobes and teeth of the leaves, and the leaf bottoms may be woolly. Near its top, the thick flowering stalk branches into several long slender stems tipped with purple, lavender, or pink flower heads. About 1½ inches (4 cm) in diameter, the rounded flower heads consist of many threadlike disk flowers. Tufts of soft down cling to the tiny seeds.

Texas thistle grows in abundance throughout most of the state along roadsides and in unplanted fields. It also occurs in Oklahoma and Mexico.

Bull thistle, a common annual or biennial herb, produces huge spiny leaves, the lower ones up to 2 feet (6 dm) long. The thick stalk is branched only in the upper portion, the branches usually topped with a solitary yellow or pink flower head 2−3 inches (4−8 cm) broad. This species is the only thistle in Texas with yellow flowers. Bull thistle grows in open sandy areas and along roadsides in the eastern third of the state, mainly near the Coast, as well as throughout the eastern United States.

Two other thistle species, one in the Trans-Pecos and one in deep East Texas, are rare. Collect thistles only if the local population is abundant and the identity is known.

CACTACEAE—CACTUS FAMILY

Few plants have such power to fascinate and frustrate us like cactus does. As its victims, we curse its injurious spines, while wondering at its curious configurations.

Native American tribes throughout the country have relied on cacti for food, medicine, dyes, and a variety of other uses for thousands of years. They eat the colorful flowers and succulent fruit of many cacti and the stems of a few species. The cactus family also includes the hallucinogenic peyote, used in the religious rituals of native American tribes in the Southwest and Mexico.

The spiny yuccas, agaves, and even mesquites are frequently mistaken for cacti, while a number of true cacti don't have spines at all. You will need to rely on other characteristics to help you identify the diverse members of this family. All cacti have areoles, which are pits or protrusions scattered across the surface of the plant. If the plant does have spines, they emerge in clusters from these unique structures. The areoles vary in appearance from rough, round spots, as seen on the prickly pear, to woolly elongations. For an excellent field guide to the identification of cacti, refer to Del Weniger's *Cacti of Texas and Neighboring States*.

Cacti have responded to a hostile, water-starved environment by developing a storehouse of unusual characteristics. A network of fine, shallow roots quickly soaks up rainwater. Bloated stems store enough water to enable the plants to withstand extended droughts. The absence of leaves cuts down on water loss through evaporation, and a thick waxy skin helps hold in the precious liquid. In fact, the waxy coating on prickly pear cacti is so effective at blocking the escape of moisture that it is harvested in Mexico to waterproof raingear.

Even the spines improve the chances for survival. The juicy interior of a cactus plant makes a fine meal for a pocket mouse, jackrabbit, or mule deer. Spines arranged in an interlacing pattern present a formidable barrier to those hungry animals. In spite of this protection, many desert creatures manage to find ways to burrow under a plant or, in the case of a prickly pear cactus, to eat between the spines. The intricate latticework of spines on some species also shades the plant, often providing the only respite from the summer sun. A large prickly pear cactus may provide shade for a desert cottontail or nesting habitat for a roadrunner or cactus wren. These adaptations to life in the desert combine to create bizarre life-forms.

In the 1800s the peculiar-looking plants became popular as ornamentals in Europe. The craze for cacti expanded over the decades, resulting in the removal of many tons of plants from the wild yearly, to be shipped all over the world. A 1974 study by the Smithsonian Institution estimated that 30 percent of the cactus species in the United States are now either endangered or threatened with extinction. In addition to the devastation of cactus populations by collectors, ranching and farming take their toll on the plants when the land is cleared for pastures and farms. While a number of cacti furnish delectable fruits and vegetables, always take into consideration their local abundance before harvesting any of these marvels of the desert.

OPUNTIA—*OPUNTIA* SPECIES

CHOLLA—*OPUNTIA IMBRICATA* AND OTHER SPECIES
(See photograph, plate 6.)

The chollas, while not as succulent as prickly pear pads, do provide some possibilities for food. The Hopis, Papagos, and various other tribes in the Southwest ate the flower buds, the yellow fruits, and the young stem joints (Niethammer 1974). Typically, the Indians baked the plants in an underground pit. Cholla has a slightly sour flavor. As a fried vegetable, the buds and stems are tasty. The small fruits have a lot of seeds, making them less desirable foods.

FRIED CHOLLA

Cholla flower buds and stem
  joints
Cornmeal
Whole wheat flour

Garlic salt
Salt and pepper
Oil

Collect the buds and tender stem joints with tongs, cutting them off at the juncture. Burn off the spines, then peel the vegetables (if you use the fruits, remove the seeds). Place the pieces in a pot of water and boil them until tender, about 15 minutes. Then make a batter with 2 parts cornmeal to 1 part flour, adding the seasonings to taste. Roll the cholla pieces in the batter, and fry them in a pan with hot oil.

The dead stems of the tall chollas, such as *Opuntia imbricata,* decay to a woody hollow cylinder. The lacelike pattern of the wood makes an ornate decoration.

Plant Characteristics

Although they are members of the same genus, the chollas do not resemble prickly pears. Instead of being flat pads, the spiny joints of the cholla stem are cylindrical and knotted, resembling thick rope, and vary from 1–3 inches (3–8 cm) in diameter. In some species the glochids, hairlike spines surrounding the longer needles, are few or may be absent. Cane cholla (*Opuntia imbricata*) branches, treelike, to a height of several feet. Some cholla species hug the ground, rising a mere 6 inches (15 cm) above the surface. Flower colors range from yellow to green to orange or deep magenta, and the usually yellow-green fruits are ropy, like the stems. Chollas grow in the western and southern parts of the state.

PRICKLY PEAR CACTUS, NOPAL, CACANAPO—*OPUNTIA ENGELMANNII* AND OTHER SPECIES

(See photograph, plate 7.)

Warning

Eating too much of the raw prickly pear fruit can cause constipation. On the other hand, too many prickly pear pads eaten at one time (and for some people three small pads can be too much) can cause diarrhea (Scooter Cheatham, interview, September 1984). The cactus contains oxalic acid and can poison cattle if no other sources of forage are available to balance their diet (Watt and Breyer-Brandwijk 1962). Cacti have been attributed with saving lives by supplying both food and water to people stranded in the desert, but considering the potential problems of overconsumption, eat them in moderation.

Prickly pear spines and glochids can cause a skin rash in sensitive individuals and, if left embedded, can cause severe infection. The glochids cause a skin rash resembling scabies (Mitchell and Rook 1979).

Prickly pears grow in abundance in Texas. The peculiar plants with their flat, round pads are a familiar sight in fields and pastures throughout much of the state. The stems, flowers, and succulent fruits of prickly pears provide tasty treats.

The pads, actually joints from the stem of the cactus, make an excellent cooked vegetable. Prickly pears are grown for food in Mexico, Greece, and Italy (Hackett and Carolane 1982). Occasionally you'll see them in the produce section of groceries in Texas. Though you can use the older pads, the young pads that are newly formed in the spring provide a more tender vegetable. If collected early enough, the tender new pads, or *nopalitos,* will not have formed long spines. But don't overlook the tiny hairlike needles, or glochids, that emerge early from the areoles. If you are not observant, you may discover the barbs embedded in your hands. The prickly pear harvester quickly learns the value of a thick pair of leather gloves.

Harvest the young pads by grasping them with tongs and slicing them at the stem joints. Hold the pads over a flame to singe both the long spines and the glochids, then scrape off any remaining spines with a knife. Rinse the pads well, and check them thoroughly for any tiny spines that may cling to the surface. Slice the pads into thin strips, and drop them into boiling water to cook for about ten minutes. Drain off the water, and rinse the *nopalitos* to wash off some of the slippery gum. The *nopalitos* now are ready for use in a variety of dishes, salads, soups, and casseroles. If you use older pads, remove the tough skin by scraping it off with a knife, and cut out the more fibrous sections (Gibbons and Tucker 1979).

NOPALITOS AND *HUEVOS RANCHEROS*

Prickly pear pads (1 small pad
  per person)
Eggs

Butter
Salt and pepper
Picante sauce

After preparing the *nopalitos* as above, sauté them in butter. Fry your eggs, sunny-side up, with salt and pepper to taste. Serve the eggs topped with picante sauce, the *nopalitos* on the side.

Or sauté the *nopalitos* with chopped onions and tomatoes, simmering them until well cooked. Then stir in beaten eggs, and cook as you would scrambled eggs or an omelet.

Nopalitos taste pleasantly sour and contain generous amounts of vitamin A and calcium. The interior of the pad is mucilaginous, yielding a slippery vegetable that's a bit difficult to get hold of with a fork. Try eating your *huevos rancheros* Mexican style, scooping them up with a tortilla or a piece of bread.

FRIED *NOPALITOS* FOR TWO

1 cup *nopalitos,* prepared
  as above
⅓ cup wheat flour
⅔ cup cornmeal

1 teaspoon chile powder
Salt and pepper to taste
Vegetable oil

Place flour, cornmeal, and spices in a small bag, and shake the bag to mix. Drop *nopalitos* into the bag, and shake till the strips are well coated. Heat oil in a skillet. Fry the strips till they are golden brown.

NOPALITOS GUMBO

½ cup *nopalitos,* prepared
  as above
2 cups cooked rice
2 slices bacon
3 tablespoons flour
1 large onion, chopped
1 celery stalk, chopped

1 clove garlic, chopped
1 can stewed tomatoes
2 cups cooked chicken, diced
Salt and pepper
Gumbo filé (powdered sassafras
  leaves)

Fry the bacon, and remove from pan. Brown the flour in the bacon fat to make a roux. Add 1 cup boiling water, and stir well. In a separate pan

sauté the onion, celery, and garlic in bacon fat or oil. Add the cooked
vegetables to the roux. Mash the stewed tomatoes, and add them with
their juice. Chop the *nopalitos,* and add them to the gumbo. Finally,
add the chicken, salt, and pepper. Simmer for at least 30 minutes.
Serve the thick gumbo over rice, with gumbo filé sprinkled on top.

These are just a few of the many ways you can incorporate prickly pear
pads into your meals. You can eat the large yellow, orange, or red flowers
of the prickly pear as well. The sweet nectar attracts bees and produces a
delicious honey. But the most delightful part of the plant is the red fruit,
called the tuna or pear. Rub or burn off the glochids, peel the fruit, and
eat it raw. The fruit is high in sugar, with some pears yielding up to 14
percent sugars, and also contains good amounts of vitamin C, calcium,
and phosphorus (Tate 1972).

You can use the raw pears in fruit salads, fruit drinks, yogurt, or gelatin
dishes. Cut the pears in half, remove the seeds, and roll slices of the
pears in confectioners' sugar for a candy-sweet treat. Mash the fruit, and
mix the juice with confectioners' sugar for a pink cake icing. Some species produce sweeter and more succulent fruits than others. If you find
one with fruit that you don't relish raw, cut out the seeds and stew the
pears with added sugar for candies and preserves or add the cooked fruit
to the ice cream freezer.

The following recipe makes a scrumptious bright red fruit jelly that
rivals anything great-grandmother ever made. For more recipes, refer to
Carolyn Niethammer's *American Indian Food and Lore.*

PRICKLY PEAR JELLY

About 15 large prickly pear
  fruits
Lemon or lime juice

Powdered pectin or Sure-Jell
Sugar

Use only fully ripe fruits. Slightly green fruits add an unpleasant sour
flavor to the jelly. After removing the spines, cover the fruit in water and
boil until tender, about 20 minutes. Mash the fruit and strain it through
cheesecloth to produce the juice. Measure the juice. (For every cup of
juice, you will need 1½ tablespoons powdered pectin or Sure-Jell, 2
tablespoons lemon or lime juice, and 1 to 1½ cups sugar. The smaller
amount of sugar yields a slightly tart jelly.) Pour the juice into a clean
pot, add the pectin, and bring to a quick boil, stirring constantly. Add
the lemon juice and sugar. Bring to a rolling boil, and cook for 3
minutes or until it passes the jelly test (refer to the index). Pour the jelly
into jars.

In the past the harvest of the tunas was a big social event for many native American tribes in the Southwest. Family groups would gather in their favorite pear patch in late summer to harvest, eat, and dry the fruits. Indeed, they would return in subsequent years to reap what archeologists call the second harvest, the extraction of the prickly pear seeds from the previous year's feces. You may choose a method that is more socially acceptable by today's standards for obtaining the nutritious seeds. Grind the flat seeds, which are high in oil and protein, into flour, or add them to soups (Newcomb 1961; Struever 1971; Scooter Cheatham, interview, September 1984).

Prickly pear cacti offer much more than just delightful, nutritious foods. In Mexico people use the plants for a variety of home remedies. When cut open, the pad forms a soothing poultice to apply to wounds and bruises, a handy remedy considering the number of wounds and bruises one earns collecting the pads and fruit. Archeologists in West Texas have uncovered prickly pear purses, dried pads hollowed out or two pads tied together to form a small container. Early desert dwellers made the pouches thousands of years ago.

The Navahos dye wool with the uncooked juice of the fruit, letting the wool soak in the fermenting juice for about a week (Bryan 1978). The pears produce spectacular pinks and magentas on wool that fade somewhat with exposure to sunlight. If you notice a cluster of small white woolly webs on the plants, brush them off and save them for dyeing wool or cotton. Inside the web is a tiny insect called a cochineal (see photograph, plate 7, photo insert), a relative of the mealybug. If you press the insect between your fingers, a scarlet juice squirts out. The body of the cochineal makes an excellent pink or red dye. The colors are fast, and a small amount goes a long way. Refer to Chapter 5 for recipes with these unusual dye materials.

Prickly pears have value as windbreaks and soil stabilizers. Unfortunately, a few species have earned a bad reputation in Texas and some other parts of the world. A Caribbean species, *Opuntia stricta,* was introduced into Australia in the early 1800s. In its new home no natural predators existed to control its growth. The plant spread rapidly, covering millions of acres of rangeland and farmland and rendering the land unusable. After many futile attempts, the government finally developed effective eradication measures (Baker 1965).

Back home, Engelmann's prickly pear (*Opuntia engelmannii*) has increased in abundance since ranching and farming transformed the Texas plains. The decimation of the prairies by grazing livestock and poor farming practices depleted the soil and rid the land of grasses and many herbaceous plants. While most cacti grow slowly, prickly pears grow rapidly. As other cacti disappeared, *Opuntia engelmannii* spread across the land at an alarming rate. Today thousands of square miles of prickly pear cover abused landscapes in Central and South Texas.

Ranchers try in vain to eliminate the spiny plants from their fields, but in times of drought the plants become welcome friends. With their spines burned off, they furnish a reliable and plentiful source of food and water for cattle, which relish the succulent pads. In fact, a United States Department of Agriculture study in South Texas found that prickly pear cacti make up "five percent of a cow's diet throughout the year regardless of range conditions" (Weishuhn 1980). The cacti also provide food for deer and javelinas. Perhaps we can find ways to turn the prickly pear problem into an advantage by harvesting this worthwhile food.

Plant Characteristics

Prickly pears, members of the genus *Opuntia,* are the cacti most widely used for food. The flat stem joints, or pads, vary from circular to egg-shaped to elongate and may be more than 1 foot (3 dm) across. Tiny conical succulent leaves, which fall off as the pad matures, appear on the new spring growth. Opuntias are the only cacti that produce on the areoles tiny hairlike spines at the base of the longer spines. These barbed needles, called glochids, are extremely difficult to remove once they grab you.

Some species of prickly pears lack the long spines but retain the glochids. A spineless cultivar is available for landscaping and is by far the easiest to work with for food preparation. Texas' many species and varieties of prickly pears vary in the color of the spines—purple, brown, white, and yellow. All opuntias produce spectacular flowers, with colors from yellow to orange to red. The fruit varies in size, shape, and palatability. Most Texas species produce red to purple fruit, but a few have yellow-green fruit. The fruit of some species becomes papery dry and therefore inedible when fully ripe. While most prickly pears inhabit the drier central, south, and western regions of the state, several species grow in the sandy soil of East Texas.

Opuntia engelmannii, our largest and most abundant prickly pear, frequently stands 4–5 feet (12–15 dm) tall, with specimens 10 feet (3 m) tall occasionally found. The species varies considerably in the shape and size of pads and the color of spines and flowers. Engelmann's prickly pear grows from the Gulf of Mexico to the Pacific Ocean and deep into Mexico.

Tasajillo, Aguijilla, Jumping Cactus—*OPUNTIA LEPTOCAULIS*

Tasajillo grows in abundance throughout most of the western half of the state. Easily overlooked until one of the joints "jumps" from the plant to your flesh, the cactus lies hidden in the shade of a tree or fence or in the brush. The plant has little value, except for its tasty red or yellow fruits.

Unfortunately, the fruits are so small, and the spines so troublesome, that the plant yields just an occasional nibble to the curious. Peel the skin back with a knife, pick out the few seeds, and toss the tiny treat into your mouth. Scooter Cheatham (interview, September 1984) reports that the fruits have a reputation for being slightly hallucinogenic, so use them sparingly.

Plant Characteristics

Tasajillo has jointed stems that are cylindrical and usually smooth, rather than knotted. The young stems, only about ¼ inch (6 mm) thick, give the spindly plant a precarious appearance, as though it were hardly strong enough to hold itself erect. Barely 1 inch (2.5 cm) thick, the older stems form a branching support for the 2−5 foot (0.6−1.5 m) tall plant. The joints detach easily from the plant. After an encounter with tasajillo, you can expect to come away with at least one joint—spines, glochids, and all—embedded in your person. The yellow flowers give way to red or yellow fruits, up to 1 inch (2.5 cm) long, which often develop short green shoots from their summit.

STRAWBERRY CACTUS—ECHINOCEREUS STRAMINEUS, ECHINOCEREUS ENNEACANTHUS
(See photograph, plate 7.)

While a number of cacti have succulent fruits, few occur as abundantly or are as easy to recognize as the opuntias. But I can't leave the cactus family without mentioning the strawberry cactus. The fruits of this cactus actually do taste like strawberries. The fruit I sampled, that of *Echinocereus stramineus,* had a pink interior speckled with tiny black seeds, even resembling a strawberry. Eaten raw or made into jellies, this incredible desert treat is not to be missed, if you can beat the wildlife to it (Weniger 1970).

Plant Characteristics

The low-growing strawberry cacti bloom in early spring, producing clusters of large pink to purple flowers. The round brown or purple fruits ripen in late summer. In Texas the plants occur mainly within 50 miles of the Rio Grande in the Trans-Pecos, and *Echinocereus enneacanthus* may be found south to Rio Grande City. Ranching operations have uprooted many plants, but strawberry cacti are still common in Big Bend National Park, where they are protected by law.

CARYOPHYLLACEAE—PINK FAMILY

CHICKWEED—*STELLARIA MEDIA*
(See illustration.)

The winter growth of chickweed provides one of the tastiest wild greens in the state. The tiny plants grow in large patches in lawns and alleyways. Pull up a few handfuls, clip off the roots, and use the whole aboveground plant. Toss the fresh plants into your salads, or cook them in a little water for just a couple of minutes. You may want to mix these mild greens with a pot of stronger-flavored greens, adding the chickweed to the pot in the last minute or two of cooking. Chickweed contains moderate amounts of vitamin C and iron (Zennie and Ogzewella 1977). You'll find the greens in abundance from late fall to spring.

In times past, chickweed was put to use in the treatment of a wide variety of ailments. A poultice of the cooked greens was applied to soothe external sores and bruises. The greens were valued in preventing and treating scurvy, caused by vitamin C deficiency. You can take advantage of this pleasant source of vitamin C by eating the greens raw or throwing them in the blender to make a liquid for drinking (Fleming 1975; Gibbons 1966; Gibbons and Tucker 1979; Elias and Dykeman 1982).

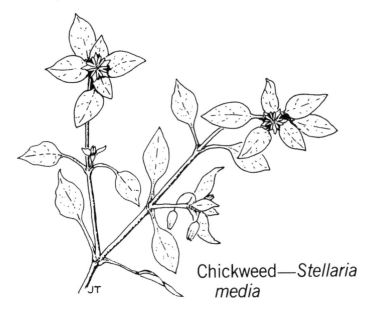

Chickweed—*Stellaria media*

62

Plant Characteristics

Stellaria media is a mat-forming winter annual. Standing but a few inches tall, the plant forms a soft ground cover. The small ovate leaves are simple and opposite, and the margins are entire. The leaf blade may reach 1.5 inches (4 cm) long but typically is less than ¾ inch (2 cm) long. To examine the tiny white flowers, you'll need a hand lens. The five petals are so deeply lobed that at first glance the plant seems to have ten petals.

From late fall through the winter, chickweed comes up in lawns, gardens, abandoned fields, and wooded areas in the eastern third of the state to the edge of the Edwards Plateau. A native of Europe and western Asia, the plant is naturalized in much of the United States.

CHENOPODIACEAE—GOOSEFOOT FAMILY

LAMB'S-QUARTERS, GOOSEFOOT, PIGWEED, QUELITE SALADO— *CHENOPODIUM ALBUM*
(See illustration.)

Warning

As does spinach, lamb's-quarters contains oxalic acid, which tends to bind calcium and prevent its proper absorption by the body. If your diet is low in calcium, don't rely on spinach or lamb's-quarters as a source of calcium (refer to "Spinach" in the index for more information) (Kohman 1939; Kingsbury 1964). On rare occasions lamb's-quarters has been known to accumulate potentially toxic levels of nitrates and may have caused livestock poisoning. Because large quantities must be consumed to cause problems, this type of poisoning is unlikely to affect humans.

Though a number of the 26 species of Chenopodium *in Texas have tasty edible leaves, do not use those with aromatic leaves, such as wormseed (*Chenopodium ambrosioides*). The Mexican people use the leaves of wormseed, or epazote, sparingly as a seasoning for beans with no problems, but in quantity the leaves can cause poisoning. An oil on the herb is an irritant and toxin. An extract of the oil of the seeds kills intestinal worms, but an overdose of the medicine can cause human and animal deaths. Wormseed has a smell similar to that of turpentine or camphor. The leaves are variable, they may resemble lamb's-quarters, or they may be oblong and coarsely toothed or pinnately lobed.*

Lamb's-quarters, an inconspicuous green weed, supplies nutritious and good-tasting greens for salads and potherbs. The young plants under

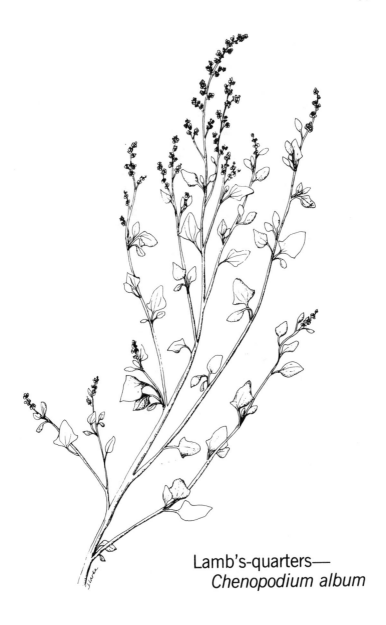

Lamb's-quarters—
Chenopodium album

a foot tall furnish the tenderest shoots and leaves. The herb does not become bitter with age, so you can use the leaves on older plants. Collect the lamb's-quarters from winter to fall. Use the leaves raw in salads, or boil the leaves and tender tips for 10 minutes and serve them with lemon or pepper sauce. Save the cooking water for use as a yellow dye for wool.

Lamb's-quarters contains generous amounts of vitamins A and C and supplies protein and minerals. The vitamin A content is comparable to that of carrots. The greens are superior or equivalent in nutrition to just about any other garden vegetable (Gibbons 1966; Scooter Cheatham, interview, September 1984; Zennie and Ogzewella 1977).

Lamb's-quarters seeds, available from summer to winter, also provide a nutritious food. Strip the seed heads from the stems, let them dry in the sun, and then rub them between your hands. Winnow the tiny black seeds by placing the seed heads in a basket and shaking the basket in a breeze. Boil or toast the seeds, or grind them to mix with wheat flour. During his military campaigns, Napoleon I relied on *Chenopodium* seed bread when other food was scarce.

Though botanists generally believe that *Chenopodium album* originated in Europe, recent archeological work in Canada has determined that the Blackfoot Indians used the seeds as early as A.D. 1500. Today *Chenopodium album* is one of the most widely distributed plants in the world.

Native Americans used various species of *Chenopodium* for food. Archeologists believe that *Chenopodium* may have been cultivated in the central Mississippi Valley before the introduction of maize and beans from Mexico (Struever 1971). *Chenopodium quinoa,* a Peruvian species, furnished a staple cereal plant of the diet of the Incas and still provides an important part of the diet of millions of indigenous South Americans. The seeds contain about 15 percent protein and 55 percent carbohydrate, higher percentages of both nutrients than corn contains (Schery 1972).

In several South African tribal communities, wild *Chenopodium* greens are frequently sautéed and served with cornbread. The Food and Agricultural Organization in 1957 found that the protein content of a meal of *Chenopodium* leaves and cornbread is markedly higher than that of corn alone (Holm et al. 1977). Cultivation of nutritious native plants adapted to local climatic and soil conditions may be an important factor in the prevention of future catastrophic famines in Africa and other drought-prone areas.

Considering the evidence in favor of these nourishing and tasty greens, it is dismaying that *Chenopodium* species are considered obnoxious weeds in the United States. The greens outdo their cousin spinach nutritionally and deserve to be as common in American diets.

Plant Characteristics

Chenopodium album, a much-branched annual weed that can reach 6—9 feet (2—3 m) in height, grows in back alleys, unmowed lawns, and vacant lots throughout the state. The slender grooved branches often are tinged with red. Appearing pale green on top, the delicate simple leaves are often whitish or gray-green underneath, and they alternate on the stems. Lower leaves typically are diamond-shaped but are variable, and the margins may have wavy teeth or lobes. The smaller upper leaves may be narrow and entire. Minute flowers cluster in tiny gray-green heads, which grow on long, slender spikes and produce minuscule black shiny seeds. This species occurs throughout North America and into South America. It also grows in Eurasia and northern Africa.

Chenopodium berlandieri, another common edible species, may be recognized by the odor of the leaves, which is reminiscent of the smell of dirty socks. Despite their odor, the leaves provide a delicious pot of greens, but the seeds retain a strong smell when cooked.

ORACH, SALTBUSH—*ATRIPLEX PATULA*
FOUR-WING SALTBUSH, SHADSCALE, CHAMIZA—*ATRIPLEX CANESCENS*

Warning

If grown in soil that contains selenium, Atriplex canescens *and* A. rosea *can accumulate levels of selenium that may be toxic to livestock, thus limiting its use as food for livestock and humans. The pollen of four-wing saltbush causes hay fever (Kingsbury 1964; Wodehouse 1971).*

Euell Gibbons (1964) reports that the young leaves and tender tips of the new growth of orach provide a tasty cooked vegetable or a fresh addition to salads. I haven't had the opportunity to try these greens, but they furnish vitamins and iron and are available practically year-round. Orach absorbs salts from the saline soils and salt marshes in which it grows. Salt deposits form on the leaf surfaces, adding a naturally salty flavor to the greens.

Numerous West Texas species, such as four-wing saltbush, grow in alkaline soil. Southwestern Indians are reported to have used the ground seeds and the ashes of the burned leaves as a substitute for baking powder (Vines 1960). Though Kirk (1975) reports that the leaves of western species of *Atriplex* may be used as a cooked vegetable, I have been unable to verify the safety of using the alkaline-soil species. The value of most species of *Atriplex* probably lies in their use in soil reclamation and livestock forage more than in human food use.

Ranchers used at least two Texas saltbushes, *Atriplex canescens* and *Atriplex argentea,* as forage crops in the early part of the century. The saltbushes contain protein, calcium, and phosphorus and are high-yielding crops. Australian saltbush, *Atriplex semibaccata,* was introduced into the United States in 1888 as a forage crop and soil binder. The salt content of these forages limits their palatability for livestock and may place them in the category of emergency feed, for use in supplementing more-palatable forage.

Because *Atriplex* species tolerate saline and alkaline soils, they could open up new areas to forage crop production. Besides, their ability to remove salts from the soil may make them desirable in the reclamation of soils that have become too saline for agriculture. If saltbushes are proved effective in soil reclamation, they may become highly valued in agriculture for that virtue alone (Ritchie 1979).

Plant Characteristics

The saltbushes grow in saline or alkaline soil in arid areas and salt marshes. *Atriplex patula,* an herbaceous annual that resembles its cousin lamb's-quarters, may be erect or partially prostrate. Lower leaves, $1-3$ inches (2.5–7 cm) long, are triangular or shaped somewhat like an arrowhead. They may be opposite on the lower stem and alternate above, with margins that are entire or have wavy teeth. Tiny flowers occur in green spikes. Orach grows along the Coast and inland. Besides occurring in much of the United States and Canada, orach is found in Europe, Asia, and northern Africa.

The fruit of *Atriplex canescens* is a four-winged membrane. The simple leaves are entire and oblong to linear, and the name *"canescens"* refers to the silvery cast given to the leaves by tiny surface scales. Growing in dry alkaline soils and salt flats in West Texas, the shrubby perennial is also found in the western United States, Mexico, and Canada.

TUMBLEWEED, RUSSIAN THISTLE—*SALSOLA KALI*
(See illustration.)

Warning

Though the young plants are good livestock fodder, tumbleweed can accumulate nitrates and has caused some livestock poisoning. Oxalic acid content, though normally low, may have also caused some problems for livestock in rare cases (refer to "spinach" in the index for more information on oxalic acid) (Kingsbury 1964; Burlage 1968). Both of these types of poisoning result from consumption of large amounts of plant material and thus are unlikely to affect humans. Mature plants contain small amounts of possibly toxic alkaloids (Watt and Breyer-Brandwijk 1962). I

Tumbleweed—*Salsola kali*

have found only limited documentation on the use of the shoots for human food, so use them in moderation.

Niethammer (1974) reports that tumbleweed, despised by ranchers and immortalized in song, furnishes edible greens. Collect the very young shoots when they are less than about 5 inches (12 cm) tall, before the spines harden, and use them as a cooked vegetable (Elias and Dykeman 1982; Gibbons and Tucker 1979). The greens are available for only a short time, in spring and early summer, and are difficult to identify as young shoots. To identify them properly, locate a stand of mature tumbleweeds one year and look for the shoots the following spring. I haven't had the opportunity to sample tumbleweed greens, but Jennifer Jones sent the following recipe from El Paso.

TUMBLEWEEDS AND BACON

½ pound tumbleweed shoots
3 slices bacon

1 medium-sized onion,
   finely chopped

Remove the roots from the tumbleweed. Wash and chop the green shoots. Slice the bacon into small pieces, sauté until crisp, and remove from pan. Add the onion to the bacon drippings, and sauté until the onions are transparent. Stir in the chopped tumbleweed shoots. Sauté for a few minutes, adding a little butter if needed. Add ¼ cup water, and simmer till tender. Serve the tumbleweed and onions with bacon bits on top.

Tumbleweed, a native of Eurasia, has become a troublesome weed in the West. The dead plant forms a characteristic rounded clump that blows across open plains and highways in high winds. The tumbling weeds often land in creekbeds, clogging them and increasing the possibility of flooding. The plant has also become a major cause of hay fever in West Texas (Wodehouse 1971). In recent years, however, research has shown that tumbleweed has commercial potential if cultivated and pressed into logs for use as fuel (Foster, Rawles, and Karpiscak 1980). Since the plant requires little water for growth, it could become a valuable crop in arid areas of the country. Tumbleweed's high alkali content has led to its use in glass making.

Plant Characteristics

The annual herb, which forms a rounded much-branched plant, ranges 2–5 feet (6–15 dm) in height but is usually about 30 inches (8 dm) tall. The slender green stems develop reddish-purple stripes, and the small spine-tipped leaves are linear to threadlike and sometimes fleshy. Tumbleweed has become naturalized throughout the western United States and western Canada, growing along roadsides and in cultivated fields and disturbed soils. Tumbleweed is found in West Texas and on the Edwards Plateau.

COMMELINACEAE—SPIDERWORT FAMILY

DAYFLOWER, WIDOW'S-TEARS—*COMMELINA* SPECIES
(See photograph, plate 7.)
SPIDERWORT—*TRADESCANTIA* SPECIES
(See illustration.)

Tradescantia and *Commelina* species both provide delightful greens. Use the leaves, stems, and flower parts of the tender young plants. The crisp plants have a pleasant distinctive flavor. Clip off the stems above ground. Chop them up, and add them raw to salads, soups, stews, and sautéed vegetable dishes. The greens need only about 10 minutes of cooking (Crowhurst 1972; Gibbons and Tucker 1979; Holm et al. 1977).

Unlike most wild greens, these greens do not become bitter with age. On older plants the stems become tough, but the leaves usually remain tender. A mucilaginous sap provides one of the well-remembered characteristics of these plants. Because of the distinctive texture of the *Tradescantia* juice, the plants are known not so fondly as snotweeds. The roots of *Tradescantia* species may contain saponins (Burlage 1968). Though I have found no records of poisoning, it would be best not to use the roots for food.

Tradescantia flowers in the spring, with a couple of species blooming through the summer, but *Commelina* blooms in the fall as well as the spring and summer. The ephemeral nature of the flowers of both genera provides the common name "dayflower." With the slightest touch, the delicate petals shrivel, seeming to disappear from sight.

Plant Characteristics

Texas provides a home for a dozen species of *Tradescantia* and six species of *Commelina*. Several species are endemic and uncommon, others widespread and abundant. Collect them only when you find plants in fair-sized colonies. Leave plenty for next year's growth, and try not to disturb the roots.

The two groups of plants have a number of similarities. They are herbaceous perennials or annuals and provide us with some of our loveliest wildflowers. Most species stand less than 30 inches (8 dm) tall and be-

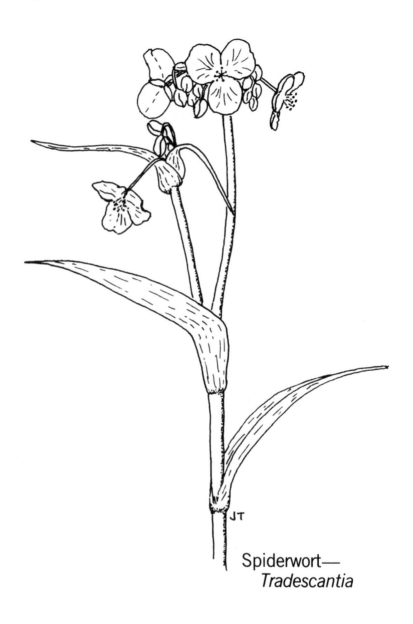

Spiderwort—
Tradescantia

come partly trailing as the stems lengthen. Long, slender grasslike leaves clasp and surround the succulent stem at regular intervals. Flowers of both genera have three petals.

In *Tradescantia* species the showy petals may be blue, purple, pink, or white. Unopened flower buds, which tend to dangle on long stems, form a cluster that fancifully reminds one of the legs of a spider.

The two top petals of *Commelina* are showy and blue, but the bottom petal on most species is smaller and may be a paler blue or a translucent white. The presence of the insignificant third petal inspired eighteenth-century botanist, Carolus Linnaeus to name the genus for the three Commelin brothers. Two became well-known botanists, but the third died before making a name in botany.

A pocketlike pair of leafy bracts encloses *Commelina* buds, and on some species a mucilaginous liquid fills the pocket. If you gently squeeze the bracts, the liquid spills out like a teardrop—thus the common name "widow's-tears." One bud opens at a time, each blossom lasting just a day. A similar species, *Commelinantia anomala,* also is edible but is endemic to the Edwards Plateau, so use it only when it is found in large colonies.

Dayflowers and spiderworts grow in a variety of habitats. Most species prefer moist well-shaded areas. Look for them on stream banks, in rich woods, or as weeds in gardens and along roadsides.

CRASSULACEAE—ORPINE FAMILY, STONECROP FAMILY

SEDUM, STONECROP—*SEDUM* SPECIES
(See photograph, plate 8.)

You can eat the fleshy leaves and stems of sedums raw, boiled, steamed, or pickled. The plants are slightly tart and crisp. They mix well with stronger-flavored greens and are available year-round.

Stonecrops are well adapted to survival in shallow soil or on rocky outcroppings. The succulent leaves and stems store water while a waxy coating helps reduce water loss through the leaves and stems. The plants can survive long periods of drought. Several Texas species are somewhat rare, so collect plants only from large colonies. The colonies help hold the precious soil in place so that larger plants may grow. Please gather plants sparingly or grow your own (Gibbons 1964; Elias and Dykeman 1982).

Plant Characteristics

Sedums are succulent perennial or annual herbs. The Latin word *"sedere"* means "to sit," perhaps referring to the tendency of sedums to grow low to the ground. Reaching only a few inches above the ground,

Texas species may trail along the surface. The smooth succulent leaves are less than ⅓ inch (1 cm) long, and the tiny flowers may be white, pink, or yellow. Two species are endemic to the Trans-Pecos mountains, and one is endemic and rare along the coast of South Texas. Do not collect stonecrops in those areas.

CUCURBITACEAE—GOURD FAMILY

BUFFALO GOURD, FETID GOURD, STINKING GOURD, CALABACILLA AMARGA— *CUCURBITA FOETIDISSIMA*
(See photograph, plate 8.)

*Warning*_____

Consider other wild Texas gourds to be potentially toxic. The gourds of Melothria *species (a tiny green cucumberlike fruit) and of balsam apple,* Momordica *species (a yellow or orange spiny fruit), have caused poisoning (Ellis 1978).*

Though related to the edible squashes, the fetid odor and the extremely bitter taste of the buffalo gourd make the fruit inedible. In spite of this, archeological studies show that native Americans have used the plant for at least nine thousand years. Various Indian tribes throughout the Southwest and Mexico have used the seeds for food, the oil as a cosmetic, the green fruit and root as a laundry detergent, and the dried fruit as rattles in ritualistic gourd dances. Recent research demonstrates that the buffalo gourd, an important resource in the past, may become a valuable source of food for people and livestock in the future (DeVeaux and Schultz 1985; Lancaster, Storey, and Bower 1983).

The Indians dried and roasted the seeds of the buffalo gourd. The seeds do not contain cucurbitacins, bitter glycosides found in the flesh of the fruit, leaves, and roots. Fruit pulp clinging to the seeds, however, will cause the seeds to taste bitter. To eliminate the bitter pulp, dry the gourds until they turn yellow or tan, cut them open, and remove the seeds. Wash the seeds, and sun-dry them thoroughly. Then roast the seeds for 15 to 30 minutes, or sauté them for a few minutes to destroy digestive inhibitors present in the seeds. You can salt the seeds and eat them like pumpkin seeds, grind them into a flour or meal, or boil them up for a mush. The leathery seed coat is a bit tough and should be well chewed or removed from the tender seed. The gourds ripen from late spring through the fall and may be harvested even after the vine is killed by frost. Handle the gourds with gloves to avoid the irritating prickly hairs that cover the vegetation (Niethammer 1974).

Color Plates

Natural dye colors on wool. Front row, left to right: indigo (blue), coreopsis (yellow), golden-rod (gold), walnut hulls (brown). Back row, left to right: soapberries (yellow), broomweed (gold), prickly pears (magenta), elderberries (lavender), elderberry leaves (tan), elderberries (gray), greenbriar berries (khaki green), bluebonnets (pale lime).

Ivy and broomsedge twined basket, created by Sue M. Smith.

Willow basket with handmade paper, created by Sue M. Smith.

AGAVACEAE

Agave, Maguey—*Agave americana*—
useful

AGAVACEAE

Lechuguilla—*Agave lechuguilla*—
poisonous

AGAVACEAE

Beargrass—*Nolina texana*—fiber and
toxic

AGAVACEAE

Sotol—*Dasylirion leiophyllum*—useful

4

AGAVACEAE

Yucca and Wisteria—Fabaceae—fiber and toxic

APIACEAE

Poison hemlock—*Conium maculatum*—poisonous

APIACEAE

Water hemlock—*Cicuta maculata*—poisonous

ASTERACEAE

Sweet goldenrod—*Solidago odora*—tea

ASTERACEAE

Greenthread—*Thelesperma filifolium*—
tea

ASTERACEAE

Gumweed—*Grindelia squarrosa*—
medicinal

ASTERACEAE

Limoncillo—*Pectis angustifolia*—tea

ASTERACEAE

Maximilian sunflower—*Helianthus
maximiliani*—edible

BERBERIDACEAE

Mayapple—*Podophyllum peltatum*—edible and toxic

BORAGINACEAE

Anacua—*Ehretia anacua*—edible fruit

BROMELIACEAE

Spanish moss—*Tillandsia usneoides*—fiber

CACTACEAE

Cholla—*Opuntia imbricata*—edible

CACTACEAE

Prickly pear—*Opuntia engelmannii*—
edible

CACTACEAE

Cochineal on prickly pear pads—
Opuntia—dye

CACTACEAE

Strawberry cactus—*Echinocereus
stramineus*—edible fruit

COMMELINACEAE

Dayflower—*Commelina erecta*—edible

CONVOLVULACEAE

Dodder—*Cuscuta*—dye

CRASSULACEAE

Sedum—*Sedum nuttallianum*—edible

CUCURBITACEAE

Buffalo gourd—*Cucurbita foetidissima*—useful

CUPRESSACEAE

Juniper, Mountain cedar—*Juniperus ashei*—useful

9

EBENACEAE

Persimmon—*Diospyros virginiana*—
edible fruit

ERICACEAE

Madrone—*Arbutus xalapensis*—
edible fruit

EUPHORBIACEAE

Bull nettle—*Cnidoscolus texanus*—
stinging plant

EUPHORBIACEAE

Candelilla—*Euphorbia antisyphilitica*—
wax

EUPHORBIACEAE

FABACEAE

Snow-on-the-prairie—*Euphorbia bicolor*—poisonous

Bequilla—*Sesbania macrocarpa*—fiber and toxic

FABACEAE

FABACEAE

Black locust—*Robinia pseudo-acacia*—toxic

Honey locust—*Gleditsia triacanthos*—edible

FABACEAE

Mescal bean, Texas mountain laurel—
Sophora secundiflora—toxic

FABACEAE

Rebud—*Cercis canadensis*—edible
flowers

FAGACEAE

Chinkapin oak—*Quercus muhlenbergii*—
edible

LAMIACEAE

Autumn sage—*Salvia greggii*—spice

12

LAMIACEAE

Henbit—*Lamium amplexicaule*—edible

LAMIACEAE

Lemon mint—*Monarda citriodora*—tea

LAURACEAE

Red bay—*Persea borbonia*—spice

LAURACEAE

Sassafras—*Sassafras albidum*—tea

MENISPERMACEAE

Snailseed—*Cocculus carolinus*—toxic fruit

NYMPHAEACEAE

Spatterdock—*Nuphar luteum*—edible

OLEACEAE

Ligustrum, Privet—*Ligustrum*—toxic fruit

ONAGRACEAE

Showy evening primrose—*Oenothera speciosa*—edible

14

PASSIFLORACEAE

Passionflower—*Passiflora incarnata*—
edible fruit

PHYTOLACCACEAE

Coralito—*Rivina humilis*—toxic fruit

POACEAE

Carrizo—*Arundo donax*—useful

PONTEDERIACEAE

Water hyacinth—*Eichhornia crassipes*—
useful

ROSACEAE

Hawthorn—*Crataegus spathulata*—
edible fruit

ROSACEAE

Laurel cherry—*Prunus caroliniana*—
toxic fruit

ROSACEAE

Mexican plum—*Prunus mexicana*—
edible fruit

SAPINDACEAE

Mexican buckeye—*Ungnadia speciosa*—
toxic seeds

SOLANACEAE *SOLANACEAE*

Buffalo bur—*Solanum rostratum*—toxic Tree tobacco—*Nicotiana glauca*—toxic

The nutritious seeds contain as much as 35 percent protein and up to 43 percent oil. The refined oil has excellent potential as a commercial cooking and salad oil. Two hundred to three hundred seeds may develop in a single gourd.

The perennial root of the buffalo gourd contains as much as 56 percent starch by dry weight. You can extract the starch by pounding the roots and then washing the starch from the fiber (see "starch extraction" in the index). Be sure to thoroughly remove all the fibers from the starch to eliminate bitterness. The root may attain a weight of more than 88 pounds (40 kg) in three or four years. Starch content is highest from late fall through the winter. Buffalo gourd starch has good potential for use in food and in industry. Starch can be hydrolyzed to produce sugars for foods, beverages, and fermentation processes, and it can be used in laundry sizing and adhesives.

Buffalo gourd is part of a research project at the University of Arizona and may soon be put into agricultural production. Because it is well adapted to arid conditions, is extremely fast-growing, and has a perennial root, the plant has tremendous potential as an agricultural product in drought-prone areas. In addition to having value as a source of protein, oil, and starch for human food, the plant may be employed as a livestock forage. The annual stem and leaf growth can exceed 650 feet (200 m) in a season. The vines are good soil binders and potentially useful as forage for ruminants, such as cattle and goats. Ruminants can also eat the seed meal, the residue left after oil extraction. Monogastric animals, such as swine and poultry, cannot digest the seed coat, but the seed meal could serve them as a food supplement in limited quantities. With so many valuable uses, buffalo gourd is one of the most exciting new crops currently under investigation in the United States (Hackett and Carolane 1982; Ritchie 1979).

Plant Characteristics

Buffalo gourd is a fast-growing vine that crawls along the ground. The large leaves, longer than broad and usually triangular in outline, are rough-textured and malodorous. The bright yellow flowers are about 4 inches (1 dm) long, and male and female parts appear on separate flowers on the same plant. The spherical to elliptic gourds, about 2–3 inches (5–8 cm) long, are green with light green or yellow stripes, the whole gourd turning yellow or tan with age. Buffalo gourd grows predominantly in the western half of the state along roadsides and in disturbed soils such as agricultural fields. It may be found from Nebraska south to central Mexico, and from Southern California almost to the Mississippi River.

CYPERACEAE—SEDGE FAMILY

The leaves and inflorescences of the grass (Poaceae), sedge, and rush (Juncaceae) families resemble each other. Though it is not always a reliable method for differentiating the families, you might find this little ditty referring to the flowering stalks helpful: "Sedges have edges; rushes have ridges; grasses are round and grow all around." The members of these three families provide innumerable sources of fibers for basketmaking, weaving, and papermaking (refer to "Poaceae" in the index for information on the uses of native grasses).

NUT-GRASS, TULILLO—*CYPERUS ROTUNDUS*
YELLOW NUT-GRASS, CHUFA, ZULU NUT—*CYPERUS ESCULENTUS*

Nut-grasses probably win the prize as the most-despised weeds in the world. They spread quickly by means of underground stems, or rhizomes, and compete with crops for water and space. Practically impossible to remove permanently from gardens and farmers' fields, the weeds cause serious crop losses annually throughout the world (Holm et al. 1977).

Despite these problems, nut-grasses have enjoyed popularity as foods in the past. Pharaohs dined on chufa tubers, and even today the nutlets are cultivated for food in northern Africa. Every few inches, each rhizome produces a small nutlike tuber that clings precariously to the threadlike rhizome. You will have to dig carefully to retrieve the well-buried tubers. Look for the young tubers from late fall to early spring.

To prepare the nutlets for eating, simply scrape off the tough outer layer and let the tuber air-dry. Then eat them raw, baked, or boiled. If you dry the tubers at a low oven temperature (about 200° F) for 2 to 4 hours until they are brittle, you can grind them for use as a flour or as grounds to brew like coffee for a pleasant beverage (Elias and Dykeman 1982; Gibbons 1966; Scooter Cheatham, interview, March 1985).

The problems caused by nut-grasses as weeds probably outweigh their value as food crops. But if you've just dug up a batch of nut-grass tubers from your lawn or garden, you might as well put them to use!

Other members of the genus *Cyperus* have had economic value throughout the world. The Egyptians made papyrus from *Cyperus papyrus,* and the Chinese make mats from the leaves of *Cyperus tegetiformis,* an export industry that produces millions of dollars of income (Hill 1952).

Plant Characteristics

Nut-grasses are perennial herbs found in lawns, gardens, and disturbed soils in most areas of the state. Grasslike leaves, several inches tall, emerge from the ground in a fan-shaped cluster and have a prominent midrib. As garden weeds, you probably won't find these sedges in bloom. The flower stalk is a triangular stem topped with a papery inflorescence, similar to the flowers of grasses. A whorl of leaves sits below the inflorescence. *Cyperus esculentus* stems are typically 1–2 feet (30–60 cm) tall. *Cyperus rotundus* stems often are less than 1 foot (30 cm) tall. Many species of native *Cyperus* occur in Texas. Some others may have succulent tubers.

EUPHORBIACEAE—SPURGE FAMILY

BULL NETTLE, MALA MUJER—*CNIDOSCOLUS TEXANUS*
(See photograph, plate 9.)

*Warning*_____

John Williams (letter to the author, July 1986) reports that some people have severe allergic reactions to the sting of bull nettle. Some species in other countries can cause dangerous reactions. Watch for symptoms, such as vomiting or swelling of the throat, that may require emergency medical care. Protect dogs from contact with the plant. Bull nettle is not a member of the nettle family, and, unlike the true stinging nettles (Urtica), the foliage cannot be eaten. The bull nettle contains a toxic and caustic milky sap (Mitchell and Rook 1979). The sap of some tropical species of Cnidoscolus *is boiled down to produce a rubbery latex (Hill 1952).*

Many of you already have been introduced to bull nettle and don't care to encounter the plant again, thank you. But every one of God's creatures is a thing of beauty, and even this much-despised plant deserves our praise.

The long, stinging hairs that coat the leaves, stems, and even the fruiting capsule defend the plant quite admirably from any hungry animal who might venture along. When brushed across unprotected flesh, the hairs inject a powerful dose of caustic juice into the skin. The sting of the bull nettle has been touted as one of the worst of any stinging plant in the country. (For further details on plants that sting and how to treat the irritation, refer to Chapter 4.)

The first time you see bull nettle in bloom, you may be surprised at the beauty of the white flowers. The funnel-shaped blossom has a fragrance that competes with the finest perfumes. (Perhaps someday we'll see bull nettle perfume at the cosmetic counter in Foley's, but with the sexploitation so common in the marketing field these days, the perfume is certain to be called Mala Mujer—"Bad Woman.") Perhaps the only creatures that dare approach the bull nettle are the sphinx moths, insects that steal its sweet nectar and pollinate the blossom in return. If you have a good sense of balance, you can lean over the plant just close enough to whiff the fragrance, but beware, lest your nose come the tiniest bit too close to the nearby stinging hairs.

Despite the various noxious properties of the herb, bull nettle harbors a delightful food. The seed capsule bears a coat of armor more formidable than steel. Inside waits a delicious nut, ripening from early to late fall (Scooter Cheatham, interview, September 1984). So what, you say? No matter how good it tastes, you're not interested in harvesting bull nettle? Well, if you should change your mind, follow these guidelines for a safe harvest. Proper dress is essential, including long sleeves and long pants. Boots and thick gloves are a good idea, but you can get by without them. Bull nettles must be one of the reasons cowboy boots were invented.

Gather the capsules when they begin turning brown. Pluck them off the top of the plant with a pair of tongs, and drop them into a large paper bag. When you return home, set the paper bag in a dry spot. As the fruits ripen, the capsules explode, releasing the seeds. After all the capsules have ejected their fruits, winnow out the seeds and throw away the stinging capsules. A thin, smooth white to brownish shell covers the oblong seeds. On one end of the shell is a cream-colored growth. Though it is considered edible, I find this growth too hard to bite into. Crack the shell open to reveal the tasty morsel within. Eat the nuts raw, or chop them up for use in nut breads.

Plant Characteristics

Compare the photograph of bull nettle with the drawings of noseburn and stinging nettle, two other plants with stinging hairs (page 300). Bull nettle usually stands about 1½–2 feet (4–6 dm) tall but may be taller. This plant is easy to recognize by its long, stinging hairs, large lobed leaves, and milky sap. The plant grows in sandy soils throughout most of the state to the eastern edge of the Trans-Pecos. It also occurs in Louisiana, Oklahoma, Arkansas, and northern Mexico.

NOSEBURN, CHICHICASTLE—*TRAGIA* SPECIES
(See illustration, page 300.)

Warning

Because little information is available on Tragia, use the herb in moderation. Do not confuse noseburn with other plants that have stinging hairs. Bull nettle, also a member of the spurge family, has poisonous leaves. Compare the photograph of bull nettle, plate 9, with the drawings of noseburn and stinging nettle (page 300).

Unlike the large bull nettle, the delicate vines of noseburn go unnoticed until they come in contact with exposed ankles and legs. Members of the genus *Tragia* bear stinging hairs that inject irritating chemicals on contact with tender skin. Fortunately, the sting of the common Texas species abates quickly. (Refer to Chapter 4 to learn more about Texas plants that sting.)

As with the true stinging nettles (*Urtica*), you can use the leaves of noseburn as a cooked green, but don't eat the leaves raw. Cooking eliminates the irritant chemicals. Use rubber gloves to strip the leaves from the vine. Rinse the leaves, and simmer them in a small amount of water for 10 minutes. Because the leaves are small and scattered on the vines, you can rarely collect more than a handful at a time. The flavor is quite bland, so add your handful of leaves to a pot of mixed greens. The leaves are available year-round (Scooter Cheatham, interview, September 1984).

Plant Characteristics

Ten species of *Tragia* grow in Texas. The most commonly encountered species occur as small-leaved vines to erect herbs with threadlike stems. These perennial herbs trail along the ground or twine across vegetation. Stiff stinging hairs and soft nonstinging hairs coat the stems and leaves. The simple, alternate leaves vary in shape across species, but the most common species have oval or elongated heart-shaped leaves with coarse teeth. On almost all species the leaves are less than 2½ inches (6.5 cm) long. The inconspicuous green flowers occur in tiny clusters opposite the leaves. Several erect species are rare or uncommon in Texas, so do not use them for food.

FABACEAE—LEGUME FAMILY (FORMERLY LEGUMINOSAE)

The legume or bean family is one of the largest families of plants in the world. More than 300 species of legume-bearing trees, shrubs, vines, and wildflowers call Texas home, with another 40 or so European and Asian immigrants now widespread in the state. Next to the grasses, which produce all our grains and cereals, the bean family is the second most economically important group of plants in the world.

All of the beans and peas found at the dinner table come from this family: limas, pintos, kidneys, navies, green beans, black-eyed peas, snow peas, and even peanuts. These edible legumes have been in cultivation for centuries. A number of wild legumes also provide excellent sources of food.

A number of herbaceous legumes reportedly bear edible tubers. These starchy vegetables provided valuable carbohydrates and protein for the earliest dwellers of our continent. Native Americans showed these plants to early European explorers, who in their turn often relied on them for survival. Almost all of them are quite rare today, and the low-growing herbs and vines can be confused with nonedible and even toxic legumes, such as the locoweeds, so I discourage wild harvests. You may want to collect a few seeds, however, and try growing your own wild tubers. Judging by their earlier importance, it seems likely that nutritional research will bear out the food value of these native tubers and indicate that they are worthy of cultivation.

Besides the plants listed below, I have also found references indicating that the following species may bear edible tubers: *Dalea lanata, Dalea terminalis, Peteria scoparia, Galactia marginalis,* and *Hoffmanseggia glauca.* Documentation on those plants was limited and usually poorly verified, however, and most of the plants are rare or uncommon.

Before taking a bite of the next wild bean you see, however, you need to know that the legume family also contains a number of highly toxic beans. *Sophora secundiflora* (mescal bean, or Texas mountain laurel) has deadly poisonous beans and foliage. The various species of locoweed (*Oxytropis* and *Astragalus*) have caused much loss of livestock in the western United States. Native Americans used certain leguminous plants as fish poisons and as powerful drugs for medicinal and religious purposes. Never experiment with an unknown wild bean. Its resemblance to something you had for dinner last night does not qualify it for tonight's dinner table. (Refer to Chapter 4 for more information on poisonous legumes.)

Some of the best sources of nectar and pollen for honeybees are members of the family, including the clovers and acacias. Many of our most beautiful ornamentals are legumes, including the redbud tree, mimosa tree, wisteria, and poinciana (*Caesalpinia* species). Texas' state flower, the bluebonnet, also belongs to the family.

Only the grasses rival the legumes for the number of valuable forage plants, soil binders, and soil improvers. Wildlife and cattle, sheep, and goats rely on many wild legumes for browse. Legumes restore nutrients and fix nitrogen in the soil, functioning as natural fertilizers on cultivated and grazed land. A number of native forage legumes have been or could be cultivated. Various other forage and cover crops introduced from Europe and Asia, including many of the clovers and alfalfa, escape from cultivation and grow wild on ranchland and farmland across America.

The best-known and longest-cultivated forage crop is alfalfa (*Medicago sativa*). The clovers, a large group of valuable forage legumes, include members of the genera *Medicago, Trifolium, Melilotus, Desmodium,* and *Lespedeza.*

Popinac (*Leucaena leucocephala*), a native of southern Mexico planted as an ornamental tree in South Texas, equals or surpasses alfalfa in vitamin and protein content. Popinac provides an excellent substitute for alfalfa as a forage crop in tropical and subtropical regions of the world (Ritchie 1979). A native South Texas tree called *tepeguaje* (*Leucaena pulverulenta*) has potential as a forage crop and natural fertilizer. This rapid-growing tree occurs from Brownsville south into Mexico.

Good native browses in Texas include feather dalea (*Dalea formosa*), Texas snoutbean (*Rhynchosia texana*), bundleflower (*Desmanthus illinoensis*), and several of the acacias, trefoils (*Lotus*), vetches (*Vicia*), and wild beans (*Phaseolus*). Some of the best forage legumes, however, such as alfalfa and sweet clovers (*Melilotus* species), also have caused considerable livestock losses.

Family Characteristics

To recognize members of the bean family, first examine the plant for fruit. The fruit of a legume will be some kind of bean pod, which may appear long and flat, short and rounded, or twisted like a corkscrew. It may contain one or many seeds of varying sizes and colors, ranging from the tiny, flat, brown, and edible seeds of the mesquite to the large, plump, red, and deadly poisonous seeds of the mescal bean. A few other plant families produce fruits similar to bean pods, so you will need some extra clues to identify the family properly.

The leaves of most Texas legumes conform to one of several basic patterns. Almost always compound, they may be either pinnately compound or palmately compound. Pinnately compound leaves may be once or twice compound. The leaflets usually have entire margins and an elliptical shape.

For good examples of typical legume leaf shapes, take a walk down the street. You are bound to find one of the ornamental legumes in someone's yard. The mimosa tree (*Albizia julibrissin*), a lovely Asian ornamental with beautiful pink puffball flowers in late spring, has leaves that are twice pinnately compound. So does the huisache (*Acacia farnesiana,* illustrated). The leaves of mescal bean (*Sophora secundiflora,* see photo) are once pinnately compound. If you familiarize yourself with the leaves of these trees, recognizing legumes in the wild will be much easier. The garden peas and beans have a compound leaf with only three leaflets. For a good example of a palmately compound leaf, get down on your hands and knees and examine the leaves of Texas' most famous wildflower, the bluebonnet.

A notable exception to the rule for leaf type is the redbud tree (*Cercis canadensis,* see photograph), a native plant commonly used as an ornamental. The leaves of the redbud are simple and heart-shaped. Though the redbud defies the legume family tradition in its leaf, you can recognize it as a legume by its flat bean pod and the shape of the pink tc purple flowers that decorate its branches in late winter or early spring, before the leaves appear.

There are several general types of legume flower. Look at the flowers of the redbud, the bluebonnet, the black locust, and any of your garden peas or beans. Though the petals of each species vary in size and shape, they all form a blossom with bilateral symmetry—one half is a mirror image of the other half, somewhat like a face. In legumes this type of flower is said to be papilionaceous, from the scientific name for swallowtail butterflies, *"Papilio;"* to some, legume flowers resemble butterflies. The petal at the top is called the banner, the two side petals form the wings, and the bottom of the flower is the keel, often resembling a tiny boat, formed by two petals that may or may not unite into one. On many of the clovers, the flowers are tiny and clustered together in a tight, rounded head, requiring a magnifying glass to observe the papilionaceous flower structure.

Some legumes produce flowers that are only slightly bilateral, with the five petals almost uniform in shape and size. The bright yellow flowers of retama (*Parkinsonia aculeata,* illustrated) and the sennas (*Cassia*) fall into this category.

A third common flower type is the puffball flower cluster, such as that of the mimosa tree and the huisache. A variation on the puffball, a cylindrical shaped puff, occurs on the mesquite tree. The pink or yellow balls or cylinders consist of many tiny flowers clustered together into a spherical head or a cylindrical spike. The stamens of each individual flower extend so far beyond the petals that the stamens themselves provide the shape and color of the inflorescence. These flowers are often quite aromatic and grace some of the best honeybee plants in Texas, the mesquites and acacias.

So now you have the clues that you need to distinguish members of the legume family from other plant families in Texas. If you find a plant that has the characteristics of at least two of the plant parts described here—leaf, flower, and fruit—you can be reasonably certain that you are looking at a legume.

ACACIA, HUISACHE, CATCLAW—*ACACIA* SPECIES
(See illustration.)

Warning

Until someone conducts research to verify the safety of using the acacia seeds for human food, they must be considered potentially toxic. Some species of Acacia contain cyanogenetic glycosides and related toxic substances in the pods and leaves. Guajillo, Acacia berlandieri, though considered a good browse plant, has caused death in cattle and sheep that have consumed large amounts over several months. Acacia greggii contains a high cyanide content in the fall and has caused livestock poisoning (Allen and Allen 1981; Kingsbury 1964).

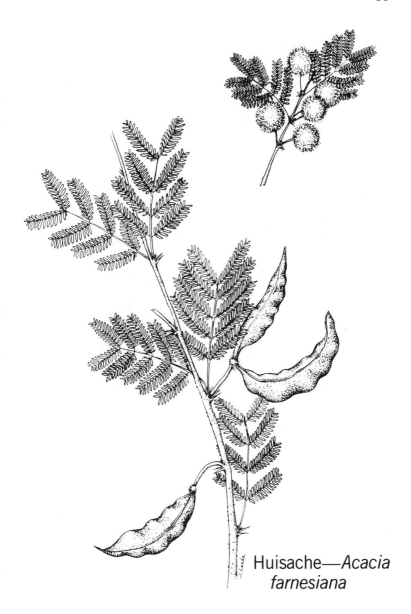

Huisache—*Acacia
farnesiana*

A dozen species of *Acacia* find a home in Texas. Native Americans in the Southwest have used the seeds of a number of these thorny shrubs and trees for food. Texas species that the Indians reportedly ate include mescat acacia (*Acacia constricta*), catclaw (*Acacia greggii*), and viscid acacia (*Acacia neovernicosa*). The Indians dried the seeds and ground them into a coarse meal. They wetted the meal and formed it into cakes that could be dried and stored for later use (Vines 1960; Kirk 1975; Warnock 1974). Because little information is available on these foods, however, and because some of the allegedly edible species have caused poisoning in livestock, I cannot recommend their use for human food. The shrubs and trees provide other useful resources, though.

Acacias furnished a valuable source of wood for tools and fuel in the early days of human life in the deserts of the Southwest. An insect called *Tachardia lacca* is found on *Acacia greggii* and produces lac, an ingredient in sealing wax, lacquers, and varnishes. Native Americans in the Southwest used lac for sealing food-storage vessels. Though not available in commercial quantities on *Acacia greggii,* the insect is extensively cultivated on other trees in India.

Though they are neglected resources in the United States today, acacias have the potential to furnish many local products, such as tannins, dyes, gums, wood, food, forage, and honey. Several species supply good browse for wildlife and livestock. A wide variety of commercially valuable products come from members of the genus found in other parts of the world. Some of the world's best tannins come from acacias. Gum arabic, from the sap of species in northern Africa, India, and the Middle East, is an important ingredient in adhesives, confections, waxes, inks, cosmetics, medicines, and watercolors (Schery 1972; Allen and Allen 1981).

The largest acacia in Texas, huisache (*Acacia farnesiana*), serves as a graceful tree for landscapes in the southern half of the state. Huisache has been put to a great variety of uses throughout the world. The French cultivate *Acacia farnesiana* for the perfume from its sweet-scented yellow flowers, which also yield a delicate honey. Tannins for tanning leather are produced by the pods and bark. The dark tannins are used in ink making and as a black dye for leather in Bengal and the West Indies. The pods provide forage for wildlife and livestock. Durable hand tools and posts can be made from the hard, dense root wood, which is also a good source of fuel and charcoal. Bark fibers have been used to make rope. In Java the gum of the pods supplies a crockery cement, and the gum extracted from the sap of the trunk is considered superior to gum arabic (Duke 1981; Vines 1960).

Plant Characteristics

Texas acacias are spiny shrubs and trees. The stiff spines may be hooked or straight, in pairs at the leaf axils or single all along the branches.

The twice pinnately compound leaves have numerous tiny leaflets. Occurring in puffball heads or puffy cylindrical spikes, flowers are white or yellow. Most of them are fragrant and valued honey-producers. The pods vary in shape and size.

ALFALFA—*MEDICAGO SATIVA*

Warning

As with some other leguminous forage plants, alfalfa causes bloat in livestock when it constitutes a high percentage of their diet. Though the factors causing bloat are not fully understood, saponins in the leaves may contribute to the problem (Kingsbury 1964). To prevent bloat in livestock, include grasses in the pasture or fodder. Humans should use the herb in moderation.

Alfalfa, probably a native of Persia, has been in cultivation for more than 3300 years. Today it is a mainstay of modern agriculture. The most important forage crop in the United States, alfalfa provides the highest yield of protein per acre of any livestock crop. It also supplies calcium, magnesium, phosphorus, and vitamins. Nitrogen-fixing bacteria in the root nodules make alfalfa an excellent soil restorer on nitrogen-depleted soils (Allen and Allen 1981; Duke 1981; Hill 1952; Schery 1972).

Humans can benefit from the nutritional herb as well. Alfalfa sprouts, grown from seeds available at health food stores, have become a popular salad addition in the United States. The sprouts provide protein, vitamins, and minerals. The Chinese and Russians cook the leaves of the tender young plants for greens. Cultivated in Texas, alfalfa often grows wild along roadsides and in abandoned fields. Collect the leaves in late winter or early spring, boil them for a few minutes, and serve them with lemon or pepper sauce.

The nectar of the flowers yields a good honey. You can make a bland tea of the dried young leaves and flowers. Alfalfa tea and concentrated alfalfa tablets, sold in health food stores, are thought to help prevent hay fever and a variety of other ailments. The herb is a mild laxative, so take care in using the concentrated tablets.

In addition to having uses in food and medicine, alfalfa seeds contain an oil suitable for use in paints and varnishes. Papermakers have used the stem fibers in their craft, and wool dyers extract a yellow dye from the seeds.

Plant Characteristics

This low-growing perennial herb has compound leaves with three obovate leaflets, each about ½−1 inch (1−3 cm) long. Violet to blue papilionaceous flowers occur in racemes, and the pod forms a loose spiral. Alfalfa grows wild in much of the state.

BLACK LOCUST—*ROBINIA PSEUDO-ACACIA*
(See photograph, plate 10.)

Warning

The seeds, leaves, stems, roots, and bark of the black locust are poisonous. (For details, see "black locust" in the index.)

Scooter Cheatham (interview, March 1985) reports that the clusters of fragrant white flowers of the black locust, removed from the stems, coated with a thick batter, and deep-fried, make good fritters. As the rest of the plant is toxic, however, I cannot recommend the flowers for food. The blooms emerge in the spring and yield good honey (Peterson 1977; Gibbons and Tucker 1979).

The strong, durable wood is used for fence posts, wooden pins in shipbuilding and telephone insulators, and furniture. Black locust serves as an important lumber tree in Romania and Hungary (Allen and Allen 1981). Though considered somewhat of a trash tree in Texas, it has value in revegetating land that has been strip-mined for coal. Nitrogen-fixing bacteria in the root nodules restore depleted soil, increasing the nitrogen supply to nearby trees, and decaying leaves of the trees recycle calcium, magnesium, and potassium into the soil.

The Mescalero Apaches also reportedly ate the rose-colored flowers of New Mexican locust, *Robinia neomexicana* (Basehart 1974). The plant is rare in Texas, found only in the mountains of the northern Trans-Pecos. It also is useful in revegetation and erosion control. The wood is a good source of charcoal and can be used for making small wooden objects.

Plant Characteristics

Black locust, a medium- to large-sized tree, bears large pinnately compound leaves with leaflets up to 2 inches (5 cm) long. Pairs of small spines appear in the leaf axils. The white papilionaceous flowers hang in loose racemes that are 4 inches (10 cm) long or more. The flat pods are 2—5 inches (5—13 cm) long and are smooth, not hairy. Probably introduced from the southeastern United States, black locust grows as an ornamental and a weedy tree in the eastern half of the state.

GROUNDNUT, INDIAN POTATO—*APIOS AMERICANA*

Warning

Groundnut is infrequent to rare in Texas. Rather than harvesting from the wild, you may want to grow your own from seed. The vine may be confused with toxic legumes, so be sure of your identification.

The root of this high-climbing perennial vine yields a string of edible tubers, which numerous Indian groups have relied on for protein. Wash and peel the tubers, then boil, roast, or fry them like potatoes. The groundnut may be the plant that Sir Walter Raleigh brought to England and called a potato (Schery 1972). Elias and Dykeman (1982) report that the seeds are edible also. Roast the pods, remove the seeds, and boil them for about 20 minutes or sauté them in butter (Peterson 1977; Elliott 1976; Gibbons and Tucker 1979).

Plant Characteristics

The brownish-red flowers are papilionaceous, and the pinnately compound leaves have five or seven leaflets. Groundnut grows in East and North Central Texas, primarily in woods. It is also found in the eastern United States and southeastern Canada.

HOG PEANUT—*AMPHICARPAEA BRACTEATA*

Warning

Hog peanut is infrequent to rare in Texas. Rather than harvesting from the wild, I recommend growing your own from seed. The vine may be confused with toxic legumes, so be sure of your identification.

Like the true peanut, the hog peanut produces flowers and seeds underground. The Dakotas used the underground seeds (not the roots) for food. Gibbons and Tucker (1979) report that the seeds are tasty if boiled like other beans. Gather the pods just below the surface, without pulling up the whole plant. Soak the pods to loosen the seeds, then boil the seeds for about 20 minutes (Fernald, Kinsey, and Rollins 1958; Crowhurst 1972; Peterson 1977).

Plant Characteristics

The vining annual has compound leaves with three leaflets. The underground flowers do not have showy petals, but clusters of lavender or nearly white papilionaceous flowers occur above ground, drooping from the leaf axils. Hog peanut grows in moist woods in the eastern United States and Canada. In Texas it occurs mainly in the eastern woodlands and is uncommon to rare.

HONEY LOCUST—*GLEDITSIA TRIACANTHOS*
(See photograph, plate 10.)

*Warning*_____

Be sure you have correctly identified the honey locust before eating the pods. Honey locust pods may be confused with the toxic pods of the Kentucky coffee tree (Gymnocladus dioica), *an occasional ornamental in North Texas. The Kentucky coffee tree has no thorns, but thornless varieties of honey locust are also used as ornamentals. Kentucky coffee tree pods, though similar to honey locust pods in shape, are flat—not twisted, as honey locust pods often are—and 3–10 inches (8–25 cm) long. While honey locust pods are thin and papery, coffee tree pods are thick and woody. Other members of the genus* Gleditsia *contain toxic alkaloids and saponins, so use only the honey locust for food (Duke 1981).*

The pods of the honey locust have a sugar-sweet pulp. Gibbons and Tucker (1979) report that while tender, the young pods may be nibbled raw or boiled and eaten like string beans. The paper-thin pulp of the mature pods varies from sweet to bitter. If it is sweet, you can suck on the pulp. The Cherokees pounded the ripe pods and soaked them in water to make a sweet beverage (Arnott 1975).

Use the heavy, tough wood of the honey locust for fuel and for making tools, fence posts, lumber, and furniture. The flowers yield a good honey. High in sugar and protein, the pods are used as animal fodder in South Africa (Vines 1960; Ritchie 1979; Allen and Allen 1981). The abundant sweet pods may be suitable for the fermentation of fuel alcohol as an alternative to gasoline.

Plant Characteristics
Honey locust forms a large tree with large once or twice pinnately compound leaves. The long, thin, smooth pods may be flat or twisted. When mature, the dark brown pods are 8–18 inches (20–45 cm) long and 1–1½ inches (2.5–4 cm) wide. The many seeds rattle when you shake the ripe pods. Wild trees produce long, branched thorns along the main trunk and branches.

INDIAN BREADROOT—*PSORALEA HYPOGAEA*
SCURFY PEA—*PSORALEA CUSPIDATA*

*Warning*_____

One Texas species, Psoralea tenuiflora, *has caused poisoning in livestock (Kingsbury 1964). Fifteen species of* Psoralea *grow in the state. Do not use any species other than* Psoralea hypogaea *and* Psoralea cuspidata *for food.* Psoralea hypogaea *is rare in Texas. It should not be harvested from the wild, but you may want to try growing your own from seed. Use wild* Psoralea cuspidata *only if you can identify it positively and you find it in abundance. See "tuber" in the index for information on other wild tubers.*

The roots, not the beans, of these two species have been used for food. A breadroot not found in Texas, *Psoralea esculenta,* served as an important food for native Americans of the northern plains, especially the Sioux. The large edible tubers sometimes weighed as much as fifteen pounds. French explorers called it *pomme blanche,* meaning "white apple." These two Texas *Psoralea* species also played a role in the diet of early native Americans and European explorers, though their tubers are not so impressive in size (Ajilvsgi 1984; Kirk 1975; Allen and Allen 1981; Fernald, Kinsey, and Rollins 1958; Gibbons and Tucker 1979).

Peel the round tuber of *Psoralea hypogaea,* then boil it or roast it like a potato. Indians and explorers often sliced the tuber, dried it, and then stored it for later use or ground it into flour. You can also dry the smaller root of *Psoralea cuspidata* and pound it into flour (Elias and Dykeman 1982).

Plant Characteristics

Both *Psoralea* species are low-growing herbaceous perennials with purple flowers and palmately compound leaves that have three to seven leaflets. They are found in the Panhandle and North Central Texas and onto the Edwards Plateau, growing north across the Great Plains.

KUDZU, KUZU—*PUERARIA LOBATA*

The kudzu vine provides a dramatic example of the potentially disastrous consequences of transporting plant species to nonnative lands. An honored ornamental and food plant in its native Indochina and Japan, kudzu came to the United States in 1876. The Japanese exhibited the attractive vine at the Philadelphia Centennial Exposition. Admiring Americans began using kudzu in the southeastern United States as an ornamental shade vine. Between 1910 and 1935 it became widely used in the South as livestock fodder and pasturage. Rich in protein and chlorophyll, the vine compares favorably with alfalfa in nutritive value. In 1935 the Soil Conservation Service put it to use as a soil binder and restorer on farmland that had suffered severe soil loss. Naming it King Kudzu, American farmers considered the vine the answer to a prayer (Allen and Allen 1981; Duke 1981; Hill 1952).

But by 1955 the blessing had become a curse. The fast-growing vine had spread beyond its desired boundaries, covering crops and pastures and destroying valuable forests. A single vine can grow 100 feet (30 m) or more in a season. The vines quickly cover all other vegetation in their path, killing trees by blocking out light and pulling down trees and telephone poles.

Today kudzu covers over one million acres of farm, forest, and pasture in the southeastern United States. I remember driving through Georgia as a child and seeing kudzu covering the fields and trees by the roadside. The dense cover produced an eerie effect that reminded me of the animal-shaped hedges in Disneyland. The vine has spread into East Texas, where it may soon present a serious problem. Fortunately, the severe winters of the northern United States and the droughts in the Southwest have restricted the spread of the vine to the warm, moist regions of the country. In Japan, insect predators, diseases, and a less hospitable climate control the spread of the plant.

Although kudzu has become so despised in the United States, the Japanese and other Oriental peoples rely on kudzu as a food and fiber, in addition to the ornamental and forage uses mentioned above. They eat the young, tender flowers, leaves, and shoots, adding them raw to salads or boiling them for soups, teas, and casseroles. Older foliage becomes too fibrous for eating. Stripped of the tough outer bark, the tuberous roots may also be boiled and eaten. The roots, which are highest in starch in fall and winter, may reach 7 feet (2 m) or more in length and can weigh more than 400 pounds (180 kg). Japanese arrowroot, a cooking starch, is extracted from the tubers and is used as a thickener for soups, a coating for fried foods, an ingredient of noodles, a gelling agent, and a medicine (see "starch extraction" in the index for information on extracting starch from roots).

To use kudzu starch as a substitute for other cooking starches, dissolve the powder in a small bowl of cold water. Then pour the liquid through a fine-mesh strainer into the cooking liquid. Kudzu starch is sold by the ounce in health food stores. *The Book of Kudzu: A Culinary and Healing Guide,* by William Shurtleff and Akiko Aoyagi, provides recipes for cooking with kudzu and much more valuable information.

The stem fibers of the kudzu vine furnish threads for fishing line, baskets, and textiles. Fine artist's paper, wallpaper, and cloth for kimonos all have been manufactured from the fibers. In the United States, researchers at Vanderbilt University have proposed that the root starch be extracted commercially and used in the fermentation of baker's yeast and ethanol fuel. Kudzu has much potential for use in the United States as well as in Japan. Perhaps we can transform the curse back into a blessing by taking advantage of the many valuable products that the plant can furnish (Shurtleff and Aoyagi 1977; Elliott 1976; Tanner et al. 1979).

Plant Characteristics

Kudzu is a woody perennial vine that easily climbs to 65 feet (20 m) and higher. Compound leaves bear three large broad, densely hairy leaflets that may be entire or deeply lobed. The fragrant papilionaceous flowers are purple, and the hairy linear pod is red or brown. Kudzu currently grows in East Texas along roadsides.

MESQUITE, HONEY MESQUITE, ALGARROBO, LA PÉCHITA—*PROSOPIS GLANDULOSA* AND OTHER SPECIES
(See illustration.)
TORNILLO, SCREWBEAN—*PROSOPIS PUBESCENS, PROSOPIS REPTANS* VAR. *CINERASCENS,* AND OTHER SPECIES

For centuries members of the genus *Prosopis* have supplied a major source of food for the Seris, Papagos, Pimas, and other native American tribes of the arid Southwest. The pods of honey mesquite (*Prosopis glandulosa*) and tornillo (*Prosopis pubescens*) may have been the most important wild foods of the Jumanos, an agricultural tribe that flourished in Southwest Texas until the eighteenth century (Newcomb 1961). Archeologists have discovered mesquite beans in storage bins in 1200-year-old Peruvian excavations. Common names for members of the genus abound worldwide. For simplicity, I will use the name "mesquite" to refer to the genus generally. "Tornillo" refers to those species with corkscrew-shaped pods.

Why have mesquites played such an important role in the American past? The bean pods yield a large annual summer-fall harvest. In drought-prone regions of the continent, these pods supply an abundant wild food that native Americans could depend on from year to year. In addition to being available in the driest part of the year, the nutritious pods could be stored to last through harsh winters. During the weeks when the pods ripened, entire families migrated to a favorite grove. Frequently, one family claimed ownership of a particular grove from generation to generation. The Seris of northwestern Mexico still harvest the pods annually.

The pods furnish protein, sugars, carbohydrates, and minerals. They contain up to 13 percent protein and 36 percent sucrose, twice as much sugar as beets or sugar cane (Ritchie 1979; Becker and Grosjean 1980). The pods are also rich in calcium, iron, and other minerals. You can chew the raw pods, green or ripe, and spit out the fibrous pulp. You can also boil the green pods to produce a nutritious syrup or grind the ripe pods into meal. The flavor of the pods varies considerably, from bitter to sweet. You may have to try a few trees to find a sweet one, but once you find a

Honey mesquite—*Proso-
pis glandulosa*

good tree, you have a friend for years to come.

Though generally a neglected food source in modern times, the highly nutritious pods still yield valuable human nutrition in some areas of the world. In a village of southwestern India, agricultural production is so low that one would expect a large portion of the local population to be under-fed. The rarity of malnutrition in the village has been attributed to the inhabitants' regularly eating the pods of the native *Prosopis cineraria* (Ritchie 1979).

The tiny seeds of mesquite yield up to 37 percent protein, 60 percent with the hard seed coat removed. In most cultures the seeds were not used, probably because they are more difficult to process than the pods.

Mesquites furnished important foods for Americans in the past, and there is no reason they cannot do so in the future. Though home process-ing of the pods is time-consuming, the results are nutritious and good-tasting foods.

GREEN MESQUITE POD SYRUP

You can boil the tender green pods, collected in early summer, to obtain a nutritious syrup. Chew the pulp of one or two pods before you gather a bagful. If they are bitter, don't waste your time. Try another tree.

When you find a sweet tree, fill your bag up with the green pods. Wash the pods and break them into small pieces. Place the pieces in a pot, cover them with water, and bring the water to a boil. Simmer the beans for 2 hours, adding small amounts of water if needed to prevent the syrup from burning. Mash the pods, and tear them apart further to re-lease more of the sweet pulp. Simmer for a few more minutes. Strain the juice through a sieve, then pour it back into a clean pot. Add sugar to taste (about 1 cup sugar to 2 cups juice for a thin syrup). Boil for 5 minutes. Mesquite syrup has a unique flavor and is excellent on pancakes.

Usually, green and ripe pods will be available at the same time on one tree. Native Americans used metates for grinding the ripe pods. Several thousand years ago the Amargosan-Pinacateño tribe of Sonora, Mexico, developed a specialized grinding stone for mesquite pods. R. S. Felger reports that he tried out one of the special mesquite crushers and found that it greatly decreased the time required to grind the pods (Simpson 1977). You can grind the dry pods in a hand-operated or electric grain mill. Scooter Cheatham (interview, September 1984) recommends a steel-plate grinder. I have successfully used a blender, but the pods can break the blades of a cheap blender. Use the ripe pods as follows.

MESQUITE POD MEAL

The dry pods, available from summer to fall, can be pulled from the trees or simply gathered off the ground. Test your tree for sweetness by breaking open a pod and sucking the pulp inside. Collect a bagful of sweet pods.

To dry out the pulp for easier grinding, toast the pods for an hour or two, at 150−200° F, until they are brittle. If not dry enough, the sticky pulp will gum up your grinder. To store the pods for later use, toast them first to kill the bruchid beetles that often attack mesquites.

Break up the pods, run them through your grinder, and sift the fragments through a coarse sieve. In the first grinding the seeds, surrounded by a hard section of the pod, will separate from the rest of the pod. Regrind the large fragments, and again sift the fragments through a sieve.

You will end up with a bowlful of shell fragments and seeds and a bowlful of grainy flour or meal. If you have a mill with variable settings, you can regrind the meal at finer settings.

Set aside the seeds and shell fragments. The Seris chew the inedible shell fragments for their sweetness and then throw them out. Soaked in water, the fragments supposedly yield a sweet beverage, but I find the drink unpalatable. Various native American groups would let the juice become slightly fermented, producing a beverage with a very low alcohol content. Highly intoxicating beverages from the sugary pods probably were unknown until colonists introduced the Indians to distillation processes.

Mesquite meal tastes great in waffles. Use the meal in place of acorn meal in the waffle recipe on page 103. The Seris make a simple bread of the mesquite meal. They add water to the meal, knead the mixture into a dough, then shape it into rolls or small round cakes. Rather than cooking the bread, the Seris merely let it dry in the sun. The dry cakes can be stored for later use or eaten immediately.

Here are a few recipes for using mesquite meal to get you started.

MESQUITE CORNBREAD

⅔ cup cornmeal	1 egg
⅓ cup mesquite meal	¾ cup milk
1 teaspoon baking powder	Cooking oil

Combine the dry ingredients, add the beaten egg and the milk, and mix well. Pour into a hot 8-inch iron skillet coated with oil. Cook slowly on top of the stove. Watch the bread carefully because mesquite flour browns quickly. When the bread has cooked most of the way through, flip it over to brown the other side.

MESQUITE PAN BREAD

| 1 cup mesquite meal | 1 cup water |
| 1 cup whole wheat flour | Cooking oil |

Combine the flours and water to make a dough. Heat a thin layer of oil in a skillet. Make small flat patties with the dough, and place them in the skillet. When the patties are well browned, turn them over. Serve them with butter and honey.

MESQUITE-HONEY COOKIES

⅓ cup mesquite meal	¼ cup butter
⅔ cup whole wheat flour	¼ cup honey
¼ teaspoon baking powder	½ teaspoon vanilla
¼ cup water	

Preheat the oven to 350° F. Mix the dry ingredients together. In a separate bowl, cream the butter and honey together, and add the vanilla. Add the dry ingredients to the butter mixture, and stir. Add the water, and mix well. Place tablespoonfuls of the dough on an oiled cookie sheet, and bake for 15 minutes.

I have read that you can grind up the tiny seeds to make a protein-rich flour that can be cooked into a porridge or mixed with other flours. Further grinding and winnowing is required however, to separate the seeds from their casings. By the time I get this far, the tiny seeds hardly seem worth the trouble. The yellow seeds, covered in brown seed coats, are very hard. I have never obtained a fine flour by grinding them in my coffee grinder—the hard grains are too large for use as a food. If you have a method for grinding the seeds into a fine powder, you can use them as a flour. As with a number of beans, though, mesquite seeds (but not the pods) contain digestive inhibitors. Research indicates that short-term heating probably is the best method for increasing the digestibility of the seed protein, but even that method has not been proved effective. At any rate, don't eat the seeds raw.

Native Americans have long used mesquite wood to build houses and corrals and to make weapons and tools. Today woodworkers prize the wood for use in tool handles, gunstocks, and carvings. The dense, hard wood dries to a lovely reddish brown. Though the size and shape of mesquite trees make them generally unsuited for lumber, good pieces carry a high price tag. The water-resistant wood provides the framework for Mexican fishing boats. In Argentina, mesquite wood was used in the past to make cobbles for streets and is still used in parquet floor tiles. Timbering of *Prosopis caldenia* for industrial purposes during both world wars had a devastating effect on Argentine forests (Simpson 1977).

Mesquite furnishes a high-grade firewood with a high heating value, good for purposes such as firing pottery. In 1985 mesquite charcoal for barbecues brought in several million dollars in sales. When Texas oil reserves run low, the maligned mesquite may take on new importance. In addition to the fuel value of the wood, the abundant sugary pods may prove to be as useful for fuel alcohol production as corn (Hope 1985).

Native Americans used the spines for sewing needles, and the root, with its outer bark removed, for cordage. The fragrant flower spikes of mesquites and tornillos provide pollen and sweet nectar for honeybees. Mesquites thus have good potential in commercial honey production. The Pimas pick the blossoms and eat them raw. Unfortunately, the highly allergenic pollen causes hay fever in South Texas and the Rolling Plains, where honey mesquite grows in dense stands.

Native American children chew the gummy sap of some sweet, white-sapped species. You can use the brown gum of honey mesquite as a brown to black dye for textiles. Until recent decades the Seris used the sap to make black face paint. The Yavapais of northern Arizona use the sap for dyeing hair. Besides coloring hair, the sap is said to kill lice. The Papagos of southern Arizona mix the gum with the red mineral hematite to yield a red paint for decorating pottery. The gum provides a cement for broken pottery and is also a good emulsifier. It may have commercial potential as a substitute for gum arabic (see "gum arabic" in the index).

Eyewashes of the leaves and gum, and a tea from the gum for sore throats, illustrate a few of the medicinal uses native American tribes have made of *Prosopis*. They also have used the inner bark and roots medicinally. Teas of the leaves and of the inner bark also have been used as emetics, however, and the boiled gum drunk as a purgative. As with all medicines, these should not be used by those unknowledgeable in their application and possible side effects.

Besides providing human food, mesquite pods supply food for livestock and deer. In Hawaii the leaves and pods of *Prosopis pallida* provide a major source of cattle food. Mesquite is an important livestock forage in India, Pakistan, South Africa, northern Argentina, and Uruguay. Livestock deaths in Texas and Hawaii, though, led to a search for possible toxic substances in mesquite. None were found, and research indicates that the problem occurs only when mesquite becomes the dominant forage. When other food is not available to dilute the sugars, the high sugar content of the pods inhibits the ability of ruminants to digest cellulose. Alfalfa, grasses, or other herbs should either be mixed with the mesquite or made available on the range to prevent illness in livestock (Ritchie 1979; Becker and Grosjean 1980; Kingsbury 1964).

Honey mesquite, *Prosopis glandulosa,* has gained a bad reputation among ranchers and farmers. In the past century the numbers of honey mesquite trees in Texas have increased vastly. Dense stands of mesquite cover much of South Texas, the Edwards Plateau, and the Rolling Plains. Ranchers and farmers consider the trees a detriment to their industries, but probably the most important factor in the increased density of mesquites has been the introduction of large numbers of grazing animals into the Southwest beginning in the 1800s.

Cattle, goats, and sheep have altered the Texas landscape considerably in a short period of time. They have eaten up the wild grasses and tender herbs, enabling topsoil to erode. By eating the nutritious mesquite pods, cattle and other livestock have aided in dispersal of the seeds, which pass through the animals' stomachs undigested and ready to germinate. The young seedlings, sprouting up in the trampled soil, with few grasses and herbs for competition, spread rapidly.

Once dense stands of honey mesquites were established, eradication of the pest became an impossible task. Chaining and burning the trees and shrubs destroys only aboveground growth. The root system, which can extend more than 200 feet down and 45 feet laterally, makes digging up the trees nearly impossible. In addition, the extensive root system makes mesquites experts at obtaining water in dry lands. Mesquites have been called water hogs and blamed for low yields of grasses and other forage plants. Thinning dense stands of mesquite does reduce competition for water and allow increased growth of other forage. In areas where mesquites do not occur in high densities, or where water is more readily available, however, mesquites do not inhibit the growth of other plants and, indeed, can be beneficial.

Mesquites provide shade for herbs and grasses and protection from trampling by livestock. As do many legumes, mesquites increase the nitrogen content of the soil around their roots by fixing nitrogen in the soil. Soil porosity and organic matter in the soil under the crown of the trees is also typically higher than that of surrounding areas. Thus, the canopy of a mesquite provides an ideal shelter for other forage herb and grass seeds to germinate and grow (Gilbert 1984).

Although ranchers and farmers often despise the tree, complete decimation of the populations could have serious side effects for wildlife. White-tailed deer and other wildlife rely on the trees for food and shelter. On a sunbaked pasture, cattle congregate beneath the only shade around, a mesquite tree.

American ranchers may find the soil-binding and restorative properties of mesquites an important aspect of future range management. In India *Prosopis juliflora* growing in shelter belts prevents the expanding desert sands from covering fields and villages. Planted in the Sudan, mesquites prevent sand from filling irrigation canals.

Though increased in numbers, *Prosopis glandulosa* has not changed its geographical range appreciably in the past century. Honey mesquite has long been an important component in dry grassland ecosystems. Even before the decimation of the prairies, mesquite was common in the arid Southwest. It is not the presence of mesquite that poses a problem for us today but its density. Though control of the spread of mesquite will continue to be a problem in Texas, it becomes more and more apparent that the management of this valuable resource, rather than its eradication, will be the goal of the future (Allen and Allen 1981; Simpson 1977; Ritchie 1979).

Plant Characteristics

Honey mesquite, *Prosopis glandulosa,* is a deciduous shrub or small tree. Straight, stout spines about 2 inches (5 cm) long arm the branches. Leaves are bipinnately compound, as though two (occasionally four) pinnately compound leaves were joined together, and the long, narrow leaflets have no teeth. Fragrant yellowish flowers occur in cylindrical puffball spikes. When mature, the slender bean pods are yellowish and often streaked with red. They grow to about 8 inches (20 cm) long and are somewhat flattened. Honey mesquite occurs throughout most of the state and the Southwest.

Two species of tornillos grow in Texas. Their leaves are similar to those of the honey mesquite, but the bean pods of tornillos coil tightly, like corkscrews. *Prosopis pubescens,* with cylindrical flower spikes, grows from Uvalde County west, near the Rio Grande in the Trans-Pecos, and across the Southwest. *Prosopis reptans* var. *cinerascens,* with flowers in round heads, grows in South Texas. All three species occur in northern Mexico.

REDBUD—*CERCIS CANADENSIS*
(See photograph, plate 11.)

The pink to lavender blossoms of the redbud tree grace the branches before the leaves appear in late winter or early spring. Add the fresh flowers and flower buds to salads, breads, and pancakes, or serve them pickled or fried. The flowers have a pleasant, slightly sour flavor and are high in vitamin C (Zennie and Ogzewella 1977). Scooter Cheatham (interview, March 1985) reports that the young green pods may be eaten raw, boiled, or sautéed. The pods appear in late spring, and by summer they are dry, papery, and no longer edible (Peterson 1977; Kirk 1975).

Redbud flowers attract bees and yield a fairly good honey. Around Lake Tahoe, California, women of the Paiute and Washo tribes used strips of the red bark of *Cercis occidentalis* for basket weaving. Redbud also produces a good-quality, high-density wood (Allen and Allen 1981).

Plant Characteristics

Redbud is a small-sized deciduous tree. The simple heart-shaped leaves have smooth margins. Papilionaceous flowers cluster along the branches, and the dark brown mature pods are flat, thin, and only about 2–4 inches (5–10 cm) long. *Cercis canadensis* is a common tree of the eastern United States and the mountains of eastern Mexico. Represented by three varieties in Texas, redbud occurs across the state except in the south. The trees are frequently used in landscaping throughout Texas.

RETAMA, JERUSALEM THORN—*PARKINSONIA ACULEATA*
(See illustration.)

Native Americans reportedly ground the seeds of retama to make a flour or meal, but I have found little information on the use of the seeds and no data on their digestibility. The seeds pop out of the papery shells easily. A thick, hard, brown seed coat covers the yellowish seeds. Although it is time-consuming to remove the seed coat, the inner seed tastes pleasant and is soft enough to grind into flour.

The fairly dense wood of retama provides a good fuel and, though brittle, is suitable for carvings. The wood has been used as pulpwood for paper in the past (Allen and Allen 1981). Considering its quick growth, perhaps the tree would be suitable in plantations for fuel and paper production in areas of the world where wood supplies are rapidly disappearing.

In Texas the tree adds a graceful touch to landscaping, but it has become a troublesome weed on ranches and farms of Central Texas and the Rio Grande Plains (Turner 1959). The flowers yield a good honey and a yellow dye for wool.

Plant Characteristics

A small to medium-sized thorny tree, retama produces beautiful yellow flowers practically year-round. The five flower petals are almost equal in shape and size. Constricted between the fat seeds, the pods have papery, thin walls and are 2–4 inches (5–10 cm) long. The once-pinnate or bipinnately compound leaves have numerous minute leaflets on a flattened stalk that may be 16 inches (4 dm) long. The bark of the tree is smooth and greenish. Retama is found throughout the warm regions of the Americas. In Texas it occurs from South Texas north to Brown County.

Retama—*Parkinsonia aculeata*

TEPARY BEAN—*PHASEOLUS ACUTIFOLIUS*

When the Spanish arrived in the New World, the Aztecs had thousands of acres of land under cultivation in beans and grains. One of the Aztec codices (ancient documents dealing with religion and history) lists the annual tribute to the emperor as 280,000 bushels of maize, 230,000 bushels of beans, and 200,000 bushels of amaranth.

Along with the more familiar pinto and kidney beans, which are varieties of *Phaseolus vulgaris,* native Americans in the Tehuacán Valley of Mexico cultivated the tepary bean, *Phaseolus acutifolius.* They grew both species for more than five thousand years before the arrival of the Spanish, who preferred the larger pinto and kidney beans (Schery 1972; Struever 1971). Today the tepary is almost an unknown food in most of the United States, but some southwestern Indians, such as the Pimas and the Papagos, still grow *Phaseolus acutifolius,* and the Zunis cultivate various colors of the small beans for ceremonial purposes.

The name "tepary" originated as a misunderstanding. When the Spanish asked the Papagos the name of their beans, the Papagos answered, "T'pawi," which means "It is a bean" (Russell 1983).

The tepary bean compares favorably with the better-known legumes in protein (21 to 32 percent), mineral, and carbohydrate content. It is also rich in calcium, containing 210 milligrams per 100 grams of cooked beans (Ritchie 1979).

Tepary beans are rare in Texas, so I do not advocate collecting them from the wild. But I do recommend planting teparies in your garden. In recent years the tepary has become a popular crop in semiarid regions of Africa, Asia, and Australia. Interest in its cultivation in the southwestern United States has been renewed because of its drought tolerance and ability to grow in a wide range of soil conditions (Hackett and Carolane 1982). The plant is also being considered as a hay and cover crop, and the bean pods can be used as fodder after the seeds are harvested.

The plant grows rapidly, producing a crop in two months, and when irrigated, it has a yield comparable to that of the more popular legumes. Indeed, the tepary has the advantage over other beans in that it grows quite well without any irrigation. A broad-leaved cultivar now is available from a few seed dealers in the United States.

Harvest the beans after they dry on the vine. Like some other beans, teparies contain digestive inhibitors. The hard beans require overnight soaking and long boiling to render them digestible and prevent gas. Niethammer (1983) recommends soaking them 12 hours, then pouring off the rinse water. Cook the beans 8 to 12 hours (the time varies depending on how long the beans have been stored) with at least 3 cups water per cup of beans. Add ⅛ teaspoon baking soda per cup of dry beans to assist in the degassing process. Niethammer also suggests pouring off the cooking water to aid in removing digestive inhibitors. If, like me, you do not want to throw off that rich soup, cook the beans for about an hour, throw off the water, then add fresh water and continue cooking. That technique works well for degassing any beans that require long cooking.

VEGETARIAN TEPARY BEAN CHILI

2 cups beans, fully cooked
Water
1 onion, chopped
2 cloves garlic, chopped
1 can whole tomatoes

Chili powder
Cumin
Salt and pepper
Cilantro, chopped

To the fully cooked beans, add the vegetables and the spices to taste. Cook for 1 hour, and serve with cornbread.

Plant Characteristics

An annual climbing herb, the tepary bean bears three linear to lanceolate leaflets per leaf. Pale lavender papilionaceous flowers occur in clusters of about two to four flowers. The pods are curved, and the beans vary in shape and color but are usually speckled. Native to Mexico and the southwestern United States, the bean grows wild in Texas only in the Trans-Pecos mountains.

FAGACEAE—BEECH FAMILY

OAK, ENCINO—QUERCUS SPECIES
(See illustration and photograph, plate 11.)

Warning

Because of the high tannic acid content of many species, eating large amounts of raw acorns for extended periods of time can cause kidney damage. Oak foliage and acorns should not be the only food available to livestock. Cattle, and occasionally goats and sheep, have died from eating large quantities of acorns and oak foliage over a period of several days. Kingsbury (1964) states that a diet of less than 50 percent oak forage is safe and nutritious for livestock. As with other livestock foods, be sure your stock have a variety of forages available (Sperry et al. 1964; Stephens 1980; Keeler, Van Kampen, and James 1978).

Used for fences, flooring, cabinets, ships, barrels, tools, and furniture, oak wood has long been a prized lumber and source of fuel. Oaks provide

Bur oak—*Quercus macrocarpa*

tannins and dyes for leather and wool and supply forage for wildlife and livestock. In addition, acorns furnish an important food for people.

Acorns played an important role in American history as one of the main foods in the diet of native Americans from coast to coast. In northeastern California the Miwok Indians relied on acorns as a major source of protein. They ground the nuts up for flour and used the oil for cooking. At Indian Grinding Rock State Historic Park in Amador County, California, I was awed by the large oak trees that surround the abandoned village site. There I marveled over the ancient grinding rock, 175 feet long, embedded with 1158 mortar holes that were formed by Miwok women as they ground acorns into flour. The Miwoks stored the acorns in large basket granaries for use through the winter.

Closer to home, the Apaches and Comanches of West Texas, the Tonkawas of Central Texas, and the Caddoan tribes of East Texas all harvested acorns (Newcomb 1961). And acorns have supplied as much as 25 percent of the diet of the poor in Italy and Spain (Hill 1952). Why have so many people relied on acorns for food? Acorns furnish protein (about 8 percent) and fats (37 percent) and are high in calcium and other minerals (Crowhurst 1972; Fleming 1975). They grow in abundance, and you can pick them for free. The question should be, Why don't more people use acorns for food? The answer: preparing a few pounds of acorn flour requires hours of labor, and most of us cannot spare the time. Nonetheless, acorn flour has a delightful rich flavor. Once you've tried acorn waffles, you'll have trouble settling for plain old waffles again.

Raw acorns have a mildly to strongly bitter taste, depending on the species. Tannic acid causes the bitterness, the same substance that makes coffee and tea dark brown in color. To prepare acorns for eating, you need to remove as much tannic acid as possible. For the Indians who ate acorns on a daily basis, reducing tannic acid levels was essential to good health. Besides being unpalatable, raw acorns consumed in large quantities over time can cause kidney damage.

To remove tannic acid, you must leach the acorns with water. The Indians set the acorns in a basket in a clean fast-flowing stream. The water rushing through the basket would leach out the tannins in a day or two. Since most of us do not have a clean fast-flowing stream nearby, we need to boil out the tannins. Start with the milder-flavored acorns to reduce the amount of leaching required. The Texas oaks reported to be the sweetest include Emory oak (*Q. emoryi*) in the Trans-Pecos, Vasey oak (*Q. pungens* var. *vaseyana*) in Southwest Texas, white oak (*Q. alba*), chestnut oak (*Q. prinus*) and coastal live oak (*Q. virginiana*) in East Texas; plateau live oak (*Q. fusiformis*) in Central Texas, bur oak (*Q. macrocarpa*, illustrated) in East and Central Texas, and chinkapin oak (*Q. muhlenbergii*, photographed), found in many areas of the state. The acorns of each of these oaks mature in one year, which may account for their lower tannic acid content (Hill 1952; Gibbons 1962; Scooter Cheatham, interview, October 1984).

The acorns of chinkapin oak and bur oak are both excellent. The meat has a pleasant nutty flavor and just a hint of bitterness when raw. The large acorns are much easier to shell than those of the live oaks, which have a wonderful flavor but smaller nuts. In general, the sweeter acorns have a fairly light-colored fleshy kernel. The nuts of the bitter species tend to be darker. Taste a few to determine that you have a fairly sweet species.

Acorns grow in abundance throughout Texas in the fall. Collect them off the ground, or spread a sheet under the tree and shake the limbs. Use the ripe acorns, with tan to brown shells, not the green ones. Collect three times as many as you think you'll need—expect at least half of them to be molded or infested with insects. Shell the acorns as you would any nut. A nutcracker works fine on larger nuts, but you may need to slit open the shell of smaller acorns with a knife. Remove the kernels. If a thin brown corky layer clings to the light-colored flesh, peel off the layer.

Toss the nuts into a large pot, and cover them with plenty of water. Bring to a boil, then boil for about 15 minutes. The water will turn brown, the color of tea, as the tannic acid is extracted from the kernels. Throw out the water (or use it to dye wool, cotton, or linen), and replace it with fresh water. To save time, have a second pot of water already boiling. Reboil the acorns, throwing out the brown water, several times until the water no longer turns brown. The boiling process takes about two or three hours, though the time varies with the amount of tannic acid in the acorns.

When you are finished, the acorns will no longer taste bitter and will have turned a darker brown. The nuts have a flavor similar to boiled chestnuts. Unless you want to use them wet, you need to dry out the nuts. Spread them out on cookie sheets, and roast them in an oven at about 200° F for an hour. You can eat the roasted nuts or chop them up to use as you would any chopped nuts.

To prepare acorn flour, run the roasted nuts through a flavor mill, food grinder, or blender. If the flour still is damp, dry it in the oven for 30 minutes. Then regrind the flour, if needed, to the fineness you want. Use it in breads, either by itself or with other flours.

ACORN WAFFLES

1 cup acorn flour	¼ cup oil
1 cup whole wheat flour	2 eggs
2 teaspoons baking powder	1½ cups water
2 teaspoons cinnamon	

Combine the dry ingredients, and mix well. In a separate bowl, mix the wet ingredients together. Then add the wet ingredients to the dry, and mix well. Use the batter in a waffle iron or for pancakes. Serve with mesquite syrup.

ACORN-OATMEAL COOKIES

½	cup butter	½ cup whole wheat flour
½	cup brown sugar	1½ cups oats
1	egg	1 teaspoon baking powder
1½	teaspoons vanilla	Raisins
1	cup acorn flour	Pecans

Preheat oven to 350° F. Cream the butter and sugar together, and stir in the egg and vanilla. In a separate bowl, mix the dry ingredients. Add them to the wet ingredients, and blend well. Stir in the raisins and nuts. Add a little water if needed to hold the dough together, then spoon the dough onto an oiled cookie sheet. Bake for 10 minutes.

In the 1800s and early 1900s the black oak (*Q. velutina*), a native of the eastern United States, supplied one of the world's most valued textile dyes. The inner bark, which yields a yellow dye known as quercitron, was shipped to Europe for dyeing cotton and wool and, because it is rich in tannic acid, for tanning and dyeing leather. Tannic acid is also used to make inks and to control the viscosity of mud in the drilling of oil wells.

The white oak (*Q. alba*) and the coastal live oak (*Q. virginiana*) also have furnished commercial tannins. All three species occur in East Texas. Oak bark contains about 15 percent tannic acid, and oak galls rate as one of the three most important natural sources of tannic acid. The galls of a certain oak in Turkey and Austria contain 60 to 70 percent tannic acid (Hill 1952; Schery 1972). Appearing as swollen growths on the tree branches, galls form where an insect has drilled a hole in the branch and laid its eggs.

You can use the bark and galls of a number of species of oak in home dyeing experiments. Tannic acid is a natural mordant (refer to Chapter 5 for information and recipes), and oaks yield an amazing variety of colors: tans, yellows, and oranges (Bryan 1978; Adrosko 1971). The inner bark of white oak and black oak have also had some value in the past as an astringent medicinal wash.

Oak foliage and acorns provide nutritious forage for wildlife and livestock. Javelinas, deer, squirrels, cottontails, and porcupines, quail, grouse, wild turkeys, and mourning doves feast on various species of oaks. The acorns of the sweet species furnish excellent food for hogs. Cattle, goats, and sheep also relish the forage.

Oaks are wind-pollinated and produce large amounts of highly allergenic pollen. Some species bloom in the spring and others in the fall, so they contribute to hay fever problems in both seasons. Live oaks are a major cause of hay fever in Texas (Wodehouse 1971).

Plant Characteristics

Oaks are shrubs or trees with alternate simple leaves. Most oak leaves are lobed, but the leaves of a few species, such as the live oaks, are mostly entire. Texas has more than 40 species of oak, and the trees hybridize to such an extent that distinguishing one species from another is often quite difficult. The genus can be roughly divided into two groups, the red (or black) oaks and the white oaks. Red oak leaves have bristle tips (short hairlike or needlelike protrusions) on the leaf lobes, while white oak lobes are smooth. The sweet acorns come from both groups.

Dead oak leaves tend to cling to the branches through the winter. The live oaks maintain green foliage through the winter, and then drop their leaves in the spring, just before the new growth emerges. In the winter a cluster of buds at the branch tips is a good clue that you are looking at an oak. Male flowers occur in drooping catkins loaded with pollen; female catkins are so small as to go unnoticed. The pollinated female flowers develop into acorns in one or two years.

FOUQUIERIACEAE—OCOTILLO FAMILY

OCOTILLO, CANDLEWOOD—*FOUQUIERIA SPLENDENS*
(See illustration.)

Ocotillo brightens up the hot West Texas desert with its scarlet blossoms. You can eat the flowers fresh or dipped in batter and fried. The nectar at the base of the blooms provides a sweet treat. The Cahuilla Indians of California soaked the flowers in water for a sweet beverage and ground up the seeds for flour. This unique desert dweller deserves our protection. If you wish to sample its flowers, take only a few without damaging the shrub.

Around the turn of the century, West Texas ranchers used the thorny shrubs as a living fence: a row of ocotillos planted close together forms a fence or corral as effective as barbed wire. Wax, resin, and gum in the bark protect the branches from the drying effects of the sun. The wax has been used for waxing leather, the gum as a thickener and adhesive, and the resin as a waterproofing agent and varnish. In Mexico the shrubs are still harvested from the wild and the resin exported for industrial use (Vines 1960; Brumgardt and Bowles 1981; Tate 1972; Latorre and Latorre 1977).

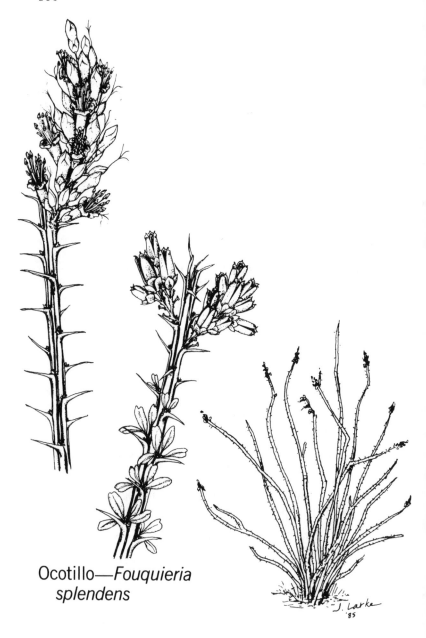

Ocotillo—*Fouquieria splendens*

Plant Characteristics

The bizarre shrub is superbly adapted to life in the desert. Most of the year the only parts of the plant visible are clumps of tall, slender wands waving in the desert breeze. Though the wands may reach 30 feet (9 m) in height, they rarely exceed 1−2 inches (2−5 cm) in diameter. Sharp spines arm the wands and protect the plant from hungry desert animals. After a rain the simple leaves, 1−2 inches (2−5 cm) long, emerge briefly, only to drop off again during dry periods. Streaks of green on the bark enable photosynthesis to continue when the leaves have fallen. The spectacular spring and summer blossoms more than make up for the otherwise drab look of the shrub. One or two large clusters of bright red blooms hang from the tip of each wand, attracting hummingbirds, bees, and bats to the nectar. Ocotillo grows from the western Edwards Plateau through the Trans-Pecos to California and Mexico.

JUGLANDACEAE—WALNUT FAMILY

HICKORY, NOGAL—*CARYA* SPECIES
PECAN, NOGAL PECANERO, NUEZ ENCARCELADA—*CARYA ILLINOINENSIS*
WALNUT, NOGAL, NUEZ—*JUGLANS* SPECIES
(See illustration, page 323.)

Warning

These nut trees all are wind-pollinated and produce allergenic pollen. Pecan cultivars, growing in abundance in many urban areas, cause a particularly severe form of hay fever in April and May (Wodehouse 1971). The juice of the hulls, particularly walnut hulls, will stain skin and can cause a skin rash in sensitive individuals.

We have all feasted on the delicious nuts of the walnut, pecan, and hickory. Fresh or roasted, salted or sugared, whole or chopped, the nuts enhance an infinite variety of dishes from salads to main courses to desserts. Texas cooks pride themselves on their pecan pies and pralines. We pay several dollars a pound for these nuts at groceries, and yet, wild nuts are available, free for the taking, every fall.

Numerous varieties of pecans have been developed from the native tree. Though the small size and hard shell of the native pecan discourages most nut collectors, the flavor of the native nut equals or surpasses that of the cultivars. When the earliest white settlers moved into Central Texas, the Tonkawas gathered pecans for barter with the Anglos (Newcomb 1961). The high price of a pound of the shelled nuts today gives an indication of the bartering power the pecan must have held 150 years ago. That the pecan is now the official state tree reflects the importance of the pecan in Texas' history and economy.

In addition to hosting the pecan, Texas provides a home for three native walnuts, including the well-known black walnut. Most of our nine native hickories also yield sweet nuts that are rich in protein, oil, and minerals. Pecans, walnuts, and hickories provide some of our best-tasting and most nutritious wild foods (Gibbons 1962). So this fall get on out there and start hunting.

MOTHER'S PECAN TARTS

CRUST
½ stick butter
1 small package cream cheese
1 cup flour, sifted

FILLING
1 stick butter
1 cup sugar
2 eggs, separated
1 teaspoon vanilla
1 cup chopped pecans
1 cup raisins or dates

To prepare the crusts, cream the butter and cheese together, then mix the flour in. Chill in the refrigerator for a few minutes. Roll the dough out thin, and cut with a biscuit cutter. Fit the crusts into muffin tins. To prepare the filling, cream the butter and sugar together, add the egg yolks and vanilla, and mix. Add the nuts and raisins, and mix well. Beat the egg whites, and fold them in. Fill the tart shells with the mixture. Bake at 350° F for 20 minutes.

WALNUT-TOFU "MEATBALLS"

1 pound tofu (soybean curd)
1 cup walnuts, chopped
2 cloves garlic, chopped
1 small onion, chopped

Powdered oregano, thyme, and sage
Parsley, chopped
Bread crumbs

Break up the tofu, and work it with your hands for a couple of minutes. Add all other ingredients except the bread crumbs, and knead them into the tofu. Form small, meatball-size balls, roll them in the bread crumbs, fry them in oil, and serve with spaghetti. My family loves to eat these vegetarian "meatballs" fresh from the frying pan.

Walnut, pecan, and hickory trees provide excellent wood for cabinets, furniture, fences, and tool handles. The quality of the woods was not unknown to the native Texans who claimed the land centuries before the Spanish arrived. The Comanches favored hickory wood for bows, and many other tribes used the wood for tools and firewood.

The leaves and green hulls of all these trees yield some of the best natural dyes available in the state. Colors range from tan and brown to almost black on wool, cotton, basketry fibers, and even human hair (refer to Chapter 5 for recipes).

Plant Characteristics

Walnuts, hickories, and pecans all bear large pinnately compound leaves that in several species are strongly aromatic. The leaves alternate on the stems, but the large serrated leaflets are arranged opposite each other on the leaf stalk. The pollen-bearing male flowers form long, drooping catkins.

Walnuts grow predominantly in rich woodlands, along streams, or in canyons. If you slice open a walnut twig lengthwise, you'll see a series of tiny hollow chambers in the pith, a characteristic that distinguishes walnuts from other members of the family. Walnut leaflets are ovate to lanceolate. A spherical hull encloses the wrinkled shell of the nut, and the hull does not split open like that of the pecan. Black walnut (*Juglans nigra*) grows in East Texas, Arizona walnut (*Juglans major*) occurs on the Edwards Plateau and in the Trans-Pecos, and little walnut (*Juglans microcarpa*), with tiny nuts, grows in South, Central, and West Texas.

Pecan is the only *Carya* species not restricted to the eastern third of the state. Pecan groves abound along river bottoms in East, Central, and North Texas. The leaflets of pecan trees are oblong-lanceolate and curved, and the oblong shell of the nut is smooth.

Hickories grow in rich woodlands and swamps, and a few produce bitter nuts. The hulls of hickory nuts split open as the nuts mature. Varying in shape from elliptical to almost spherical, the shells of the nuts may be smooth, ridged, or wrinkled.

LAMIACEAE—MINT FAMILY (FORMERLY LABIATAE)

HENBIT, DEAD NETTLE—*LAMIUM AMPLEXICAULE*
(See photograph, plate 12.)

The leaves, stems, and flowers of henbit serve as a tasty addition to salads or soups. A few fresh sprigs add a pleasant flavor to salads (Elias and Dykeman 1982; Fernald, Kinsey, and Rollins 1958). Henbit is a weedy plant, common in lawns and gardens and along roadsides. The plant blooms year-round but is most abundant in the fall and winter. Refer to Chapter 2 for information on wild mints suitable for teas and spices.

Plant Characteristics

Henbit is an annual or biennial herb, typically just a few inches tall, though occasionally up to 18 inches (45 cm) high. To appreciate the unusual deep pink to purple flowers, get down on your knees with a hand lens. The minute flower buds are red to purple. The five petals of the opened flower unite to form a long, slender tube. At the top of the tube the bilateral flower is strongly lipped, and the bottom lip is spotted. If you have a lively imagination, the flower, barely ½ inch (13 mm) tall, may remind you of a long-necked puppy or rabbit. Occurring in pairs that clasp the stem, the tiny simple leaves have rounded teeth and a wrinkled appearance. The leaf shape and hairs give the plant a superficial resemblance to a nettle, but *Lamium* lacks the sting—hence the common name "dead nettle."

The square stems, opposite leaves, and two-lipped flowers are clues that henbit is a member of the mint family (see "mint" in the index for more information on recognizing mints). Unlike most mint leaves, the leaves of henbit are not aromatic. Henbit occurs as a weed throughout much of the state. Another species, red henbit (*Lamium purpureum*) has purplish leaves and grows in East Texas. Red henbit can also be used for food. Both henbits are natives of Europe that are now naturalized throughout the United States.

LILIACEAE—LILY FAMILY

The lily family includes many beautiful wildflowers, such as the trout lilies, Solomon's seals, the true lilies, and *Trillium*. While some of these lovely wildflowers bear edible parts, they occur rarely in Texas and deserve to be left alone. A few important edible members of the family are discussed below. The lily family also includes the deadly poisonous death camas (*Zigadenus*), which resembles the edible blue camass mentioned in this section. Additional confusion arises with the use of the common name "lily." A number of members of the amaryllis and iris families are commonly called lilies. Though you can boil and eat the bulbs of the true lilies, *Lilium* species, many of the so-called lilies contain highly toxic alkaloids.

Descriptions of the lily, iris, and amaryllis families are given together in Chapter 4, "Poisonous and Harmful Plants" (see the index). The bulbs, leaves, and flowers of toxic iris and amaryllis species often resemble those of the lily family. Familiarizing yourself with the characteristics of all three families may prevent a disastrous misidentification.

BLUE CAMASS, WILD HYACINTH—*CAMASSIA SCILLOIDES*

Warning

I mention this unusual plant mainly to distinguish it from the very similar-looking and highly toxic death camas, Zigadenus nuttallii, and other species (see the index for information and illustration) (Wells 1982). The best way to distinguish blue camass from death camas is by the color of the flowers. Those of death camas are creamy white, greenish, or yellowish, while those of blue camass are pale blue.

The ornamental hyacinth (Hyacinthus orientalis), also in the lily family, has toxic bulbs. The possibility of confusing the blue camass with either of these two poisonous plants is more than enough of a reason to leave the lovely blue camass alone.

The northwestern Indians introduced quamash, *Camassia quamash,* to members of the Lewis and Clark Expedition. The starchy bulb occasionally provided the only reliable source of food for the explorers. Our native blue camass, *Camassia scilloides,* also is edible. You can eat the bulb raw, boiled, or baked like a potato. Although the camass furnished a valuable source of nutrition in the past, the wildflower is uncommon in Texas. Unless you grow your own supply, I do not recommend removing this graceful wildflower from its natural setting (Peterson 1977; Gibbons and Tucker 1979; Weddle 1980; Scooter Cheatham, interview, March 1985).

Plant Characteristics

Blue camass has an erect spike of spring-blooming pale blue flowers on a leafless stalk. The small flowers have six tepals. Grasslike leaves crowd the base of the flower stalk. Blue camass grows from Central Texas northward in fields and prairies and open woodlands. It is scattered throughout the eastern United States.

DAY LILY—*HEMEROCALLIS FULVA*
(See illustration.)

Warning

Eat the day lily in moderation, as it is a mild laxative (Elias and Dykeman 1982). If eaten raw, the green buds can cause throat irritation.

The leaves of narcissus, daffodil, and iris somewhat resemble those of the day lily. Do not mistake these poisonous garden flowers for the day lily

Day lily—*Hemerocallis fulva*

(see the index for further information on the toxic look-alikes in the iris and amaryllis families).

The Greek words "hemera" and "kallos" translate to "day beauty." The handsome day lily blooms for a day and then withers. Though not often found growing wild in Texas, this common garden flower deserves mention because of its wide array of uses. Besides adding beauty to a summer garden, the plant can serve as a source of food, fiber, and dye.

In the spring the crisp white tuberous swellings on the roots yield a delicious succulent vegetable. After scrubbing them, eat them raw, boil for 15 minutes, or bake them like potatoes. Later in the year the tubers become tough but not bitter and may still be used if cooked. Collect only the firm tubers, and leave plenty for next year's crop.

Use the white heart of the late-winter to early-spring shoots as a vegetable—raw, steamed, or boiled for 5 to 10 minutes. Euell Gibbons (1966) found that the flower buds provide a good source of vitamins A and C. The green buds are tasty steamed or boiled but irritate the throat if eaten raw.

You can even eat the large showy flowers of the day lily. Add the fresh petals to a salad. In China and Japan the flowers are dried and stored for year-round use as a thickener for soups. The petals also add a delicate flavor to clear soups. Add the fresh, withered, or dried flowers to soup in the last few minutes of cooking. The flowers of most cultivars bloom in late spring and summer (Crowhurst 1972; Elliott 1976; Peterson 1977; Gibbons 1962). The leaves, collected in the fall as they fade to lovely shades of brown and gold, work well in weavings, and the plant yields a yellow dye for wool.

Plant Characteristics

The day lily, an ornamental perennial from Eurasia, occasionally occurs wild. Cultivars may be purchased with blossoms in red, orange, yellow, or pink, the blooms appearing in the spring, summer, or fall. The large funnel-shaped flowers, which may be more than 4 inches (10 cm) wide, have six tepals. The inner three tepals have wavy edges and are slightly broader. Unlike the tepals of true lilies, day lily tepals are not spotted. The flowers stand erect, not nodding. The leaves are basal, and none occur on the tall flower stalk, which can reach 6 feet (2 m) in height. The tips of the long, swordlike leaves arch over to touch the ground. The day lily has a fleshy or tuberous, but not bulbous, root.

GREENBRIAR, CATBRIER, BLASPHEME-VINE, STRETCHBERRY, ZARZAPARRILLA—*SMILAX BONA-NOX*
(See illustration, page 332.)

114

_____

Some individuals report developing a skin rash after being scratched by the prickles of the vine (Scooter Cheatham, interview, March 1985). The snailseed vine Cocculus carolinus, *which has toxic foliage and berries, looks very similar to* Smilax bona-nox. *Snailseed does not bear thorns and has red berries (see photograph, plate 13).*

If you have ever tangled with the greenbriar vine, you can appreciate its various common names. The thorns cling like the claws of a cat and have induced more than one blasphemous response from this explorer. But in spite of its thorns, the greenbriar supplies a number of useful products.

The succulent growing tips of the vines, as they emerge in the spring, furnish a delightful nibble. You can boil the tips, but with cooking, the stem becomes fibrous and the leaf flavor rather bland. I prefer the nutty flavor of raw tips (Peterson 1977).

The roots of a tropical *Smilax* provided the essential ingredient in sarsaparilla, an old-fashioned soft drink similar to root beer (Schery 1972). Gibbons (1966) reports that a reddish meal obtained from the tubers of *S. bona-nox* makes an interesting jelly. The flesh of the tough root turns pink to red on exposure to the air. I have followed his instructions and obtained the starchy material he mentioned, but I have never gotten my jelly to gel, and the starch was too astringent to be considered palatable. The red color of the starch gave me an idea however. I tried dyeing some wool with it, and sure enough, I obtained an attractive reddish-brown color on my wool (see "greenbriar" in the index for the recipe for extracting the starch for use as a dye). Digging up, chopping, and pounding the root involves some heavy labor. Maybe you can find a neighbor willing to pay you to remove the weedy vine from his/her yard.

Though the blue-black berries of *S. bona-nox* probably are not toxic, they are not considered edible. I found reports that the berries of two other species, *S. herbacea* (rare in Texas) and *S. pseudo-china,* are edible, but Gibbons and Tucker (1979) state that the berries of *S. herbacea* are not palatable (Medsger 1966; Fernald, Kinsey, and Rollins 1958). The berries have the consistency of rubber, giving the plant another common name, "stretchberry." They produce beautiful dyes for wool, including a rich forest green. You can find the berries practically year-round, but they grow abundantly in the fall and winter.

Plant Characteristics

With one exception, Texas greenbriars (*Smilax* species) are woody to shrubby perennial vines with spines scattered on the stems. The vining branches climb with the help of paired tendrils. Leaf shapes vary among species and may be oval, linear, or triangular. The simple leaves may be entire, lobed, or have spiny protrusions on the margins. *Smilax bona-nox,* an abundant weedy species, occurs throughout the eastern two thirds of the state. It grows along fences, in thickets, and on hillsides in a variety of habitats. Eight other species occur predominantly in East Texas, with one (*Smilax renifolia*) endemic to the Edwards Plateau. The only Texas species that is an herbaceous annual and thornless is the extremely rare carrion flower, *Smilax herbacea,* of East Texas. The smell of its flowers gives away its common name. Because several similar-looking species are rare, collect greenbriar only when it is growing in abundance.

LILY—*LILIUM* SPECIES

Warning_____

Many wild and garden flowers commonly called lilies contain highly toxic alkaloids. Rain lilies (Cooperia species), atamasco lilies (Zephyranthes species), spider lilies (Hymenocallis species), and lily of the valley (Convallaria majalis) all are toxic. Use only members of the genus Lilium.

Two beautiful wild lilies grow in Texas, one in the mountains of the Trans-Pecos and one in the woods of Southeast Texas. Please don't dig up these rare wildflowers. If you grow any of the perennial lilies in your garden, though, you may want to try the bulbs for food. Peterson (1977) reports that you can use the cooked rough, scaly bulbs in soups and stews. Collect them at any time of the year, scrub them, and boil or bake them like potatoes. In the Orient, lilies are cultivated for their tasty bulbs (Weddle 1980; Kirk 1975; Elliott 1976).

Plant Characteristics

The large showy flowers of the true lilies somewhat resemble those of the day lily, but the six large tepals of lilies are all the same size and usually are spotted. The flowers may be funnel-shaped, or the tepals may curve backward. Colors vary from yellow to orange or orange-red (some nonnative species may be white). One to several flowers appear at the top of a single smooth stalk, possibly 3 feet (1 m) tall, and may be erect or nodding. The leaves may be alternate or whorled on the smooth flower stalk, but not basal. The bulbous roots of lilies are covered with scales, an important identifying characteristic. Lilies that may be found in gardens include the tiger lily, Canada lily, and Turk's-cap lily.

ONION, GARLIC, CHIVES—*ALLIUM* SPECIES
(See illustration.)

After a warm spring rain, as you walk along your favorite creek, you may notice a faint odor of onions. Looking down, you find that the thick bed of grasslike leaves below you is a bed of wild onions. Onions, garlic, and chives all belong to the genus *Allium*. You can use the bulbs and leaves of all species in any recipe calling for onions—salads, soups, stews, meat dishes, casseroles, omelets. You can even use the green bulblets that top the stalks of the wild garlic *Allium canadense* var. *canadense*. The wild onions and garlics have a stronger flavor than cultivated varieties, so use them sparingly.

Medicinally, onions and garlics have a number of uses. The plants supply a natural antiseptic and contain high levels of vitamin C (Zennie and Ogzewella 1977). Soldiers in World War I applied garlic juice to wounds to prevent infection (Elliott 1976). Cold sufferers sometimes chew garlic, a treatment not appreciated by close family members.

The skins of cultivated yellow and red onions yield excellent dyes. Whenever you peel an onion, save the skins in a nylon stocking. When you have filled the stocking, use them to produce bright yellow, gold, and orange dyes on wool.

Plant Characteristics
A dozen species of wild onion grow in Texas. Leaves and bulbs of the biennial or perennial herbs bear a distinctive oniony odor. Leaves are basal and linear, like tall blades of grass. Most Texas species bloom in the spring. The six tepals form small flowers that may be white, yellow, pink, red, or purple. Flowers occur in umbels at the top of the slender flower

Wild garlic, wild onion—
Allium canadense var.
canadense

Crow poison—*Nothoscor-
dum bivalve*

stalk and may stand erect or nodding. Seeds are black and wrinkled. Wild onions grow in a variety of habitats from East Texas to the mountains of the Trans-Pecos. Some occur in abundance along stream banks.

MALVACEAE—MALLOW FAMILY

Warning

A few mallows, such as Malva parviflora, *have caused some poisoning in livestock when large quantities of plant material are eaten (Kingsbury 1964; Mitchell 1982).*

The mallow family includes the economically important plants cotton and okra and the ornamental shrubs hibiscus, althaea, rose of Sharon, and hollyhock. The beautiful Texas wildflowers rose pavonia, wine-cup, Turk's cap, and velvetleaf mallow belong to the family.

A number of the mallows produce good dyes for wool. Indian mallow (*Abutilon incanum*) and chingma (*Abutilon theophrasti*), a Eurasian species that is sometimes found growing wild in the High Plains, contain strong fibers in their stems.

The fruit, flowers, and leaves of a number of mallows have been used for food. I have frequently sampled the tiny capsules of *Sida* species while they are green and tender. The young leaves of *Malva parviflora* and other *Malva* species are considered edible as a potherb. Like okra, many mallows have mucilaginous sap. The root sap of the European marshmallow originally provided the gummy juice for making marshmallows. The green capsules of the dwarf mallow (*Malva rotundifolia*), a West Texas weed, can be boiled down to a mucilaginous liquid, then whipped with sugar for a tasty confection (Gibbons 1966).

Various members of the family have been put to use as medicinal herbs. Research is needed to determine what compounds provide the medicinal effects.

Family Characteristics

Texas mallows are either herbaceous wildflowers or shrubby plants and have simple and alternate leaves. The five petals of the flowers twist around each other in the bud. The petals are brightly colored, from yellow to orange, pink, purple, or bright red. Numerous stamens unite to form a long tube that usually protrudes beyond the petals. An excellent large-scale example of the typical mallow flower is the garden hibiscus.

TURK'S CAP—*MALVAVISCUS ARBOREUS* VAR. *DRUMMONDII*
(See illustration.)

I can recall plucking Turk's cap flowers as a child and sucking the sweet nectar from the base of the petals. The bright red flowers and plentiful nectar attract hummingbirds, making the shrubby plant a welcome addition to your yard. Growing in front of a picture window, the wildflowers provide a stage for viewing the hummers at work.

You can eat the flowers, fruit, and young leaves of Turk's cap either raw or cooked (Scooter Cheatham, interview, September 1984). The leaves are a bit too fuzzy and tough to yield a very good salad or potherb alone, so you may want to mix them with other greens. Have you ever tasted hibiscus tea? You may like a tea of Turk's cap flowers. Dry the flowers and store them for year-round use. Though the flowers and fruits can be found just about any month of the year, they are most abundant in the late spring and late fall. The beautiful red flowers produce mealy red fruits about ¾ inch (2 cm) in diameter. The flavor of the raw fruit is reminiscent of that of a watermelon or an apple. The five large seeds fill up much of the pulp, so as a raw food, they provide little more than a nibble. Cooked down, however, the fruits produce a delightful jelly or syrup.

TURK'S CAP JELLY

2 cups ripe and slightly underripe fruit
2 tablespoons pectin
½ cup sugar

Cover the fruit with water. Heat and simmer until soft, about 20 minutes. Crush the fruit and strain it through cheesecloth or a jelly bag. Add the pectin to the liquid, and bring it to a rolling boil. Add the sugar, bring to a boil, and cook for 2 or 3 minutes, until the liquid passes the jelly test (see the index). Turk's cap fruits gel with a minimum of pectin and sugar. The amber-colored jelly has a distinctive but subtle flavor.

The Mexican people use a strong decoction of the flowers to treat diarrhea, and a poultice of the leaves and roots externally to treat chest congestion. Use the leaves and flowers to produce dyes for wool.

Plant Characteristics

Turk's cap can be found both wild and in landscaping throughout Central and South Texas. Usually 3−4 feet (1 m) tall, the shrubby perennial

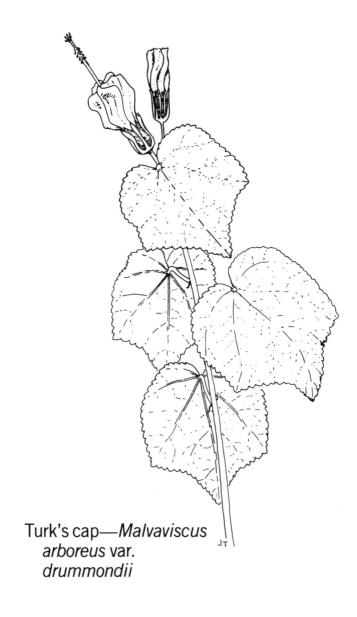

Turk's cap—*Malvaviscus arboreus* var. *drummondii*

JT

may reach 10 feet (3 m). The leaves, about 2–3 inches (5–8 cm) long, usually have a heart-shaped base and are about as broad as they are long. They are simple and alternate, with toothed margins and three shallow lobes. The upper surface of the leaves has the texture of velveteen cloth. The bright red flowers never fully open. Turk's cap grows in shady areas on limestone hills, along wooded streams, and in palm groves from Texas to Florida, and into Mexico and Cuba. Two other varieties are found in the Rio Grande Valley.

MARTYNIACEAE—UNICORN PLANT FAMILY

DEVIL'S CLAW, UNICORN PLANT, RAM'S HORN, UÑA DE GATO, TORITO—
PROBOSCIDEA LOUISIANICA, PROBOSCIDEA PARVIFLORA,
AND OTHER SPECIES
(See illustration, page 374.)

The fruit of devil's claw has been put to a variety of uses for centuries in the Southwest and in Mexico. *Mexicanos* eat the seeds and young pods, and southwestern Indians use the ripe pods in weaving baskets. The plant is also cultivated as an ornamental for its attractive flowers.

To prepare pods of *Proboscidea louisianica* and *Proboscidea parviflora* for eating, collect the green pods in early summer. Gather the small, tender pods only. After they grow to more than about one or two inches long, they become very bitter. Wash the pods, brush off the sticky hairs, and remove the stems. Then cover the pods in water, and boil them for 15 to 20 minutes. Slice them and serve with butter. The pods have the consistency and flavor of okra and can be used as a substitute for okra in gumbos. The pods reportedly make good pickles (Schery 1972). In the early 1900s *Proboscidea louisianica* was cultivated in Michigan and Massachusetts, and the pods canned commercially (Bretting 1984).

Mexicanos commonly eat the seeds of both species fresh from the fields. In a few areas of Mexico the seeds are sold in markets. You can collect the seeds from the ripe seed pods. Cut off the woody hull from the mature seeds to extract the tender seed. The immature seeds are preferred in Mexico because they can be eaten without removing the seed coat. Devil's claw seeds have an excellent flavor. Eat them fresh, toasted, or ground into meal. Researchers collected seeds from *P. louisianica, P. louisianica* subsp. *fragrans,* and *P. altheaefolia* in Texas for evaluation and found them to be high in protein and to produce a good-quality oil (Berry, Bretting, and Weber 1981).

Anthropologists studying groups in Mexico and South America have found additional uses of the plants. In some areas campesinos feed the roots of *Proboscidea altheaefolia* to livestock. The Seris remove the outer corky layer and eat the middle layer of the root themselves. The Tarahumara Indians of Mexico boil and eat the leaves of *Proboscidea loui-sianica* subsp. *fragrans* with beans. Nutritional evaluation has not been done to confirm the food value of these plant parts.

When the pods of devil's claw ripen, they become woody and split into two black claws. The Papagos cultivate varieties with large pods and weave them into beautiful baskets. The Pimas also weave with the hard pods. Use the pods in children's crafts, decorated as insects or birds, and in dried flower arrangements. If nothing else, you can always use them as pothooks or coat hangers (Niethammer 1974; Bretting 1984; Gibbons and Tucker 1979).

Plant Characteristics

Proboscidea louisianica is a branching annual herb. Mature plants are shrublike, up to 3 feet (1 m) tall. The large ill-scented plants often topple over and wither by the end of the summer. Sticky hairs cover the branches, leaves, and immature pods. The simple leaves vary in shape but often are heart-shaped. They have long petioles and may be 6−12 inches (1.5−3 dm) wide. Most of the leaves occur in pairs. Leaf margins may be entire or strongly wavy. Spotted and mottled with purple and yellow on the interior, the showy flowers are creamy, pink, or lavender. The flower forms a bell-shaped tube that opens into a four-lobed bilateral blossom, about 2 inches (5 cm) wide. The distinctive pods, about 4 inches (1 dm) long, are curved like claws or horns. When ripe, they pop open to form a woody double claw.

Proboscidea louisianica grows in Northeast Texas and the Edwards Plateau westward to about Schleicher County. Look for it in disturbed areas, at the edges of ranchland and farmland, and along stream banks and roadsides. Native to the southern United States and Mexico, the plant is now found wild farther north, because of its cultivation. The subspecies *fragrans*, with purple flowers, grows in the Trans-Pecos.

Proboscidea parviflora occurs in sand, gravel, and clay in the Trans-Pecos. Its white, pink, or reddish-purple flowers may have little or no mottling, with perhaps a single yellow band inside the lower lobe. The leaf margins are entire or wavy or have several shallow lobes. *Proboscidea altheaefolia,* with yellow flowers and small leaves, grows in the Trans-Pecos and part of South Texas. Several other species also occur in Texas, but I have found no information about their uses.

NYMPHAEACEAE—WATER-LILY FAMILY

LOTUS, YELLOW LOTUS, WATER CHINQUAPIN—*NELUMBO LUTEA*
(See illustration.)

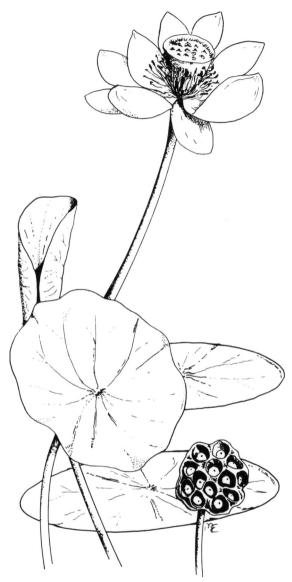

Lotus—*Nelumbo lutea*

SPATTERDOCK, YELLOW COW-LILY— *NUPHAR LUTEUM*
(See photograph, plate 13.)
WATER-LILY, WHITE WATER-LILY, NINFA ACUÁTICA—*NYMPHAEA ODORATA*

Nymphaeaceae is named for the water nymphs of Greek mythology, who lived in ponds and secluded lakes. Though I have found various reports that all three of these members of the water-lily family have edible parts, the plants in general contain bitter compounds and do not produce palatable foods. As they tend to be uncommon to rare in Texas, I discourage their use for food unless you have them in your own pond. Only the seeds can be gathered without harming the plants.

Although native Americans have used the underwater rootstock of the spatterdock and some other species of water-lilies for food, only the lotus comes well recommended for our modern palates. The starchy tuberous swellings on young lotus roots can be baked, peeled, and eaten like a sweet potato. The tubers are bitter and inedible when raw. Collect them in the late fall and winter in unpolluted water (Elliott 1976; Gibbons and Tucker 1979; Peterson 1977).

Two native American tribes who once lived along the Texas coast used yellow lotus for food. The Bidais collected lotus seeds and tubers, and the lotus probably was the "wild potato" of the Akokisas (Newcomb 1961). Though Elias and Dykeman (1982) report that the flowers, young unfurling leaves, and stems can be used as cooked vegetables, I find the foliage quite bitter even when boiled. *Nelumbo lutea* is the only lotus in the Americas. The Chinese cultivate *Nelumbo nucifera* for its seeds and rootstocks (Hackett and Carolane 1982).

You can eat the immature seeds of the lotus. Look for them in the summer and fall. They contain up to 19 percent protein. Crack off the thin shell, and eat the immature seeds raw, boiled, roasted, or ground into flour. Before cooking, remove the bitter green undeveloped leaf attached to the seed. The mature seeds become rock hard, practically inedible. If you want to try using them, roast them, then crack off the thin, hard shell, and grind the nuts in a coffee grinder. I have read that you can soften the hard nuts by removing the shells first and boiling them.

Elias and Dykeman (1982) report that the ripe seeds of spatterdock and the white water-lily also are edible. I haven't tried them, but here is the recommended procedure. Parch them to loosen the shell. Crack them, and then either fry the nuts like popcorn for eating or grinding for flour, or boil them like rice. The two other Texas water-lilies, a yellow-flowered species (*Nymphaea mexicana*) and a blue-flowered species (*Nymphaea elegans*) may have edible seeds, but I have found no references for them.

Plant Characteristics

These aquatic plants grow in quiet ponds, shallow lakes, and slow-moving streams. Spatterdock occurs mostly in East Texas and on the Edwards Plateau, lotus grows from East Texas to the eastern Edwards Plateau, and the white water-lily grows from Southeast Texas inland to Erath County. All are occasionally found planted as ornamentals in ponds in other areas of the state.

The lotus flower, up to 10 inches (25 cm) across, may have 20 or more light yellow tepals. Usually the leaf stalks hold the spherical leaves out of the water. The unusual flat-topped receptacle that holds the acornlike nuts may be 4 inches (1 dm) in diameter.

Spatterdock has a bright yellow waxy flower about 1¾ inches (4.5 cm) in diameter. The numerous small petals resemble thick stamens, and the six large sepals (often all yellow, or three green) form a rounded cup over the petals. Floating on or emerging from the water, the leaves are oval to almost circular and have a rounded notch at the base. The round leathery fruit holds many seeds and matures underwater.

The fragrant white water-lily has numerous sharp-pointed petals and four sepals. The bloom may be 2–6 inches (5–15 cm) across. The floating (occasionally emerging) leaves are circular, with a sharply cut wedge on one side. Like that of spatterdock, the leathery fruit matures underwater.

ONAGRACEAE—EVENING PRIMROSE FAMILY

SHOWY EVENING PRIMROSE, AMAPOLA DEL CAMPO—
OENOTHERA SPECIOSA
(See photograph, plate 13.)

The young leaves of the showy evening primrose taste delightful raw as an addition to salads or cooked as a green (Scooter Cheatham, interview, September 1984). The leaves tend to turn bitter after the plant flowers. To ensure proper identification, collect the leaves of young plants growing next to blooming plants. Pink blooms appear from the early spring to midsummer. Since this plant is a perennial, don't pull it up by the roots. The effects of eating large amounts are unknown, so use the greens sparingly.

Recent research has uncovered a number of valuable uses for the seed oil of *Oenothera biennis* as a source of vitamin F, a nutritional supplement, and a medicine (Horrobin 1981). Elias and Dykeman (1982) report that the leaves, young shoots, and roots of this yellow-flowered biennial species are edible in their first year. Boil them for 20 to 30 minutes in two changes of water to render the bitter herb palatable. Accurate identification of the basal rosette is difficult without the flowers, so I don't recommend its use unless you are very familiar with the plant. It grows only in the northeast corner of the state. I have found no reference to the use of *Oenothera* species other than these two.

Plant Characteristics

The showy evening primrose is a beautiful low-growing perennial wild-flower. The stems may stand 18 inches (45 cm) tall but are only a few inches tall in mowed areas. Typically less than 3 inches (8 cm) long, the narrow simple leaves alternate on the stem. The toothed, lobed, or nearly entire margins are often wavy-edged. The large flowers have four pink to rose, occasionally white, delicate petals that are similar in size and shape, each about $1-1\frac{1}{2}$ inches (2.5−4 cm) long. Usually the center of the flower is yellow. The flower bears eight large stamens, and the style ends in a cross-shaped stigma. A cylindrical capsule, the fruit is up to $\frac{1}{2}$ inch (1.5 cm) long, with no pedicel.

Showy primrose may be found in fields, open woods, and lawns and along roadsides. The flower grows in much of Texas but is rare in the northern and western parts of the state. In Central and East Texas, large masses of blooms may be seen. The plant occurs from Kansas and Missouri south to northeastern Mexico.

OXALIDACEAE—WOOD SORREL FAMILY

WOOD SORREL—*OXALIS* SPECIES
(See illustration.)

Warning

The sour taste of wood sorrels is caused by oxalic acid. When wood sorrel is eaten in moderation, the oxalic acid poses no problem (see "spinach" in the index for information on problems caused by overconsumption of spinach, another plant high in oxalic acid). Use very tart wood sorrels in small quantities as a flavoring for salads and soups rather than a large quantity as a main course. Livestock should not be allowed free access to fields covered with wood sorrels. Sheep in Australia have been poisoned by Oxalis pes-caprae, *which contains as much as 14 percent oxalic acid, after feeding on a large stand for two weeks (Kingsbury 1964; Lampe and Fagerström 1968).*

Nearly a dozen species of *Oxalis* grow in Texas, several as common weeds. Next time you are weeding your garden, instead of throwing the

Wood sorrel—*Oxalis dillenii*

wood sorrel in the garbage, toss the leaves into a salad or use them to flavor a soup. The fresh leaves and tender green fruit pods add a zingy sour flavor to vegetable dishes. Wood sorrel is high in vitamin C and was used in the past to prevent and treat scurvy, which is caused by a vitamin C deficiency. Wood sorrel is available year-round (Gibbons and Tucker 1979; Fleming 1975; Zennie and Ogzewella 1977).

Plant Characteristics

Some species of *Oxalis* provide attractive wildflowers, some are cultivated as ornamentals, and others are common lawn and garden weeds. The small herbs, typically less than 1 foot (3 dm) tall, bear yellow, pink, or purple flowers. Wood sorrel flowers have five delicate petals of equal size and shape. The common Texas species have compound leaves with three heart-shaped leaflets that meet at a point. The leaflets have no teeth on the margins. Some species may have triangular, round, or oval leaflets. Wood sorrels are often mistaken for clovers. Clover (*Trifolium*) leaflets are not heart-shaped, however, and the flowers are bilateral.

PINACEAE—PINE FAMILY

PIÑON, PINYON PINE—*PINUS EDULIS, PINUS CEMBROIDES*
(See illustration.)

The small cones of the piñon produce large edible nuts in the fall. A thin hard shell surrounds the delicious nuts. Use these excellent nuts raw or roasted (Peterson 1977; Kirk 1975; Schery 1972). The tasty treats are high in protein, carbohydrates, and oil. Piñon is reported to have been the major source of protein in the winter for the Utes and Paiutes of the Great Basin (Blanchard 1977). Today the Navahos and other native Americans and Anglo Americans in the Southwest harvest the nuts for food and for sale in local markets. Unfortunately, some overzealous harvesters cut down whole trees to reach the valuable fruits.

These pines are not abundant in Texas, growing mainly in the mountains of the Trans-Pecos. Other pines also produce edible seeds, but they are too small to be worth the trouble. Pignolias, expensive nuts sold in specialty shops, come from a European pine. Pignolia nuts furnish one of the essential ingredients in pesto, an Italian sauce for pasta. Here's a pesto recipe using piñon nuts.

Piñon—*Pinus edulis*

PESTO

2 cloves garlic, chopped
1 cup fresh basil leaves
½ cup piñon nuts,
  chopped

1 cup grated parmesan cheese
½ cup olive oil

Use an electric blender to make this rich sauce. Toss the garlic and basil into the blender, and turn it on for a few seconds. Then add the nuts and parmesan, and blend further. Gradually add the oil to the blender mix, and blend to a smooth paste. Serve on noodles.

The Navahos use piñon lumber in building hogans and as a firewood. The Mescalero Apaches caulked baskets with pine resin to make them watertight.

You can fashion beautiful coiled baskets from pine needles. The needles of the piñons are too short and stiff for use, but the long needles of several East Texas pines and the ponderosa pine, the largest pine in the mountains of West Texas, work well for coiling. Pine needles and resin both produce brown dyes for wool (Bryan 1978). Refer to Chapters 5 and 6 for more information.

I never pass up an opportunity to enjoy an encounter with *Pinus ponderosa*. The furrowed bark of this magnificent tree has a strong aroma of vanilla. To experience this olfactory delight fully, stand in the sunshine, arms outstretched around the regal trunk, and inhale.

Pine resin has various industrial applications, in turpentine, glue, tar, pitch, and rosin. And, of course, pines furnish us with fuel, timber, and pulp for paper.

Several native American tribes used the inner bark of some species of pines for food. The eastern white pine (*Pinus strobus,* not found in Texas) was a favorite (Gibbons 1966; Crowhurst 1972). The turpentine flavor of pines makes boiled bark undesirable by modern standards, though the bark provides a nutritious starchy food. Pine bark is sometimes called an emergency food. Roughly translated, that means a food that tastes so bad, you would probably never want to eat it except in an emergency. The powdered inner bark has a number of medicinal applications and is used today as an ingredient in cough remedies. The tender needles of the white pine produce a pleasant tea and contain vitamin C. Though other species may be suitable for such use, the needles of ponderosa pine and loblolly pine (*Pinus taeda*) both have caused livestock poisoning, so I don't recommend using the bark or the needles of those species (Kingsbury 1964; Keeler, Van Kampen, and James 1978).

Plant Characteristics

Pines are evergreen cone-bearing trees. The leaves consist of one to five needles tied together in bundles known as fascicles. Pine trees are wind-pollinated, and the small male cones produce prodigious amounts of yellow pollen. According to Wodehouse (1971), pine pollen rarely causes hay fever.

The piñons are both small trees with cones less than 2 inches (5 cm) long. In Texas they grow predominantly on mountain slopes in the Trans-Pecos. *Pinus edulis* typically has two short stiff needles per fascicle, and *Pinus cembroides* usually has three. *Pinus cembroides* var. *remota,* with two needles per bundle, occurs on the Edwards Plateau.

PLANTAGINACEAE—PLANTAIN FAMILY

PLANTAIN—*PLANTAGO MAJOR, PLANTAGO LANCEOLATA*
(See illustration.)

Plantago major and *Plantago lanceolata* grow along roadsides, in lawns and fields, and up through cracks in sidewalks throughout the United States. Though a forgotten herb in America today, early European settlers brought plantains with them for use as potherb and medicine (Gibbons 1964; Crowhurst 1972; Silverman 1977; Kirk 1975). Native Americans named the plant white man's foot, as it followed the settlers west. The people of various Southwestern tribes have utilized both the introduced species and numerous native species of *Plantago.* The Tarahumaras of northern Mexico still use plantain as one of their main vegetables (Bennett and Zingg 1935; Simpson 1977).

As a food, the young leaves of plantains can be used fresh or cooked. Add them to salads, or boil them for 15 minutes with just a little water. The nutritious herb provides calcium and other minerals (Holm et al. 1977). One hundred grams furnish as much vitamin A (11,000 international units) as a large carrot (Zennie and Ogzewella 1977). Look for the greens from the late fall to spring. Older leaves may become too fibrous and bitter for use. A few native species are uncommon, so use plantains only when you locate fairly large populations.

The Chinese used the leaves and seeds of plantains for food in the past and still use them medicinally for a variety of ailments (Lust 1974). Psyllium seeds, a laxative, come from *Plantago psyllium* (Mitchell and Rook 1979). The crushed fresh leaves of *Plantago major* provide an astringent juice, used to soothe wounds, sores, insect bites, and the rash of poison ivy.

Plantain—*Plantago lanceolata*

Plant Characteristics

Plantago major and *Plantago lanceolata,* both introduced from Europe, occur in North Central Texas and the Trans-Pecos. Perennial or biennial herbs, they consist of a basal rosette of leaves with a slender flower stalk emerging from the center. The strongly ribbed simple leaves may be smooth or hairy, and the margins may be entire or undulating or have small teeth. *Plantago major* has broadly ovate leaves to 1 foot (3 dm) long, including the wide petiole. The narrow leaves of *Plantago lanceolata* are up to 1½ inches (3.5 dm) wide and about 1¾ feet (5 dm) long. Flower stalks of both species may extend above the leaves and are tipped with a dense spike of minute greenish-white flowers with transparent paper-thin petals.

POACEAE—GRASS FAMILY (FORMERLY GRAMINAE)

The grass family contains the most economically important plants in the world—the cereal grains rice, wheat, and corn. Several other grains, such as rye, millet, and barley, also have worldwide economic importance. More than five hundred species of wild grasses grow in Texas. Many southwestern Indian tribes relied on the seeds of the grasses as a dietary staple. Native Americans gathered the seeds of dozens of species from the wild and partially cultivated several species. Possibly the most important wild grain, used by the Paiutes, Hopis, Navahos, and several other tribes, was Indian ricegrass, *Oryzopsis hymenoides* (Doebley 1984). Like many other wild grasses, Indian ricegrass no longer grows in abundance in Texas. The introduction of grazing livestock reduced the native prairies to almost nothing. Today mesquite and creosote bush cover lands that once were waist-high in grasses.

Grasses have round, typically hollow stems. The leaves, usually linear, sheath the stem. Because grasses are wind-pollinated, they do not need to produce showy flowers to attract insects. Instead, the flowers are reduced to scaly bracts that enclose the male and female parts. The grains form within the papery bracts after pollination.

CARRIZO, GEORGIA CANE—*ARUNDO DONAX*
(See photograph, plate 14.)
GIANT CANE—*ARUNDINARIA GIGANTEA*
REED—*PHRAGMITES COMMUNIS*

You can grind the seeds of these three cane-forming grasses into flour. If you can find the very young shoots before they become too fibrous, you can boil or bake them. The tender young stems of the common reed have been used to produce a candy—dried, ground into flour, moistened, and roasted, the stems yield a sugary mass (Elias and Dykeman 1982; Fernald, Kinsey, and Rollins 1958).

While many grasses furnish good grains, the woody-stemmed canes have a wide variety of nonfood uses as well. The thin hollow stems of *Arundo donax* have provided reeds for woodwind instruments for more than five thousand years. Panpipes, brushes, and paper have been constructed from the canes (Baker 1965). The common reed holds an important spot in the economy of Romania. The Romanians make paper, cardboard, cellophane, and synthetic fibers from the reed. They also use it as thatch, cement reinforcement, insulation, and fertilizer and for fuel alcohol production. Reeds can be made into writing pens and woven into mats and sandals. Reeds also are an important windbreak and a shelter for fish and waterfowl (Holm et al. 1977). Dr. B. C. Wolverton (1982), with NASA's National Space Technology Laboratories, has conducted studies that show the usefulness of reeds in treating wastewater.

Giant cane, carrizo, and common reed, as well as many other species of canes and bamboos, have been used for centuries in various parts of the world to construct buildings, furniture, fishing rods, and baskets. In the United States we rely heavily on our large supply of tree lumber for building construction, but in many parts of the world, lumber is a rare commodity. In South America, Africa, and the Orient, canes and bamboos often form the basis for construction of homes, bridges, and even large buildings, such as apartment houses and factories (McClure 1966). Bamboos and canes supply lightweight, resilient building materials that are rot and insect resistant.

Today the destruction of forests has become a worldwide problem. Since many forest products can be replaced by the fast-growing canes and bamboos, perhaps it is time to consider growing grasses for industry and leaving some of our forests alone.

Plant Characteristics

Probably a native of the Mediterranean, *Arundo donax* now grows throughout the warmer areas of the world. Carrizo was planted for erosion control in the southern United States. It grows commonly along rivers and lakes from Southeast Texas through Central Texas and follows the Rio Grande into the Trans-Pecos. The canes reach 20 feet (6 m) high.

Although *Arundinaria gigantea* once formed large canebrakes in East and Southeast Texas, grazing livestock have all but eliminated the native cane from Texas. The woody canes grow to 25 feet (8 m) tall and occur throughout the southeastern United States.

Phragmites communis can be found throughout the state along rivers and creeks and in marshes, frequently growing alongside carrizo. The common reed is shorter and more slender than the other two canes, reaching a height of about 10 feet (3 m). The reed grows all over the world in the warmer regions.

POLYGONACEAE—KNOTWEED FAMILY

DOCK, CANAIGRE, CAÑAIGRÍA, SORREL—*RUMEX* SPECIES
(See illustration.)

Warning

Docks contain oxalic acid, which imparts the sour flavor, and chrysophanic acid. Both can irritate the skin and mouth of sensitive persons. Because the very sour species are higher in oxalic acid, use them in small portions. Normal servings of the milder greens are probably no more harmful than spinach, a vegetable that also contains oxalic acid. Avoid very bitter plants. Since tannic acid is harmful in quantity, I do not recommend using the roots for food.

Consumption of large amounts of plants high in oxalic acid, or consumption of moderate amounts over several weeks, can cause severe calcium deficiency. In rare circumstances docks have been blamed for livestock poisoning. All such reports that I have encountered occurred outside North America. Rumex acetosa, not found wild in Texas, has been blamed for the death of sheep in England. The sheep became ill after a day of grazing an area covered with little else but that plant. Curly dock, a common weed in Texas, and sheep sorrel (Rumex acetosella), rarely seen in Texas, have both been suspected of livestock poisoning. Large amounts must be consumed to cause problems, however, and I have found no reports of any human poisonings from any species. But if your diet is low in calcium, use dock and spinach only as an occasional part of your diet (for more information on oxalic acid in spinach, see "spinach" in the index) (Holm et al. 1977; Mitchell and Rook 1979; Lampe and Fagerström 1968; Kingsbury 1964; Watt and Breyer-Brandwijk 1962).

The young tender leaves of docks furnish tasty, nutritious greens. The different species vary in flavor, from mildly tart to slightly bitter to pickle-sour. Use the sour species to spice up salads or soups. Substitute the milder docks, such as curly dock (*Rumex crispus*), for spinach in salads or as cooked greens.

Collect the young basal rosettes of leaves from fall to early spring, before the flower stalk emerges. If they are not bitter, use them fresh, or simmer them about 10 minutes. The greens tend to become watery when

Curly dock—*Rumex crispus*

cooked, so add very little water and don't overcook them.

If the leaves taste slightly bitter, boil the greens in a small amount of water about 5 minutes, then discard the water. Add a small amount of fresh boiling water to the pot, and simmer for about 10 minutes. Season and serve the greens. After the flower stalk emerges, young stem leaves may be mild enough for this same treatment. Later in the spring and summer, the leaves become too bitter for use. The greens may act as a slight laxative, so eat them in moderation (Elias and Dykeman 1982).

Euell Gibbons (1964; 1966) found that the leaves of curly dock are high in vitamin C and contain more vitamin A than carrots. The mineral content is also quite good. Combining flavor and nutritional value, curly dock provides one of the most desirable wild foods in Texas and one that deserves consideration for use in the vegetable garden (Medsger 1966; Crockett 1977; Crowhurst 1972; Fernald, Kinsey, and Rollins 1958; Niethammer 1974).

Native Americans also ground dock seeds and used the meal in breads. Removing the papery seed cover and grinding the seeds involves a lot of work, though, to obtain even a small amount of meal.

The roots of *cañaigría, Rumex hymenosepalus,* contain as much as 35 percent tannic acid (Schery 1972). The species thus has potential as a commercial source of tannins for tanning leather. Docks also yield excellent colorful dyes for wool (refer to Chapter 5 for recipes).

Recently researchers with the National Cancer Institute have hydrolyzed agents from the tannins in *Rumex hymenosepalus* that are useful in cancer treatment. Native Americans used the powdered yellow roots of *Rumex crispus* as a tooth cleanser, a laxative, an astringent, and an antiseptic (Lewis and Elvin-Lewis 1977). They applied the juice of the plant and a poultice of the leaves to rashes caused by stinging nettles and poison ivy.

Plant Characteristics

Rumex species are perennial or annual herbs. A basal rosette of leaves appears in the fall, followed in spring by a leafy flower stalk that reaches 3 feet (1 m) tall in several species. Leaves are simple and alternate, their stems sheathing the flower stalk and their margins entire. The shape of the leaves varies among species, from lanceolate to oblong to arrowhead-shaped. Six green, white, or pinkish sepals make up the tiny flowers. Three-angled rusty-brown papery wings enclose the seeds.

Twelve species of *Rumex* occur in Texas. Curly dock, introduced from Eurasia, occurs throughout much of the state. Curly dock has coarse, dark green leaves with undulating, crisped margins. The narrow long-stalked leaves may be 1 foot (3 dm) long. *Rumex hastatulus* and *R. aceto-sella,* both commonly called sheep sorrel, have a pickle-sour flavor similar to that of *Oxalis.* The two species have arrowhead-shaped leaves.

PONTEDERIACEAE—PICKERELWEED FAMILY

PICKERELWEED—*PONTEDERIA CORDATA*

Elias and Dykeman (1982) report that the tender young leaves of the pickerelweed, as they begin to unfurl in the spring, are edible raw in salads or cooked as a vegetable. Boil the leaves for about 10 minutes. The seeds, available in the summer and fall, also can be eaten raw, roasted, or ground into flour. Use the plant only when it is found growing in large colonies in clean, unpolluted water (Crowhurst 1972; Peterson 1977; Fernald, Kinsey, and Rollins 1958; Elias and Dykeman 1982).

Plant Characteristics

Pickerelweed, an aquatic perennial herb, grows in colonies in shallow, slow-moving water, such as marshes and ditches. The flower stalk reaches as high as 3 feet (1 m). A dense spike of blue showy flowers tops the stalk. Six petals unite into a bilateral funnel-shaped flower, and two yellow spots appear on the upper lobe of the blossom. Several long-stalked leaves emerge from the base of the flower stalk, with one leaf attached halfway up the stalk. The large leaf blades are triangular, often with a heart-shaped base. A single seed is found in each inflated angular fruit. Pickerelweed grows from East Texas to the edge of the Edwards Plateau. The plants are found throughout the eastern United States and eastern Canada.

WATER HYACINTH, WAMPEE—*EICHHORNIA CRASSIPES*
(See photograph, plate 14.)

Long considered a costly weed that destroys fishing grounds and clogs waterways, the water hyacinth has received attention lately for its potential as a food supplement and a source of medicines and for a variety of other unusual uses.

Though some sources maintain that water hyacinth leaves can be eaten when cooked, the leaves contain irritating chemicals. I have found that the raw leaf causes my mouth to itch. Fernald, Kinsey, and Rollins (1958) report that cooking does little to improve the palatability. The water hyacinth has excellent potential, however, as a worldwide food source for the future. Let's see why.

The story of the worldwide proliferation of the water hyacinth provides a startling example of what can happen when a plant is introduced into a new environment. Before 1884 the plant, a native of South America, grew predominantly in Brazil. South American exhibitors introduced the beautiful aquatic to gardeners in the United States at the 1884 Cotton States Exposition in New Orleans. Several individuals, admiring the beautiful flowers, carried home a pailful of the herbs. A Floridian planted his in the Saint Johns River. By 1895 the plant not only had disrupted navigation on the Saint Johns but had also spread from the Atlantic Coast to the Pacific and north to Virginia.

Carried to Africa in 1951, the plants soon clogged hundreds of miles of rivers and streams. Today *Eichhornia crassipes* causes severe problems in waterways the world over. Governments have spent millions of dollars in vain attempts to clear navigable waters, such as the Panama Canal, of the pest. Water hyacinth crowding has caused flood damage in the millions of dollars. The plants block out sunlight and deplete fresh water of dissolved oxygen, causing the death of fish and other aquatic life (Monsod 1979).

A number of factors combine to allow the water hyacinth its great success. The stalks of the leaves, spongy and inflated like balloons, float on the surface of the water. Currents and breezes transport the herbs from one spot to another. The plants reproduce vegetatively from their root tips at an alarming rate. In an experimental setting, two parent plants produced 1200 offspring in four months (Holm et al. 1977). The flowers yield large numbers of seeds, which sink to the bottom of the stream and remain viable for a number of years. The plants tolerate limited exposure to salty water and drought. These superb adaptations explain why dredging, burning, and even poisoning are ineffective at eliminating the water hyacinth. Though the living plants may be destroyed, seeds and roots survive to regenerate the colony.

In the past few decades a number of researchers have studied ways to put this otherwise noxious weed to good use. Dr. Godofredo Monsod (1979), in the Philippines, developed a process for converting the protein in water hyacinths into a food supplement for livestock and a flour additive for human use. The additive is high in protein, minerals, and vitamins A, E, and B_{12}. The nutrients can be extracted from the leaves in a saltwater solution. Dr. Monsod also developed processes for producing pulp for paper and antibacterial drugs from the plants.

Researchers with the National Aeronautics and Space Administration, looking for plants that might be useful on long-term space voyages, have experimented with the water hyacinth. Their findings have led to some down-to-earth applications of the weed. Because of the remarkable ability of the water hyacinth to purify polluted water, the weeds are now in use at several sewage treatment plants in Texas. Water hyacinths planted in settling ponds extract suspended solids and toxic metals, such as lead, cadmium, and mercury, from the sewage. NASA scientists also advocate the use of the plants for human and livestock food and for the production of methane gas by fermentation (McDonald and Wolverton 1980; Wolverton and McDonald 1981; B. C. Wolverton, letter to the author, 4 December 1985).

In an age when hundreds of millions of people in Third World countries are malnourished, and much of the world's fresh water is contaminated, the water hyacinth offers the potential for filling a wide variety of human needs. Perhaps in the future the water hyacinth will be looked upon as a blessing and not a curse.

Plant Characteristics

Eichhornia crassipes, a floating aquatic herb, forms large colonies in lakes, rivers, streams, ditches, and marshes worldwide. In Texas it grows predominantly in the eastern third of the state, to the edge of the Edwards Plateau. A short flower stalk, topped with a dense spike of blue to lavender flowers, emerges from the center of the floating leaves. The showy six-petaled flowers unite to form a tube and funnel about 2 inches (5 cm) broad. A large orange spot appears on the upper lobe of the bilateral flower. Shiny rounded leaf blades top bloated spongy leafstalks.

PORTULACACEAE—PURSLANE FAMILY

PURSLANE, VERDOLAGA—*PORTULACA OLERACEA*
(See illustration.)

Warning

Purslane contains about 9 percent oxalic acid (about the same amount as spinach—see "spinach" in the index for details). Oxalic acid binds with calcium, preventing its absorption by the body. Eaten as an occasional vegetable, purslane causes no problems and is nutritious. But if your diet is low in other sources of calcium, you would not want to include purslane as part of your daily diet. Livestock should not be allowed free access to large stands of purslane. In rare cases sheep in Australia have died from oxalic acid poisoning after eating large amounts of purslane in a short period of time or from eating moderate amounts daily for several weeks (Kingsbury 1964).

Purslane grows as a weed in gardens and flowerbeds and up through cracks in the concrete. The succulent annual weed has caused serious crop damage in a number of areas of the world. And yet, purslane has been used as a food for more than two thousand years in India and Persia. Europeans today grow the herb as a garden vegetable. So the next time you are weeding your yard, save the purslane for the table rather than the garbage can.

The succulent stems and leaves taste slightly tart. Chop up the fresh leaves and stems for salads. Use the entire aboveground plant boiled,

Purslane—*Portulaca oleracea*

steamed, fried, or pickled. Purslane provides a tasty addition to a mixture of sautéed vegetables, and the mucilaginous juice of the stems makes a good thickener for soups. The plant tends to hold on to a lot of sand and grit, so wash it thoroughly, as you would spinach. Flowering from spring to fall, purslane reaches its prime in the heat of the summer, a time when most other wild greens have wilted.

Besides having a good flavor, purslane is high in vitamin A, containing 8000 international units per 100 grams (Zennie and Ogzewella 1977). It also provides iron, calcium, and vitamin C. Even the tiny black seeds are nutritious. To collect the seeds, gather the plants in late summer, and set them on a sheet or a piece of plastic to dry in the sun. The seed capsules explode as they ripen. Crumble up the plants, and sift out the seeds. Grind the seeds, and mix them half-and-half with wheat flour when you are ready to use the seed flour (Crowhurst 1972; Peterson 1977; Gibbons 1962; Holm et al. 1977; Kirk 1975; Gibbons and Tucker 1979; Elias and Dykeman 1982).

Plant Characteristics

A low-growing annual, purslane produces numerous prostrate and erect succulent stems, and its fleshy leaves alternate on the stem. The simple leaves, with entire margins, are ¼–1 inch (6–25 mm) in length. The yellow flowers are about 0.2 inch (6 mm) in diameter. Native to the Middle East, purslane now grows throughout the world. It occurs throughout Texas in sandy soil, salt marshes, and waste areas. Native southwestern species of *Portulaca* are all allegedly edible. Moss rose is an ornamental *Portulaca* with pink to purple flowers, but I have had no reports on its edibility.

RUBIACEAE—MADDER FAMILY

BEDSTRAW, CLEAVERS, GOOSEGRASS—*GALIUM APARINE*

The very young leaves and stems of bedstraw, particularly the unfolding leaves at the stem tips, provide a mildly flavored potherb. Place tender leaves and stems in a pot with a small amount of water, simmer them for 10 minutes, and serve them with butter and lemon. The herb can also be mixed with other greens. The prickly hairs make the plant difficult to swallow raw, but boiling or steaming softens the prickles. If the stems seem a bit fibrous, use just the leaves. On older plants the stiff hairs make the plant inedible even cooked. Look for bedstraw from late fall to early spring (Scooter Cheatham, interview, March 1985; Crowhurst 1972; Gibbons and Tucker 1979; Elias and Dykeman 1982).

Gibbons (1966) reports that the roasted fruits furnish a good coffee substitute. The prickly, round fruits ripen in the late spring and summer. Strip them off the stems with a gloved hand. Roast them in the oven until they are dark brown. Then grind the fruits in a coffee grinder, and brew them like coffee.

The dried foliage of bedstraw forms a matted strawlike material. In times past, the dried plants of an aromatic European species provided a stuffing for mattresses. Thought to be a native of Eurasia, bedstraw has become a costly weed infesting rice and grain fields worldwide (Holm et al. 1977). So if you have a mattress that needs stuffing, feel free to pull up the weedy plant by the bucketful. But it is probably best to leave the plant alone on wooded slopes, where it helps prevent soil erosion.

Bedstraw roots may yield a red dye. The plant is related to madder, one of the best plant sources for a red dye. The roots of bedstraw consist of short threads, however, and are hardly worth the trouble to collect enough for a strong dyebath.

A tea and a poultice of the herb have been used to treat a variety of ailments. The tea is said to be a tonic, a strong diuretic, and a mild laxative. A cool tea is also reported to soothe sunburn.

Plant Characteristics

Bedstraw is a familiar plant to children, who like to stick a handful of the herb on each other's clothing. *Galium aparine,* a trailing annual, covers large patches of ground from late fall to summer. The common weed grows in lawns, on gentle slopes in rich woods, in abandoned fields, and along the shore. Stiff, prickly hairs cover the leaves, stems, and fruits. The succulent square stems are lined with whorls of six to eight leaves. Usually the linear to oblanceolate leaves are less than 1 inch (2 cm) long, but they can extend to about 3 inches (7 cm). The tiny flowers are white. *Galium aparine* grows in the eastern two thirds of the state and was probably introduced from Europe.

Nearly a score of *Galium* species occur in Texas. Though species other than *Galium aparine* may also be palatable, most of them occur in restricted areas of East Texas or the mountains of the Trans-Pecos. A few are rare or endemic. To distinguish *Galium aparine* from its less common cousins, first note that it does not occur in the Trans-Pecos. The combination of the trailing manner, the number of leaves per whorl, and the prickly leaves, stems, and fruit separate *Galium aparine* from most other species in its range. The additional characteristics mentioned above should distinguish it from the rest.

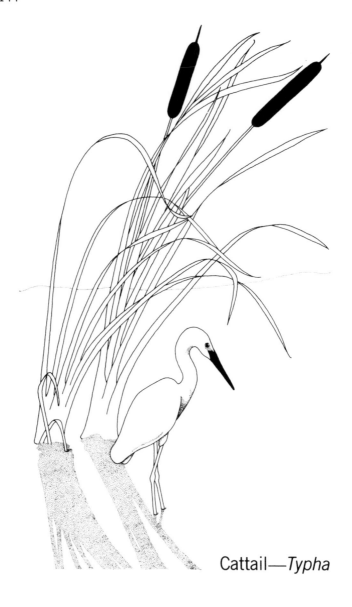

Cattail—*Typha*

TYPHACEAE—CATTAIL FAMILY

CATTAIL—*TYPHA* SPECIES
(See illustration)

*Warning*_____

Cattail roots should not be eaten raw. If the plants are growing in polluted water, don't use cattails for food. Runoff from roads, lead from automobile exhaust, and pesticides are all possible sources of contamination (Erickson and Lindzey 1983).

Euell Gibbons called cattails the supermarket of the swamps. Virtually every part of the plant has a use, from the root to the flowers. People throughout the world have used cattails for food and fiber for thousands of years (Gibbons 1962; Elias and Dykeman 1982; Elliott 1976; Fernald, Kinsey, and Rollins 1958).

You can harvest cattails in any season. From the late fall until new growth emerges in the spring, starch is concentrated in the roots. Researchers at the Cattail Research Center of Syracuse University found the starch to contain as much protein as corn or rice and more carbohydrate than potatoes (Morton 1975). Cattails also furnish calcium (Mason and Bryant 1975).

Plan to get wet and muddy while collecting the roots. Usually you can gather a good quantity of the long, ropy rootstock without damaging next year's crop. Scrub the root, and peel off the spongy layer surrounding the stiff white core. Use sections of core that approach ½ inch (1.5 cm) in diameter. Thinner sections do not have much starch in them. When full of starch, the wet core feels slippery.

Here's Euell Gibbons' technique for washing the starch out of the root. Cut the core into small sections, and place the pieces in a large bowl of cold water. Work the core with your hands, separating all the fibers and scraping out the starch with your fingernails or a knife. Slosh the fiber around in the water until you have removed all the starch. Pour the water through a coarse sieve to extract the fibers. Let the water settle for half an hour. The starch will sink to the bottom of the container. Carefully pour off the water, leaving the starch in the bowl. To obtain a cleaner starch, fill the container with more cold water, stir up the starch, and let it settle again. Pour off the water.

You can use the wet cattail starch immediately in pancakes, breads, and biscuits. Mix it half-and-half with wheat flour, or use the starch alone. If you want to store the starch for later use, you can let it dry. Besides being directly used for food, starch has numerous industrial and household uses, for example, as a sizing and as a medium for fermenting fuel alcohol. The starch also can be converted into various sugars for use in food and beverages. Note that the root should not be eaten raw. Some species may cause vomiting if much is consumed uncooked (Morton 1975).

When you pull up the roots, you'll probably pull up a few newly emerging buds. You can eat these tender white buds, scrubbed and peeled, raw or boiled. The buds have a texture and flavor similar to those of cabbage. The swollen white joint between the bud and the root is starchy. Peel it, then roast or boil it for a potatolike vegetable. Like the roots, this part should not be eaten raw.

From winter to spring, look for the first green shoots, up to 2 feet (6 dm) tall. Wade out into the water, grasp the shoot at about water level, twist, and pull. Peel off the outer green layers of the shoot to reach the tender lighter-colored center section. The shoots can be eaten raw in salads if you gather them before they turn bitter. If they are slightly bitter, try boiling them in one or two changes of water. Known as cossack asparagus, the shoots furnished a popular vegetable for the cossacks of the Don Valley in Russia. Older shoots become too bitter for eating.

In the spring a woody flowering stalk shoots up from the base of the leaves. The flower spikes resemble two corny dogs placed end to end. The top cluster is composed of male flowers, the bottom cluster holds the females. While they are still green, cut off a few clusters. Remove the papery sheath surrounding the flowers. Boil the clusters for a few minutes. Eat them like corn on the cob, coated with butter. Cattail-on-the-cob is a delightful food. The core of the cluster, like that of a corncob, is hard and inedible.

As the flower clusters mature, the male flowers yield large quantities of golden pollen. The Navahos and Apaches value the pollen for religious ceremonies. The golden powder is high in protein. To collect the abundant pollen, bend the stalk over and rub the pollen into a paper bag or bucket. Sift the fine powder, and mix it with flour for use in breads and muffins. It adds an attractive yellow color to rice dishes. Wodehouse (1971) reports that the pollen is not particularly allergenic and only occasionally causes hay fever, but if you are highly allergic to other pollens, don't use any kind of pollen for food.

The female flowers produce a mass of brown seeds after they are fertilized. Though the cylindrical brown clusters may or may not remind you of a cat's tail, somewhere in your childhood memories you can recall brushing the velvety "tails" against your cheek and then scattering the fluff-covered seeds in a summer's breeze. The pulverized seeds make a nutritious, protein-rich flour. Add it to breads, cakes, and pancakes. Separating the seeds from the silky fluff hardly seems worth the trouble, though. Native Americans extracted the seeds from the fluff and parched them at the same time. Remove the cattail fluff from the stem, and lay it out on a flat surface. Then ignite the fluff and let it burn off, leaving the parched seeds ready for eating. Researchers at the United States Department of Agriculture found that the seeds contain a drying oil that has industrial value. The seed meal left after extracting the oil can be used for cattle and chicken feed (Morton 1975).

Cattails provide useful fibers as well as foods. The silky fluff attached to the seeds can be put to a variety of uses. The silk is buoyant and water-repellent and makes a good insulator. During World War II, imported supplies were difficult to obtain, and nations on both sides of the line were forced to rely on homegrown products. The Germans manufactured compressed boards from cattail floss for heat insulation and sound insulation in buildings. The U.S. Navy needed a substitute for the kapok used in life vests. Our kapok supply came from the Dutch East Indies, which was then in the hands of the Japanese. Cattail and milkweed floss were both found to be excellent replacements for kapok (Allan 1980; Hill 1952). After the war we again turned to imported products and eventually to petroleum substitutes for insulating substances.

You can use cattail silk for stuffing pillows, cushions, even mattresses, and as a substitute for down in comforters, vests, and sleeping bags. Collect the brown seed heads while they are still firm. They are easier to gather and work with before the clusters explode. Pull the fiber from the core, and make sure it's dry before you use it. Stuff it loosely into whatever you choose. The floss tends to mat into lumps after a while, but it's free and it works, so who's complaining? The floss can be spun like cotton to produce thread for weaving textiles. If you don't want to bother with removing the tiny brown seeds from the fluff, you can leave them in place. But remember that the seeds can be used for food. It's a good idea to freeze the fluff for a few days before using it—that will kill any insect larvae that may be living in the seeds or floss. Another use of the fine fiber is as a tinder. Cattail down will ignite with a spark, making it a handy fire starter to carry along on camping expeditions. The entire cattail head, immersed in kerosene, makes an effective torch.

The leaves of this marvelous plant have been put to use all over the world for just about any type of woven article you can imagine. Cattail mats more than 10,000 years old have been recovered from an archeological dig in a Nevada cave (Schery 1972). The Mexican Kickapoo Indians use cattails to cover their wigwams and to make floor mats (Latorre and Latorre 1977). Cattails harvested from Lake Cayuga, in Ithaca, New York, go into the manufacture of rush-bottomed chairs. The leaves furnish a good caulk for canoes and log cabins. The leaves and stems have been woven into sandals, baskets, thatching for roofs, and room partitions, and they yield good pulp for papermaking. Perhaps the most fascinating use of the stems is that of the people who live on Lake Titicaca in Bolivia.

The lake dwellers live on floating islands that they weave out of cattails and bulrushes (Morton 1975).

For weaving, collect the leaves and stems at any time of the year, while they are green or after the plants die. In either case, dry them in the shade and then store them until needed. Soak the cattails in water when you are ready to start weaving, and keep them damp as you work to prevent brittleness. If you collect green leaves, the final product will be greener than that of the sun-dried leaves. The stems provide a good coil foundation for baskets (Smith 1983).

Fibers in cattail stems can be used as a substitute for jute, and those of the leaves can be used like linen to produce textiles. Loosen the fibers by soaking the plant material in water for several days.

Besides all these uses, peoples the world over have used cattail roots and leaves for a wide range of medicinal purposes, and the floss was used in a Paris hospital in the 1940s as a dressing for burns (Morton 1975).

Though often considered a noxious weed that blocks drainage canals and moves into rice fields, cattails also serve as valuable wildlife habitat. The roots fix nitrogen in the soil and act as soil stabilizers, preventing erosion. Planted along the Nile River, cattails reduce soil salinity.

With its many uses, the cattail deserves consideration as a cultivated plant. It grows quickly and, according to studies at Syracuse University, yields more usable food per acre than most grain crops. The weedy plants have even been considered as a source of biomass for alcohol fuels (Biesboer 1984; Morton 1975).

A small pond or old stock tank in your back yard could easily be converted into a cattail pond, a ready source of food and a valuable home for wildlife. Your backyard wildlife habitat can provide you with years of melodious spring evenings, filled with the song of the red-winged blackbird defending his nests in the cattails and the call of the bullfrog as he welcomes his mate.

Plant Characteristics

More than a dozen species of cattail (*Typha*) grow throughout the world. The tall grasslike leaves, standing several feet tall, are easy to spot protruding from the water. Three species grow throughout Texas in fresh and brackish water. They may be found scattered in clumps in a roadside ditch in Houston, crowding a freshwater pond in a quiet neighborhood in Austin, blowing in the breeze in a brackish marsh on Padre Island, or standing placidly at the bottom of a waterfall in the midst of the desert in Big Bend National Park.

URTICACEAE—NETTLE FAMILY

PELLITORY, CUCUMBER PLANT—*PARIETARIA* SPECIES
(See illustration.)

Try a nibble of the small leaves and juicy stems of *Parietaria*. Though not related to the cucumber, the flavor of this tiny herb comes close to that of the garden cucumber. The herb provides a refreshing addition to salads (Fleming 1975; Scooter Cheatham, interview, September 1984). Though you can use the plant as a cooked green, pellitory becomes bland when cooked. I much prefer it fresh. Young growth is best. Look for the herb year-round, particularly in late winter and spring. Though related to stinging nettles, the soft hairs that coat the stems of *Parietaria* do not sting, though the hairs on older plants may be disagreeable to some people. Occasional stands of pellitory have little flavor, so sample them before collecting.

Pellitory—*Parietaria pensylvanica* var. *obtusa*

Plant Characteristics

Two species of these small annuals are found in Texas. The low-growing herbs occur in colonies that cover the ground in small patches. They rarely stand more than a few inches high, the slender succulent stems spreading along the ground as they lengthen. The narrow leaves are alternate and simple, with three prominent veins, and the margins are entire. Soft hairs cover the stems and leaves. The tiny green flowers go unnoticed.

I have found pellitory on rocky ledges, on the shoulders of roads, along riverbanks, in lawns, and in gardens in Central Texas. *Parietaria pensylvanica* and *Parietaria pensylvanica* var. *obtusa* grow in the northern two thirds of the state. The leaves vary somewhat in shape from lanceolate to elliptic and are less than 2¾ inches (7 cm) long. *Parietaria floridana* grows predominantly in sandy soil, cedar brakes, and palm groves and occurs from the Coast to the Trans-Pecos. Its leaves are usually ovate and less than 1¼ inch (3 cm) long.

STINGING NETTLE, ORTIGA—*URTICA* SPECIES
(See illustration, page 300.)

Stinging nettles often go unnoticed until you brush up against one with bare legs or arms. Even as your flesh burns with the sting, you may not know what hit you. Search the ground closely for the inconspicuous plant. You'll discover a slender herb with tiny hairs coating stems and leaves. The plant belongs to either the genus *Urtica* or the genus *Tragia* (see *"Tragia"* in the index). The hairs of the true stinging nettles (*Urtica*) act like hypodermic needles on contact, injecting tiny needlelike crystals and irritating chemicals into your flesh (Mitchell and Rook 1979). The irritation and mild rash may take 24 hours to subside fully. (Refer to Chapter 4 if you would like to know more about the various Texas plants that sting and how to treat the itch.)

Despite their bad reputation, stinging nettles are renowned for their good qualities. Members of the genus *Urtica* provide nutritious cooked greens. An analysis of *Urtica dioica* leaves instigated by Euell Gibbons (1966) showed some astounding results. The greens contain more protein than any other leafy vegetable known, 6.9 percent protein for the fresh greens and 42 percent by dry weight. The vegetable also contains generous portions of vitamins A and C and iron. No wonder nettles are a popular food and medicinal herb in the British Isles. The surprising thing is that they have never caught on in the United States.

Warning

Do not confuse members of the genus Urtica *with bull nettle,* Cnidoscolus texanus. *Bull nettle leaves are toxic. Compare the photograph and illustration of these plants (see plate 9 and page 300).*

To collect and prepare nettle greens, wear gloves. Gather the new winter shoots and the leaves before the plant flowers. And don't eat any nettles raw! Clip off the whole plant above the root. If you want only the leaves, grasp the base of the stem with one hand and strip off the leaves by sliding your other hand up the stem. To cook nettles, rinse the leaves and young shoots, and place them in a pot. Add just a little water, and simmer for about 10 to 15 minutes. The heat eliminates the irritant quality of the herbs. Serve them mixed with other greens or with plenty of seasoning, as the flavor is rather bland. You can add the nutritious cooking liquid to soups or drink it as a tea, with lemon and honey (Peterson 1977; Crowhurst 1972; Scooter Cheatham, interview, March 1985; Gibbons and Tucker 1979).

As the plant matures, especially after it flowers, the stems and leaves become covered with tiny hard calcium grains. These make the herb gritty and undesirable for food. The stems on older plants are too fibrous to eat.

The outer layer of the stems of nettles yield excellent fibers. You can loosen the fibers by soaking the stems in water for a few days. In years past, the Scottish wove a cloth said to be as fine as linen from nettle fibers.

The British and Scottish have used nettles as medicinal herbs for centuries. The value of the herb is derived from its high nutritional content. Nettles were once used to treat scurvy and other vitamin-deficiency diseases.

Plant Characteristics

Stinging nettles are annual or perennial herbs covered with stinging hairs. Five species occur in Texas. The plant may consist of a single erect stem, or the stems may branch. Stems and branches are slender and ridged. Varying in shape from ovate to elliptic to lanceolate, the simple leaves occur opposite each other on the stem and are coarsely toothed. Tiny green or white flowers emerge in clusters from the leaf axils. Nettles usually grow in moist soils, along stream banks, and in shady canyons. Nettles are not common in Texas, so collect them only where they occur in large colonies.

Urtica urens, a native of Europe, grows wild in South Texas, and *Urtica chamaedryoides* grows mainly in South and Central Texas. Both are slender annuals, usually less than 2 feet (6 dm) tall, with small leaves. A large-leaved variety of *Urtica chamaedryoides* is extremely rare, found only in Cameron County. *Urtica gracilis,* a slender herb up to 3 feet (1 m) tall, is possibly a variety of the European native *Urtica dioica.* The plant grows from the Panhandle to the Trans-Pecos.

Two Trans-Pecos species (*Urtica serra* and *Urtica gracilenta*) grow only in the mountains. Besides being relatively scarce, these large coarse nettles bear long, fierce stinging hairs, good reasons to leave them alone. These species reach 3–6 feet (1–2 m) in height.

VIOLACEAE—VIOLET FAMILY

VIOLET—*VIOLA* SPECIES

Warning_____

The leaves of violets, particularly some yellow-flowered species, are laxative (Elias and Dykeman 1982). I recommend that you use only the blue-flowered species. The roots of some violets reportedly are emetic, so use only the leaves and flowers (Burlage 1968). The popular greenhouse plants known as African violets are not related to wild violets and are not edible.

Greek mythology (Bulfinch 1959) contributes an explanation for the existence of the well-loved wildflowers the violets. Hera, the queen of the gods, caught her husband, Zeus, flirting with Io, the daughter of the river god. To hide Io's beauty from his wife, the king of the gods turned Io into a heifer. Hera suspected her fickle husband's trick. She demanded that he give her the heifer, which she kept under guard. Zeus created the violet as a fragrant food for Io to eat until he could set her free. The Greek word for violet is *"ion."*

The leaves and flowers of the blue violets furnish tasty, nutritious additions to salads. The blooms appear in the spring. Gather the leaves from late fall to early spring—they turn bitter later. You can use both flowers and leaves raw. The leaves also make a fine cooked vegetable. Boil them in a small amount of water for 10 minutes, or mix them with stronger-tasting greens. Add the leaves to soups as a thickener, or dry them for use as a tea. The flowers can be candied or made into jellies and jams. Euell Gibbons (1966) gives several wonderful violet recipes in his book *Stalking the Healthful Herbs.*

Gibbons had the vitamin content of violets analyzed and found that the leaves and blossoms provide an excellent source of vitamin C. The leaves are also high in vitamin A. A half-cup serving of leaves furnishes as much vitamin C as four oranges and more than the minimum daily requirement of vitamin A!

Collect violets only where they are found in abundance. Clip the leaves off above ground, leaving the roots intact. Most species reproduce vegetatively, so picking the flowers does not inhibit next year's growth. A few do rely on seeds for reproduction, however. To ensure their rejuvenation next spring, never pick more than a small percentage of the flowers you find (Crowhurst 1972; Stahl 1974; Peterson 1977; Gibbons and Tucker 1979).

Plant Characteristics

Nineteen species of herbaceous violets are listed for Texas. All occur in East Texas, with a few extending into Central Texas. Only three species produce erect, leafy stems. Others are stemless perennial herbs only a few inches tall. Solitary flowers emerge from a small basal rosette of leaves. Usually the leaves are heart-shaped and toothed, though several species have leaves that are lobed or entire. Forming a spur in the back, the five blue to purple petals (yellow or white in a few species) open into a bilateral bloom. Most violets grow in moist soils, rich woods, and lawns, along roadsides, and in open fields.

Limoncillo—*Hedeoma
drummondii*

2 Teas and Spices

Many Texas plants make delightful teas and spices. A certain satisfaction comes from collecting your own fresh herbs from the wild. Teas and spices from fresh plants have a fuller flavor than the dried concoctions we pay dearly for at groceries. By using fresh herbs, you also receive the benefits of the vitamins, particularly A and C, that many contain. If carefully dried and stored, the herbs will retain their good flavor for up to a year.

To collect wild teas and spices, pick only fresh, undamaged plant material. Never use wilted or molding leaves or flowers. When possible, clip off small portions from several plants, minimizing damage to plants. Protect local populations by collecting a small number of plants, and collect plants only when they are found growing in abundance. Dry the herbs that you cannot use right away. Either tie the plants in small bundles to hang up for drying, or lay them out in a single layer on a clean surface. If necessary, dry them for about half an hour in the sun to drive off surface dew. Then set them in the shade in a well-ventilated area to complete the drying. If you want to oven-dry them, the temperature should not exceed about 100° F (115° F for roots). Higher temperatures will drive off the volatile oils that provide the aroma and flavor of the herbs. The herbs are dry when they become brittle and break easily.

In addition to the references cited in the text, the following references were used for information on many of the teas and spices described in this chapter: Scooter Cheatham, interviews, September 1984 and March 1985; Correll and Johnston 1970; Crowhurst 1972; Elias and Dykeman 1982; Fernald, Kinsey, and Rollins 1958; Fleming 1975; Gibbons 1962, 1964, 1966; Gibbons and Tucker 1979; Kirk 1975; Medsger 1966; Peterson 1977; Stahl 1974.

Before storing dried herbs, remove unneeded plant parts, such as stems, from leaves and flowers. To preserve the flavor in storage, protect the herbs from oxygen, light, and moisture. Store them in glass jars that can be set in a dark place or in airtight canisters. When you are ready to use your home-prepared herbs, crumble them into tiny bits. A number of tea plants also serve as spices, and a number of spices add an interesting touch to a pot of tea.

Warning_____

Use spice and tea plants only in small quantities. Just as you would not sit down to a bowlful of black pepper, you cannot make a meal of a wild spice. Unless noted otherwise, assume that none of the tea and spice plants listed here are edible plants. Like salt and pepper, some wild spices and teas, such as juniper and epazote, are harmful or highly poisonous if consumed as a food. Some teas are diuretics or laxatives or have other medicinal effects and thus should be used in moderation. Limit consumption of teas to one or two cups a day until you are familiar with the effects the herbs have on your system. If you are allergic to pollen, you may want to avoid teas made with flowers. The volatile oils that provide the flavor of many herbs also can cause dermatitis in sensitive individuals.

Teas

Wild teas vary considerably in flavor. Some bland teas are high in vitamins and can be combined with more-flavorful teas. Some medicinal teas have unpleasant flavors that you may want to hide with honey or lemon. If you prefer the stronger flavor and the caffeine kick of black teas, you may want to add one of the caffeine-free herb teas, such as peppermint, to your more traditional brew. Yaupon tea makes a rich black tea that does contain caffeine. A number of pleasant alternatives exist to your usual drink. Mix 'em and match 'em. Some you'll love, and some just won't be your cup of tea. Any herb tea can be turned into a refreshing summer beverage simply by putting it on ice. Many of these plants also yield good dyes for wool (look them up in the index).

Most members of the mint family, Lamiaceae, have highly aromatic leaves that furnish excellent teas. Many mints used for teas have been put to a variety of medicinal uses by peoples the world over, so use them in moderation. Not all mints are safe for teas. Burlage (1968) reports that the bitter skullcaps (*Scutellaria* species) are toxic.

Members of the mint family are herbs or shrubs with square stems and simple paired leaves. The small bilateral flowers, which form tight clusters in the leaf axils or in spikes along branch tips, are tube-shaped and open out into flaring upper and lower lips. Fruits are clusters of four tiny nutlets.

Some members of Verbenaceae, the verbena family (*Lantana,* for example) are highly toxic but have leaf and stem characteristics similar to those of mints. Verbenas may be distinguished from mints by the flowers. Verbena flowers may be clustered into round or flat-topped heads or may be scattered along a tall spike. Also bilateral, with five united petals, verbena flowers form a short tube that opens out to a cupped or flattened face. The petals are almost equal in size and do not have flaring lips.

In general, 1 teaspoon of dried herbs, or 2 teaspoons fresh, will make a cup of tea. Two basic methods may be used in brewing teas—infusion and decoction. To make an infusion, place the crumbled herb into the tea pot or tea strainer. Pour boiling water over the herb, and let it steep for 5 to 10 minutes. Unless noted otherwise, the teas mentioned in this chapter are infusions. For a decoction, place the herb in water, bring the water to a boil, and simmer for a set time, usually 10 minutes or less. Take the pot away from the heat, and let it steep for a couple of minutes more. For almost all leaves and flowers, an infusion extracts the flavor without driving off the volatile oils. For roots and bark, a decoction may be needed to extract the flavor.

ALFALFA—*MEDICAGO SATIVA*—FABACEAE

The young leaves and flowers make a bland tea that can be combined with more-flavorful teas. High in vitamins and minerals, the perennial is reported to be good for hay fever and is mildly laxative. Use it in moderation. The plant flowers in spring and summer. For other uses of alfalfa, see the index.

BASSWOOD, LINDEN—*TILIA* SPECIES—TILIACEAE

Use the fragrant white to yellowish flowers of the basswood tree for tea. Two tablespoons of flowers make one cup of tea. You can nibble the mucilaginous leaf buds or add a few to salads. These large East and Central Texas trees produce flowers in spring and summer. The flower cluster and the round fruits are attached by a slender stalk to a leaflike bract. Several inches long, the bract is linear to oblong. The alternate, simple leaves are ovate to heart-shaped. The blades are about 4–6 inches (10–15 cm) long and have sharply pointed teeth.

BEE BALM, HORSEMINT, BERGAMOT—*MONARDA* SPECIES—LAMIACEAE
(See photograph, plate 12.)

I find that a tea of the leaves and flowers of some bee balms is too strongly flavored to be enjoyed on a regular basis. These mints have been used for centuries by the Cherokees and other tribes, however, to treat fevers and to help them sleep (Ajilvsgi 1984). The Shakers used a tea of the lavender-flowered *Monarda fistulosa* to soothe sore throats. Thymol, an ingredient in cough syrups, is derived from the oil of the yellow-flowered *Monarda punctata*. An aromatic substance, citronellol, is extracted from the volatile oil of *Monarda citriodora,* an abundant lavender species found throughout Texas. Citronellol is used in perfumes and as an insect repellent.

Monarda species are tall annual or perennial herbs, some up to 3 feet (1 m) high. The flowers are large for a mint, some more than 1 inch (3 cm) long, with narrow lips. The flowers of most species form dense clusters at the leaf axils, surrounding the stem. Most species are hairy. Colors range from white to lavender to purple or yellow, often with darker spots inside flowers. The plants are available in the summer. Various species grow across the state. Collect only those plants growing in abundance.

BEE BRUSH, QUEBRADORA—*ALOYSIA GRATISSIMA*—VERBENACEAE

The Mexican Kickapoo Indians use the leaves and flowers as a tea (Latorre and Latorre 1977). The deciduous shrub with white aromatic flowers grows in the southern half of the state and the Trans-Pecos. The leaves and flowers are available all year except in winter. Bee brush is an excellent honey plant.

BLACKBERRY, DEWBERRY—*RUBUS* SPECIES—ROSACEAE

Blackberry leaves may be used for teas. Do not use wilted or molded foliage, as it develops some toxicity. For information on other uses of *Rubus* species, refer to the index.

CATNIP—*NEPETA CATARIA*—LAMIACEAE

If you can keep catnip away from the cat, you might try it for tea. High in vitamins C and A, this mint has a strong aroma that is enjoyed by humans as well as by felines. Serve a tea of the leaves with lemon. The perennial may reach 3 feet (1 m) in height. The large toothed leaves are gray-green and hairy. The white to lavender flowers are spotted and grow in terminal spikes. A native of Europe, catnip grows wild in disturbed soil in East and Central Texas and is available from spring to late summer.

CLOVER—*TRIFOLIUM* SPECIES—FABACEAE

RED CLOVER—*TRIFOLIUM PRATENSE*
WHITE CLOVER—*TRIFOLIUM REPENS*

These low-growing perennial herbs, often found in lawns in the eastern half of the state, have three oval leaflets per leaf. They bloom in spring and fall. The tiny flowers, with the typical legume shape, occur in dense, oval heads about an inch long. The dried flowers make pleasant teas. Introduced from Europe, the plants now grow wild in many areas of the country. Clover can cause a skin rash in sensitive individuals.

GOLDENROD, SWEET GOLDENROD—*SOLIDAGO ODORA*—ASTERACEAE
(See photograph, plate 4.)

Though some other goldenrods also may be used for teas, sweet goldenrod is the best by far. Leaves and yellow flowers of the fall-blooming wildflower smell and taste like licorice or anise. The tea was highly valued as a substitute for imported tea during the American Revolution (Silverman 1977). A slender perennial herb, sweet goldenrod usually stands less than 3 feet (1 m) tall and grows in sandy soil in East and Southeast Texas and in Bastrop County. Collect plants only when they are growing in abundance. It is identified by its distinctive aroma. Clip a few flowering branches from several plants, leaving the roots and other branches undamaged. Though the flowers can be used in teas, the pollen is allergenic to some individuals. Refer to the index for more information on this delightful wildflower, including a recipe for goldenrod jelly. Goldenrods also produce lovely yellow dyes for wool.

GREENTHREAD, NAVAHO TEA, COTA—*THELESPERMA* SPECIES—ASTERACEAE
(See photograph, plate 5.)

The flowers and leaves of these tall spring and summer wildflowers make a fine tea. Several perennial species grow commonly on the Edwards Plateau, but several annuals are endemic to restricted areas of the state and are somewhat rare. Collect plants only when they are growing in abundance. Cut one of the flowering stalks from the branched herb, leaving the roots and the rest of the flower stalks undamaged. To store the plant, fold the whole stalk accordion-style, tie it together with a piece of the flower stalk, and dry it. One bundle made from a 12- to 18-inch stalk is good for one cup of tea. Different species of greenthread are available from spring to fall. These tall, branching herbs have opposite leaves. The leaves of many species are dissected into linear or threadlike sections.

160

The yellow ray flowers, when present, surround yellow or reddish-brown disk flowers. For information on identifying members of the sunflower family, see the index.

HOREHOUND, MARRUBIO—*MARRUBIUM VULGARE*—LAMIACEAE
(See illustration.)

A medicinal infusion may be made from the strongly flavored leaves of horehound, which has been used for centuries in Europe for a wide variety of ailments. Like bee balm, the bitter horehound is a tea that some individuals won't like. But flavored with honey, the mint makes a soothing remedy for coughs and sore throats. Horehound candy is an old-time cough remedy. You can make your own horehound cough drops. First make a strong decoction of the leaves by simmering them in water for 20 minutes. Strain out the leaves, and add sugar to the liquid (1 cup sugar per cup of tea). Boil the liquid till a teaspoon of the concoction forms a hard ball when dropped into cold water. Pour the candy onto waxed paper, and let it sit till it hardens. Cut into cough drop–size pieces. My husband came to the conclusion that anyone with a sore throat would recover quickly with this treatment, if only to avoid the bitter remedy.

The erect perennial, up to 3 feet (1 m) tall, is covered with a dense cobweb of gray wool. Rounded teeth occur on the wrinkled leaves. Tiny white flowers form dense clusters around the stems at the leaf axils. Horehound is another European herb that now grows wild in abandoned fields and along roadsides across the state and is available practically year-round.

LIMONCILLO—*PECTIS ANGUSTIFOLIA, PECTIS PAPPOSA*—ASTERACEAE
(See photograph, plate 5.)

The leaves and flowers of the low-growing annual herbs provide a pleasant lemony tea. Limoncillo blooms in summer and fall. The young, edible leaves may be added as a flavoring to stews. The volatile oil can be used to scent perfume, and the herb furnishes a yellow dye for wool. The pollen can cause hay fever in sensitive individuals. Found growing on calcium-rich soil from the Edwards Plateau to the Trans-Pecos, these fragrant wildflowers provide one of the best wild teas in West Texas. Collect the herbs only when they are found in large colonies. The bright yellow flower heads are small, about 0.5-inch (1 cm) across, and the leaves are about ½–1½ inches (1–4 cm) long and less than ⅛ inch (1–2 mm) broad. Other aromatic species also may be used in a similar manner. (For information on identifying members of the sunflower family, see the index).

Horehound—*Marrubium vulgare*

LIMONCILLO, MOCK PENNYROYAL—*HEDEOMA* SPECIES—LAMIACEAE
(See illustration, page 154.)

Warning

A species not native to Texas, pennyroyal (Hedeoma pulegioides), was used in the past as part of a compound to induce abortion (Lust 1974). Because the potential effects of our local species are not documented, do not use any members of the genus Hedeoma during pregnancy.

The small sweet-scented hedeomas provide delightful teas that I consider among the best wild teas in the state. Use both the leaves and the flowers of these mints to produce a lemony or minty-flavored infusion. You can also use the plants as insect repellents.

The various perennials and annuals are less than 2 feet (6 dm) tall, and some are such low-growing herbs that they are practically ground covers. The delicate herbs may be coated with soft hairs. Tiny pink, blue, or lavender flowers cluster in the leaf axils. Hedeomas are available from spring to fall. Two Trans-Pecos species are very rare, so collect plants only east of the Pecos and only when they are found in abundance.

MORMON TEA, JOINT FIR, POPOTE, CAÑATILLA—*EPHEDRA ANTISYPHILITICA*—EPHEDRACEAE

The green branches of this unusual shrub can be used for tea. Cut off a few branches from the plant in any season, taking care not to damage the rest of the shrub. Brew a decoction by boiling the twigs for 10 minutes. The tea is a diuretic and an antiseptic. Mormon tea is one of many plants that was erroneously thought to cure syphilis before the days of antibiotics. Found in the western two thirds of the state, the shrub, typically under 3 feet (1 m) tall, consists of many vertical jointed stems with minute scalelike leaves at the joints. The Spanish names mean "broom straw" and "little reeds," quite descriptive of the stems of the shrub. Other *Ephedra* species may also be used for tea.

The powdered twigs of a Chinese species, mahuang, contain a large dose of the alkaloid ephedrine (Lust 1974). Mahuang is a powerful medicinal, to be used only by individuals familiar with the proper dosages. Some drugstore antihistamines contain pseudoephedrine, a synthetic substitute for mahuang. Texas species of *Ephedra* are reported to contain only minute amounts of ephedrine.

MULLEIN—*VERBASCUM THAPSUS*—SCROPHULARIACEAE
(See illustration, page 316.)

Use the first-year leaves of mullein to make a soothing decoction for coughs and sore throats. Boil the leaves in water for 10 minutes, then strain the liquid through cheesecloth to remove the tiny hairs. Add honey and lemon for an even more soothing tea. The leaves and flowers also produce a strong yellow dye for wool. Roman women used the tea as a yellow hair dye.

Mullein is a biennial wildflower. The first year, the plant produces a basal rosette of large velvety leaves. The second year, the plant produces a flowering stalk up to 6 feet (2 m) tall. Roman soldiers dipped these stalks in tallow and used them as torches. The small yellow flowers occur in a dense spike more than 1 foot (3 dm) long. This European native grows wild across the state and is available year-round.

PEPPERMINT—*MENTHA PIPERITA*—LAMIACEAE

One of the best-known mints, peppermint has a familiar aroma that is the best clue to its identity. The leaves are high in vitamins A and C. Use them in teas, as fresh additions to salads and sandwiches, or in mint jelly. Peppermint has been used as a relaxing, healthful herb for centuries. The dark green leaves are toothed, and the upper surfaces smooth. The stems of the perennial may recline or stand 2–2½ feet (6–8 dm) tall and may be tinged with purple. Growing in dense clusters at the tips of the branches, the flowers are white to purple. This native of Europe may be found from spring to fall in wetlands and along streams in Central and West Central Texas. Collect plants only from large colonies.

PERSIMMON—*DIOSPYROS VIRGINIANA*—EBENACEAE

(See photograph, plate 9.)

The dried leaves of the orange-fruiting persimmon can be used as a tea. Collect young leaves in the spring. I find the flavor to be bland, but the leaves are high in vitamin C. For further information on persimmons, refer to the index.

PRAIRIE TEA—*CROTON MONANTHOGYNUS*—EUPHORBIACEAE

(See illustration.)

Warning

Watch for allergic reactions to Croton monanthogynus, *a member of the spurge family.* Croton fruticulosus, *with soft hairs on the leaves, can also be used for tea or spice, but it is difficult to distinguish from other species of* Croton, *some of which are skin irritants and may be toxic (Mitchell and Rook 1979; Kingsbury 1964; Kinghorn 1979). Species other than these two are reported to contain a carcinogenic component (Scooter*

Prairie tea—*Croton monanthogynus*

Cheatham, interview, September 1984). Croton texensis, *a toxic species, is used as an insecticide. For further details on toxic spurges, see the index.*

The leaves of these sweet-smelling herbs produce a mildly flavored golden tea. Dried leaves produce a stronger flavor than fresh. Where it is abundant, pull up the whole plant. Hang bundles of the plants to dry. Then strip the leaves from the stems. Prairie tea can also be used like basil as a spice. One foot (35 cm) tall or shorter, the tap-rooted annual forms a rounded much-branched herb with tiny leaves. The herb is available from spring to fall and grows in abundance on calcium-rich soil in much of the state, especially on the Edwards Plateau.

REDROOT, NEW JERSEY TEA—*CEANOTHUS AMERICANUS*—RHAMNACEAE

The dried leaves of this small shrub were a popular substitute for imported tea during the American Revolution (Schery 1972; Peterson 1977). The shrub is not common, so collect leaves sparingly. Gibbons and Tucker (1979) recommend the following technique for preparing the leaves. Separate out the imperfect leaves and twigs. Boil these in water for a few minutes. Then dip the unspotted, undamaged leaves, a few at a time, in the liquid for about a minute. Remove the scalded leaves from the liquid, roll them up, and place them in a bowl. Cover the bowl with a damp cloth. Stir the leaves every few hours, and redampen the cloth each time. This procedure will darken the leaves. The next day, place the leaves in an oven or dehydrator at about 100° F. When they are dry, pack the leaves in airtight containers. Medicinally, the plant is an antiseptic astringent. Typically less than 3 feet (1 m) tall, redroot grows in sandy soil in East and Central Texas. The alternate, simple, oval leaves are 2–4 inches (5–10 cm) long and half as wide. They are finely toothed. The tiny white flowers grow in ovoid clusters. *Ceanothus herbaceus,* of Central Texas, the Edwards Plateau, and the Panhandle, may also be used for tea, but it too is uncommon.

ROSE—*ROSA* SPECIES—ROSACEAE

The red fruit of the rose, known as the hip, is high in vitamin C. Make an infusion by pouring boiling water over the fresh or dried hips. You can eat fresh rose petals as an addition to salads and as a flavoring in teas. Though Texas has several species of wild roses, they are not common. Use the larger hips of the cultivated roses, and leave the small natives alone.

166

SAGE—*SALVIA* SPECIES—LAMIACEAE
(See photograph, plate 11.)

Use the leaves of any fragrant wild sage as a tea or a spice for soups and meats, as you would the culinary sage. The leaves of this mint contain moderate levels of vitamins A and C and can be added fresh to salads and sandwiches. Use them sparingly, though. Various species occur as annuals, perennials, and shrubs. Sage flowers vary in color from white to scarlet to bright blue, and many are showy wildflowers. The tubular flowers may be 1½ inches (4 cm) long, and each flower has two stamens. The plants are available year-round. Collect them only when they are found in abundance.

SASSAFRAS—*SASSAFRAS ALBIDUM*—LAURACEAE
(See photograph, plate 12.)

*Warning*_____

Safrole, a concentrated extract of sassafras oil, is reported to be carcinogenic (Elliott 1976).

Use the bark of sassafras root as a tea and the leaves as a spice. The root has an aroma similar to that of root beer. Brew a decoction by boiling the chopped root about 30 minutes or until the liquid turns reddish in color. The root can be reused several times. Sassafras trees grow in East Texas and can be recognized by their leaves. Three variations of the oval leaves appear on a single tree: with no lobes, with a lobe on one side (mitten-shaped), or with two or more lobes. The large smooth leaves have a lemony aroma, and the twigs are greenish. Where the trees are abundant, pull up a few small seedlings to collect the root.

Sassafras tea has been one of America's favorites for more than four hundred years. The Indians in Florida introduced the Spanish to the aromatic tree in the 1500s. Sassafras was the first cash crop of the Virginia colony and rivaled tobacco as a major export to Europe for many years. It became popular in Europe because it was said to be a cure-all. When some people started using the tea to treat the sores of syphilis, however, it suddenly became quite an unfashionable beverage.

In modern times sassafras has been used as a flavoring for medicines, tobacco, root beer, soaps, perfumes, toothpaste, and gum. The aromatic wood has also been used as a moth repellent. The lemony-flavored leaves are dried and powdered to make filé, which is used with creole gumbo.

SPEARMINT, YERBA BUENA—*MENTHA SPICATA*—LAMIACEAE

The familiar aroma is a clue to the identity of this popular mint. A tea of the leaves is soothing to the stomach and relaxing, and it acts as a diuretic. A tea of the flowers is reported to be stimulating. High in vitamins A and C, the leaves may be eaten fresh in salads and sandwiches or used in mint jelly. Oil of spearmint is a flavoring for candy and chewing gum and is also an insect repellent. Spearmint is a native of Europe that occurs in wetlands in Central and West Texas. The branched stems of the perennial may be more than 3 feet (1 m) tall and often are tinged with purple. The smooth leaves are toothed. The white to lavender flowers grow in small interrupted whorls on the upper portion of the stems. Spearmint is available from spring to fall. Collect this mint only from large colonies.

STRAWBERRY—*FRAGARIA* SPECIES—ROSACEAE

Use strawberry leaves for a tea high in vitamin C. For further information on wild strawberries, see the index.

YARROW—*ACHILLEA MILLEFOLIUM*—ASTERACEAE

(See illustration, page 5.)

Though yarrow is used the world over as a medicinal tea, I discourage its use as a beverage. Yarrow contains more than 120 chemical compounds, some known to be quite toxic. Yarrow is suspected of causing the death of a calf who ate a single plant. The aromatic leaves also can cause skin irritation (Chandler, Hooper, and Harvey 1982). See the index for further information on yarrow.

YAUPON, CASSINA—*ILEX VOMITORIA*—AQUIFOLIACEAE

(See illustration.)

Warning_____

The berries of yaupon and the other hollies are highly toxic. See "holly" in the index for details.

The leaves of the evergreen yaupon yield a dark tea. Yaupon, a relative of the South American maté (*Ilex paraguayensis*) is the only wild tea in Texas that contains caffeine. Gather a mixture of young and older leaves

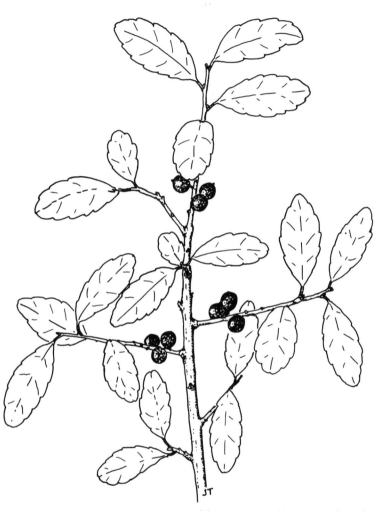

Yaupon—*Ilex vomitoria*

in any season. To make a good drink, the leaves must be roasted in an oven at 200° F until they turn brown (Gibbons 1964). They can then be used to brew tea or stored for later use. The name *"vomitoria"* refers to the belief that some Indian tribes used yaupon tea as an emetic. Gibbons (1964) states that yaupon was not the plant used in the purging "black drink." Ellis (1978) confirms that the leaves contain no toxic substances, though the berries are poisonous. Yaupon is an evergreen shrub of Southeast and Central Texas. The small, simple leaves alternate on the stems. The margins of the oval leaves are lined with rounded teeth. To distinguish yaupon from the possum haw holly (*Ilex decidua*), note that possum haw is a deciduous shrub—it loses its leaves in winter. Also, if you bend a fresh leaf of yaupon, it will crack before the leaf is bent in half. The leaves of possum haw are more flexible. Possum haw leaves are not desirable for tea.

The leaves of American holly, *Ilex opaca,* may be used for tea but do not contain caffeine. This tree is an East Texas evergreen with spiny leaves. Six other East Texas species of *Ilex* are very rare.

Spices

Use wild spices in small quantities, as you would any kitchen spices. If you are adding spices to soups, stews, or other vegetable dishes, the flavor may be enhanced by sautéing the spices in oil before adding the vegetables.

The seeds and young leaves of many members of the mustard family, *Brassicaceae,* have been used as peppery seasonings. The young leaves of plants that are mild in flavor and tender in texture may be used fresh in salads or as cooked greens. Care should be taken when using the spicy-hot mustards. The oil, which is usually concentrated in the seeds, is a strong skin irritant that can burn and blister the skin (Schmutz and Hamilton 1979).

Several mustards are described in detail below, but seeds of the following mustards also may be used as a peppery seasoning: pennycress (*Thlaspi arvense*), bladderpod (*Lesquerella* species), whitlow grass (*Draba* species), tansy mustard (*Descurainia* species), and *Sisymbrium* species. The root of spring cress (*Cardamine bulbosa*) is reported to have the flavor of horseradish and is used grated and mixed with vinegar.

Members of the mustard family may be recognized by the combination of the following characteristics. All are herbaceous plants. The four petals of the flowers form the shape of a cross, giving rise to the old family name, "Cruciferae." The flowers are white, yellow, or lavender. In most species the stamens are distinctive: four are long and two are short. The fruit is a dry silique, a many-seeded capsule occurring in a wide variety of shapes. The earliest leaves may form a basal rosette on which the leaves often are pinnately lobed. On the flowering stalk the leaves are usually alternate and may be entire or toothed, pinnately lobed, or pinnately compound.

CHILE PEQUÍN, BIRD PEPPER, CHILTIPIQUÍN—*CAPSICUM ANNUUM*—SOLANACEAE
(See illustration, page 217.)

Warning

*The leaves contain toxic alkaloids and cannot be used as a spice. Don't confuse this plant with the Jerusalem-cherry (*Solanum pseudocapsicum*), which has toxic fruits. See the index for descriptions and more information on both plants.*

The small green to orange-red berries of chile pequín furnish a very hot pepper, high in vitamins. Chile peppers, cayenne, and bell peppers are cultivars of this wild plant. Since they are hotter than the domestic varieties, you should wear gloves when collecting the wild fruits to protect your hands and eyes from the irritants in both the fruits and the leaves. Add a few boiled berries to a shaker full of vinegar for a spicy pepper sauce to use on your wild greens. Chile pequín is available year-round on the Edwards Plateau and in South and Southeast Texas.

EPAZOTE, WORMSEED—*CHENOPODIUM AMBROSIOIDES*—CHENOPODIACEAE

The aromatic leaves of *epazote* are used in Mexico as a seasoning for beans. **The oil of the seeds is used to expel worms, but overdoses have caused death in infants. The oil contains a toxic alkaloid. Use only the leaves and use them in small quantities.** Wormseed resembles lamb's-quarters (*Chenopodium album*, illustrated on page 63), but some wormseed populations have leaves with strongly lobed margins. The leaves have an aroma similar to that of turpentine or menthol. This native of tropical America grows as a weed in Texas in disturbed soils and along coastal shores and salt marshes. Leaves are available practically year-round.

JUNIPER, CEDAR, SABINO, TLÁXCAL—*JUNIPERUS* SPECIES— CUPRESSACEAE
(See photograph, plate 8.)

Warning_____

The astringent fruits are not edible. Use only as a spice in small quantities. Two or more fruits may cause poisoning if eaten by a child (Michael Ellis, interview, January 1986; Schmutz and Hamilton 1979).

The astringent ripe blue or reddish-brown fruits of juniper trees may be used as seasonings for meats, stews, and sauerkraut. The fruits are available year-round but are most abundant in the fall. I've eaten a tasty baked chicken that was basted with a mixture of two juniper fruits sautéed with onions. One or two of the woody fruits is enough for each dish, as the volatile oil is strong in flavor and toxic in quantity.

Junipers have been put to a variety of uses throughout the ages (Fleming 1975; Crowhurst 1972; Peterson 1977; Bryan 1978; Hill 1952). The strongly scented foliage is used in Christmas ornamentation. The volatile oil of the fruits has been used as a flavoring for gin, perfume, soaps, and cosmetics. The bark, roots, twigs, and cones furnish dyes for wool. Junipers provide wood for fence posts, building construction, furniture, and pencils. Juniper fence posts are durable and resistant to rot and insect infestation. American Indians rubbed juniper oil on their skin as an insect repellent, and cedar shavings and cedar chests are used by modern peoples as moth repellents. Junipers provide an important source of food and shelter for wildlife. Urban sprawl has eliminated most of the nesting habitat of the golden-cheeked warbler, an endangered Texas bird that relies on thick stands of mountain cedar, *Juniperus ashei,* for its summer home. For humans, however, mountain cedar is despised because of the severe winter hay fever caused by its pollen. Refer to the index for further information and descriptions of junipers.

KNOTWEED, SMARTWEED, PINKWEED—*POLYGONUM AVICULARE*— POLYGONACEAE

Warning_____

The leaves and seeds of some species are so pungent that they can raise blisters on the skin (Mitchell and Rook 1979; Kingsbury 1964). Use peppery species only as a spice as they could cause intestinal irritation if eaten as a salad or cooked vegetable.

The leaves and seeds of several species of *Polygonum* are a peppery spice. Use the pungent plant sparingly in soups and stews, just as a seasoning. Those plants that are mildly flavored may be eaten raw or used as a cooked vegetable. Collect the young leaves and stems in winter and spring before the plant flowers. The leaves also yield a good dye for wool.

Polygonum aviculare resembles a trailing grass. The annual or weakly perennial herb usually is vinelike, though it may also grow erect. Linear or oblong leaves, with blades about ⅔ inch (15 mm) long, sheath the stem. They are simple, alternate, and entire. The tiny pink or white flower buds never open. Knotweed is probably a native of Europe and grows throughout Texas.

MINTWEED, REDBRUSH LIPPIA, HIERBA DULCE, ORÉGANO CIMARRÓN— *LIPPIA GRAVEOLENS*—VERBENACEAE

The leaves of this small deciduous shrub are reported to be used as a spice similar to oregano. The slender shrub grows throughout much of South Texas, the coastal area, and the Trans-Pecos in dry, rocky soil. Mexican Kickapoos use this species and *Lippia alba,* in South Texas, as a spice and a tea (Latorre and Latorre 1977). Mintweed leaves are available in all seasons except winter.

MUSTARD—*BRASSICA* SPECIES—BRASSICACEAE

Warning_____

Mustard oil is a dangerously caustic irritant. Mustard plaster, made from the powdered seeds, is a long-used remedy for aches and pains, but it can discolor and blister skin if left on too long and is reported to have caused the death of a small child (Mitchell and Rook 1979).

All of the brassicas growing wild in Texas were introduced from Eurasia as garden greens. The early basal leaves that appear in winter and spring may be used in salads or as cooked greens. The very young greens are not bitter at all, but older leaves become too bitter for use. For use as a potherb, simmer the coarse leaves in water about 30 minutes. The leaves may be mixed with milder greens or boiled twice to reduce the slightly bitter flavor that some greens have, but a true East Texas native is recognized by her/his eager consumption of the bitter greens laced with hot pepper sauce. Mustard greens are rich in vitamins A, B_1, B_2, and C and the minerals calcium and potassium (Gibbons 1962). A number of other garden vegetables, such as turnips, rutabaga, rape, and charlock, come from this genus. Broccoli, cauliflower, cabbage, and brussels sprouts are all cultivars of *Brassica oleracea.*

The seeds of the brassicas may be used to make mustard. Culinary mustard comes from the seeds of black mustard, *Brassica nigra*. To make your own mustard, collect the seeding stalks of any spicy species and dry them in the sun for a few days. Beat the stalks to release the seeds. Brown some wheat flour by toasting it in the oven or on a griddle. Then grind the mustard seeds, and mix them with equal amounts of toasted flour. Moisten the concoction with a mixture of half water and half vinegar.

Texas' wild mustards are annuals or biennials and are available from winter to summer. The flowering stalks may reach 3 feet (1 m) in height. The basal leaves are pinnately lobed. The flowers are yellow, and the siliques linear and sometimes cylindrical. The round seeds of most plants are reddish to black.

ONION, GARLIC—*ALLIUM* SPECIES—LILIACEAE
(See illustration, page 117.)

Wild onions and garlic are relatives of the culinary herbs. Wild onions are stronger in flavor than the domestic varieties. For information on distinguishing wild onions from similar-looking toxic plants, refer to "Onion" in the index.

PEPPERGRASS, LENTEJILLA—*LEPIDIUM* SPECIES—BRASSICACEAE
(See illustration.)

Use the seeds of peppergrass as a peppery spice. Add the young basal leaves that appear in winter and spring to salads, or use them as cooked greens. High in vitamin C and a good source of iron, the leaves can be mixed with milder-flavored greens. For the Tarahumara and a number of other indigenous tribes in Central and South America, *lentejilla* is a valued food (Bennett and Zingg 1935). Euell Gibbons (1962) reports that *Lepidium virginicum* is a farm crop in New Jersey.

Peppergrasses, members of the mustard family, are annuals, biennials, or perennials and are available from fall to early summer. The herbs are often much-branched, forming a rounded mass of seeding stalks around 1–2 feet (2–7 dm) tall. The Spanish name, meaning "little lentil," refers to the more or less circular, partly flattened siliques. The edges of the silique are winged, the wings forming a shallow V-shaped notch at the top of the pod. The siliques are ⅛–¼ inch (3–5 mm) wide.

RED BAY—*PERSEA BORBONIA*—LAURACEAE
(See photograph, plate 12.)

The leaves of red bay have an aroma similar to that of culinary bay leaves. Use them in spaghetti sauce, soups, and stews. Red bay is an

Shepherd's purse—*Capsella bursa-pastoris*

Peppergrass—*Lepidium virginicum*

evergreen tree or large shrub growing in rich woods and swamps in Southeast Texas, along the Gulf Coast. The shiny, leathery leaves, available year-round, are simple, entire, and elliptical. Alternating on the branches, they are about 4−8 inches (1−2 dm) long. The branches may be covered with reddish hairs.

SHEPHERD'S PURSE, PANIQUESILLO—*CAPSELLA BURSA-PASTORIS*—BRASSICACEAE
(See illustration.)

The green pods of *paniquesillo* are a peppery spice. Add the pods and the young leaves and stems to soups and stews. The herb is high in vitamins A and C (Zennie and Ogzewella 1977). The species name of this low-growing member of the mustard family literally means "shepherd's purse." The triangular flattened silique, only ¼−⅓ inch (6−8 mm) wide, resembles a tiny purse. Usually less than 1 foot (3 dm) tall, shepherd's purse must be viewed from only a few inches away to admire the tiny white flowers and pods. The introduced annual grows as a weed in lawns, along roads, and in fields worldwide. Shepherd's purse blooms in winter, and young plants are available from fall to early spring.

SPICEBUSH—*LINDERA BENZOIN*—LAURACEAE

The dried and ground leaves, twigs, bark, and berries of the spicebush have been used in the past as a spice and a tea. It is reported that the dried berries were used during the American Revolution as a substitute for allspice. Spicebush has become very rare and endangered in Texas, however, and efforts should be made to preserve and propagate this beautiful shrub. Many of the moist, rich wooded areas on the Edwards Plateau and in East Texas where spicebush once thrived have been eliminated by urban sprawl and clear-cutting for timber. The attractive shrub is well worth cultivating as an ornamental.

SWEET BAY—*MAGNOLIA VIRGINIANA*—MAGNOLIACEAE

The leaves of this semievergreen tree have an aroma similar to that of bay leaves and are reported to be used in the same manner to spice meats and sauces (Vines 1960; Medsger 1966). The leaves are available practically year-round. The flowers provide a fragrance for perfumes. The East Texas tree has leathery leaves with whitish hairs on the bottom side. Sweet bay is closely related to the evergreen giant magnolia commonly grown as an ornamental.

WATERCRESS—*RORIPPA NASTURTIUM-AQUATICUM*—BRASSICACEAE

Watercress, a popular salad green, was brought from Europe by early immigrants. It now grows in streams, shallow pools, marshes, and springs throughout the United States. The raw greens and flowers of this member of the mustard family add a peppery flavor to salads and sandwiches. The greens also make a fine potherb, cooked briefly like spinach or added to soups. The herb is high in vitamins A, C, and E and is a fair source of minerals (Fleming 1975).

Though it is not so unusual to find the aquatic vegetable in Texas streams, finding it in uncontaminated water is practically impossible. For this reason, harvesting wild stands may already be a thing of the past. Some people suggest soaking the greens in water with Halazone or Chlorazene tablets for 30 minutes, then rinsing them in clean water before eating them, but this is not a proven method for eliminating all contaminants. You might try growing your own in a small pond.

Watercress is readily identified by its leaf shape and the presence of small white cruciform flowers. It often appears as a floating or creeping mat of foliage at the quiet edge of a stream. The shiny leaves are pinnately compound, with the oval terminal leaflet larger than the others, and the cylindrical siliques are about ¾ inch (2 cm) long. The greens are available year-round. Watercress is a perennial, so try to clip off the greens without disturbing the roots.

WAX MYRTLE, BAYBERRY—*MYRICA CERIFERA*—MYRICACEAE

Use the evergreen leaves of bayberry as a substitute for bay leaves in seasoning meats, sauces, soups, and stews and as a tea. The leaves are available year-round. The tiny hard black fruits, covered with white wax, were used in the past for making bayberry candles, providing both the fragrance and the wax (Hill 1952). To extract the wax, boil the fruits in water, strain out the seeds and the trash, and let the wax float to the surface of the water to harden. The leaves can be used as an insect repellent. Both the leaves and the fruits provide dyes for wool. The shrub or small tree grows in moist forests in the eastern third of the state. Its alternate simple leaves, typically less than 3 inches (7 cm) long, are narrow and oblanceolate. The margins may be entire or bear fine teeth near the tips.

WORMWOOD, WESTERN MUGWORT, ESTAFIATA—*ARTEMISIA LUDOVICIANA*—ASTERACEAE

Growing throughout the state, wormwood is a perennial herb covered with grayish hairs. The aroma resembles that of sage, and the leaves may be used like sage to season meats and stews. A variety of medicinal effects are attributed to wormwood, including the expulsion of roundworms and abortion, so use the herb in moderation (Fleming 1975). Several Old World species are cultivated and used as kitchen herbs and medicinals. Wormwood is available from spring to fall.

Texas persimmon—
Diospyros texana

3 Edible and Poisonous Berries and Other Fleshy Fruits

A number of trees, shrubs, and herbs found in Texas produce delicious succulent fruits. A number of others yield highly poisonous fruits, especially some of the common ornamental shrubs. Most poisonings from wild and ornamental fruit happen to children under five years old. Children attracted to the bright colors may pop the fruits into their mouths before parents can stop them.

But how can you tell an edible fruit from a poisonous one? Can you rely on the color, following the adage that certain colors of berries are safe and others are not? No, you cannot. As the information in this chapter demonstrates, both edible and poisonous fruits come in a variety of colors. For example, you can eat dewberries and blueberries, but the purple berries of the pokeweed have caused deaths in children. What about red berries? Strawberries are red, but so are the poisonous berries of yaupon. Colors cannot help us distinguish the good guys from the bad guys. How about the berries that birds eat? Are those safe for humans? Not necessarily. Many fruits that birds and other animals relish can poison us. The only reliable method for distinguishing an edible from a toxic berry is to make a positive identification of the plant and then refer to a reliable source for information on its safety. The lists of toxic and edible berries in this chapter provide invaluable information for parents and Scout leaders.

If you have small children, you can begin teaching them today which fruits in their surroundings can cause poisoning. If someone ingests any of the toxic fruits listed here or any plants with unknown toxicity, contact a doctor or Poison Control Center immediately. Refer to page 231 for first aid instructions.

This chapter includes native plants with fleshy fruit and a few ornamental plants that grow wild in abundance in Texas. For other plants found in your house and yard, refer to the section on toxic ornamentals in Chapter 4.

To provide a quick reference for identifying fruits, the plants in this chapter are grouped according to the color of the ripe fruit (most unripe fruit is green so you will need to know the color of ripe fruit to use this key). The toxic fruits are presented first. The edible fruits, with recipes for their use, begin on page 195.

This chapter includes only fleshy fruits for two reasons: (1) these are the fruits that attract children most frequently and have caused a number of severe poisonings, and (2) since you can use many edible fleshy fruits for making jellies and pies, it is convenient to have them all together in one chapter. For plants with nonfleshy fruits, refer to the index. For example, edible beans (members of the legume family), such as mesquite, are listed together in the chapter on edible plants. Toxic beans, such as the red beans of the Texas mountain laurel, are grouped together in Chapter 4.

If you come across a fruit not mentioned in this book, do not assume that it is safe to eat. The potential toxicity of a number of plants is unknown.

A few definitions will help you in identifying some of the common types of fleshy fruit. Refer to the glossary for definitions of other botanical terms.

Aggregate fruit—A dense cluster of berries, like a blackberry.

Berry—A fleshy fruit without a hard stone. A tomato is a berry. The small seeds of edible berries usually can be swallowed.

Bloom—A white waxy coating found on the surface of some fruits.

Drupe—A fleshy fruit with a single hard stone, like a cherry. The stone may contain one or several seeds. The stones of edible drupes should not be swallowed.

Poisonous Fruit

Blue, Purple, or Black Fruit: Toxic

CHERRY—*PRUNUS* SPECIES—ROSACEAE

The seeds, leaves, and bark of the cherries can cause severe poisoning and death. The astringent fruits of wild cherries generally require cooking to make them palatable. See the index for further information on wild cherries.

COYOTILLO—*KARWINSKIA HUMBOLDTIANA*—RHAMNACEAE

(See illustration.)

The shiny reddish-brown to black drupe, ⅜ inch (1 cm) long, looks tempting but is highly poisonous. The fruit ripens in the fall. Coyotillo fruit, seeds, and leaves are all toxic to humans and livestock (Ellis 1978; Kingsbury 1964; Hardin and Arena 1974). Symptoms may not occur for several days or weeks, but medical treatment should begin immediately to minimize nerve damage. The poison can cause paralysis. With treatment, recovery may be complete but may involve lengthy hospitalization. A small child nearly died in Mexico recently from eating the succulent fruit (Michael Ellis, interview, January 1986).

Coyotillo is an attractive rounded shrub with smooth simple leaves. About 2 inches (5 cm) long, the oblong leaves occur in pairs, and the margins are entire. The delicate secondary veins of the leaves lie parallel to each other and are slightly raised. Coyotillo grows on the arid plains of South Texas to the southern part of the Edwards Plateau and the southeast edge of the Trans-Pecos.

EVE'S NECKLACE—*SOPHORA AFFINIS*—FABACEAE

The black leathery bean pod of this lovely Texas tree is thought to be poisonous (Turner 1959). The pod, ripening in the fall, resembles a string of black pop beads several inches long. No data are available on the degree or type of toxicity. It is closely related to the highly toxic mescal bean (see the index for a description and information on mescal bean).

The legume Eve's necklace is a shrub or small tree with pinnately compound leaves. Its elliptic leaflets have entire margins. The spring inflorescence is a drooping cluster of papilionaceous white to rose-colored blossoms. The tree grows from the Edwards Plateau to North Central Texas.

Coyotillo—*Karwinskia humboldtiana*

JUNIPER, CEDAR, SABINO, TLÁXCAL—*JUNIPERUS* SPECIES— CUPRESSACEAE
(See photograph, plate 8.)

The small blue or reddish-brown fruits of junipers resemble berries. Junipers are evergreen conifers, however, and their fruits are miniature woody cones. Eight species occur in Texas. The round or knobby cones range from ¼–½ inch (5–12 mm) in diameter and frequently are coated with a bloom. Junipers contain an astringent resin that makes the fruit unpalatable and can cause gastrointestinal distress if eaten in quantity. The disagreeable flavor will probably prevent just about anyone from eating enough to cause serious harm, but Michael Ellis of the Texas State Poison Center considers ingestion of two or more berries potentially toxic (interview, January 1986). A decoction made with *J. sabina,* not found in Texas, has been used as an herbal abortifacient with disastrous consequences. A single strong dose of the drink can be strongly cathartic, and repeated smaller doses have proven deadly (Lampe and Fagerström 1968; Schmutz and Hamilton 1979).

The southwestern Indians used the less resinous fruits of a few western species for food, a practice that I do not advocate for any Texas junipers (Elias and Dykeman 1982). You can use the fruits of our native species in very small quantities as a spice for flavoring meats, sauerkraut, beans, and vegetables. The aromatic oil of a European juniper is used to flavor gin (Hill 1952). For further information on other uses of junipers, refer to the index.

Junipers are evergreen shrubs or trees. The tiny needles cover the branchlets and are shaped like either sharp-pointed awls or tiny scales. Some species produce male and female flowers on separate trees, but only female trees develop the berrylike cones.

LANTANA, ALFOMBRILLA HEDIONA—*LANTANA CAMARA,* *LANTANA HORRIDA*—VERBENACEAE
(See illustration, page 184.)

The shiny blue-black fleshy fruits of the lantanas, about ¼ inch (6 mm) in diameter, occur in small tight clusters. Though some previous publications assert that the ripe fruit is edible, experimental studies show that both ripe and unripe fruit are potentially lethal. The green unripe fruits have caused the death of several children. Symptoms may not appear for several hours, but treatment should begin as soon as possible after ingestion of the plant. Prompt medical treatment that includes gastric lavage has been shown to be an important factor in preventing death (Lampe and Fagerström 1968; Kinghorn 1979; Kingsbury 1964; Ellis 1978;

Lantana—*Lantana
horrida*

Hardin and Arena 1974). Sheep and calves have died from eating the leaves and the fruit. The rough, hairy foliage also causes a skin rash in sensitive individuals (Mitchell and Rook 1979; Holm et al. 1977).

Lantana camara, an introduced ornamental shrub, grows wild in Central and South Texas. *Lantana horrida,* a native also used as an ornamental, grows nearly throughout the state. These shrubs have simple, opposite, strong-smelling leaves and may be mistaken for a member of the mint family. The rough-textured, wrinkled leaves are broadly ovate and toothed. The ridged branches may be armed with prickly hairs. The colorful tiny tubular flowers are arranged in hemispherical heads, about 1 inch (2–3 cm) in diameter. Flowers of two or more different colors—cream, yellow, orange, pink, or red—appear in each head. Other native *Lantana* species also may be toxic.

LIGUSTRUM, PRIVET—*LIGUSTRUM* SPECIES—OLEACEAE
(See photograph, plate 13.)

The blue-black oval drupes, about ¼ inch (4 mm) in diameter, occur in clusters. Ripening in the fall, the fruit may cling to the shrub through the winter. The fruit and possibly the leaves of the ornamental shrubs can cause poisoning. Children have died from eating the fruits of *L. vulgare* in Europe, a species grown as an ornamental in the eastern United States. So far, poisoning in the United States has been rare, but all species should be considered potentially toxic. Violent gastrointestinal upset may come on rapidly (Lampe and Fagerström 1968; Hardin and Arena 1974; Ellis 1978).

Several ornamental *Ligustrum* species are planted in Texas. *Ligustrum japonicum* has become a persistent weedy shrub in the eastern half of the state. The evergreen shrub or small tree has simple, opposite, oval leaves that are 2–4 inches (5–10 cm) long. The top surface of the thick textured leaves is waxy and smooth, the margins entire. Attractive fragrant clusters of tiny white flowers appear in the spring and summer.

NIGHTSHADE, BLACK NIGHTSHADE, HIERBA MORA NEGRA—*SOLANUM AMERICANUM* (FORMERLY *SOLANUM NIGRUM*)—SOLANACEAE

Black nightshade has shiny black berries, about ¼ inch (5–8 mm) in diameter. The green unripe berries contain higher concentrations of the toxic glycoalkaloid solanine than the ripe berries do and have caused the death of children. The foliage and ripe fruits can also cause poisoning, however. The toxicity of the species is quite variable in different varieties and in different parts of the world (Hackett and Carolane 1982). Euell Gibbons (Gibbons and Tucker 1979) reports using the ripe berries in pies, and numerous other references indicate that the ripe cooked fruit may be safe. Personally, I consider the whole plant potentially deadly and leave it alone (Heiser 1969; Kingsbury 1964; Emboden 1979).

Black nightshade is a small annual herb with white to purplish flowers that bloom year-round. The lobe tips of the five-lobed flower bend back, and the five yellow stamens form a protruding beak. The thin translucent leaves are ovate or oval, up to 4 inches (1 dm) long. The margins are quite variable and may be entire or have coarse or wavy teeth. Black nightshade grows in disturbed soil throughout the state. The large genus *Solanum* contains numerous toxic species in Texas. See the index for information about the nightshade family.

POKE, POKEWEED, ÑAMOLI—*PHYTOLACCA AMERICANA*—PHYTOLACCACEAE
(See illustration, page 267.)

All parts of the poke can cause severe poisoning. Pokeberries are dark purple but leave a bright red stain. The berries, about ⅓–⅜ inch (8–10 mm) in diameter, are clustered on a long drooping stem that may be bright red. The leafy perennial herb sends up a woody purple or red stalk to 10 feet (3 m) tall, that dies back in the winter. For details on toxicity, uses, and further characteristics of poke, refer to the index.

VIRGINIA CREEPER—*PARTHENOCISSUS QUINQUEFOLIA*—VITACEAE
(See illustration.)

The blue-black berries, about ¼ inch (5–7 mm) in diameter, strongly resemble grapes. The toxic fall fruits of Virginia creeper have caused fatalities. Even in moderately toxic cases, the oxalic acid in the fruits can cause permanent kidney damage. Symptoms may be delayed nearly 24 hours, but medical treatment should be sought as soon as possible after ingestion. The leaves may also be toxic. The closely related cow itch vine (*Cissus incisa*) also contains toxic concentrations of oxalic acid (Lampe and Fagerström 1968; Stephens 1980; Ellis 1978; Kingsbury 1964; Hardin and Arena 1974).

Virginia creeper is a common vine throughout the eastern half of the state. The woody climbing vine has palmately compound leaves with five leaflets (rarely seven). The elliptic leaflets are serrated and may be up to about 6 inches (15 cm) long. Two other similar species of *Parthenocissus* occur in Texas, one in West Texas and one with seven fleshy leaflets on the Edwards Plateau. Cow itch vine is a climbing vine with black berries and palmately three-lobed leaves that are thick and fleshy.

Virginia creeper—
*Parthenocissus
quinquefolia*

Red Fruit: Toxic

CORALITO, SMALL POKEWEED, ROUGE PLANT—*RIVINA HUMILIS*—PHYTOLACCACEAE

(See photograph, plate 14.)

The tiny translucent berries of *coralito* are ⅛ inch (2–3.5 mm) in diameter and orange or bright scarlet. All parts of the plant are considered toxic, with toxicity similar to that of its larger relative poke, listed above with purple fruit (Lampe and Fagerström 1968).

Coralito is a low-growing delicate perennial herb. The erect or vining stems may appear beneath the shade of a tree. Though usually just a few inches tall, the herb can reach 5 feet (15 dm). The small simple alternate leaves typically are ovate and may have entire or wavy margins. The tiny flowers may be white, greenish, or pink. *Coralito* grows in much of the state except the Panhandle and the far east.

HOLLY, YAUPON—*ILEX* SPECIES—AQUIFOLIACEAE

(See illustration, page 168.)

The yellow to bright red (black in a few uncommon species) berries of the hollies are toxic. The round fleshy fruits, ⅜ inch (6–10 mm) in diameter, of Texas' eleven species contain several stones and ripen in late fall and winter. As few as 6 berries have caused a child to vomit, and 20 to 30 berries have caused fatalities in children (Lampe and Fagerström 1968; Ellis 1978; Gibbons and Tucker 1979; Hardin and Arena 1974). The leaves of yaupon, *Ilex vomitoria,* have been safely used for tea, though. Refer to the index for information on preparing the tea and other uses of yaupon.

Members of the genus *Ilex* are shrubs or trees with alternate, simple leaves. They may be evergreen or deciduous, and a number of our native hollies are grown as ornamentals. The leaf margins may be entire or spine-tipped or have rounded teeth. Male and female flowers develop on separate trees.

JERUSALEM-CHERRY—*SOLANUM PSEUDOCAPSICUM*—SOLANACEAE

The toxic globose yellow to orange to bright red fruits of the Jerusalem-cherry are ⅓–¾ inch (1–2 cm) in diameter and may be confused with those of the chile pequín (an edible red fruit discussed below; see illustration, page 217). The peppery fruits of chile pequín usually are oval to long and tapering rather than spherical. All parts of the Jerusalem-cherry are toxic. Keep this houseplant out of the reach of small children and pets (Kingsbury 1964; Keeler, Van Kampen, and James 1978; Lampe and Fagerström 1968; Ellis 1978).

Jerusalem-cherry is an ornamental houseplant and garden shrub that occasionally grows wild along roadsides and in disturbed soil in Southeast Texas. The narrow or oblong leaves, to 4 inches (1 dm) long, are simple and have entire or wavy margins. The small white flowers are five-lobed and about ½ inch (12 mm) in diameter. Other members of the genus *Solanum* also are toxic. Refer to the index for information on and characteristics of the nightshade family.

SNAILSEED—*COCCULUS CAROLINUS*—MENISPERMACEAE
(See photograph, plate 13.)

The red succulent drupes of the snailseed vine are about ¼ inch (6 mm) in diameter and form attractive clusters in late fall. Though the toxicity of these fruits is poorly documented, Michael Ellis of the Texas State Poison Center assumes that they can cause poisoning and advises inducing vomiting if any are ingested (interview, January 1986). Commonly used as an ornamental, the vine is native to the eastern half of the state. The heart-shaped or ovate, shallowly lobed leaves resemble those of the greenbriar, but the vine has no thorns.

WAHOO, STRAWBERRY-BUSH—*EUONYMUS* SPECIES—CELASTRACEAE

The fruit, seeds, leaves, and bark are purgative and potentially toxic. The fall fruit of the two Texas species consist of a three- to five-lobed capsule that may be pink, red, or purple. The capsule splits open to expose the seeds, each encased in an orange-red or scarlet membrane. No toxic incidents have been reported in the United States, but poisonings in Europe have caused convulsions and coma. Ornamental and native species should all be considered potentially dangerous (Hardin and Arena 1974).

Texas native species are shrubs with four-angled green to brown branches. The simple leaves occur in pairs and have finely toothed margins. The seeds of the closely related vine bittersweet (*Celastrus scandens*) also may be toxic.

Yellow, Cream, or White Fruit: Toxic

CHINABERRY—*MELIA AZEDARACH*—MELIACEAE

The cream- to yellow-colored leathery drupes, about ⅝ inch (15 mm) in diameter, occur in large clusters hanging from the tree in the fall. The ridged stone contains several small seeds. Toxicity varies considerably from tree to tree. Children have eaten the fruit of some trees with no harmful effects. On the other hand, as few as six to eight fruit have killed a child (Ellis 1978). The poison has a narcotic effect, sometimes producing mental confusion and stupor. Symptoms may occur rapidly or several hours after ingestion and may include severe gastrointestinal distress, paralysis, or convulsions. All parts of the tree can cause poisoning in humans and pets. Though wild birds eat the fruit, fermented fruit can cause toxic effects in birds. The fruit and leaves have been used as an insect repellent, and the bark has been used as a fish poison (Vines 1960; Lampe and Fagerström 1968; Hardin and Arena 1974; Kingsbury 1964).

Chinaberry, an ornamental tree, now grows wild in abundance in the eastern half of the state in thickets and woodlands. The medium-sized tree has a large rounded crown with dark green foliage. The twice pinnately compound leaves alternate on the branches. The leaves may be 1−2 feet (3−6 dm) or more in length and bear many toothed leaflets. The aromatic spring-blooming flowers are white to purple.

MISTLETOE, INJERTO—*PHORADENDRON TOMENTOSUM*—VISCACEAE
(See illustration.)

The waxy white berries, and indeed the entire mistletoe plant, are highly toxic. The translucent stemless berries, about ¼ inch (4−6 mm) in diameter, mature in late fall and winter. Women have died from drinking a tea of the berries in an attempt to cause abortion. Children also have died from eating the berries. Death may occur within twelve hours (Lampe and Fagerström 1968). I recommend leaving Christmas mistletoe out of homes with small children. Cattle usually avoid the plant but have died from browsing on the foliage (Ellis 1978; Hardin and Arena 1974; Kingsbury 1964).

Our most common mistletoe, *Phoradendron tomentosum,* grows throughout the state as a parasite on mesquite, hackberry, ash, oak, willow, sycamore, and cottonwood trees. In winter, when the trees lose their leaves, the evergreen leaves and branches of mistletoe become highly visible. The much-branched plant may form a bushy clump 3 feet (1 m) or more in height and breadth. The simple entire leaves grow opposite on the branches.

Birds spread mistletoe by feeding on the berries and then dropping the seeds on tree branches. The mistletoe sends its roots into the tree branch, deriving water and minerals from the tree. The green leafy species of mistletoe produce their own starches through photosynthesis and thus can live for years without killing the host tree. They may weaken the

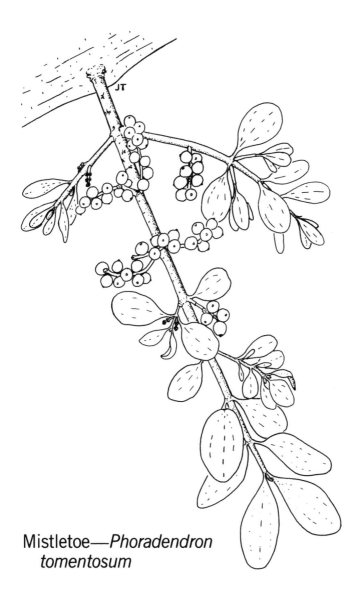

Mistletoe—*Phoradendron
tomentosum*

tree, however, reducing its growth and making it more susceptible to disease and insect infestation. The juniper mistletoes (other *Phoradendron* species) and dwarf mistletoes (*Arceuthobium* species that are parasitic on pines) in the Trans-Pecos are more likely to cause death of the host tree. *Phoradendron tomentosum* intergrades with the eastern *P. serotinum*. *Phoradendron villosum* grows on oaks in the Trans-Pecos. All three species are toxic. No information is available on the possible toxicity of the juniper and pine mistletoes.

NIGHTSHADE, SILVERLEAF NIGHTSHADE, TROMPILLO—*SOLANUM ELAEAGNIFOLIUM*—SOLANACEAE
(See illustration, page 274.)

Both the green unripe berries and the ripe yellow to black fruit can cause severe poisoning. The hard berries about ⅝ inch (15 mm) in diameter, resemble tiny tomatoes, and ripen in the summer and fall. All parts of the herb are poisonous. The weedy prickly perennial herb grows abundantly in disturbed soils throughout the state. The purple flowers, blooming year-round, have five lobes forming a star and five yellow stamens that form a protruding beak. Other species of *Solanum* also cause poisoning. For further information on the toxicity, uses, and characteristics of nightshades, refer to the index.

POISON IVY, POISON OAK, POISON SUMAC—*TOXICODENDRON* SPECIES—ANACARDIACEAE
(See illustration, page 290.)

The round creamy-white berries, about ¼ inch (5–7 mm) in diameter, appear on the vines and shrubs in spring and summer. The majority of people in the U.S. are sensitive to poison ivy and its relatives, including poison sumac (*Toxicodendron vernix*). Even if you have never contracted the rash, consider ingestion of the berries as potentially dangerous. Ingestion of any part of the plant can cause severe swelling and irritation of the lips, mouth, tongue, throat, and anus within a day or two. For descriptions and details on the treatment of external contact with *Toxicodendron* species, refer to the index. Contact your doctor or the Poison Control Center for information on treating the ingestion of any parts of these plants.

SOAPBERRY, JABONCILLO—*SAPINDUS SAPONARIA* VAR. *DRUMMONDII*—SAPINDACEAE
(See illustration, page 395.)

Soapberries contain toxic saponins. The round drupes are about ½ inch (13 mm) in diameter, ripening in summer and fall. The dark seed is visible through the translucent amber flesh of the drupes. I have found no reports of human poisonings in the United States, but you can expect possibly severe gastrointestinal distress from ingestion of the fruit (Lampe and Fagerström 1968; Schmutz and Hamilton 1979). The saponins can cause a skin rash in sensitive individuals.

Villagers in Mexico use the berries for laundry soap and to stupefy fish. To make soap, simply place the mashed fruits in water and stir up a lather. The fruits also yield a bright yellow dye on wool.

Soapberry is an attractive native tree with pinnately compound leaves that alternate on the stems. While the leaflets of most compound leaves occur in pairs, those of the soapberry may be almost alternating on the leaf petiole. The narrowly lanceolate leaflets reach 4 inches (1 dm) long and have entire margins. The white spring and summer flowers grow in dense inflorescences. Soapberry occurs throughout the state along streams and the edges of woods and is sometimes planted as an ornamental.

TALLOW TREE, CHINESE TALLOW TREE—*SAPIUM SEBIFERUM*— EUPHORBIACEAE

Though not a fleshy fruit, the hard white seeds of the Chinese tallow tree, ¼ inch (7–8 mm) in diameter, occur in such abundance in the fall that the ornamental tree is included here. The mature seeds have been ingested without causing toxicity, perhaps because the hard seed prevents poisoning. Nevertheless, since the immature green to blackish-brown fruit that encloses the seeds has caused rapid and severe gastrointestinal distress in humans, it is wise to consider the seeds potentially toxic also. The leaves and white milky sap of the tree also can cause poisoning (Ellis 1978; Mitchell and Rook 1979).

A drying oil with industrial value, perhaps useful in paints or varnishes, can be pressed out of the seeds. The Chinese cultivate the tallow tree for the hard white wax on the seeds, which they boil off for use in making candles and soap (Hill 1952).

Now growing in abundance throughout the eastern half of the state, the tall ornamental Chinese tallow tree bears simple alternate leaves. The diamond-shaped leaves, 1–3 inches (3–7 cm) long, have entire margins, and the leaf tip tapers to a long point. A three-celled capsule about ⅜ inch (1 cm) long, the fruit encloses the three white seeds.

Fruits With Unknown Toxicity: Avoid Eating Them

AMERICAN BEAUTY-BERRY, FRENCH MULBERRY—*CALLICARPA AMERICANA*—VERBENACEAE

The native shrub, often used in landscaping, produces tight clusters of lilac to purple drupes in the leaf axils. I have found several sources stating the fruit is safe to eat, and several stating that it is inedible (Gibbons and Tucker 1979; Fernald, Kinsey, and Rollins 1958). I have talked to one woman who reported feeling slight nausea after eating beauty-berry jelly. Personally, I discourage its use for food. The raw fruit has an unpleasant flavor.

AMPELOPSIS, HEARTLEAF—*AMPELOPSIS CORDATA*—VITACEAE

Leaves and berries of the climbing vine strongly resemble grapes. The blue or greenish berries are inedible and taste horrid, but I have found no reports of toxicity. The plant may cause dermatitis.

CAROLINA BUCKTHORN—*RHAMNUS CAROLINIANA*—RHAMNACEAE

Though Euell Gibbons (Gibbons and Tucker 1979) considers the black fruit of the tree edible, several other species have toxic, cathartic fruit (Lampe and Fagerström 1968; Peterson 1977; Kingsbury 1964; Hardin and Arena 1974). I find the fruits of Carolina buckthorn to have a bad taste, and I consider them inedible.

DOGWOOD—*CORNUS* SPECIES—CORNACEAE

Dogwoods may have blue, red, or white fruit. Some berries may be toxic. Of the cases of berry ingestions on record with the Texas State Poison Center, Michael Ellis (interview, January 1986) reports nothing more severe than stomach upset.

ELBOW-BUSH—*FORESTIERA PUBESCENS*—OLEACEAE

The blue drupes probably are not toxic in small quantities, but they are not considered edible.

GREENBRIAR—*SMILAX* SPECIES—LILIACEAE

(See illustration, page 332.)

The blue-black fruits of greenbriars probably are not toxic. Michael

Ellis (interview, January 1986) reports no problems from the cases of berry ingestions on record with the Texas State Poison Center. I have found several reports that two species, *Smilax herbacea* and *S. pseudochina*, have edible fruit. No information is available on the edibility of the common Texas species *S. bona-nox*. For a description and information on other uses of the thorny vine, see the index.

HERCULES' CLUB, DEVIL'S WALKINGSTICK—*ARALIA SPINOSA*—ARALIACEAE

Black berries may be toxic if eaten raw in quantity (Hardin and Arena 1974).

HONEYSUCKLE—*LONICERA* SPECIES—CAPRIFOLIACEAE

Lampe and Fagerström (1968) report that the red berries of three *Lonicera* species not found in Texas are highly toxic and have caused fatalities. Euell Gibbons (Gibbons and Tucker 1979) considers the blue berries of two northern species to be sweet and edible. Assume that Texas species and the Japanese honeysuckle are inedible, although Michael Ellis reports only stomachaches from the ingestion of honeysuckle berries in Texas (interview, January 1986).

INDIAN STRAWBERRY—*DUCHESNEA INDICA*—ROSACEAE

An ornamental ground cover, Indian strawberry now grows wild in East Texas. The red strawberry-shaped fruit probably is not toxic, but it is not palatable.

PEPPERVINE—*AMPELOPSIS ARBOREA*—VITACEAE

(See illustration, page 340.)

This climbing vine has twice pinnately compound leaves with coarsely toothed leaflets. Its black berries are inedible and taste awful, but I have found no reports of toxicity. Peppervine may cause dermatitis.

Edible Fruit

Texas has a delightful variety of edible wild fruits. Many provide a pleasant snack on an outdoor walk. The high acidity of others, such as wild grapes, makes them unpleasant to eat raw in quantity but excellent for jellies, juices, or pies. The native Americans who greeted the first Spanish explorers in Texas used many wild fruits. The Caddoan tribes harvested wild plums, cherries, mulberries, blackberries, and grapes. The Comanches used wild currants, grapes, persimmons, and cactus fruits (Newcomb 1961). Besides providing food for people, wild berries furnish valuable food for wildlife. Wild fruits also yield beautiful dyes for wool (see Chapter 5).

Collecting fruit from the wild takes time and patience. Most wild plants produce tiny fruits. Collecting enough for a good batch of jelly or a pie may take an hour or longer. Carry along a sheet to spread out beneath a tree or shrub to catch the fruit as it falls. And be prepared to fight your way through thorns, ant beds, and poison ivy to the treasure house of wild edible fruits.

Standard Jelly and Jam Recipes

This section includes several jelly and jam recipes, but since any sweet soft fruit can be used to make jellies and jams, here are two standard recipes. The amount of pectin and sugar required for a good gel and a good flavor varies with the fruit. If the jelly does not gel within a few hours after you pour it into jars, you can reboil it with an extra tablespoon or more of pectin or sugar. Boil fruits in nonreactive containers, such as glass, stainless steel, or enamel-coated pots. Iron and copper pots may affect the color of the jelly and destroy vitamin C. Acidic fruits can corrode and pit the surface of aluminum and galvanized steel pots.

For instructions on sterilizing and canning jelly for long-term storage, refer to a cookbook or the instructions in a box of Sure-Jell. I often make small batches of jelly to be eaten within a few weeks, so I just pour the jelly into a clean jar and store it in the refrigerator. When I am not concerned about preserving the jelly or jam for several months, I often use much less sugar than is called for in the standard recipe.

STANDARD JELLY RECIPE

4 cups prepared fruit
1 package Sure-Jell pectin
   (amount needed varies with
   different fruit)

Sugar (about 1 cup per cup
   of juice)
2 to 3 tablespoons lemon
   juice

To prepare fruit, remove the stems and blossom ends from the fruit, also removing large seeds from drupes. Measure the fruit, place it in a pot, and barely cover it with water. Crush soft fruit. Heat and simmer—about 10 minutes for very soft fruits, 15 to 20 minutes for harder fruits. Mash the fruit, and strain it through a large screen sieve or colander to remove seeds and skins. Then strain the liquid through a jelly bag or cheesecloth, and squeeze the bag to extract more juice.

Pour the liquid into a clean pot, and add the pectin. Also add lemon juice to low-acid fruits. Bring the liquid to a rolling boil, then pour in the sugar all at once. Bring the liquid to a rolling boil again. Stir constantly, and boil for 1 to 5 minutes. When the liquid passes the jelly test, pour it into jars.

JELLY TEST
To test the liquid to see if it has gelled, scoop up a teaspoonful, and let it cool for a few seconds. Pour the liquid back into the pot. If the last few drops run together to form a sheet as they slide off the spoon, the jelly is ready to pour into jars. If the liquid pours off the spoon in a single stream, cook it for another minute and test it again.

STANDARD JAM RECIPE

4 cups prepared fruit
1 package Sure-Jell pectin (amount needed varies with different fruit)

4 cups sugar (amount needed varies)
2 to 3 tablespoons lemon juice

To prepare fruit, remove the stems, blossom ends, and any hard seeds from the fruit. You may want to run the pulp through a food grinder or blender to chop up skins and firm flesh. Crush soft fruit. Measure the prepared pulp, and place it in a pot. Barely cover the fruit with water (to very juicy fruits, add just a bit of water).

Add the pectin (also add lemon juice if needed for low-acid fruits) before cooking the fruit. Bring the mixture to a rolling boil, stirring constantly. Add the sugar all at once. Bring to a rolling boil again. Stir and boil the mixture for 1 minute. Pour the jam into jars. Some jams take a few days to gel after cooking.

In addition to the references cited in the text, the following references provided information on many of the wild edible fruits included in this chapter: Correll and Johnston 1970; Crowhurst 1972; Elias and Dykeman 1982; Fernald, Kinsey, and Rollins 1958; Gibbons 1962, 1964, 1966; Gibbons and Tucker 1979; Kirk 1975; Medsger 1966; Peterson 1977; Simpson 1982; Vines 1960; Scooter Cheatham, interviews, September 1984, March 1985.

Blue, Purple, or Black Fruit: Edible

BLACKBERRY, DEWBERRY—*RUBUS* SPECIES—ROSACEAE

Blackberries and dewberries form juicy blue-black aggregate fruits (one Texas species, *Rubus louisianus,* has whitish fruit). The delicious berries make excellent juices, jams, cobblers, and pies. Use them fresh on cereal or ice cream. These delightfully tart remembrances of childhood are abundant in late spring and early summer. During the dewberry season in June and July, roadsides in East Texas abound with fruit stands. The hardy folk who wade through prickles, chiggers, and poison ivy to collect the luscious fruits of *Rubus trivialis,* the southern dewberry, make it possible for the less enthusiastic to enjoy Texas' most popular wild berry.

To make dewberry juice, cover the raw berries with water, crush them, and strain them through cheesecloth. Add sweetening to taste. Uncooked juice should be refrigerated and consumed within a day or two. You also can use the young leaves of *Rubus* species in teas. The fruits and the young shoots provide dyes for wool.

Nearly a dozen species of blackberry and dewberry grow in the eastern half of the state. Prickly hairs and spines cover the vines and shoots. Those with trailing vines are known as dewberries. The shrubby species with arching shoots, or canes, are called blackberries. Lovely white flowers appear in the spring and summer, soon followed by the fruit. The plants grow in woods and thickets, along streams, railroad tracks, roadsides, and fences.

BLACKHAW—*VIBURNUM PRUNIFOLIUM*—CAPRIFOLIACEAE
RUSTY BLACKHAW—*VIBURNUM RUFIDULUM*
WITHE ROD—*VIBURNUM NITIDUM*

Blackhaws bear blue-black drupes with a rather dry sweet pulp and a flat seed. The oval fruits, about ½ inch (1.5 cm) in diameter, are coated with a bloom. Available from late summer to fall, the fruits can be used in jellies or meat sauces, but they are best eaten raw. The flavor varies from tree to tree. Collect fruit only when it is found in quantity.

The shrubs or small trees grow in woodlands and thickets. The finely toothed leaves are simple and opposite. Tiny white flowers grow in large clusters. Blackhaw and withe rod occur in East Texas. Rusty blackhaw is found in East and Central Texas. Other Texas species of *Viburnum* are reported to have bitter fruit.

BLUEBERRY, WHORTLEBERRY—*VACCINIUM ARKANSANUM, VACCINIUM DARROWII, VACCINIUM ELLIOTTII*—ERICACEAE
FARKLEBERRY, SPARKLEBERRY—*VACCINIUM ARBOREUM*

Texas' blueberries have been overlooked as a source of edible fruit. The fleshy blue-black berries, frequently with a bloom, look like the cultivated blueberries. Collect wild fruit only when it is found in quantity. The best-flavored wild species, *Vaccinium arkansanum,* has the largest fruits, about ¼–⅓ inch (7–10 mm) in diameter. This species deserves consideration for cultivation. The two smaller *Vaccinium* shrubs yield smaller, less favorable fruits. Available in summer, the berries can be used fresh or in pies, jellies, and jams. Farkleberry bears tiny dry reddish to black fruit in the summer and fall. Though not very tasty raw, the berries yield a pleasant pink jelly that is slightly tart.

FARKLEBERRY JELLY

2 cups farkleberries
   Sugar
½ package Sure-Jell pectin

Place the berries in a pot, and barely cover them with water. Heat, and simmer for 15 minutes. Crush the fruit. Pour the fruit and liquid through cheesecloth or a jelly bag. Squeeze the bag to release more juice. Measure the juice, and pour it into a clean pot. Add the pectin, and bring the liquid to a rolling boil. Add the sugar all at once (1 cup sugar per cup of juice). Bring to a rolling boil again, stirring continuously. Boil for 1 to 3 minutes, or until the liquid passes the jelly test.

Texas vacciniums are low-growing bushes to large shrubs. The small, alternate, simple leaves are entire or serrate. *Vaccinium darrowii* is a dwarf evergreen species. Of the eight Texas species, only these four are reported to have palatable fruit. Most species occur in East or Southeast Texas. Farkleberry grows in East and South Central Texas. While most blueberries grow in wetlands, such as swamps, streamsides, or bogs, farkleberry and *Vaccinium darrowii* grow in dry sandy soils. Collect fruit only when it is abundant.

BRASIL, BLUEWOOD, CAPUL NEGRO—*CONDALIA HOOKERI*—RHAMNACEAE
(See illustration.)

The purple-black fruit of brasil is a juicy round drupe, about ¼ inch (5–7 mm) in diameter, with a large pit. Eat the sweet shiny drupes raw or cooked in jellies (Latorre and Latorre 1977). They ripen in late summer and fall. Brasil is a shrub or small tree. Its stiff branches end in spines, adding a challenge to the gathering of the fruits. The tiny leaves are obovate, about ⅝–¾ inch (15–20 mm) long and ⅜–½ inch (9–12 mm) broad. They are alternate, simple, and entire. Brasil grows from South Texas to the southern Edwards Plateau. Several other *Condalia* species with edible fruit occur in Texas.

CHERRY—*PRUNUS* SPECIES—ROSACEAE

Black Cherry—*PRUNUS SEROTINA*
Chokecherry—*PRUNUS VIRGINIANA*

Warning

Unripe cherries are too astringent for use and may be toxic. The seeds, bark, leaves, and roots of cherries contain highly toxic hydrocyanic acid (Hardin and Arena 1974; Ellis 1978). Remove the seeds before cooking. Kingsbury (1964) reports that children have died from eating the seeds of Prunus serotina. *Do not eat the fruit of the laurel cherry,* Prunus caroliniana, *used in landscaping in the eastern half of the state. Laurel cherry, a native of East and Central Texas, is a shrub or small tree with shiny, evergreen leaves. Its black fruit is very astringent and inedible (see photograph, plate 15).*

The purplish-red or black cherries are small, only about ¼–⅓ inch (7–10 mm) in diameter. The fruit ripens in the summer. Black cherries vary in their palatability and may be somewhat bitter. The astringent quality of chokecherries usually makes the raw fruit inedible, but cooked with sugar or honey, Texas' wild cherries are suitable for pies, jellies, jams, and sauces (Stárry 1981). American Indians used dried cherries in making pemmican, a dried mixture of fruit, suet, and meat carried while traveling. The wood of black cherry also furnishes a fine high quality lumber.

Cherries are medium to large trees that are uncommon in Texas. Collect fruit only when it is found in quantity. The dark green leaves are ovate, simple, alternate, and finely toothed. In spring the aroma of the white flower clusters fills the air. Several varieties of black cherry grow in the state—in East Texas, on the Edwards Plateau, and in the Trans-

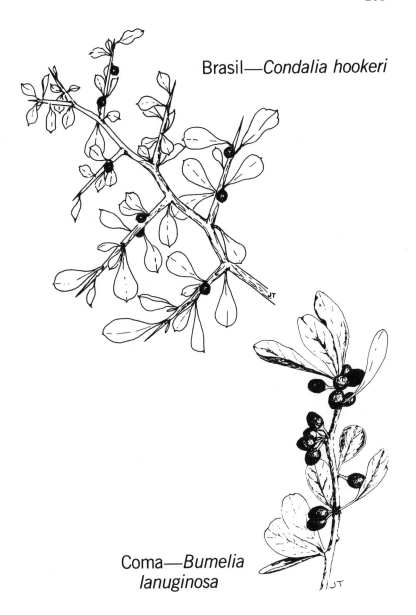

Brasil—*Condalia hookeri*

Coma—*Bumelia lanuginosa*

Pecos. They are found in woods and canyons and on mountain slopes. Chokecherry grows in open woods and on rocky slopes in East Texas, the Panhandle, and the Trans-Pecos.

COMA, GUM BUMELIA, GUM ELASTIC—*BUMELIA LANUGINOSA*—SAPOTACEAE
(See illustration.)

Warning_____

Robert Vines (1960) reports stomach disturbances and dizziness from eating a quantity of raw coma fruits that were not sweet. I recommend eating raw fruits only if they are fully ripe and sweet. Palatability may vary from tree to tree.

From late summer to mid-fall the tree produces shiny black oval drupes about $\frac{1}{3}-\frac{1}{2}$ inch (7−12 mm) long. The fruits are sweetest when they are slightly shriveled. Dried, they have the same texture and flavor as raisins. They contain a large shiny seed that breaks into two halves. The seed makes it difficult to use the whole fruits in baked goods, as you can raisins. Collect a handful of *Bumelia* fruits, and nibble on them as you take a stroll through the neighborhood on a cool fall evening. The fruit makes an excellent dark purple jelly.

COMA JELLY

2 cups drupes
¼ sugar
3 tablespoons pectin

Place the drupes in a pot, and cover them with water (you do not have to remove seeds). Heat, and simmer 15 minutes. Crush the fruit, and strain it through cheesecloth. Add the pectin, and bring the liquid to a rolling boil. Add the sugar, and return to a rolling boil, stirring constantly. Boil the liquid for 1 to 3 minutes, until it passes the jelly test.

The small coma tree bears simple, entire leaves that may alternate or form clusters on the twigs. Typically obovate, the leaves are about three times longer than wide. The leaf margin curls under slightly, and the young leaves and the underside of the older leaves may be covered with woolly hairs. Coma occurs in much of the state. Other Texas species of *Bumelia* may not be palatable.

CURRANT—*RIBES* SPECIES—SAXIFRAGACEAE

The juicy black or purplish-brown (occasionally yellow) round currant berries range from ¼–⅜ inch (6–10 mm) in diameter. Withered flower petals cling to the tops of the fruits. The tart currants make wonderful jellies and jams. Dried, they resemble tiny raisins. Currants, a favorite of the Comanches and Apaches, who roamed the western half of the state, are available from summer to fall (Newcomb 1961). Collect currants only when they are found in quantity.

Currants grow on small shrubs with small, rounded, alternate leaves. The leaves are simple, toothed, and palmately lobed. Several Texas species bear stout spines on long, slender branches. Four species of *Ribes* grow in the Trans-Pecos and the western half of the state, but none are common. Only one species, with greenish fruit, grows in East Texas.

ELDERBERRY—*SAMBUCUS CANADENSIS*—CAPRIFOLIACEAE
(See illustration.)

Warning

Although the cooked ripe berries are harmless, raw ripe elderberries can cause nausea if eaten in quantity. The green berries and the leaves, twigs, and roots of the shrub are moderately toxic. I have found no reports of severe poisoning or fatalities (Kingsbury 1964; Stephens 1980). The red-berried species (not found in Texas) are not considered edible.

Elderberry shrubs produce an abundant supply of fruit each summer, fruit that makes excellent jellies and jams. The blue-black berries grow in large clusters, but the individual berries are minute, barely more than ⅛ inch (4–5 mm) in diameter. Available in midsummer, the juicy clusters can be gathered by the bucketful in a single outing. With stems removed, the berries cook down to a considerably smaller volume of juice, so collect more than you think you'll need. The raw berries have an unpleasant flavor and should not be eaten in quantity, but cooking or drying the fruit eliminates the unpleasant taste. Dried fruit, stewed with sugar, can be added to pies, muffins, and pancakes. Elderberries are high in vitamins A and C and are a good source of minerals (Gibbons 1962, 1966). Before using the berries, remove all green fruit and twigs, as they are slightly toxic.

Elderberry—*Sambucus canadensis*

ELDERBERRY JELLY

1 pound berries (2½ cups)
½ package Sure-Jell pectin

1 cup sugar per cup of juice
1 tablespoon lemon juice

Remove ripe berries from stems and foliage. Place the berries in a pot, and mash them. Without adding water, heat the fruit and simmer for 10 to 15 minutes. Strain the fruit through cheesecloth or a jelly bag. Press the pulp to release more juice. Measure the juice (1 pound of berries yields only about 1 cup of juice).

Pour the juice into a clean pot. Add the lemon and pectin. Heat to a rolling boil, stirring continuously. Toss in the sugar all at once. Bring to a rolling boil again. Boil and stir the liquid for 1 to 2 minutes, until it passes the jelly test. Pour it into jars.

I spent hours picking the tiny berries off the twigs before I came across this suggestion in *Mother Earth News*. George Luther (1979) recommends detwigging the berries by rubbing the clusters across a piece of ½-inch-mesh hardware cloth.

To make elderberry juice, heat and extract the liquid as you would for jelly. Boiling the fruit may damage the flavor of the juice, but you need to heat it to at least 190° F for pasteurization. Strain the liquid through cheesecloth or a jelly bag, then dilute and sweeten to taste. Drink the juice within a few days, or can it.

You also can eat the showy white flower clusters. If you gently shake the flower petals off the shrub into a bucket, undamaged fertilized ovaries will develop into fruit. Add the loose flowers to pancake batter. Wine from elder flowers and elderberries has been a home-brewed favorite for many years. Besides being used for food, elderberry juice is used widely as a meat stamp dye (Hackett and Carolane 1982), and the berries and foliage provide dyes for wool.

Elderberry is a medium-sized shrub of wetlands, growing particularly along streams and the edges of swamps. The long, slender branches are covered with corky bumps. The pinnately compound leaves occur in pairs and have five to eleven long, slender serrated leaflets. Elderberry occurs mainly in the eastern and central sections of the state. Two less common *Sambucus* species occur in the Trans-Pecos: *Sambucus caerulea,* found only on Emory Peak, and *Sambucus mexicana.* Both have edible fruit, but leave these rare plants alone.

GRAPE—*VITIS* SPECIES—VITACEAE
(See illustration, page 312.)

*Warning*_____

Though most people recognize grapevines, a few other plants may be confused with them. I once mistook the heartleaf ampelopsis, Ampelopsis cordata, *for a wild grape and popped one of the similar-looking but inedible fruits in my mouth. The horrid flavor told me of my error. Heartleaf ampeloposis leaves resemble the leaves of some species of grapes, but the fruits are slightly flattened and occur in looser clusters than do grapes. Though I found no reports to indicate that the* Ampelopsis *berries are toxic, they most definitely are not edible. Virginia creeper (*Parthenocissus quinquefolia, *illustrated) has poisonous berries that strongly resemble grapes, but the creeper bears palmately compound leaves (see the index for further information).*

The wine grape, *Vitis vinifera,* has been in cultivation in the Old World since before 5000 B.C. (Schery 1972). Texas has more than a dozen species of wild grapes, ranging in size from the tiny graybark grape (*Vitis cinerea*), ⅛–⅜ inch (4–9 mm) in diameter, to the famous sweet muscadine (*Vitis rotundifolia*), as large as 1 inch (25 mm) in diameter. The juicy purple to black fruits grow in abundance from midsummer to late fall.

You can use any of the Texas grapes for juice or jelly, though palatability and sweetness varies from vine to vine. A frost or two may sweeten the fruit, but several species are too sour to eat raw in quantity. The mustang grape (*Vitis mustangensis*), the most common grape in the eastern half of Texas, bears fruit so pungent that it can irritate your hands while you're picking. You'll need plenty of sugar to make the sour species palatable.

WILD GRAPE JELLY

Several cups fully ripe grapes,
    with a few unripe grapes
Sugar (1 cup per cup of juice)

If you add a few unripe grapes to the jelly, they will supply enough natural pectin to gel the juice. Remove the stems, wash the grapes, and place them in a pot. Barely cover the grapes with water. Mash them, and simmer for 10 minutes. Push the pulp through a coarse sieve or colander to remove seeds and extract more liquid. Strain the pulp and liquid through cheesecloth or a jelly bag, then squeeze the bag to extract more juice.

Grape juice forms a precipitate of tartaric acid that will cloud the jelly. To remove the precipitate, let the juice stand in the refrigerator undisturbed overnight. The next day, pour the liquid off, leaving the dregs at the bottom of the container. Measure the juice, and pour it into a clean pot. Add the sugar. Bring the liquid to a rolling boil, stirring continuously. Boil it for about 3 to 5 minutes, or until it passes the jelly test. Pour the jelly into jars. If it does not gel within a day, there was not enough pectin in the grapes. Reboil the jelly for a minute with a tablespoon or two of pectin.

GRAPE JUICE

1 gallon or less fully ripe
  grapes
Sugar or honey

Heat and extract the juice as you would for jelly. Let the juice sit undisturbed in the refrigerator overnight to enable the precipitate to settle. Pour off the liquid the next day.

Add sweetening to taste, about ½ cup sugar per cup of juice for the very sour species. To pasteurize the juice, reheat it to 190° F, simmering for 20 minutes. To preserve the flavor and vitamins, do not boil the juice.

Grape leaves have long been used in the Greek delicacy *dolmadakia*. Some wild grapes, such as the mustang grape, produce hairy, tough leaves that are unsuitable for eating. But if you find some young tender leaves in late winter or early spring, try the following recipe.

DOLMADAKIA

Several cups young grape   Italian spices
  leaves   Cooking oil
3 cups cooked rice   Several lemons
1 small onion, chopped   Salt and pepper
1 clove garlic, chopped

In a frying pan, sauté the onion, garlic, and spices in oil. Add the cooked rice and the juice of two lemons to the pan. Simmer for a few minutes. Clean the grape leaves, picking out tender undamaged leaves. Boil the leaves in water for about 5 minutes, until they are tender but

208

not falling apart. Wrap one or two grape leaves around a heaping table-spoon of the rice mixture. Place a steam basket in a large pot, and fill the pot with water to below the bottom of the steamer. Place the *dolmadakia* in the steaming basket. Cover the pot, and steam them for 30 minutes. Serve as an appetizer with lemon.

Besides using grapes for food, you can use both fruits and leaves to dye wool. Boil strips of the loose shaggy bark of the thick vines for use in weaving. The slender vines, with tendrils attached, make an attractive handle for a basket.

To distinguish grapevines from other similar-appearing vines, some of which may have toxic fruits, look for the following features. Grapes have simple, alternate, heart-shaped or broadly ovate leaves. The margins are lined with teeth and may be lobed. A dense mat of woolly hairs coats the bottom surface of the leaves of mustang grape and several other species. Grapevines do not have spines. The climbing vines can be found on hillsides and roadsides and along rivers, streams, and canyons from deep East Texas to the mountains of the Trans-Pecos.

MULBERRY, MORAL—*MORUS* SPECIES—MORACEAE
(See illustration.)

Warning

Unripe fruit and milky sap of mulberry leaves can cause gastrointestinal distress and some toxicity (Schmutz and Hamilton 1979; Peterson 1977). The sap can cause a skin rash. Paper mulberry (Broussonetia papyrifera), though related to Morus *species, is not a true mulberry and does not have edible fruits. The red fruits of paper mulberry form a dry spherical cluster.*

The oblong aggregate fruits of mulberries, 3/8−1 inch (10−25 mm) long, resemble raspberries or blackberries. Our native mulberries are purple when ripe. White mulberry, *Morus alba,* introduced from China and frequently used as an ornamental in Texas, bears an edible white, red, or purple fruit.

Though quite tasty, the fruits of the native mulberries and the white mulberry are smaller and less sweet than those of the black mulberry, *Morus nigra,* more common as an ornamental in the eastern United States. The abundant mulberries often go unnoticed, left to drop from the trees and stain sidewalks in late spring and early summer. Remembering the mulberry pies of my youth in Florida, I eagerly made a pie from the fruits of *Morus alba* one spring. I was disappointed in the rather bland flavor of the pie and decided the mulberries are better eaten fresh. Use

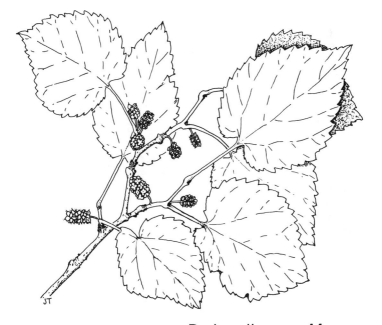

Red mulberry—*Morus rubra*

them on cereal or ice cream, or boil them down for jelly or preserves. Dried, the fruit tastes somewhat like a raisin. As with many fruits, be wary of overconsumption, which can cause diarrhea.

To make a cold drink from the berries, add water, crush them, and strain the mixture through cheesecloth. Add sweetening and lemon juice to your taste. If you don't drink it up the same day, heat the juice to 190° F and simmer it for a few minutes to pasteurize it. The Caddoan and Tonkawa tribes of Texas used the inner bark of mulberries to manufacture a crude cloth (Newcomb 1961).

Mulberries form small to medium-sized trees. The alternate simple leaves have toothed margins and are ovate. They may be unlobed or may bear a deep lobe on one or both sides of the leaf, resembling a mitten. Leaves of the white mulberry form the food for silkworms in the Orient. The medium-sized tree was introduced to the eastern United States in the 1800s in attempts to start a silk industry there. Though the industry failed to produce a profit, the trees became popular ornamentals and now grow wild in much of North America and Europe. In Tucson, Arizona, the ornamental trees have become common enough to cause severe hay fever problems (Newman 1984).

White mulberry grows in South and Central Texas and is particularly abundant along streams. Both white mulberry and red mulberry (*Morus rubra*) grow in similar habitats, and because the white mulberry has red- and purple-berried varieties, it is commonly mistaken for red mulberry. The unripe fruit of the red mulberry is red, turning purple when ripe. Red mulberry grows in East and Central Texas and also is used as an ornamental. Mountain mulberry, *Morus microphylla,* with small fruit, occurs less commonly in the western two thirds of the state, mostly in limestone canyons. Its fruit turns nearly black when ripe.

PERSIMMON, TEXAS PERSIMMON, CHAPOTE—*DIOSPYROS TEXANA*— EBENACEAE
(See illustration, page 178.)

The round black fruit of the Texas persimmon is about ¾–1 inch (2–2.5 cm) in diameter and contains several large seeds. When fully ripe, the sweet rich fruit has a flavor that resembles that of a prune. The astringency of the unripe fruit makes your mouth pucker and leaves a horrid taste, so use only the soft juicy fruit.

Gather the abundant persimmons in late summer or early fall. These delightful fruits produce excellent jams, puddings, cream pies, and quick breads. The flowers are a good honey source. Another persimmon, *Diospyros virginiana,* also occurs in Texas and has an edible orange fruit (see the index). The hard, dense wood of persimmons works well for tools and for wood sculpture (Vines 1960).

The Texas persimmon is a small graceful tree. The smooth gray bark reminds small children (and imaginative adults) of the wrinkled legs of an elephant. The small obovate leaves are simple and alternate, and the untoothed margins curl under slightly. Texas persimmon grows in rocky woodlands of the western two thirds of the state.

PRICKLY PEAR CACTUS, NOPAL, CACANAPO—*OPUNTIA* SPECIES—CACTACEAE
(See photograph, plate 7.)

Ripe in summer and fall, prickly pears may be eaten raw in small quantities, and they yield excellent jellies and confections. Many species and varieties of prickly pear cactus grow in Texas. You can use the purple or reddish fruits of all of them, though they vary considerably in flavor. Minute hairlike spines cover the cup-shaped fruits of prickly pear cactus. The pears are about the size of a child's fist. Refer to the index for numerous recipes and further information on the many uses of the prickly pear cactus.

SABAL PALM, TEXAS PALMETTO, PALMA DE MÍCHAROS—*SABAL TEXANA*—ARECACEAE (FORMERLY PALMAE)

*Warning*_____

The fruit of some other palm trees is inedible. Cycads, which resemble small palms, have toxic fruit.

You can eat the fresh ripe black fruits of our large native palmetto (Vines 1960; Latorre and Latorre 1977). The round fruit, about ¾ inch (2 cm) in diameter, has a crusty skin and a thin layer of sweet pulp. The flattened brown seed ½ inch (11 mm) in diameter, is smooth and shiny. Available in summer and early fall, the fruit has a datelike flavor. Remove the seed, and pour boiling water over the pulp to soften it for use in sweet breads. You can use the fibrous bark of the trunk and leaf petioles for weaving.

Sabal palm is a medium-sized tree, with a trunk less than 3 feet (1 m) in diameter. The huge fan-shaped palm frond, 4—6 feet (1—2 m) long and broad, is not flat like that of some other palms. Instead, the accordionlike fan folds upward along the downwardly curved midrib. The very long leaf petiole has no spines on its edges. The sabal palm has almost been eliminated from its natural habitat along the Rio Grande in far South Texas. It is widely used as an ornamental, however, north to Travis County. Harvest fruit only where the tree is used as an ornamental. Though a number of palms grow in South Texas today, only *Sabal texana* and one other palm, the dwarf palmetto (*Sabal minor*), are native to Texas.

SERVICEBERRY, SHADBUSH, JUNEBERRY—*AMELANCHIER* SPECIES— ROSACEAE

The reddish to purplish-black (occasionally yellow) fruits of the serviceberries resemble blueberries and are ¼−⅓ inch (6−8 mm) in diameter. Though some northern species yield sweet juicy fruit, the three Texas species are less favorable. Indians in the Southwest used the Utah serviceberry, *Amelanchier utahensis,* as an ingredient in pemmican, a nutritious dried mixture of fruit, suet, and meat that they carried during journeys. All three Texas species are rare or very rare in the state, mostly growing in national parks in the Trans-Pecos, so most Texans will never see them. Please, do not harvest wild fruits from these rare trees. The attractive trees could be cultivated as native ornamentals, however, to provide berries for birds and people. Serviceberries ripen in late summer. Use the fruits raw or cooked in pies and jellies.

Serviceberries are shrubs or small trees that have small ovate or oval leaves with serrated margins. The leaves are simple and alternate. Serviceberries do not have thorns. Utah serviceberry grows in the Guadalupe Mountains, and *Amelanchier denticulata* in the Chisos Mountains of Big Bend. *Amelanchier arborea* grows in northeast Texas.

Brown Fruit: Edible

PAWPAW, CUSTARD APPLE—*ASIMINA TRILOBA*—ANNONACEAE

Warning_____

Raw pawpaw fruit disagrees with some individuals, causing severe gastrointestinal distress (Kingsbury 1964). Some people contract a skin rash from handling the fruit.

The unusual banana-shaped fruit of the pawpaw is allegedly edible. The fruit, 4−5 inches (1 dm) long, turns brown to black when ripe in the fall. The fruit may drop from the tree while still green and hard. Let it ripen (or freeze it) till the skin turns brown and the yellow pulp is soft. Remove the large, bony seeds, and eat the pulp raw or baked. The flavor varies from tree to tree. Pawpaw fruit is available in the fall. Collect it only where it is found in quantity.

The pawpaw is a shrub or small tree with alternate simple leaves, 4−11 inches (1−2.8 dm) long, 2−6 inches (5−15 cm) broad. The leaf margins are entire. Rust-colored woolly hairs may coat the young leaves. Pawpaw grows in the moist woodlands of East Texas. The dwarf pawpaw, *Asimina parviflora,* grows in the pinelands and oak thickets of Southeast Texas. Its smaller black fruits are considered edible also.

Green Fruit: Edible

CRAB APPLE—*PYRUS IOENSIS, PYRUS ANGUSTIFOLIA*—ROSACEAE

*Warning*_____

As with cherries, the seeds and leaves of the crab apple are toxic (Hardin and Arena 1974).

Texas native crabs produce yellowish-green apples about 1 inch (2–3 cm) in diameter. The waxy fruit ripens in early fall. Crab apples are hard and too sour to eat raw, but they make excellent jelly and cider. You can also make vinegar from crab apples. When combined with other fruits in jelly, crab apples provide natural pectin.

Both Texas species are spiny shrubs or small trees. The simple alternate leaves of *Pyrus ioensis* have large teeth. Those of *Pyrus angustifolia* have entire or finely serrated margins and may be evergreen. Fragrant showy white to rose-colored blossoms appear in spring. Crab apples are very rare in Texas; thus, wild fruits should not be harvested. Crab apples are worthy of cultivation as ornamentals, however. *Pyrus ioensis* var. *texana* is restricted in Texas to Blanco, Kerr, and Kendall counties. *Pyrus angustifolia* grows in the southeastern part of the state.

Red, Orange, or Yellow Fruit: Edible

AGARITA, AGRITO, ALGERITA—*BERBERIS TRIFOLIOLATA*—BERBERIDACEAE
(See illustration.)
BARBERRY—*BERBERIS HAEMATOCARPA, BERBERIS SWASEYI*

These three species of *Berberis* produce round succulent red berries about ⅜ inch (1 cm) in diameter. The fruit ripens in spring or early summer. Stiff spiny leaves make collecting the tiny fruit a challenge. The spines can cause a skin rash in sensitive individuals (Mitchell and Rook 1979). The highly acidic fruit can be eaten raw only in small quantities. If you can collect a quantity, the berries make excellent jellies, pies, and cobblers. To prepare a refreshing cool drink from the berries, mash the fresh fruit, add water, heat to 190° F, and simmer for 10 minutes. Strain the liquid through cheesecloth, and sweeten to taste. *Berberis* wood provides a light yellow dye for wool.

These spiny evergreen shrubs produce fragrant yellow blooms in late winter or early spring. The hard wood beneath the bark is yellow. The compound leaves have stiff spine-tipped leaflets resembling holly leaves. Agarita has three leaflets per leaf, and the other two species have five to

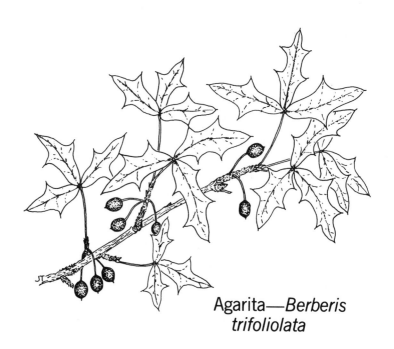

Agarita—*Berberis trifoliolata*

nine leaflets. Agarita grows across much of the state and is the only *Berberis* in Texas that is fairly common. Please, do not collect wild fruit from the other Texas species. *Berberis swaseyi,* rare and endemic to the Edwards Plateau and one location in the Panhandle, makes a particularly attractive ornamental shrub. *Berberis haematocarpa* grows in the mountains of the Trans-Pecos. A blue-berried species, *Berberis repens,* grows in the Guadalupe Mountains.

ANACUA, SUGARBERRY—*EHRETIA ANACUA*—BORAGINACEAE
(See photograph, plate 6.)

The fruit of the anacua tree is yellow to reddish orange. A thin layer of sweet pulp surrounds two hemispherical seeds, forming a drupe about ¼ inch (7 mm) in diameter. The withered flower parts cling to the top of the fruit, and the five sepals remain at the base. Anacua fruit provides a sweet refreshing snack while you are out for a walk in late summer or early fall. Collecting enough drupes to make anacua jam is time-consuming, but the fruit yields a delicious sauce with a unique flavor.

ANACUA JAM

2 cups anacua fruits
¾ cup honey

Place the fruits in a pot, and cover them with water. Heat, and simmer for 30 minutes. Mash the fruits, and strain the pulp and juice through a sieve to extract skins and seeds. With the back of a spoon, push the soft pulp through the sieve. Return the juice to a clean pot, and bring to a boil. Add the honey. Simmer and stir until the sauce thickens, about 10 minutes. Pour the liquid into a jar. The thin jam is good on toast, pancakes, and waffles.

A medium-sized evergreen tree, the anacua has stiff dark green leaves, typically about 2½ inches (6 cm) long, with the texture of sandpaper. Leaves are alternate, simple, and oval. The margins are entire or may have a few large teeth. Anacua trees grow from northeastern Mexico into the southern half of the state to Hays and Travis counties.

CHILE PEQUÍN, BIRD PEPPER, CHILTIPIQUÍN—*CAPSICUM ANNUUM*— SOLANACEAE

(See illustration.)

Warning

*The leaves of chile pequín contain toxic alkaloids, so don't use them as a spice (Fleming 1975). Protect your skin and eyes from the irritants in the leaves and fruit. The introduced ornamental Jerusalem-cherry (*Solanum pseudocapsicum*), which has a toxic red fruit, resembles the chile pequín (see the index). Jerusalem-cherry has spherical fruits and generally longer leaves than those of chile pequín and occasionally may be found growing wild in disturbed soils and woodlands of Southeast Texas (see "Solanaceae" in the index for further information on other toxic members of the family).*

Chile pequín, the wild progenitor of the jalapeño pepper, packs a wallop surpassing that of most cultivated hot peppers. The small yellow to bright red berries (shiny and bright green before ripening) are about ⅝ inch (15 mm) long. They may be conical, egg-shaped, oval, or nearly spherical. Collect them in summer and fall. Use them fresh, or dry and store them for later use as needed. One or two berries or a half-teaspoon of the powder will spice up your chili, enchiladas, or tamales. The berries provide an excellent source of vitamins C, B, and A (Hackett and Carolane 1982). Because of the irritant nature of the fruits, however, use them only as a spice and in moderation.

You will encounter *Capsicum annuum* more often in the garden than in the wild. More than fifty cultivars occur, including bell peppers, hot peppers, cayenne, and pimento. Several species of *Capsicum* were in cultivation in Mexico when the Spanish first arrived (Struever 1971). Seeds of *Capsicum* species have been discovered in Mexican archeological sites nine thousand years old and may have been in cultivation since 5000 B.C.

The pepper used in Tabasco pepper sauce is a cultivar of the closely related *Capsicum frutescens* (Schery 1972). It's easy to make your own pepper sauce to serve with cooked greens. Sterilize chile pequín fruit by placing the peppers in water, then boil the water, and simmer for 15 minutes. Pour off the water (use it to spice up a pot of beans). Then place a few chiles in a jar with a shaker-type lid, and fill the jar with vinegar. The flavor of the peppers will spice up the vinegar in a few hours. Whenever you serve some of the wild greens mentioned in this book, put the jar of pepper sauce on the table. Shake some of the hot vinegar on your greens, but beware—this pepper sauce is hotter than any Tabasco sauce you can buy in a store. Refill the jar with vinegar when it gets low.

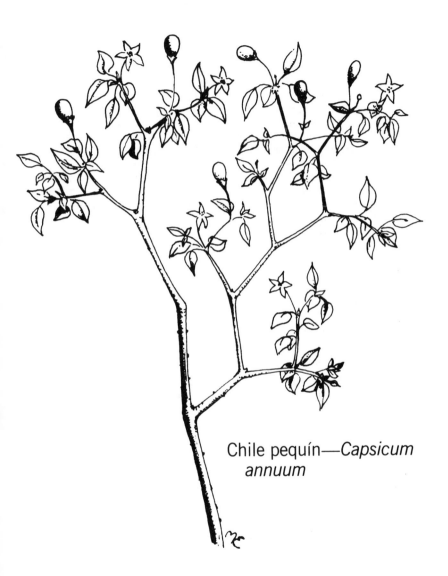

Chile pequín—*Capsicum annuum*

Peppers have been used medicinally in Mexico perhaps as long as they have been used as a spice. Rubbed on the skin, the dry pepper is a stimulant. The Spanish recorded instances of South American Indians using the smoke of burning peppers as a gas to fight off the Spanish (Heiser 1969). In the United States the oleoresin of the peppers is used as a tear gas carried by postal workers (Fisher 1973).

The cosmetic industry uses a red variety of *Capsicum annuum* as a red coloring. The common name "bird pepper" is derived from the practice of feeding cayenne to canaries to produce bright red feathers. Robert Stroud (1964), the birdman of Alcatraz, found that the mild paprika, another *Capsicum* cultivar, worked as well and discouraged the use of the spicy cayenne.

A small delicately branching shrub with zigzagging branches, *Capsicum annuum* makes an attractive ornamental. Its rounded shape and colorful fruits add to its appeal. The small, simple, alternate leaves are ovate to lanceolate and may have entire or finely toothed margins. The white star-shaped flower is only ¼ inch (7 mm) in diameter, and the anthers may be bluish. Chile pequín grows on the Edwards Plateau, along the Coast, and in South Texas.

DESERT YAUPON, CAPUL, PANALERO—*SCHAEFFERIA CUNEIFOLIA*— CELASTRACEAE

Warning_____

*Desert yaupon is not related to the yaupon holly (*Ilex vomitoria*), of East and Central Texas. Yaupon holly has poisonous berries (see the index).*

Desert yaupon produces translucent orange to bright red fruit about ⅛–¼ inch (3–5 mm) in diameter. The nearly round fruit is slightly flattened, with a groove on one side. The thin layer of flesh around the two seeds provides a sweet nibble in late summer. Scooter Cheatham (interview, September 1984) reports that the root and the berries produce dyes for wool.

This small evergreen shrub grows from the southern Trans-Pecos and the Rio Grande Plains into Mexico. The branches are slender and rather spiny. The small, simple, obovate leaves are alternate or clustered, and the margins are entire (occasionally with rounded teeth near the tips).

HACKBERRY, SUGARBERRY, PALO BLANCO—*CELTIS* SPECIES—ULMACEAE

Hackberries bear red, brown, or orange fruits, about ⅙–⅓ inch (5–8 mm) in diameter. A thin layer of sweet dry pulp surrounds a large pit. The fruit of some species is notably sweeter than that of others. Available from late summer to late fall, the fruit is good raw as a nibble or cooked down for an unusual syrup. Though most have hard stony seeds, the seeds of a few species are soft enough to chew up. Hackberries with chewable seeds can be ground up, pulp and seed together, for eating.

HACKBERRY SAUCE

1 cup hackberries	2 tablespoons lemon or orange juice
2 cups water	¼ cup sugar

Remove the stems, and wash the fruits. Place them in a pot with water. Cover the pot, and simmer for 30 minutes. Mash the fruits, and strain them through a sieve to remove seeds and hard skins. With the back of a spoon, push the soft pulp through the sieve. Return the sauce to a clean pot, adding the lemon juice and sugar. Heat to a boil. Simmer and stir the syrup until it thickens, about 10 to 15 minutes. Use the sweet sauce on pancakes or as a glaze for baked chicken.

Use hackberry leaves as a tan dye for wool and the long, hanging shoots in basketmaking. Native Americans used the horizontally spreading roots as cordage.

Six species of these shrubs or trees occur in Texas. Several grow in abundance. The smooth gray bark of some species develops large corky protuberances in older trees. Viewing these ridges at close range through a hand lens, I imagine myself staring into the Grand Canyon. The simple, alternate leaves are ovate to lanceolate, and the margins may be entire or serrated. The leaf texture may be smooth or sandpapery. One species (*Celtis pallida*), a shrub of West and South Texas, bears spines.

HAWTHORN—*CRATAEGUS* SPECIES—ROSACEAE
(See photograph, plate 15.)

Most hawthorns produce small orange-red to crimson fruit. A few species bear green, yellow, or even blue or purple fruit. The round or oblong fruits of some species are as small as ¼ inch (6 mm), others as large as ¾ inch (2 cm) in diameter. They are similar in appearance to a rose hip or small apple. Hawthorns ripen from early to late fall.

Palatability of the fruit varies from tree to tree and species to species. A number of species of *Crataegus* have fruit that is too dry, mealy, or astringent to use. Even the edible ones may not taste very sweet when raw. Look for trees with juicy haws that have a pleasant flavor. The fruits provide vitamin C. Use them for jelly, or steep them for tea. If you include a few barely ripe fruits when making jelly, you won't need to add pectin. In fact, you can combine the haws with other fruits, letting the hawthorn fruit provide the pectin.

Hawthorns are shrubs or small trees. Long, straight thorns arm the slender smooth branches. The small leaves are simple and alternate. The margins bear sharp serrations and may be lobed. Small five-petaled white flowers (occasionally pink or red) appear in spring and summer. More than 30 species are listed for Texas. Hawthorns often hybridize, making it virtually impossible to distinguish one species from another. If you find a species with good-tasting fruit, you have made a wonderful discovery. Most species grow in the eastern part of the state, but several are endemic to restricted regions of Texas. Harvest fruit only when several trees are found bearing fruit in abundance.

JUJUBE—*ZIZIPHUS JUJUBA*—RHAMNACEAE

The olive- or date-shaped drupe of the jujube tree has a thin yellow, reddish-brown, or black skin and white, yellow, or brown pulp. Up to 1 inch (2.5 cm) long, the fruit ripens in late summer and fall. Eat the sweet fruit raw, dried, or candied. The Chinese have cultivated the shrub for more than four thousand years, and the dried fruits are known as the Chinese date (Hill 1952; Schery 1972). Use the sweet fruit as you would dates. Refer to the index for a recipe for amaranth-jujube bread. You can eat the tiny flat kernel inside the large pit, but you'll need a hammer to crack the hard pit open.

The introduced ornamental is a shrubby tree found occasionally growing wild along streams and in thickets in various parts of the state. The simple glossy leaves are serrated and ovate, about 1−2 inches (2.5−5 cm) long, and have three prominent veins. Paired spines may appear at the leaf bases and along the zigzagging branches. The Mexican Kickapoo Indians eat the fruit of the native lotebush, *Ziziphus obtusifolia,* but I found no other reference to its use as food (Latorre and Latorre 1977).

MADRONE, MADROÑA—*ARBUTUS XALAPENSIS*—ERICACEAE
(See photograph, plate 9.)

Madrones bear soft, fleshy red to orange fruit about ¼−⅜ inch (8−10 mm) in diameter. Minute bumps cover the brightly colored round fruits. The tree has become rare in Central Texas because of the reduction of its habitat. Unless one grows in your back yard, you will seldom be able to collect more than a small handful of the sweet fall berries. Eat them fresh or on cereal (Lynch 1981).

The madrone is a small to medium-sized evergreen tree with attractive smooth white or pink bark that peels off the tree in thin sheets. The leathery oblong leaves, up to 4 inches (10 cm) long, are simple and alternate. The margins are entire or occasionally toothed. Small white urn-shaped flowers grace the trees in spring. Madrone grows predominantly in canyons and on mountain slopes in the Trans-Pecos, on rocky hills of the Edwards Plateau, and on the plains of South Texas.

MAYAPPLE, MANDRAKE—*PODOPHYLLUM PELTATUM*—BERBERIDACEAE
(See photograph, plate 6.)

*Warning*_____

In some individuals, eating a quantity of ripe raw mayapples can cause temporary intestinal pain and diarrhea. The leaves, roots, and green, unripe fruits of the mayapple are highly poisonous and can cause death (Lampe and Fagerström 1968; Kingsbury 1964; Kinghorn 1979). The Monominee Indians made a decoction of the plant to use as an insecticide on potato plants (Elliott 1976).

The solitary oval berry of the mayapple is about 2 inches (5 cm) long. Use the tasty fruit only when it is fully ripe. Look for the fruit in late summer, as the leaves die back and the fruits are falling off the herb. The flesh will be golden yellow or purplish, and the pulp translucent and jellylike. The pulp has a distinctive aroma. Eat the berry raw, pureed as a refreshing summer drink, or cooked in jams and jellies. Chemicals in the toxic roots, long used in herbal medicine, have been shown effective in treating certain cancers (Meijer 1974).

The fragrant flower of the mayapple provides one of the most attractive spring wildflowers in the lush forests of East Texas. Two large leaves form an umbrella canopy over the single white blossom, which develops into a single fruit. Collect fruit only where plants grow in abundance.

PASSIONFLOWER, MAYPOP, PASIONARIA—*PASSIFLORA INCARNATA*—PASSIFLORACEAE
(See photograph, plate 14.)

Passiflora incarnata yields orange-yellow fruit up to 2 inches (5 cm) long, twice as large as the fruit of any other Texas passion vine. Suck the juicy flesh from around the seeds. Use passionflower juice as a cold beverage, or cooked into jellies and jams. Several species not found in Texas are raised commercially for their fruit in Brazil and other tropical countries (Martin and Nakasone 1970). Passionflower fruit provides vitamin A and niacin. Native passionflower vines are uncommon. Collect the fruit only where the plant is found in quantity or is cultivated.

The delicate climbing vine produces an elaborate flower. Colored bright purple, red, and white, the flowers may be nearly 3 inches (7 cm) wide. The large leaves have three deeply cut, sharp-pointed lobes. The East Texas native is sometimes grown as an ornamental in other areas of the state. Texas has several other species of *Passiflora,* but only two others are reported to have palatable fruit. *Passiflora foetida,* in South Texas, has similar large purple and white flowers and a smaller yellow fruit. Its hairy leaves may be sticky and have an unpleasant odor. *Passiflora lutea,* in East and Central Texas, has greenish-yellow flowers 1 inch (2.5 cm) in diameter and tiny dark purple fruits.

PERSIMMON—*DIOSPYROS VIRGINIANA*—EBENACEAE
(See photograph, plate 9.)

You don't have to wait till after a frost to eat the fruit of the persimmon. I have tasted the most delightful persimmons, soft and calling to be eaten, in the late fall in Central Texas. The brightly colored orange to reddish-orange fruit of our native persimmon, smaller than the cultivated persimmons found in groceries, grows to about 2 inches (5 cm) in diameter. Several large brown seeds develop in each fruit. The astringent unripe fruit causes an unwelcome pucker. Eat the fruit when it is soft and mushy. You can collect unripe fruit and ripen it in the sun, though tree-ripened fruit tastes best.

Use persimmons fresh or in jams, pies, sweet breads, or puddings. The Latin name "Diospyros" translates to "fruit of the gods," a name you will espouse once you have tasted your own homemade persimmon jam. See Vines (1960) for additional recipes.

PERSIMMON JAM

3 cups persimmon pulp
2 cups water
2 tablespoons pectin

2 cups sugar
2 tablespoons lemon juice

Remove the astringent seeds from the ripe persimmons before cooking the pulp. Place the pulp in a pot, add water, and simmer for 5 minutes. Push the pulp through a coarse sieve to remove the skins. Place it in a clean pot, add the pectin, and heat to a rolling boil. Add the sugar and lemon juice. Boil vigorously for 1 to 3 minutes, stirring continuously. Pour the jam into a jar. If it does not gel in the refrigerator overnight, reboil it with a bit more pectin.

PERSIMMON BREAD

1 cup persimmon pulp
½ cup butter
½ cup sugar or ⅓ cup honey
2 eggs
1 cup whole wheat flour

1 cup rice flour, oat flour, or white
wheat flour
2 teaspoons baking powder
Walnuts

Preheat oven to 350° F. Prepare the pulp by removing the seeds and skins from ripe persimmons. Mash the pulp thoroughly. Cream the butter, and mix in the sweetening, eggs, and persimmon pulp. Mix the dry ingredients together in a separate bowl. Add the dry mixture to the wet. Blend well, and add the chopped walnuts. Add a bit of water if more moisture is needed. Bake for 1 hour. Serve topped with persimmon jam.

Though Fernald, Kinsey, and Rollins (1958) report that the leaves, high in vitamin C, make a good tea and that the roasted seeds can be ground up for a coffee substitute, I have had little success with either. The leaves have a very bland flavor, and my coffee grinder barely put a dent in the rock-hard seeds. The dense black wood, related to ebony, is used for tool handles and golf clubs.

The persimmon forms a medium-sized to tall slender tree with large leaves up to 6 inches (15 cm) long and 3 inches (8 cm) broad. The ovate or oblong leaves are simple and alternate, with entire margins, and the upper surface of the leaf is dark green and shiny. *Diospyros virginiana* grows mainly in East Texas and, less commonly, west to North Central Texas. It also is planted as an ornamental. (For information on the Texas persimmon, *Diospyros texana,* see the index.)

PLUM, WILD PLUM—*PRUNUS* SPECIES—ROSACEAE
(See photograph, plate 15.)

Six species of succulent wild plums grow in Texas. The plums vary in color from red to purple to yellow, and most are coated with a bloom. The round fruits reach about ½–1¼ inch (1.5–3 cm) in diameter. Raw wild plums tend to be sour but make excellent jellies, jams, and fruit sauces. The common plums are Mexican plum (*Prunus mexicana*), hog plum (*Prunus rivularis*), and Chickasaw plum (*Prunus angustifolia*). Look for plums along a stream bank or fencerow. Harvest only when fruit is found in abundance, as other species are uncommon. The bark and flowers of plums provide dyes for wool. The bark, leaves, and seeds are toxic (refer to *"Prunus"* in the index).

PLUM JAM

1   pound fresh ripe plums
1   tablespoon pectin
1½ cups sugar

Slice open the plums and remove the pits. Place the plums in a pot, and barely cover the fruit with water. Simmer for 5 minutes. Push the pulp through a sieve to remove the skins, or leave the skins in the jam. Place the pulp in a clean pot, add the pectin, and heat to a rolling boil. Add the sugar and reheat. Boil vigorously and stir continuously for 1 to 3 minutes. Pour the jam into jars.

Texas plums are shrubs or small trees. Several species have smooth, reddish, or chestnut-brown bark that may be covered with soft hairs. The simple, alternate leaves are ovate to elliptic and have finely serrated margins. In early spring the trees are covered with clusters of fragrant white flowers. Native plums make good ornamentals.

PYRACANTHA, FIRETHORN—*PYRACANTHA* SPECIES—ROSACEAE

This evergreen, ornamental shrub produces large clusters of orange to red pulpy fruits in late fall and winter. The round berries are about ¼ inch (5 mm) in diameter. The mealy fruits are unpalatable raw but make a tasty pink jelly (Sperry 1982). "Pyracantha" means "fire thorn." Protect yourself from the nasty thorns while collecting the fruits. The thorns can cause a skin rash in sensitive individuals.

Pyracantha berries have a reputation of being poisonous, but I have found no evidence to support the assertion. Michael Ellis, with the Texas State Poison Center (interview, January 1986), reports that the raw berries, especially when green, have caused stomachache in children when eaten in quantity but have produced no worse symptoms.

The introduced ornamental is a common trimmed hedge in Central and East Texas. Its slender branches are lined with short, stiff thorns. The small alternate, simple leaves are oblong and entire. Clusters of white flowers cover the shrub in spring.

ROSE—*ROSA* SPECIES—ROSACEAE

The red to orange fruit of the rose is called a hip. The dry elongated fruit ripens in the fall. On the wild species, which you will rarely encounter, the fruits grow to about ¼–½ inch (8–12 mm) long. More than likely, you will use the cultivated roses, with their larger hips.

You can eat rose hips raw, though they have little flavor. The hips provide better-tasting food when cooked. Use them with other fruit or alone for jelly. Euell Gibbons (1966) remarks that a cup of rose hips contains as much vitamin C as ten to twelve dozen oranges. Rose hip jelly on toast is certainly a pleasant way to get your vitamins.

Rose hip tea has long been a favorite of health food enthusiasts. Cut off the stems and the leafy protrusions at the tops of the hips. Chop up the fruits, pour boiling water over them, and let the mixture steep for a few minutes. You can also use fresh rose petals in a salad or made into jelly. Euell Gibbons (1966) offers numerous recipes using rose hips in *Stalking the Healthful Herbs*. Attar of roses is still one of the most highly valued oils in the perfume industry.

STRAWBERRY, WILD STRAWBERRY—*FRAGARIA VIRGINIANA, FRAGARIA BRACTEATA*—ROSACEAE

If you have never eaten a wild strawberry, you have missed a summer delight unparalleled in the grocery store. Though much smaller in size than the cultivated fruit, wild strawberries furnish a sweeter and more flavorful treat. Unfortunately, wild strawberries are uncommon in Texas. Rarely will you find enough for more than a mouth-watering bite or two. If you find a good colony in East Texas (the plants in the Guadalupe Mountains are protected by the National Park), you might try transplanting a few to your garden. Remember that they require acidic soil, just like the cultivated varieties. Use the delightful fruit in pies and preserves, on waffles and cereal—all the ways you ever have used strawberries. Strawberry leaf tea furnishes a good source of vitamin C (Gibbons and Tucker 1979).

Fragaria virginiana grows in East Texas, and *Fragaria bracteata* occurs in the Guadalupe Mountains. The low-growing perennials are easily overlooked in fields, at the edges of woods, and on hillsides. The plants grow in colonies. Look at ground level for clusters of three serrated leaflets. White to pink flowers appear in spring, followed by the luscious fruits in summer.

SUMAC—*RHUS* SPECIES—ANACARDIACEAE
(See illustration, page 36.)

*Warning*_____

Some people have an allergic reaction to sumac leaves and fruit. Sumacs are related to cashews, mangoes, poison ivy, and poison sumac, all of which can cause a skin rash in sensitive individuals. Poison sumac, with white fruits, is easily distinguished from the red-berried sumacs. See the index for further information on dermatitis.

Sumacs produce clusters of hard red drupes, each about ⅛–¼ inch (3.5–7 mm) long in the early fall. The acidic fruits are flattened and coated with minute hairs and an oily substance. You cannot chew up the hard fruits, but pick one and suck on it. A refreshing sour drink, reminiscent of lemonade, can be made from the acidic juice of the fruit.

You can use the fruit of any of the seven species of Texas sumacs. The Mescalero Apaches ground up the seeds and used them to season meats (Basehart 1974). Sumacs are shrubs with pinnately compound leaves. They provide dyes and mordants for wool and tannins for tanning leather. Refer to the index for details of identification and uses of sumacs.

RHUS JUICE OR SUMAC-ADE

Collect several clusters of the red berries. Remove the leaves and large twigs. Rinse the fruit quickly. Bruise the berries by rubbing them gently with the back of a spoon. Extract the juice by soaking the clusters in enough cool to warm water to cover the fruit fully. Since sumacs contain high levels of tannic acid, use warm rather than hot water so that little or no tannic acid will be extracted. Let the berries soak for 30 minutes. Strain the juice through cheesecloth to remove twigs, hairs, and seeds. Sweeten the sour beverage with sugar or honey.

TOMATILLO, GROUND-CHERRY, HUSK-TOMATO—*PHYSALIS* SPECIES— SOLANACEAE
(See illustration.)

*Warning*_____

As with other members of the nightshade family, the leaves and green, unripe fruits of Physalis *are toxic (Lampe and Fagerström 1968; Kingsbury 1964; Stephens 1980). Use only plants with sweet, juicy fruit. Two other genera bear similar-looking but inedible fruit.* Chamaesaracha

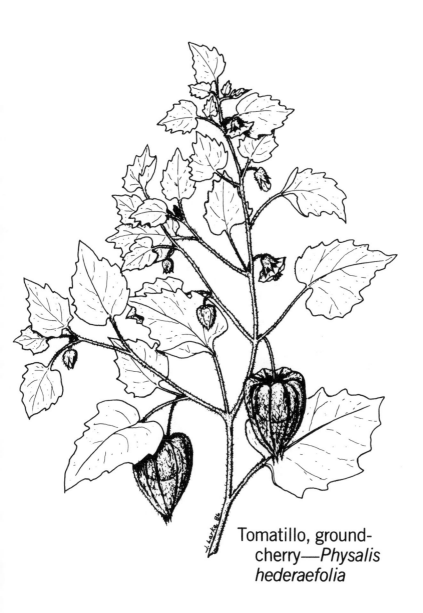

Tomatillo, ground-
cherry—*Physalis
hederaefolia*

berries are surrounded by a husk that fits more tightly around the berry rather than being inflated. The husk is not ribbed and is not completely closed around the berry. The husks of Margaranthus, *in South and West Texas, resemble those of ground-cherries, but the flowers are cylindrical and barely* ⅙ *inch (4 mm) long. The husk typically is less than* ½ *inch (12 mm) long. It completely encloses and is inflated around the tiny berry, which is much smaller than those of most species of ground-cherry (see the index for information on toxic members of the nightshade family).*

A ground-cherry resembles a miniature tomato but has an inflated husk completely enclosing the berry. Both plants belong to the nightshade family. The lanternlike husk is ribbed and may be ⅓–1½ inches (1–4 cm) long, depending on the species. The ripe berries may be brown, yellow, red-orange, or purple, and they range from about ¼–¾ inch (5–18 mm) in diameter. The berry is full of minuscule seeds, like tomato seeds. The Chinese lantern is an ornamental variety with a red husk.

You can gather ground-cherries while they are green, but you must let them ripen before eating. Store them in a cool spot with the husks on, or let them ripen in the sun. The husk will turn tan and papery as the fruit ripens. The fruit will be soft and sweet when fully ripe, in late summer or fall. Eat the delectable fruit raw, cooked down to a jam, or baked in a pie, but do not eat the husk surrounding the fruit. Ground-cherries contain generous amounts of vitamin A (Zennie and Ogzewella 1977).

John Williams (letter to the author, July 1986) offers the following recipe for use with spicy tomatillos.

ENCHILADAS CALABACITAS

TOMATILLO SAUCE

1 pound tomatillos

2 to 3 ounces chopped green chiles

2 tablespoons cumin

Salt and pepper to taste

1 handful freshly chopped cilantro

Husk and wash tomatillos, place them in saucepan, and cover with water. Boil about 10 minutes, stopping before the fruit bursts open. Drain the water from the pan. Cut the tomatillos with two blunt knives, being careful not to get the spicy juice on your hands. Add chiles, cumin, salt, and pepper. Cook and stir gently another 5 to 10 minutes until thickened (be careful—the mixture burns easily). Add cilantro, and stir well.

ENCHILADAS

12	corn tortillas	1	garlic clove, minced
2	cups cooked rice	1	can black olives
1	zucchini, chopped	1	poblano pepper, chopped
1	onion, chopped	2	cups grated cheese

In a bowl, mix the rice, zucchini, onion, garlic, olives, pepper, and one cup of the cheese. Fill each tortilla with the mixture, rolling up the tortillas and placing them in a baking pan. Pour the tomatillo sauce over the filled tortillas, and sprinkle the rest of the cheese over the enchiladas. Bake at 350° F for 20 minutes. Serve with sour cream on top.

Texas has fourteen species of ground-cherry. The low-growing leafy herbs may be a few inches or a few feet tall. The simple leaves are ovate to lanceolate, with toothed or entire margins. The herbs produce five-lobed yellow or purple flowers that may be bell- or wheel-shaped. Ground-cherry flowers and fruit often hide below the foliage. Several species grow as common weeds in fields and vacant lots. Not all species have good fruit, though. Some produce tan, dry, tasteless berries.

TURK'S CAP—*MALVAVISCUS ARBOREUS* VAR. *DRUMMONDII*—MALVACEAE
(See illustration, page 120.)

The red fruit of this common wildflower furnishes a delightful trail snack practically year-round, appearing in abundance in late summer and early fall. The mealy fruit, typically ¾ inch (2 cm) in diameter, is round but flattened at the top and bottom. The fruit divides into five pie-shaped wedges, each with a single seed. The flavor resembles that of watermelon or apple. Turk's cap fruit produces a delicious amber-colored jelly. For a jelly recipe and details on other uses of the perennial, refer to "Turk's cap" in the index.

White Fruit: Edible

WHITE MULBERRY, MORAL BLANCO—*MORUS ALBA*—MORACEAE

The white mulberry produces a sweet, juicy aggregate fruit. The color varies from white to reddish or purplish. For more information on mulberries, see the index and the illustration on page 209.

4 Poisonous and Harmful Plants

Along with many wonderful wild edibles, a generous number of toxic and harmful plants also grow in the Lone Star State. The following chapter is divided into several sections. The first section includes information on the wild plants that most commonly cause poisoning. These plants are grouped by their botanical family names. In some families, such as Solanaceae (the nightshade family), most of the species contain toxic compounds. If you learn to recognize the characteristics of the family, you eventually can identify related species in the field. You will find toxic wild berries and other soft fruits listed in Chapter 3.

Following the section on toxic wild plants, look for information on toxic ornamental houseplants and yard plants (listed in alphabetical order by common name). The next section discusses the toxic plants found in our vegetable gardens and on our spice racks. Another section includes information on plants that can make you itch, prick you with their thorns, or sting you. Finally, for the many hay fever sufferers in the state, the chapter ends with a section on plants that can make you sneeze.

First Aid for Toxic Plant Ingestion

What should you do in the case of a possible poisoning by plant ingestion? Poison Control Center personnel recommend the following steps:

1. Call a doctor or your local Poison Control Center immediately. If your doctor is already familiar with this valuable resource, have him or her call the Texas State Poison Center in Galveston or Houston for the latest information on plant toxicity and emergency care (Galveston: 409-765-1420; Houston: 713-654-1701).

2. When you talk to the doctor or Poison Control Center personnel, have the following information available if possible:
   • The name of the plant (collect a sample to show the doctor)
   • How long ago the plant was eaten
   • How much of the plant was eaten and which parts were consumed
   • The age and approximate weight of the person who ate the plant
   • What symptoms of poisoning have occurred already
   • What first aid has been given

3. If you are unable to contact a doctor or Poison Control Center, and if you cannot get to a hospital quickly, administer the following first aid. If less than one or two hours has passed since the plant was eaten, AND if the person is not unconscious, convulsing, or vomiting already, induce vomiting. Administer syrup of ipecac followed by one or two glasses of fluid—anything but milk. Give more liquids if the victim can swallow them safely. (Other methods, such as putting a finger down the victim's throat or giving salt water, are not as effective. In addition, salt is highly toxic—two level tablespoons of salt is a lethal dose for a small child.) Ipecac is toxic and calls for different dosages for different ages of children. Ask your doctor now about recommended doses of ipecac for all the people in your family. Save the vomitus for laboratory analysis. (Note: It is always preferable to contact a Poison Control Center or a doctor to verify that the plant eaten is toxic before you induce vomiting.)

Plant Poisoning: Dispelling Some Myths About Poisonous Plants

How can you tell a poisonous plant from a nonpoisonous one? Contrary to some popular ideas about plants, no generalizations can help you distinguish one from the other. Reliance on popular folklore about edible plants can result in poisoning. Let's take a look at some of the myths that are sometimes perpetuated about plants.

Myth Number One: If Animals Eat It, It Must Be Safe for Humans

Watching our dogs and cats devour house plants may be the closest that many of us come to observing animals eating living plants. Unfortunately, cats and dogs eat many different plants that can poison them. Neither do cattle, sheep, and other livestock provide reliable indicators of plant safety. Richard Keeler (Keeler, Van Kampen, and James 1978) estimates that wild plants poison 5 percent of all grazing livestock annually. Though cattle usually avoid distasteful plants, some highly toxic plants, such as locoweeds and death camas, are quite palatable and have caused extensive losses. If suitable forage becomes scarce, livestock will eat even bitter plants, such as the toxic milkweeds.

Observing what an animal eats may give us information on the toxicity of the plant, if the animal becomes ill or dies. But we cannot rely on the diet of animals to tell us which plants are safe to eat. Most animals have somewhat different digestive systems than do humans. Pronghorn antelopes have evolved special digestive adaptations, such as a large liver and large kidneys, that enable them to consume plants high in selenium and alkaloids, substances that can kill livestock. Birds eat many plants that are toxic to us. For example, at least 75 different species of birds will eat poison ivy berries.

Myth Number Two: The Color of the Berry Tells You If It Is Edible

The first problem with this old husbands' tale (surely, for every old wives' tale, there are a dozen old husbands' tales) is that I can never remember which colors allegedly indicate poisonous and which indicate edible berries. But even if I could, the knowledge wouldn't help. Some white berries are edible (white mulberry) and some toxic (poison ivy). Some red fruits are tasty (agarita), and some will put you six feet under (yaupon). Some blue berries are scrumptious (grape), but others (ligustrum) will make you wish you'd never heard the adage that blue berries are safe to eat. Enough said. Because berries and other soft fruits attract small children, this book devotes a separate chapter to edible and poisonous wild fleshy fruits, with the plants listed by the color of the fruit.

Myth Number Three: All Flowers Are Edible

A lot of flowers—for example, Turk's cap and prickly pear flowers—provide a sweet nibble. Nevertheless, a number of plants in Texas produce highly toxic flowers. Recently, children have come close to death from eating the flowers of the Carolina jasmine and from a tea of the flowers of oleander. These flowers not only are toxic to eat but also are said to produce poisonous honey.

You cannot rely on generalizations as a guide to the safety or toxicity of plants. Even if you find no reports of a plant's toxicity, you cannot assume that the plant is safe to eat. The term "nontoxic" does not mean the same thing as "edible." Many nontoxic plants are unpalatable.

Who Is Affected by Plant Poisonings?

How do plant poisonings occur, and who is most often affected? According to recent reports of the National Clearinghouse for Poison Control Centers (1981), about 80 percent of the cases involve children under age five. Young children put many strange objects in their mouths. Since small children spend most of their time indoors or in their own yards, they are most likely to eat ornamental plants. Sixty to 70 percent of the plant poisonings reported to the Texas State Poison Center in Texas occur when small children chew on philodendrons (*Philodendron* and *Monstera* species) and dieffenbachias (Michael Ellis, interview, January 1986).

Unfortunately, most parents cannot properly identify the plants their children eat. As a result, the doctor may have to induce vomiting or perform stomach lavage without knowing whether the plant truly was poisonous. If you learn to identify the plants in your local environment, you may prevent an unnecessary trauma for your small child. You can begin to teach your children about poisonous plants at an early age, thus preventing ingestion of toxic plants. At six years old, my daughter became irate when she discovered oleander bushes planted around a children's playground in a state park. Her concern about the safety of other, less well-informed children showed me how seriously she had taken the warnings I had given her several years earlier.

Among adults, plant poisonings most frequently occur from the ingestion of mushrooms (see the index for more information) and flowering plants mistaken for edible ones, and from hallucinogenic or mind-altering plants, particularly jimsonweed.

Some plants that are considered poisonous cause only mild discomfort for a short period, while others cause more pronounced nausea, diarrhea, and some vomiting. A number of other plants can be deadly poisonous. Despite the fairly large number of plants known to cause some degree of toxicity, serious human poisonings rarely occur. Statistics for 1982 from the National Clearinghouse for Poison Control Centers (NCPCC) indicate that about 10 percent of the cases handled by Poison Control Centers in the country involve ingestion of plants, but only 10 percent of those plant ingestions result in the development of any symptoms of toxicity (Mark Fow, letter and documents to the author, 21 November 1984). Toxic symptoms often do not develop either because the victim did not eat enough of the plant to cause poisoning, or because the plant was not poisonous.

In the case of ingestion of a highly toxic plant, rapid emergency treatment often prevents severe illness and fatalities. I have found reports of only two deaths in the past few years in the United States from eating a wild plant other than a mushroom. In the summer of 1985, an employee of Yellowstone National Park died from eating water hemlock (*Cicuta douglasii*) root. The man mistook the plant for an edible member of the carrot family (Sayre 1986). The other death, in Seattle, was caused by a fern, *Pteris* species (Michael Ellis, interview, January 1986).

Livestock Poisoning

Some plants cause more problems for livestock than for humans. Many wild plants eaten by cattle, sheep, goats, horses, pigs, and chickens would not be a tempting meal for humans. Few of us would sit down to a meal of locoweed, so we do not have to concern ourselves much with locoweed poisoning. Nonetheless, plants that are poisonous to livestock may also poison us.

Livestock poisoning usually occurs for one of the following reasons:

(1) Normally safe forage crops that suddenly become a large percentage of an animal's diet may cause bloat or other illness.
(2) Moldy and frost-wilted forage can develop toxicity.
(3) Some highly toxic plants taste good to livestock.
(4) Livestock may eat toxic bitter plants when more palatable forage is scarce.
(5) Toxic plants sometimes are accidentally included in hay and other cut forage.

Though this book emphasizes plants that are poisonous to humans, information on plants that also cause problems for livestock is included. For further details on plants poisonous to livestock, refer to Kingsbury (1964) and Keeler, Van Kampen, and James (1978).

The Toxins in Plants

Poor documentation of past poisoning cases and a lack of adequate research on the degree of toxicity and the chemical makeup of plants continue to create large stumbling blocks to proper medical treatment. A lot of questions remain unanswered concerning plant toxicity. The complex nature of plants exacerbates the problem. The degree of toxicity may vary in a single species depending on the part of the world in which it grows. Variables such as soil type, moisture content, amount of sunlight, and stage of development of the plant all can influence the concentrations of toxic chemicals. A single plant may contain dozens of chemical compounds in varying amounts. The researcher faces a monumental task in determining which substances, at what level of concentrations, cause toxic effects.

Surprisingly, a plant can contain toxic substances and yet not cause poisoning in humans or animals. The toxins must be present in high enough concentrations and in a form that the animal's body can assimilate to cause poisoning. Chemical analysis alone may not be sufficient to show that a plant can poison humans. Much of what we know about the toxic effects of plants comes from range reports of toxic reactions in livestock. Laboratory research with mice and rats, animals that have digestive systems similar to ours, has been instrumental in helping to determine the toxic potential that certain plants hold for humans.

Plants cause poisoning in a variety of manners. Some normally nontoxic plants, including a number of agricultural crops, can accumulate substances from the soil, such as selenium and nitrates. Nitrate and selenium poisoning usually affects only livestock. Humans rarely would eat enough of the plants to become poisoned. Some plants contain toxic substances in small doses. Oxalic acid, for example, occurs in small amounts in wood sorrel and spinach. Only when the plants are eaten as a major part of the diet does the oxalic acid cause problems. Again, livestock are much more likely to experience adverse reactions to these types of plants.

Human poisoning usually results from the ingestion of plants that contain toxic compounds as part of their natural makeup. Much still remains unknown about the toxic substances in plants, including the basic question of why plants produce them in the first place. Some probably develop as waste products of plant metabolism. Others may serve important functions in plant maintenance. Secondarily, toxins do serve an important function for plants. They furnish an effective means of defense from insect predators, although they generally are less effective at protecting the plants from large animal predators. Other plant mechanisms, such as thorns and stinging hairs, provide a better defense against mammals.

The toxins in plants come in a wide variety of forms. Many have only recently been discovered through chemical analysis, and many more remain to be found. Alkaloids are the toxins most frequently encountered in plants. Alkaloids, which are complex organic compounds, include nicotine and the compounds in opium. The poisonous carbohydrates called glycosides include cyanogenetic glycosides (with cyanide as a by-product), saponins, mustard oil glycosides, and cardiac glycosides, such as digitalis. A variety of other substances, such as resins, acids (including oxalic acid), and amines, can cause toxicity.

Toxic Wild Plants by Family

AMARYLLIDACEAE, IRIDACEAE, LILIACEAE—AMARYLLIS, IRIS, AND LILY FAMILIES

These three families furnish many spectacular wildflowers and garden beauties. A number of these well-known plants can cause poisoning. The three families share several similar characteristics. Most species are herbaceous. Commonly, the leaves are grasslike and linear and have entire margins. The flowers consist of six tepals, usually all colorful and showy. The blossoms are radially symmetrical or nearly so. The roots of many are bulbs, corms, or tuberous rhizomes. Even the fruits of the three families are similar, usually being a capsule with numerous seeds.

The poisonous members of the amaryllis, iris, and lily families resemble the edible members of the lily family mentioned in Chapter 1. For this reason, you must pay close attention to identifying characteristics. Frequently, toxicity is concentrated in the bulbs of the poisonous species. So when you collect edible bulbs, dig them up while the plant is in flower, unless you grow them in your own yard where you can mark them for later use. One of the few documented cases of poisoning from a daffodil happened because someone confused the bulb for an onion.

The most reliable distinguishing characteristics of these three families are found in the flower. In the iris family the flowers have only three stamens. The ovary is below the base of the tepals, buried in the tip of the flower stem (this is called an inferior ovary). In the iris family, and particularly in the genus *Iris*, the three inner tepals often differ from the outer three in shape and size. The basal leaves of most species in the family also are distinctive. They fold in half and partially enclose the adjacent leaf.

Flowers of the amaryllis family also have an inferior ovary but have six stamens (rarely three). Flowers of the lily family have six stamens (rarely three), and the ovary sits above the base of the petals (a superior ovary).

Death camas—
Zigadenus nuttallii

You may have to tear the flower apart to see the ovary, as it may be hidden if the petals are joined into a funnel or tube.

Amaryllis Family

The amaryllis family contains nearly two hundred alkaloids (Swain 1972). Virtually all members of the family are potentially highly toxic. Livestock deaths have resulted from the ingestion of a number of species. Human ingestions rarely occur but can cause severe poisoning. The toxicity is usually concentrated in the roots, but all parts of the plant should be considered potentially toxic (Lampe and Fagerström 1968; Kingsbury 1964).

The garden flowers that belong to this family include jonquil, daffodil, narcissus, tuberose, amaryllis, atamasco lily, spider lily, crinum, snowdrop, and snowflake. Wild native Texas species are the spider lilies (*Hymenocallis* species), star-grass (*Hypoxis* species), rain lilies (*Cooperia* species), zephyr lilies (*Zephyranthes* species), copper lily (*Habranthus texanus*), and crinum (*Crinum* species).

Iris Family

Members of the genus *Iris* contain an acrid toxic resin that is concentrated mainly in the tuberous roots but apparently also is present in the foliage and flowers. People who raise irises sometimes come down with a skin rash from handling the tubers. Calves have died from eating relatively large quantities of the plants. In humans, severe gastrointestinal distress can occur if small quantities are consumed (Lampe and Fagerström 1968; Kingsbury 1964; Stephens 1980).

Lily Family

Though the lily family includes such nutritious plants as the onion and the day lily, an number of toxic plants also exist in the family. Nearly two hundred alkaloids and numerous glycosides occur in the family (Swain 1972). Toxic garden flowers include crocus, lily of the valley, glory lily, and hyacinth.

Of the native members of the family, the plants known as death camas (*Zigadenus* species, illustrated on page 238) are the ones to avoid. All species of *Zigadenus* contain highly toxic alkaloids. All parts of the plants are toxic. Several western species have caused extensive loss of life in livestock, particularly sheep. Humans have died from eating the bulbs, which can easily be mistaken for edible members of the lily family, particularly the very similar *Camassia* species (refer to the index). Death camas flowers also have caused severe poisoning in children. The flowers may be white, yellow, or greenish. The basal leaves are grasslike, and the stem leaves are reduced to bracts. Several species grow in Texas, from the deep east to the far west sections of the state (Kingsbury 1964; Weddle 1980).

Another member of the lily family, *Nothoscordum bivalve,* is commonly called crow poison. I have found no information to indicate whether or not it truly is toxic, so we can only assume that it could cause poisoning. The small herb strongly resembles a wild onion and may grow in the same habitat. The musky smell of crow poison distinguishes this herb from the onion, with its characteristic odor (see illustrations of onion and crow poison, page 117). Other distinguishing characteristics are difficult to pin down. Crow poison may bloom in the spring or the fall and sporadically year-round. It occurs throughout the state. The flowers grow in a terminal umbel very similar to that of the wild onions. The tepals are creamy white, with a dark stripe down the outside of each one. The flower pedicels, ¾–2 inches (2–5 cm) long or more, are longer than those of onions, and they become quite stiff and erect as the fruit develops.

APIACEAE—CARROT FAMILY (FORMERLY UMBELLIFERAE)

The carrot family includes a number of well-known garden vegetables and spices: carrots, parsley, celery, parsnips, caraway, dill, coriander, cumin, chervil, and fennel. Most books on edible plants of the United States list several wild members of the carrot family as edible. Most of the edible plants mentioned in other books do not occur in Texas, however, and the few that do are either not very common or not very good to eat. On the other hand, Texas more than makes up for its lack of edible species by the presence of a number of highly toxic plants.

Distinguishing the toxic species from the edible ones is no simple task. The first-year leaves of poison hemlock, for example, look very much like the leaves of a garden carrot. Because of the danger of confusing the species, I strongly discourage the use of any wild members of this family for food. The various Texas species commonly dubbed wild carrot produce scrawny tough roots that are unsuitable for a meal. The true wild carrot, or Queen Anne's lace (*Daucus carota*), appears only sporadically in Texas. I find that as a food, the thin colorless roots of this carrot gone wild are far inferior to those of the cultivated carrots. Considering the dangers of confusing wild carrots with poisonous plants, it is far safer to grow your own carrots or buy them at the produce market.

Family Characteristics

So many wild members of Apiaceae look like the garden vegetables that the best way to learn the family characteristics is to examine some of the garden plants, such as carrot, parsley, and dill. The plants typically are herbaceous and may be annuals, biennials, or perennials. The tiny flowers grow in a special inflorescence known as an umbel, a curved or flat-topped cluster with the flower stems converging at one point. You can remember the term "umbel" if you relate the shape and structure of the flower cluster to that of an umbrella. A hard, ribbed coating covers the small seeds. The seeds may be flattened or rounded. Take a close look at celery seeds and caraway seeds for good examples. The seeds of the common Central Texas weed beggar's-ticks, *Torilis arvensis,* are coated with prickles that cling to your socks when you walk through a vacant, unmowed lot in the summer.

Many species in Apiaceae develop a basal rosette of leaves in the winter. Usually pinnately compound, the leaves may be so dissected that they resemble a soft fern leaf. The tall erect stalk that bears the flower clusters may be hollow. The bases of the leaves usually enclose, or sheathe, this stalk.

Of course, there are exceptions to these characteristics. For example, the purple eryngo (*Eryngium leavenworthii*), a beautiful wildflower, has flowers in a cylindrical congested spike rather than an open umbel, and the leaves and the bracts around the flowers are stiff and spiny. But the above characteristics will enable you to recognize most members of the carrot family when you see them.

In addition to the hemlocks described below, several other Texas members of the carrot family have been suspected of livestock poisoning. They include cowbane (*Oxypolis rigidior*), water parsnips (*Sium suave* and *Berula erecta*), and bishop's-weed (*Ammi visnaga, Ammi majus*) (Crowhurst 1972; Kingsbury 1964).

Now let's look at the most dangerous members of this family, the hemlocks. "Hemlock" is an old Anglo-Saxon word that was used generally to designate poisonous plants. The evergreen cone-bearing northern tree known as the hemlock is not poisonous, however, and is not related to these deadly poisonous herbs.

POISON HEMLOCK—*CONIUM MACULATUM*
(See photograph, plate 4.)

Poison hemlock deserves our respect. Only slightly less lethal than the water hemlocks below, poison hemlock has caused severe poisoning and death in humans and all classes of livestock. The root is the least toxic part of the plant, though toxic it is. Toxicity increases in the leaves and stems, reaching its highest concentration in the seeds. The leaves may be mistaken for carrot or parsley leaves, and the seeds may be confused with those of dill or anise. Symptoms of poisoning, such as vomiting, appear within minutes. Convulsions may follow, and death may occur within a few hours or after several days (Kingsbury 1964; Lampe and Fagerström 1968; Elliott 1976; Hardin and Arena 1974; Keeler, Van Kampen, and

James 1978). In some cases death is caused by muscle paralysis. Poison hemlock was used as a form of capital punishment in ancient Greece. In Plato's *Phaedo: The Death of Socrates,* Phaedo describes the death of the great philosopher from a tea of hemlock, as Socrates' limbs become numb and he is finally completely paralyzed.

Plant Characteristics

Poison hemlock, a biennial herb, has a hairless, usually purple-spotted stem that is 2−9 feet ((1−3 m) tall. The white flowers occur in umbels. The first-year plant sprouts a basal rosette of large compound leaves, each up to 1 foot (3 dm) long. The leaves are strongly dissected and resemble carrot leaves. Poison hemlock foliage often has an unpleasant musky odor. The root usually is a single tuber similar to that of a wild carrot.

Poison hemlock, a native of Eurasia, grows throughout the United States and Canada. In Texas it is found mainly in the southern half of the state but is also fairly common along the Pedernales River on the Edwards Plateau. It grows in wetlands, and along rivers and streams.

WATER HEMLOCK, MUSQUASH ROOT, SPOTTED COWBANE— CICUTA MACULATA

(See photograph, plate 4.)

The water hemlock is possibly the most violently poisonous and most deadly wild flowering plant in the United States. A single mouthful of the root can kill a man or a cow. Children have been poisoned from using the hollow stems as peashooters. Symptoms, such as vomiting, begin almost immediately. Convulsions develop rapidly, and death may follow within fifteen minutes to eight hours after ingestion. Toxicity is highest in the roots, young leaves, and stems and is lowest in the flowers and seeds. The plant has caused numerous deaths in humans and livestock (Lampe and Fagerström 1968; Kingsbury, 1964; Hardin and Arena 1974).

Plant Characteristics

Water hemlock is a perennial herb with a hairless, sometimes purple-spotted flowering stalk that is 2−8 feet (0.6−2.5 m) tall. The flowers, white or greenish, form attractive rounded umbels. The leaves alternate on the stalk and are up to 1 foot (3 dm) long. They may be twice or thrice compound, with narrow serrated leaflets. The leaf resembles a dill leaf in structure.

The following characteristics are particularly useful in distinguishing this plant from other members of the carrot family. Not all of these characteristics will be present in every plant, but the presence of all of them in one plant will positively identify the genus. The rootstock usually con-

Indian hemp—
*Apocynum
cannabinum*

sists of a cluster of tubers rather than a single taproot. The part of the stem just above the roots is swollen. When cut in half, the pith of this swollen section may be hollow or solid but will contain a series of horizontal layers that form small chambers in the pith. A yellowish oil may seep out of the cut stem. The oil and root have a pleasant odor, similar to that of parsnips.

Water hemlock grows in swamps and wetlands and along rivers and streams in the eastern United States. In Texas it may be found along the Coast, through East Texas, and onto the Edwards Plateau to Tom Green County. *Cicuta mexicana,* in East Texas, also is deadly poisonous.

APOCYNACEAE—DOGBANE FAMILY

Many species in Apocynaceae contain highly toxic alkaloids and cardiac glycosides. Chemists have isolated at least 765 alkaloids from the family (Lewis and Elvin-Lewis 1977). Among these poisonous plants you will find several attractive wildflowers and ornamentals. Oleander (*Nerium oleander*), one of the most deadly poisonous plants found in Texas, is a beautiful flowering ornamental shrub. The cardiac glycosides in one leaf can kill an adult (Kinghorn 1979; Kingsbury 1964). The ornamental periwinkles, *Vinca* species, contain toxic alkaloids that have been put to use in treating cancer (Larkin 1983; Lewis and Elvin-Lewis 1977). The attractive Texas wildflowers known as blue-stars, *Amsonia* species, are also poisonous members of the dogbane family. And the powdered leaves of a West Texas native, *Haplophyton,* are used as an insecticide, providing the local name "cockroach plant." (Burlage 1968; Correll and Johnston 1970). Most members of the dogbane family have milky sap.

DOGBANE, INDIAN HEMP—*APOCYNUM* SPECIES
(See illustration, page 243.)

The dogbanes contain highly toxic glycosides and resins. Though I have found no cases of human poisonings in the United States, cats and dogs have died from chewing on the plants (Schmutz and Hamilton 1979). Livestock usually avoid the bitter plants when more palatable forage is unavailable. Horses and cattle have died from eating as little as 0.5 to 1 ounce (15–30 g) of plant material (Sperry et al. 1964).

Native Americans found a use for the Indian hemp *Apocynum cannabinum*. They used the stem fibers extensively as cordage and in textiles. Archeologists uncovered a net made of the fibers in Danger Cave, Utah, dated at about 5000 B.C. (Schery 1972). You can extract the fibers by retting the stems—soaking them in water until the fibers loosen from the bark. Recent research indicates that the cardiac glycosides in Indian hemp may be useful in treating malignant tumors. *Apocynum cannabinum*

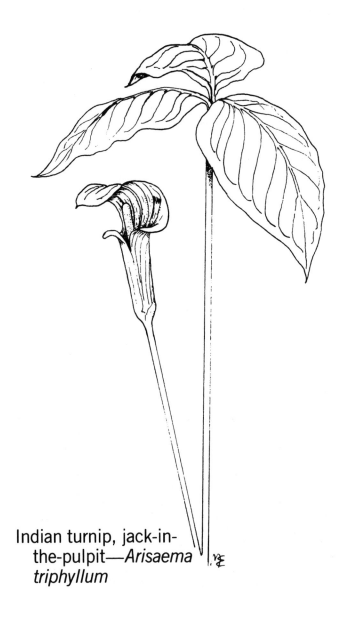

Indian turnip, jack-in-
the-pulpit—*Arisaema
triphyllum*

grows in the northeastern two thirds of the state. Other species may also have usable fibers.

Plant Characteristics

Dogbanes are herbaceous perennials with erect branching stems and milky sap. The leaves are opposite and the margins entire. *Apocynum* species may be confused with milkweeds, which are also toxic. Compare the pods and flowers of the two groups (see page 248). Dogbane flowers have five sepals and five petals. The petals unite to form a small radially symmetrical bell. Texas' dogbanes have white, greenish, or pink flowers. Like those of milkweeds, the pods of dogbanes fill up with tufts of silky hair attached to the seeds. The pods are long, slender, and cylindrical and usually occur in twos. The tips may be joined together.

ARACEAE—ARUM FAMILY

The arum family includes a number of popular ornamental house-plants and garden plants and some of our most unusual wildflowers. You can consider virtually all members of the arum family toxic. The plants contain acrid irritants. When someone, usually a small child, bites into an arum, the victim experiences painful itching and burning in the mouth, with possible swelling and blistering. In most cases the child immediately spits out the plant material, preventing further poisoning. If the mouth and throat become very swollen, however, the victim may lose the ability to speak or swallow for several days. There also is the danger of suffocation from the swelling of the tongue and throat. For these reasons you should treat the ingestion of any of these plants as a medical emergency. Contact your doctor or Poison Control Center immediately. The acrid juice causes the skin to itch and blister and can cause eye damage and temporary blindness if rubbed into the eyes. Swallowing the plant causes gastrointestinal distress and is potentially fatal. I have found no cases of human deaths in the United States, but numerous fatalities have occurred when cats and dogs have consumed the ornamental species.

Further research is needed to ascertain all the factors involved in the toxic reactions. The presence of bundles of needlelike calcium oxalate crystals, injected on contact with moisture, and a proteinaceous substance that causes histamine release may both be involved (Kinghorn 1979; Kingsbury 1964; Lampe and Fagerström 1968).

The roots of several members of the arum family have furnished valuable sources of food in the past (Gibbons 1966; Gibbons and Tucker 1979; Elliott 1976; Elias and Dykeman 1982). Native Americans have utilized Indian turnip (*Arisaema triphyllum,* illustrated on page 245), green arrow arum (*Peltandra virginica*), and calamus (*Acorus calamus*) as starchy foods. Long periods of drying (in some cases, several months) and baking are necessary to render the acrid roots palatable, though. Calamus, the least acrid of the three, requires only boiling in several changes of water to reduce its pungency, but the Food and Drug Administration has determined that oil of calamus is carcinogenic, and so the marketing of the oil is prohibited (Larkin 1983). Considering the potential for poisoning and the scarcity of these beautiful wetland wildflowers in Texas, I strongly discourage digging up any of these plants for use as food.

A number of ornamental plants come from this family. The name "dumbcane," for *Dieffenbachia* species, refers to the possibility that the unwary nibbler may become unable to speak. The luxuriant plant known as elephant ear (*Colocasia antiquorum*), often used in landscaping in South Texas, grows in abundance along the San Marcos River. A variety known as taro provides a major root crop in the South Pacific and is the main ingredient in the Hawaiian dish poi (Ellis 1978; Baker 1965). Like other members of the family, taro is toxic raw and must be carefully prepared for food use. For a full list of the common ornamental members of the arum family, see page 278.

Family Characteristics

Plants of the arum family occur as perennial herbs with thick roots. Arums produce distinctive inflorescences. The inconspicuous flowers, usually white, green, or yellow, are crowded on a succulent dense spike called a spadix. A specialized leafy bract called a spathe often encompasses the spadix. The spathe may be green or colored.

ASCLEPIADACEAE—MILKWEED FAMILY

Milky sap in the stems, leaves, and flowers inspired the common name for the milkweed family. The sap contains latex and, in a few species, may yield industrially important hydrocarbons. Only a few individuals in the family, such as the orange-flowered butterfly weed (*Asclepias tuberosa*) do not have white sap.

Besides the well-known milkweeds, Texas members of Asclepiadaceae include several other plants, most of them vines. Members of the genera *Matelea*, *Sarcostemma*, *Cynanchum*, and *Periploca* produce floss-filled seed pods, as do the milkweeds, but the flowers may be quite different from those of *Asclepias*. The milky sap of these vines, which I will collectively call milkvines, indicates the likely presence of toxic substances. The sap of some, such as *Sarcostemma viminale*, are used as fish poisons in other countries (Lewis and Elvin-Lewis 1977).

Green milkweed—
Asclepias asperula

MILKWEED—*ASCLEPIAS* SPECIES

(See illustration.)

At least eight Texas milkweeds are deadly poisonous to livestock. Probably all 36 species contain some of the toxic cardiac glycosides, resinoids, and alkaloids found in the genus (Kingsbury 1964; Stephens 1980). Some Texas species contain toxic levels one hundred times greater than the levels of some eastern species (Sperry et al. 1964). Two to three ounces of *Asclepias subverticillata,* found in West Texas, can kill a sheep. Cattle, sheep, goats, horses, and even chickens and turkeys have been poisoned by milkweeds. In general, livestock avoid the bitter milkweeds as long as more palatable forage is available. Poisonings occur when better forage becomes overgrazed or when milkweeds are accidentally included in fodder. The most highly toxic Texas species include *Asclepias subverticillata, A. latifolia, A. pumila, A. asperula, A. verticillata,* and *A. curassavica. Asclepias speciosa* and *A. incarnata* also are toxic, but apparently much larger quantities of plant material must be consumed to produce poisoning in livestock. Besides being bitter-tasting and toxic, the milky sap is somewhat caustic. Fortunately, the taste discourages children from eating milkweeds. I have found no records of human poisonings in North America (Keeler, Van Kampen, and James 1978; Van Emon and Seiber 1985).

The name "Asclepias" refers to Asklepios, the Greek god of medicine. Milkweeds have been put to a variety of medicinal uses in folk medicine for hundreds of years. The powdered root of several species, including the orange-flowered butterfly weed (*Asclepias tuberosa*), are reported to have been used to treat wounds, pulmonary diseases, rheumatism, and gastrointestinal problems, among other ailments. Many modern medicines were originally derived from poisonous plants. Perhaps research will validate some of the medicinal uses of milkweeds and provide us with new medicines from the old (Gaertner 1979; Elliott 1976; Lewis and Elvin-Lewis 1977).

One of the oldest and most fascinating uses of the toxic glycosides in milkweeds is that of the monarch butterfly. These beautiful creatures lay their eggs on the leaves of milkweeds. The caterpillars that emerge from the eggs feed and grow on the plant. The bitter glycosides of the milkweed are incorporated into the body of the caterpillar and the adult butterfly. Birds in search of dinner quickly learn that the monarch is an unpalatable food that can make them vomit. In turn, the color pattern of another butterfly, the viceroy, mimics that of the monarch, hopefully fooling any bird who may have already tasted a monarch. The relationship between the milkweed, the monarch, and the viceroy is only one of thousands of astounding examples of the coevolution of adaptations for survival between the plant and insect worlds (Wickler 1968).

Practically every book on edible plants in the United States lists milkweed as an edible plant (Crowhurst 1972; Gibbons 1962; Peterson 1977; Fernald, Kinsey, and Rollins 1958). Unfortunately, most of those books were written for the eastern United States, where the common eastern milkweed, *Asclepias syriaca,* grows in abundance. This eastern milkweed does not grow in Texas. It contains toxic substances, but apparently in low dosages. The bitter taste of the eastern milkweed can be dispelled by boiling the young shoots, flower buds, or immature pods twice. Place the plant pieces in boiling water. Let them boil for 3 to 4 minutes. Then pour off the water, and reboil them until they are tender enough to eat. The only Texas species repeatedly referred to in articles and books on edible plants is the showy milkweed, *Asclepias speciosa,* which is found in the Panhandle (Kirk 1975; Harrington 1972; Gibbons and Tucker 1979). Although this plant has been used for food, it also is toxic.

Besides the difficulties of distinguishing the highly toxic species from the moderately toxic ones in Texas, milkweeds may be confused with the poisonous dogbanes, *Apocynum* species (see *Apocynum* illustration on page 243). I discourage the use of any Texas milkweed as a wild food. Not only are milkweeds toxic and bitter-tasting, but three species—*A. involucrata, A. scaposa,* and *A. prostrata*—are also rare and endangered in Texas. Let's leave the milkweeds to the butterflies and the wildflower photographers, and go in search of more palatable vegetables.

In years past the silky floss found in mature milkweed seed pods was used in making candlewicks. You can spin the fiber like cotton. The floss is buoyant and water-resistant and makes a good insulator. During World War II, Canadian schoolchildren harvested two million pounds of milkweed floss from the wild for the U.S. Navy's use as a substitute for kapok in life vests (Berkman 1949). The United States species that produce the best floss fibers include *Asclepias incarnata* and *Asclepias curassavica,* both in Texas, and *Asclepias syriaca,* the eastern species (Hill 1952). Besides using the floss from the pods, you can use the stem fibers for cordage and papermaking. Archeologists have discovered clothing that was made from the fibers more than 10,000 years ago. The long stem fibers can be extracted by retting—soaking the stems in water until the strands separate from the pulp. Unfortunately, the stem fibers are brittle and so are not suitable for commercial textiles.

Indian tribes in Southern California coagulated milkweed sap by placing it near a fire and then chewed it as a gum. The gummy latex may be put to future use in the production of hydrocarbons for fuel and chemical manufacture. Showy milkweed, *Asclepias speciosa,* has good industrial potential. Milkweed pods also contain oil and wax, and the whole plant produces strong yellow dyes for wool. Milkweeds have the potential to furnish an exciting array of products for industry and homecraft. In the future, as petroleum resources dwindle, perhaps we will find ourselves taking a closer look at the possibilities of cultivating milkweeds for fiber, hydrocarbons, and medicines.

Plant Characteristics

With 36 species in Texas, milkweeds vary considerably in appearance. All but one Texas species are perennial herbs. The introduced tropical *Asclepias curassavica,* in South Texas, is an annual. To recognize milkweeds, look for milky sap and examine the type of flower and pods. The small flowers often congregate in large rounded inflorescences. The flowers are radially symmetrical and come in a variety of colors: white, pink, red, orange, yellow, green, or brownish. Each flower bears five often showy sepals. The five petals usually form five tiny clubs or horns, attached at their bases to a crown-shaped appendage in the middle. When mature, the pods fill up with silky floss that is attached to the flat seeds. The pods vary in shape and size, some curved and plump, others long and slender. The leaves may feel fuzzy, rough, or smooth in texture but often are stiff. They may be threadlike, narrow and lanceolate, or broad and oblong. They may alternate on the stem or occur in pairs or whorls. The leaf margins of most species are entire or undulating.

ASTERACEAE—COMPOSITE FAMILY, SUNFLOWER FAMILY (FORMERLY COMPOSITAE)

Members of the Asteraceae often are herbaceous plants with attractive flowers. A few have caused extensive livestock loss, particularly in cattle and sheep. Though most of the toxic species are distasteful to cattle and sheep, livestock will eat them when other forage is scarce. Humans rarely attempt to use those members of the Asteraceae for food, so for most of those plants human cases of poisoning are unknown. For descriptive information on the family and the edible species, refer to the index.

White snakeroot (*Eupatorium rugosum*), highly toxic to livestock, has caused human illness and death indirectly through milk produced by cows eating the plants. This milk sickness does not occur throughout the entire range of white snakeroot, but before the twentieth century the disease caused so many human deaths that people were forced to move out of certain areas of the eastern United States. White snakeroot grows in East and Central Texas. *Eupatorium wrightii,* from the Trans-Pecos, also is toxic to livestock. One other Texas plant, jimmyweed (*Isocoma wrightii*), has caused milk sickness in the Southwest (Kingsbury 1964; Lampe and Fagerström 1968; Hardin and Arena 1974; Holm et al. 1977).

The following Texas plants also have caused considerable livestock poisoning: broomweeds (*Xanthocephalum texanum, X. sarothrae, X. diversifolium, X. microcephalum,* and probably others), sneezeweed and bitterweed (both *Helenium* species), bitterweed (*Hymenoxys odorata*), rubberweed (*Hymenoxys richardsonii*), paperflowers (*Psilostrophe* species), groundsels (*Senecio* species), and cockleburs (*Xanthium strumarium, X. spinosum*). This list includes only those species that have caused the most problems. For details and information on other members of the Asteraceae that have caused livestock poisoning, refer to John Kingsbury's *Poisonous Plants of the United States and Canada* (1964).

FABACEAE—LEGUME FAMILY (FORMERLY LEGUMINOSAE)

Many of our common foods, the beans and peas, come from the legume family. As we saw in the chapter "Edible and Useful Wild Plants," a number of wild Texas legumes also are edible. Quite a few legumes are toxic, though. In this section we'll look at some plants that have caused fatalities in humans and some that have caused problems only for livestock. See "Fabaceae" in the index for the clues to recognizing the members of this family, one of the largest families of flowering plants in the world.

In addition to the toxic plants mentioned below, other legumes have caused minor losses of cattle, horse, sheep, goats, swine, or poultry (Kingsbury 1964; Allen and Allen 1981; Ellis 1978; Lampe and Fagerström 1968; Turner 1959; Sperry et al. 1964; Hardin and Arena 1974). Wild indigos (*Baptisia* species) and partridge pea (*Cassia fasciculata*) and its relatives the sennas contain toxins. Rattlepod (*Crotalaria sagittalis*) caused many deaths in livestock, particularly in horses, before the turn of the century. Two other members of the genus, *Crotalaria spectabilis* and *C. retusa,* were propagated as hay crops by the Bureau of Plant Industry in 1921, before it was discovered that the plants are highly toxic to livestock.

A number of legumes provide valuable wild forage and cultivated fodder for livestock. Some forage plants cause serious illness or death, however, when they are allowed to serve as the major food source for the animals. Alfalfa, ordinarily an excellent source of fodder, can cause bloat in cattle and sheep if the diet is not supplemented with grasses. Mesquite pods provide a wonderful source of nutrition for cattle, but if they are not supplemented with other forage, the high sugar content in the pods disrupts digestion and can cause death. The lead trees (*Leucaena* species) contain a toxic alkaloid, mimosine, which causes hair loss if the forage comprises 10 percent or more of the animal's diet (Ritchie 1979; Duke 1981). The lesson here seems to be that you can get too much of a good thing. Balanced with other forage, each of these plants provides good sources of protein and carbohydrates to livestock. Other fodder that seem to cause problems only when overeaten include the clovers (*Trifolium*) and vetches (*Vicia*). Guajillo (*Acacia berlandieri*), considered a good wild forage in West Texas, can cause deaths if sheep and goats consume it as a major part of the diet over several months.

Moldy hay from the sweet clovers (*Melilotus* species) and Korean bush clover (*Lespedeza stipulacea*) have caused death in cattle and other livestock. In sweet clover hay the mold forms coumarin, which breaks down into dicoumarin. Dicoumarin causes severe hemorrhaging. The discovery of coumarin in sweet clover mold led to the development of several important products, such as warfarin, which is used in rodent poisons, and an anticoagulant used medicinally to treat blood clots (Lewis and Elvin-Lewis 1977). Other wilted or moldy fodder crops, such as bird's-foot trefoil (*Lotus corniculatus*), can form hydrocyanic acid, which is also highly toxic.

BLACK LOCUST—*ROBINIA PSEUDO-ACACIA*
(See photograph, plate 10.)

The bark, leaves, sprouts, seeds, and pods of the black locust have poisoned horses, cattle, sheep, poultry, and humans. Small quantities of plant material can cause rapid and severe poisoning, but fatalities are rare. Horses have been poisoned by stripping the bark from a tree while tethered to it. Children have been poisoned from eating the seeds and from chewing the inner bark or sucking on the twigs (Kingsbury 1964; Lampe and Fagerström 1968; Ellis 1978; Watt and Breyer-Brandwijk 1962). Refer to the index for a description and further information on uses of the trees.

BLUEBONNET, LUPINE, GARBANCILLO—*LUPINUS* SPECIES

Several species of *Lupinus* have caused extensive loss of sheep in the western United States. As many as a thousand sheep have died at a time in Montana, Idaho, and Utah. The toxic species contain several deadly alkaloids. Sheep become ill and may die within one day if they graze an area heavy with the seeds, the most toxic part of the plants. Cattle and horses rarely become poisoned; they probably tend to avoid the seeds (Kingsbury 1964; Allen and Allen 1981; Stephens 1980; Schmutz and Hamilton 1979).

But not all lupines are toxic, and the Texas species furnish us with our best-loved wildflowers, the bluebonnets. Several species of lupines provide good forage and serve as cover crops, restoring nitrogen to depleted soils. In some areas of the world, sweet varieties that are low in toxicity have been developed for human food (Duke 1981; Summerfield and Bunting 1978). I have found no reports of livestock poisoning from

Texas species of *Lupinus*. Apparently, cattle avoid Texas' state flower, *Lupinus texensis*, and it may be a good cover crop (Turner 1959).

Plant Characteristics

Texas has six species of bluebonnets, all of them designated the state flower. The annual herbs (one is a perennial) sprout a basal rosette of palmately compound leaves in the winter. The showy spikes of blue to lavender flowers emerge in the spring.

CORAL BEAN, COLORÍN—*ERYTHRINA HERBACEA*
(See illustration.)

All parts of the coral bean shrub contain toxic alkaloids, but most poisonings occur when small children chew up the bright red seeds. Ingestion of one seed can cause serious illness. The toxic alkaloids have an action similar to that of curare, causing death from muscle paralysis. *Erythrina crista-galli*, a South American species sometimes planted as an ornamental in Texas, is one of the most toxic members of the genus (Allen and Allen 1981). The Mexican people use seeds of several species as a rat poison, and the leaves and bark as a fish poison. Surprisingly, the flowers and leaves of some Mexican species are used for food (Turner 1959; Schmutz and Hamilton 1979; Watt and Breyer-Brandwijk 1962).

Plant Characteristics

The thorny shrub has compound leaves with three triangular or three-lobed leaflets. The long, slender bright red flowers, though papilionaceous, appear tubular. The dark pods are constricted between the seeds, which are scarlet. Coral bean grows in sandy woods in East Texas, particularly near the Coast and inland to the Balcones Escarpment.

DEVIL'S SHOESTRING, CATGUT—*TEPHROSIA VIRGINIANA*

Native Americans have long used the root of this and several other species of *Tephrosia* as arrow poisons, fish poisons, insecticides, and even medicines (Ajilvsgi 1984). All parts of the plants are highly toxic. The insecticide rotenone comes from the leaves and seeds of an African species, *Tephrosia vogelii*. In restocking inland fisheries, only ten parts per million of the powdered seeds are needed to poison carp (Allen and Allen 1981; Duke 1981).

Plant Characteristics

Tephrosia species are not common in Texas and one species, *T. tenella*, is very rare. The low-growing perennial herbs usually have hairy foliage. The pinnately compound leaves may have few or many leaflets. The pa-

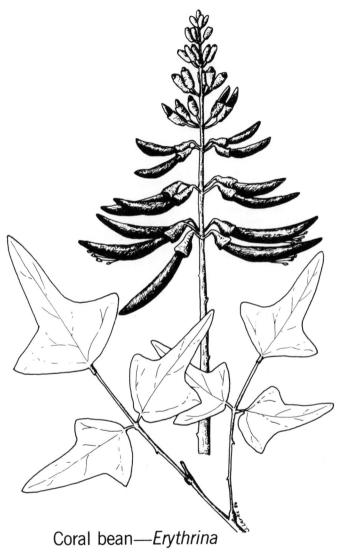

Coral bean—*Erythrina herbacea*

pilionaceous flowers may be reddish, purple, yellow, or creamy. Flattened and linear, the pods are 1 – 2 inches (3 – 6 cm) long. The common names are descriptive of the sinewy roots.

LOCOWEED, HIERBA LOCA, MILK VETCH—*ASTRAGALUS* SPECIES
(See illustration.)

Locoweeds and other members of the genus *Astragalus* have caused extensive loss of cattle, horses, sheep, and goats in the western United States (Ajilvsgi 1984; Burlage 1968; Kingsbury 1964; Turner 1959; Warnock 1970). Decades of research into the problems associated with these plants have not fully defined the toxic principles of the genus. To add to the difficulties, not all species produce poisoning. In fact, some provide good forage for wildlife and domestic livestock.

Because poisoning usually results from cumulative consumption of the plants, human poisoning is unlikely. The beans of one species, however, the ground plum (*Astragalus crassicarpus*), have a long history of use for human food (Gibbons and Tucker 1979; Allen and Allen 1981). Dozens of *Astragalus* species occur in the United States, with 27 species listed for Texas. Because of the complexities of distinguishing one species from another, and the uncertainties about causes of poisoning, ranchers have difficulty determining whether the plants on their land are likely to cause problems. Poisoning has produced vastly different symptoms and has occurred under widely different sets of circumstances (Kingsbury 1964; Keeler, Van Kampen, and James 1978). Let's look at the members of the genus *Astragalus* as three separate groups.

Locoweeds

The locoweeds contain a poorly documented alkaloidlike substance. Domestic animals, particularly horses, avidly seek out the plants, apparently becoming addicted to them. The toxin accumulates in the system of the animal, taking perhaps two months for symptoms of poisoning to appear. If the diet remains uncorrected after symptoms appear, the animals die in a few more weeks. The poison affects the central nervous system, and animals may become uncoordinated or excitable. They may tremble or become listless, unable to eat or drink. Extensive livestock loss has occurred from locoweed poisoning in the Southwest. Texas species known to cause locoweed poisoning are *Astragalus mollissimus*, *A. wootonii*, and *A. mollisimus* var. *earlei*. *Oxytropis lambertii*, a closely related species, also causes the same type of poisoning.

Selenium Accumulators

About two dozen species of *Astragalus* grow only in soils that contain selenium. These plants can accumulate enough selenium to cause death

Woolly locoweed—
Astragalus mollissimus
var. *earlei*

in livestock. A single large dose of highly toxic plant material or a cumulative amount of less toxic plants can cause poisoning. Fortunately, plants high in selenium are distasteful to livestock, and animals won't usually eat them unless other forage is unavailable. Nonetheless, these plants also have caused extensive losses in cattle and sheep in the West. In Texas only *Astragalus racemosus* is a known selenium accumulator.

An interesting side benefit has developed from the discovery of plants that grow only in selenium soils. Scientists can use the plants to map areas high in selenium for the purpose of mining the valuable element. Some *Astragalus* species also provide good indicators of uranium ore and copper-molybdenum deposits.

Other Types of Poisoning

Locoweed poisoning and selenium accumulation do not account for all toxic cases involving *Astragalus. Astragalus emoryanus,* an acceptable forage plant in some areas, seems to cause toxicity only in certain parts of its range, such as in the limestone of the Trans-Pecos and the red sands along the Llano River. Relatively small quantities of plant material can be fatal. A recent USDA study determined that the toxic substances occurring in this plant and several others, including *A. canadensis,* were nitro compounds (Keeler, Van Kampen, and James 1978). Thus, a third type of poisoning exists, and perhaps others will be discovered, as poisonings by other toxic species, including *A. praelongus* and *A. allochrous,* are studied.

Plant Characteristics

Astragalus species are low-growing perennial or annual herbs. They bear pinnately compound leaves, often with many tiny leaflets. The leaves may be basal or alternate on a leafy stem, but usually they form a clump close to the ground. The flower spikes emerge from the leaf axils. The papilionaceous flowers of most species are lilac to purple, though some species have greenish-white or creamy-yellow blossoms.

MESCAL BEAN, TEXAS MOUNTAIN LAUREL, FRIJOLILLO—*SOPHORA SECUNDIFLORA*
(See photograph, plate 11.)

All parts of the mescal bean can poison livestock and humans (Sperry et al. 1964; Turner 1959; Allen and Allen 1981; Ellis 1978). A quarter-pound of foliage can kill a hundred-pound calf. One well-chewed seed may be enough to kill a person (Schmutz and Hamilton 1979; Kingsbury 1964). Fortunately, the highly toxic seeds have a hard seed coat. The seed can go through the digestive tract intact and cause no harm, which probably explains why human poisonings are very rare (Lampe and Fagerström 1968). The hard red seeds are commonly used by children in games. Children refer to them as hot beans because if you rub the bean rapidly on the sidewalk, it becomes hot to the touch. Though Warnock (1970) reports that the aroma of the flowers can cause nausea, the Texas State Poison Center has no reports of such problems.

Native Americans in the Southwest used powdered mescal bean seeds as a hallucinogenic drug (Ricciuti 1978; Emboden 1979; Vines 1960). Archeologists digging in rock shelters in the Trans-Pecos (Adovasio and Fry 1976) have determined that groups living in the shelters used the seeds from at least 8400 B.C. until after A.D. 1000. The seeds may still be in use in ceremonies of the Plains Indians, though perhaps only as decoration. Peyote gradually has replaced mescal bean as a hallucinogen, probably because peyote is much less dangerous to use.

Plant Characteristics

Mescal bean forms an attractive shrub and often is used as an ornamental in Central Texas. The evergreen leaves and the beautiful spring flowers give it year-round appeal. The pinnately compound leaves have smooth shiny leaflets. Hanging in large showy clusters, the blue to purple flowers have a strong aroma very much like that of grape Kool-Aid. The dark-colored woody pod is constricted between the large seeds.

The foliage and leathery black pods of Eve's necklace (*Sophora affinis*) and other species probably also can cause poisoning (Turner 1959). The long pods of Eve's necklace are so deeply constricted between the seeds that they resemble a string of black pop beads (refer to the index for further description).

RATTLEBUSH, BAGPOD, BEQUILLA—*SESBANIA* SPECIES
(See illustration, page 260, and photograph, plate 10.)

All four Texas species of *Sesbania* have poisoned livestock. The seeds contain the highest level of toxic saponins, but the foliage and flowers also are toxic. At least one child has died from eating the seeds of the rattlebush, *Sesbania drummondii*.

Deaths in cattle, goats, sheep, and fowl have occurred from single doses or from cumulative small doses of the toxic seeds. As few as nine seeds of Brazil rattlebush (*S. punicea*) will kill a hen, and a couple of ounces of *S. drummondii* or bagpod (*S. vesicaria*) seeds can kill a sheep (Kingsbury 1964; Vines 1960; Sperry et al. 1964).

The Yuma Indians used the stem fibers of *bequilla* (see photograph, plate 10), *Sesbania macrocarpa,* as cordage for making fishing nets. Extract the fibers from the bark of the long, slender stems by soaking them in water for a few days. A fine paper, similar to rice paper, can be made from the soft pith of *bequilla*. This species is planted in citrus orchards in

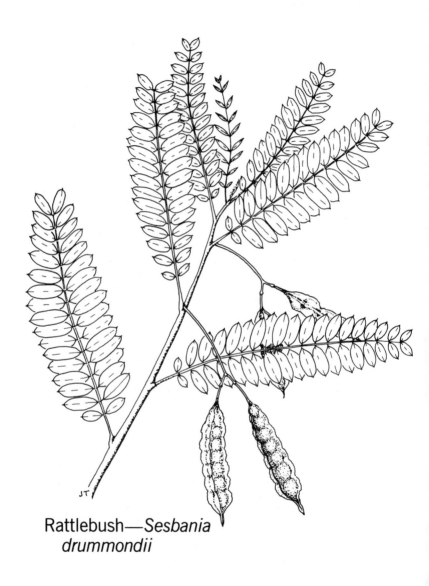

Rattlebush—*Sesbania drummondii*

the United States for soil restoration (Schmutz and Hamilton 1979; Allen and Allen 1981; Duke 1981; Schery 1972).

Plant Characteristics

Bequilla and bagpod are tall annuals, and the two rattlebushes are shrubs. All four species have large pinnately compound leaves with numerous leaflets. The papilionaceous flowers are yellow or red. The most distinctive characteristics are the pods. Bagpod has two seeds in a smooth papery pod that is about 3 inches (8 cm) long and ¾ inch (2 cm) wide. The pod is inflated and splits open when dry. *Bequilla* has a smooth, many-seeded linear pod 8–12 inches (2–3 dm) long and only about ⅛ inch (4 mm) wide. The rattlebushes bear dry, somewhat woody pods with four winged edges. About 3 inches (8 cm) long and 0.5 inch (12 mm) wide, the pods hold several seeds that rattle inside when the pod is dry.

SINGLETARY PEA—*LATHYRUS HIRSUTUS, LATHYRUS PUSILLUS,* AND OTHER SPECIES
SWEETPEA—*LATHYRUS LATIFOLIUS, LATHYRUS ODORATUS*

Members of the genus *Lathyrus* have caused many cases of illness and death in humans and livestock over the centuries in Europe, Russia, India, and northern Africa. Livestock become poisoned when the seeds mature on forage vines and become a significant part of the animal's diet. Human poisoning from *L. sativus,* rarely found wild in the United States, has occurred during times of drought and famine when people have relied on the seeds as a major food source (Allen and Allen 1981; Kingsbury 1964; Lewis and Elvin-Lewis 1977).

The sweetpeas and singletary peas are Old World vines cultivated in the United States and occasionally found growing wild in Texas. Farmers grow singletary peas as cover crops and occasionally as winter forage. Livestock poisoning from the forages led to experiments with other species, including the ornamental sweetpea *Lathyrus odoratus* and the perennial sweetpea *Lathyrus latifolius. Lathyrus latifolius* was found to be the most highly toxic, causing convulsions and death. With the forage species and *L. odoratus,* symptoms appear when the seeds become a major part of the animal's diet, typically greater than 25 percent for a period of days or weeks. The seeds cause paralysis, skeletal deformity, birth defects, and, if the diet remains unaltered, death.

Plant Characteristics

Lathyrus species typically are vining herbs. The pinnately compound leaves are tipped with a tendril. The showy papilionaceous flowers may be white, pink, red, or bluish. The linear to oblong pods have thin walls.

WISTERIA—*WISTERIA* SPECIES
(See photograph, plate 4.)

The native and the introduced ornamental vines have toxic seeds, pods, and bark. I have found no human deaths reported from the plants in the United States. Nonetheless, ingestion of even one or two seeds has caused severe poisoning in children. Violent vomiting, diarrhea, and gastrointestinal pain come on quickly, but with immediate medical treatment, recovery is rapid (Kingsbury 1964; Ellis 1978; Lampe and Fagerström 1968). Though some people maintain that the flowers are edible, the Texas State Poison Center reports cases of violent vomiting due to the ingestion of the flowers.

Plant Characteristics

Wisterias form thick high-climbing vines and have large pinnately compound leaves with leaflets that may be 2½ inches (6.5 cm) long. Fragrant purple papilionaceous flowers hang in long, loose racemes. The straight, rather flat pods are several inches long, and those of the widely cultivated Chinese wisteria (*Wisteria sinensis*) are covered with velvety hairs. The native East Texas species, *Wisteria macrostachya,* has smooth pods and is not common.

HIPPOCASTANACEAE—BUCKEYE FAMILY

BUCKEYE, HORSE-CHESTNUT—*AESCULUS* SPECIES
(See illustration.)

The seeds of *Aesculus* species resemble a chestnut, but the buckeyes and horse-chestnuts are poisonous. The true chestnut tree (*Castanea dentata*) bears an edible nut, but an infestation of chestnut blight virtually exterminated the chestnut tree in North America. The exact nature of the toxins in *Aesculus* remain undetermined but may include the saponin glycoside aesculin.

All parts of the shrubs and trees can cause poisoning (Hardin and Arena 1974; Ellis 1978; Lampe and Fagerström 1968; Kingsbury 1964). A few fatalities in children are on record. Children have been poisoned from eating the seeds and the green capsules and from drinking a tea of the leaves of the European horse-chestnut (*Aesculus hippocastanum*), a tree planted as an ornamental in the northeastern United States. All of the species found in Texas have caused illness in livestock. Cattle have become ill from grazing on seedlings and sprouts. Even honey produced from the nectar of the flowers may be poisonous to humans.

Fernald, Kinsey, and Rollins (1958) report that native Americans poi-

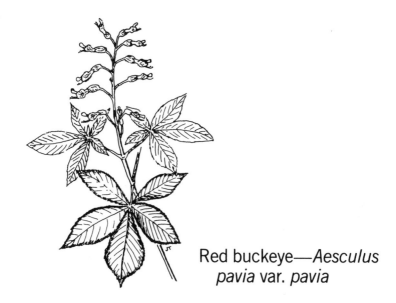

Red buckeye—*Aesculus pavia* var. *pavia*

soned fish by throwing the powdered seeds and branches into ponds. The stunned fish floated to the surface, making them easy to catch. Lewis and Elvin-Lewis (1977) state that the European horse-chestnut contains an agent that may be useful in medicine for treating shock. The roots of *Aesculus pavia* have been used for making soap, and Vines (1960) reports that the compound aesculin in ointment form can be used to treat sunburn.

Plant Characteristics

Of the buckeye family, only the genus *Aesculus* occurs in North America. Buckeyes and horse-chestnuts are shrubs or trees with large palmately compound leaves that occur opposite each other on the branches. The deciduous leaves of some Texas species fall from the shrub by midsummer. The margins of the large leaflets are serrated. The beautiful showy flowers, which are bilateral, five-lobed, and bell-shaped, form large erect inflorescences that bloom in spring. A leathery tan capsule, the fruit may be smooth or spiny. The capsule holds one to three shiny brown seeds, each about $1-1\frac{1}{2}$ inch (2.5–4 cm) in diameter with a pale spot at one end.

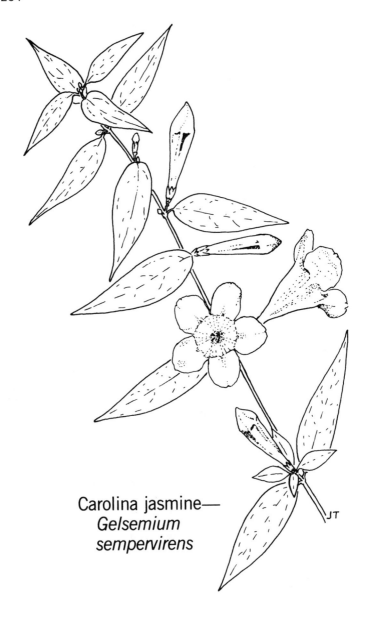

Carolina jasmine—
*Gelsemium
sempervirens*

In Texas, buckeyes grow along stream banks and river bottoms, in woods, and on rocky slopes. Our native species make attractive ornamentals. The scarlet-flowered shrub *Aesculus pavia* grows in East Texas to the edge of the Edwards Plateau, while a yellow-flowered variety occurs on the Edwards Plateau and near Houston. Ohio buckeye (*Aesculus glabra*), a tree with pale yellowish-green flowers, may be found in the northeast corner of the state. Texas buckeye (*Aesculus arguta*), a shrub to medium-sized tree with pale yellow flowers, occurs from the Edwards Plateau to Northeast Texas. These species may hybridize, resulting in flowers with color combinations of yellow and red.

LOGANIACEAE—LOGANIA FAMILY

JASMINE, CAROLINA JASMINE, YELLOW JESSAMINE, JAMÍN AMARILLO— *GELSEMIUM SEMPERVIRENS*
(See illustration.)

This high-climbing or trailing vine has caused severe poisoning in humans. All parts contain toxic alkaloids. Recently a child nearly died from eating the flowers (Michael Ellis, interview, January 1986). The toxic nectar may produce poisonous honey. Numerous adult poisonings occurred early in the century when the root was used as a medicinal herb. Familiarize your children with the hazards of Carolina jasmine since the vine is often used as an ornamental (Hardin and Arena 1974; Kingsbury 1964; Lampe and Fagerström 1968).

Plant Characteristics

The smooth slender vine grows in open woods on sandy soil in East Texas and along the Texas coast, throughout the southeastern United States, and into Mexico. The simple semievergreen leaves occur in pairs. They are lanceolate to ovate and about 1−3 inches (2.5−7.5 cm) long and half as wide, with entire margins. The petals unite to form a funnel-shaped blossom with five lobes. The fragrant yellow flowers are radially symmetrical and about 1−1½ inches (2.5−3.5 cm) long.

PHYTOLACCACEAE—POKEWEED FAMILY

CORALITO, SMALL POKEWEED, ROUGE PLANT—*RIVINA HUMILIS*
(See photograph, plate 14.)

All parts of *coralito* are considered toxic, with toxicity similar to that of the larger pokeweed, described below (Lampe and Fagerström 1968).

You can use the red berries of this low-growing perennial herb as an ink and a dye. Refer to the index for more information.

POKE, POKEWEED, ÑAMOLI—*PHYTOLACCA AMERICANA*
(See illustration.)

For those people who are aware of the pitfalls of its misuse, the poke can provide a tasty potherb. The berries yield delightful dyes for wool, and in the past, poke has had value in folk medicine. But misused, poke is a deadly poisonous plant.

The toxic compounds, including an alkaloid called phytolaccatoxin, concentrate in the bark, root, green berries, and older leaves of poke. All plant parts contain some degree of toxicity, however, including the un-cooked shoots and the tempting purple berries. Though the ripe berries reportedly have been cooked in pies, a few raw berries can cause severe poisoning or death in infants. Consider the cooked berries potentially toxic also. Poke is emetic, purgative, and narcotic. Poisoning may cause severe cramps, vomiting, diarrhea. Convulsions can also develop. With proper treatment, though, recovery usually is rapid, and fatalities rare (Ellis 1978; Hardin and Arena 1974; Kingsbury 1964; Lampe and Fagerström 1968; Watt and Breyer-Brandwijk 1962).

In recent cases of poisonings from the berries, pathologists have noted changes in the chemistry of the blood cells of the victims (Barker, Farnes, and LaMarche 1966). The blood changes have had no apparent harmful effects, and the substance involved apparently is inactivated by cooking. Nevertheless, as this mitogenic property (the substance affecting blood cells) can be absorbed through open wounds in the skin, it is advisable to wear gloves when handling the berries and roots, the parts of the plant that contain the mitogens (Lewis and Elvin-Lewis 1977).

The young spring shoots are gathered wild for food throughout the eastern United States and are cultivated in Europe and northern Africa. As most people who grew up using the greens know, if the plant is collected at the wrong stage or if it is eaten raw, it can cause poisoning. But poke greens furnish a fine vegetable for those who can positively identify the young spring growth. Gather only the very young shoots, less than about 8 inches (20 cm) tall, taking care not to collect any of the highly toxic root. Don't let the common name "poke salet" confuse you. The term "salet" does not have the same meaning as "salad." Poke salet is a potherb, not a raw vegetable. Cook the greens thoroughly, changing the water once, to extract the toxic compounds. First, boil the shoots in water for about 10 minutes. Then pour off the water. Recook the greens in a small amount of water, adding seasonings such as onions and bacon fat. Cook the greens slowly for about 30 minutes, and serve them with cornbread and pepper sauce (Abbott 1982; Arnott 1975; Peterson 1977).

Poke—*Phytolacca
americana*

The Cherokees and other native American tribes and early European settlers used poke roots to treat a variety of ailments. From 1820 to 1916 *The United States Pharmacopeia* listed poke as a medicinal, as did the *National Formulary* until 1947. The roots are highly toxic, though, and the herbal remedies occasionally have caused poisoning. Recent research indicates a number of potentially valuable uses for poke in modern medicine. The mitogens present in the berries and root may prove useful for studying immune responses and diagnosing certain diseases. Microbiologists at Southwest Texas State University have investigated a protein present in the leaves that may provide an antiviral agent for treating cold sores and influenza. Leaf extracts also may have antibacterial effects. As it has in the past, poke seems destined to continue as a valued medicinal in the future (Kinghorn 1979; B. E. Barker, letter to the author, 27 December 1985).

The crimson juice of the purple berries yields a pink to red dyebath, or "lake." Though the dye fades considerably with exposure to light, it is one of the few bright red dyes from plants. You can even obtain blue to black dyes from pokeberries. During the Civil War, people used the juice as an ink. Fernald, Kinsey, and Rollins (1958) report that in the 1780s the Portuguese intensified the color of poorly made red wines by adulterating them with pokeberry juice.

Plant Characteristics

Poke, a perennial herb, sends up a woody much-branched stalk 4–9 feet (1–3 m) tall. The smooth bark is bright red to purple. The simple alternate leaves may be 5–10 inches (1–2.5 dm) in length. The smooth leaves typically are broadly lanceolate and have entire margins. White flowers appear in a large raceme from summer to fall, and the drooping berry clusters form in late summer and fall. The stalk that holds the berries is often bright red. The berries, about ⅓ inch (8–10 mm) in diameter, turn dark purple when ripe, and the juice leaves a red stain.

Poke grows in rich low ground, particularly in disturbed open areas throughout the eastern United States and southeastern Canada. It occurs throughout much of Texas, except the far west.

SAPINDACEAE—SOAPBERRY FAMILY

MEXICAN BUCKEYE, MONILLA—*UNGNADIA SPECIOSA*
(See photograph, plate 15.)

The seeds of Mexican buckeye contain cyanogenetic lipids, the highly toxic cyanide bound up in lipid form (Seigler, Seaman, and Mabry 1971).

Toxic effects of the seeds have been poorly documented. Toxicity may vary considerably, as some individuals have eaten the seeds with no ill effects (Scooter Cheatham, interview, March 1985). A single seed gave me mild stomach discomfort, warning me not to eat any more. David Seigler (letter to the author, 31 March 1986) warns that five or six seeds could be deadly.

Native Americans may have used the seeds as a fish poison and an arrow poison. Archeologists surveying rock shelters in West Texas discovered Mexican buckeye seeds frequently stored with mescal bean seeds (*Sophora secundiflora*). Southwestern native Americans have used the highly toxic mescal beans as a hallucinogen for centuries. That the beans were stored together indicates that the Indians may also have used Mexican buckeye seeds as a hallucinogen. Chemical analysis of the seeds, however, indicates that they do not contain any psychoactive chemicals (Adovasio and Fry 1976).

Plant Characteristics

Mexican buckeye is not directly related to the true buckeye (see "buckeye" in the index). *Ungnadia speciosa* is a shrub or small tree with pinnately compound leaves that alternate on the branches. The large leaflets are serrated. Fragrant rose-colored flowers appear in the spring. The tree is most readily recognized by its pods. Often reddish, the three-lobed woody pod holds three round seeds. The hard shiny seeds, about ½ inch (1.5 cm) in diameter, are dark brown to black with a pale scar. The pods cling to the branches long after the seeds have dropped to the ground. Mexican buckeye grows in the western two thirds of the state to Dallas County and in New Mexico and Mexico. The tree is found in wooded canyons and on rocky hillsides.

SOLANACEAE—NIGHTSHADE FAMILY

The name "nightshade" brings to mind poisonous plants such as the deadly nightshade (*Atropa belladonna*), a European plant used as a source of the medicinal drug atropine. In spite of its bad reputation, the nightshade family includes many important garden vegetables. Tomatoes, potatoes, eggplant, bell pepper, and Texas' favorite, the jalapeño, all are nightshades. "Solanum" probably comes from the Latin "solamen" (meaning "quieting"), referring to the sedative properties of some species. Perhaps the most infamous family member in that regard is tobacco.

Most of these agricultural crops come from the New World, with eggplant originating in tropical Asia. When the tomato first was imported to Europe, people were aghast to think of eating a nightshade. Nonetheless, Europe and the rest of the world soon gained a taste for these curious fruits and their relatives. Even the edible nightshades have their darker side, though, and can cause poisoning. Take a look at the section "Poisons in the Garden" in this chapter for a discussion of the poisonous potential of tomatoes, potatoes, and their relatives.

The highly diverse genus *Solanum* comprises more than a thousand species worldwide, including the potato and the eggplant. Solanine is the predominant glyco-alkaloid, though others may also be present. Solanine is highly toxic and can cause death, but the degree of toxicity varies from species to species and within a species. A single species, such as the black nightshade (*Solanum nigrum* or *S. americanum*) may be highly toxic in one area of the world and yet considered edible in another area (Hackett and Carolane 1982). Black nightshade is described in Chapter 3.

Three Texas plants called wild potatoes allegedly have edible but bitter tubers (Gibbons and Tucker 1979). All three are rare species found only in the mountains of the Trans-Pecos, so whether or not the tubers are safe for food, they are not available. You can consider all 20 Texas species of *Solanum* to have toxic foliage and berries. Besides silverleaf nightshade and Jerusalem-cherry, described in more detail below, the foliage and fruit (ripe and unripe) of the following species are known to have caused human or livestock poisoning: black nightshade (*Solanum americanum* or *Solanum nigrum*), buffalo bur (*Solanum rostratum;* see photograph, plate 16), horse nettle (*Solanum carolinense* and *Solanum dimidiatum*), cutleaf nightshade (*Solanum triflorum*), cockroach berry (*Solanum aculeatissimum*), and hairy nightshade (*Solanum villosum*).

A very few wild Texas species of Solanaceae may be used for food. The ripe fruit of the ground-cherry (*Physalis*) is edible, and the ripe fruit of the chile pequín (*Capsicum annuum*) furnishes a peppery spice. Refer to the index for information and cautions on using these two nightshades. Meanwhile, you will do well to assume that the fruit of all other Texas members of the family can cause poisoning, and that the foliage of all species, including those with edible fruit, is toxic. In addition to references cited below, I relied on Kingsbury (1964), Hardin and Arena (1974), Lampe and Fagerström (1968), Ellis (1978), Heiser (1969), and Keeler, Van Kampen, and James (1978) for information on toxic members of Solanaceae.

Family Characteristics

Nightshades grow as herbs, vines, shrubs, or small trees. The best characteristics to assist you in recognizing the family are those of the flowers. Examine a petunia or a tomato blossom as an example. The flowers vary considerably in size, from the half-inch blooms of Jerusalem-cherry to the six-inch flowers of jimsonweed, but they all have five petals joined together to form either an open star, a bell, a tube, or a trumpet.

The flowers are radially symmetrical, and the stamens (usually five) may merge together to form a prominent yellow beak. The fruit may be a succulent berry or a dry capsule. The leaves are often simple and usually alternate on the stems.

JERUSALEM-CHERRY—*SOLANUM PSEUDOCAPSICUM*

The fruit and leaves of Jerusalem-cherry are highly poisonous. A shrubby plant, it is used as an ornamental indoors and outdoors and may be found growing wild in disturbed soils and woodlands in Southeast Texas. The plant may be confused with the chile pequín (*Capsicum annuum*). The yellow to red succulent berry of the Jerusalem-cherry is round. The narrow or oblong leaves, up to 4 inches (1 dm) long, have entire or slightly wavy margins. The fruit of varieties of chile pequín may be nearly round but are usually oval, or long and tapering. For further descriptions of both plants, refer to the index.

JESSAMINE, JASMINE—*CESTRUM* SPECIES

Three ornamental *Cestrum* shrubs occasionally may be found wild in South Texas and along the Coast. All parts are toxic to humans, livestock, and pets. The succulent berries attract small children and have caused severe poisoning. In the greenish unripe fruits, the alkaloid solanine predominates while the ripe berries are high in tropane-related alkaloids. The variable alkaloid content makes symptoms unpredictable. The poisons can cause severe gastrointestinal distress, hallucinations, paralysis, and death.

Plant Characteristics

Jessamines are evergreen or deciduous shrubs. The simple leaves are alternate, the margins entire. The oblong or lanceolate blades may be 2—6 inches (5—15 cm) long. The small, fragrant flowers form a slender tube or trumpet about 1 inch (2.5 cm) long. Round or oval, the berries are about ⅜ inch (1 cm) long. The day-blooming jessamine *Cestrum diurnum* has white flowers and black berries. The night-blooming jessamine *Cestrum nocturnum* has greenish-white to yellowish flowers, particularly fragrant at night, and white berries. Willow-leaved jessamine, *Cestrum parqui,* has yellowish-green flowers, also especially fragrant at night, and purplish-brown berries.

Jimsonweed—*Datura wrightii*

JIMSONWEED, TOLOACHE—*DATURA* SPECIES
(See illustration.)

In 1676, during the colonial rebellion in Jamestown, Virginia, Royalist soldiers boiled a pot of greens gathered from the wild. The greens caused the men to hallucinate and become partially crazed for several days. The plant the soldiers consumed, *Datura stramonium,* still carries the name jamestown weed, or jimsonweed, in memory of the event (Beverley 1947). Various species of *Datura* have been put to use as hallucinogens by the Algonquins in their manhood initiation rites and by the Hopis, the Zunis, and several other native American tribes, sometimes resulting in the death of the initiates (Emboden 1979). In India, criminals called dhataureas used the drug in knockout drops.

All parts of jimsonweed are highly toxic, with the seeds, leaves, and roots containing high concentrations of the alkaloids atropine, hyoscyamine, and scopolamine. During both world wars, when doctors in the United States faced a shortage of atropine, jimsonweed was cultivated as a substitute source.

According to the 1981 report of the National Clearinghouse for Poison Control Centers, 89 percent of cases of jimsonweed ingestion resulted in poisoning. Adult poisonings usually occur from attempts to use the plant to induce hallucinations. Small children are accidentally poisoned from eating the seeds, chewing the leaves, or sucking the nectar from the flowers. Adults usually recover from the toxic effects, but a few grams (a fraction of an ounce) of the leaf or seeds can kill a child. Livestock and pets also succumb to this highly toxic plant. Even honey made from the poisonous nectar is considered dangerous.

Plant Characteristics

Several species of *Datura* grow in Texas. The Texas species are annual or perennial herbs with lush bad-smelling foliage. The fragrant trumpet-shaped flowers, 3–6 inches (7–15 cm) long, are white to violet. The fruit is a round often spiny capsule about 1–2 inches (3–5 cm) in diameter, with numerous large seeds. *Datura stramonium* is occasionally used as an ornamental.

NIGHTSHADE, SILVERLEAF NIGHTSHADE, TROMPILLO—*SOLANUM ELAEAGNIFOLIUM*
(See illustration.)

Trompillo is a noxious weed in crops, particularly cotton. In Texas the plant has caused considerable loss of cattle, which are highly susceptible to poisoning from the fruit. Unlike the fruit of some other members of the genus, the ripe berries are more toxic than the unripe fruit. A few ounces

Silverleaf nightshade, trompillo—*Solanum elaeagnifolium*

can cause severe poisoning or death in livestock and humans, though human fatalities are rare.

In spite of its toxicity, the plant has been put to a variety of practical uses. The Pimas used the berry as a substitute for rennet in making cheese. The Kiowas combined the fruit with brain tissue for tanning hides. Silverleaf nightshade contains solasodine, a chemical used in the manufacture of steroids (Boyd, Murray, and Tyrl 1984). The unripe fruit or the whole plant can be used to dye wool.

Plant Characteristics

Trompillo is a spiny (occasionally spineless) perennial herb 2−3 feet (6−9 dm) tall. The stems and bottoms of the leaves have a coating of silvery hairs. The oblong simple leaves, 2−6 inches (5−15 cm) long, have entire to wavy margins. Appearing from spring to fall, the purple (occasionally white) blossoms are about 1 inch (2.5 cm) in diameter. The flowers are star-shaped with the yellow stamens forming a protruding beak. About ⅝ inch (15 mm) in diameter, the round, hard berry resembles a tiny tomato. The unripe berry is green, turning yellow, then black in summer and fall. Trompillo grows throughout the state and is particularly abundant in dry limestone and disturbed soils.

TOBACCO—*NICOTIANA TABACUM*
TREE TOBACCO, DESERT TOBACCO—*NICOTIANA* SPECIES
(See photograph, plate 16.)

The members of the genus *Nicotiana* contain the deadly poisonous alkaloid nicotine and several other alkaloids. People have died from eating the raw or cooked leaves of the wild tree tobacco (*Nicotiana glauca*) and the desert tobacco (*Nicotiana trigonophylla*). The flower nectar is also toxic. Ingestion of cultivated tobacco leaves has caused numerous human and livestock deaths. Children have died from swallowing small amounts of tobacco. For further information on tobacco poisoning, see the index.

Plant Characteristics

Tree tobacco is a tall slender shrub with alternate simple leaves that have entire margins. A waxy white coating covers the smooth ovate leaves. The tubular yellow flowers are about 1−2 inches (2.5−4.5 cm) long. The plant grows in far South Texas, the Trans-Pecos, and the eastern part of the Edwards Plateau.

Desert tobacco is a biennial or perennial herb up to 3 feet (1 m) tall. The oblong leaves are covered with sticky hairs, and the tubular flowers, about 1 inch (2.5 cm) long, are greenish-white or yellowish. It grows in South and West Texas.

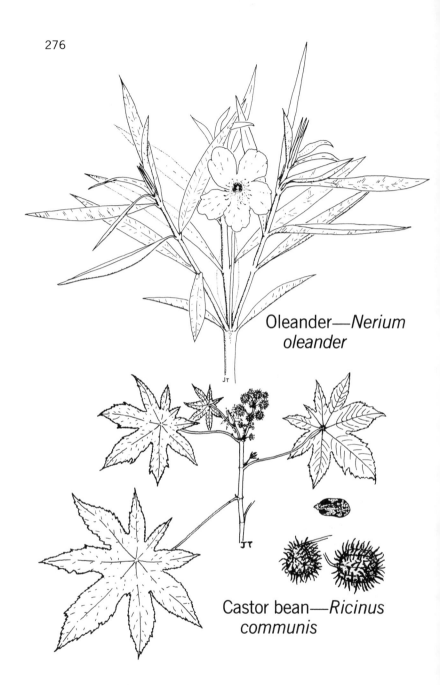

Oleander—*Nerium oleander*

Castor bean—*Ricinus communis*

Toxic Ornamental Houseplants and Yard Plants: The Enemy Within

In 1982 approximately two thirds of the plant ingestions reported to the National Clearinghouse for Poison Control Centers (NCPCC) involved ornamentals, and more than 80 percent of the victims were children under five years old (Mark Fow, letter and documents to the author, 21 November 1984). These statistics emphasize the importance of learning the identity and toxic potential of the plants in and around your own home.

Many plants that poison humans can also poison small pets, such as canaries, parakeets, cats, and dogs. Michael Ellis (interview, January 1986) notes that 10 percent of all poisoning cases reported to the Texas State Poison Center involve pets. While human deaths from wild and ornamental plants are extremely rare, the death of a pet is more likely. Every year a number of cats and dogs die from chewing the leaves of houseplants, such as schefflera and philodendron, and birds are poisoned from toxic seeds. The small body size of children and pets makes them more susceptible to toxins than adults. In addition, the delicate metabolism of cats makes them vulnerable to poisoning by plants that are harmless to humans and other animals.

For the safety of your family and pets, review this list and note which plants grow in your home environment. The list includes ornamentals commonly used in landscapes and as houseplants in Texas. These plants can cause moderate to serious illness. A number of them are considered highly dangerous and have caused numerous deaths in humans, pets, and livestock. Toxic symptoms may begin immediately or be delayed several hours or even days.

If anyone, including your pets, consumes any quantity of the plants listed here or any plant of which you are unsure, you should contact your doctor, veterinarian, or Poison Control Center. Start now to teach your children about the possible hazards of eating ornamental and wild plants. Refer to page 231 for recommended first aid procedures and further information on plant poisoning.

Other plants native to Texas that are used in landscaping may be listed in the chapters on toxic wild plants. If you have a plant not found on this list or elsewhere in this book, do not assume that it is safe. For many plants, reliable information on toxicity simply is not available. Some ornamentals that have been considered nontoxic in previous publications may in fact be toxic. The 1982 NCPCC report shows cases of poisoning occurring with some plants that other regional Poison Control Center publications list as nontoxic. Recent studies on rats and mice, conducted by

Der Marderosian and Roia, indicate that a number of plants previously considered to be nontoxic can cause poisoning (Kinghorn 1979).

For details on the toxicity of wild plants in your environment, refer to the index and to chapters on toxic plants and toxic fruits. Also refer to the index for possible additional information on plants listed here.

In addition to references cited below, I relied on the following for information on toxic ornamentals: Ellis 1978; Kinghorn 1979; Kingsbury 1964, 1965; Hardin and Arena 1974; Lampe and Fagerström 1968; Keeler, Van Kampen, and James 1978; Peterson 1977; James 1973; Mitchell and Rook 1979; Ricciuti 1978; Schmutz and Hamilton 1979; Larkin 1983; National Clearinghouse for Poison Control Centers 1981 bulletin and documents for 1982 (Mark Fow, letter and documents to the author, 21 November 1984); Michael Ellis, interview, January 1986.

AMARYLLIS FAMILY—AMARYLLIDACEAE

Many members of the family contain toxic alkaloids, including the following garden flowers: *Amaryllis, Crinum,* daffodil, jonquil, and narcissus (all three *Narcissus* species), spider lily (*Hymenocallis*), and atamasco lily (*Zephyranthes atamasco*). Though all parts may potentially cause poisoning, the bulbs are the most toxic part. Human poisoning rarely occurs unless the bulbs are mistaken for onions or other edible bulbs. I have found no reports of human deaths from these plants, but pets and livestock have died from consuming them. The bulbs can cause an allergic dermatitis in sensitive individuals. For further information on toxic wild members of the family, refer to the index.

ARUM FAMILY—ARACEAE

Caladium—*CALADIUM* SPECIES
Calla—*CALLA PALUSTRIS, ZANTEDESCHIA AETHIOPICA*
Dumbcane—*DIEFFENBACHIA* SPECIES
Elephant Ear—*COLOCASIA ANTIQUORUM*
Giant Elephant Ear—*ALOCASIA* SPECIES
Philodendron—*PHILODENDRON* SPECIES, *MONSTERA* SPECIES

Several common houseplants belong to the arum family. Chewing on the leaves, stems, or roots of these plants can cause burning and swelling of the mouth, tongue, and throat. Needlelike calcium oxalate crystals and histamine release are two possible causes of the reaction. The swelling can inhibit speech for several days, accounting for the common name "dumbcane" for the *Dieffenbachia* species. Gastrointestinal distress may also occur. The sap of the plants can irritate the skin and cause eye damage. The dumbcanes and the philodendrons account for more than half of all plant poisonings handled by the Texas State Poison Center (Michael Ellis, interview, January 1986). Because the plants burn the mouth, children rarely swallow them, and so human poisoning is usually moderate. Cats and dogs have died, however, from chewing on a number of these species. Some have the potential to cause death in humans, both from the toxic compounds in them and from suffocation, in the event of severe swelling of the tongue and throat. In addition, some individuals develop an allergic dermatitis reaction to these plants. Refer to the index for information on toxic wild members of the family.

AZALEA, RHODODENDRON—*RHODODENDRON* SPECIES—ERICACEAE

All parts of these shrubs can cause poisoning. Paralysis, convulsions, and deaths have occurred in humans. Children have been poisoned from eating the flowers or making a tea of the leaves. Even honey from the nectar can be toxic.

BOXWOOD—*BUXUS SEMPERVIRENS*—BUXACEAE

All parts of this evergreen shrub are toxic and are reported to have caused livestock deaths when consumed in large amounts.

CASTOR BEAN—*RICINUS COMMUNIS*—EUPHORBIACEAE
(See illustration, page 276.)

All parts of the shrub are toxic, especially the seeds. One to three seeds can kill a child, but the hard seed coat may prevent intoxication. The plant can cause a skin rash in sensitive persons. Castor beans occasionally grow wild in Texas.

CHINABERRY—*MELIA AZEDARACH*—MELIACEAE

All parts of the tree are toxic. Although berries of some plants have been eaten with no ill effects, as few as six to eight berries have killed a child. Berries can poison pets and have been used as an insecticide and fish poison. Chinaberry often grows wild in Texas (see the index for details).

CROCUS—*COLCHICUM AUTUMNALE*—LILIACEAE

All parts of the garden flower are toxic, especially the bulbs. For information on the lily family, see the index.

CYCAD, FALSE SAGO PALM—*CYCAS* SPECIES, *ZAMIA* SPECIES—CYCADACEAE

All parts of the palmlike shrubs are toxic to humans and pets. Paralysis and death have occurred from eating the fleshy fruits.

FOUR-O'CLOCK—*MIRABILIS JALAPA*—NYCTAGINACEAE

The roots and seeds of this flowering shrub have caused severe gastrointestinal distress in children.

FOXGLOVE—*DIGITALIS PURPUREA*—SCROPHULARIACEAE

All parts of the garden flower are deadly poisonous. Children have been poisoned by drinking water from a vase that held the cut flowers. Foxglove is the source of numerous important medicinal cardiac glycosides and steroids.

HOLLY, YAUPON—*ILEX* SPECIES—AQUIFOLIACEAE

(See illustration, page 168.)

The red or black berries of the shrubs are toxic. Fatalities have occurred in children who consumed 20 to 30 berries. For further details, refer to the index.

HYACINTH—*HYACINTHUS ORIENTALIS*—LILIACEAE

All parts of the garden flower are toxic, especially the bulb, and cause severe gastrointestinal distress. Sensitive individuals can contract a skin rash from the plant. For further information on toxic and edible members of the lily family, see the index.

HYDRANGEA—*HYDRANGEA* SPECIES—SAXIFRAGACEAE

All parts of the shrub are toxic. The flower buds and leaves have caused human poisoning.

IRIS—*IRIS* SPECIES—IRIDACEAE

The bulb or rhizome and leaves of these garden flowers have caused poisoning. The unpleasant taste of the plant probably has prevented human fatalities. The plant can also cause a skin rash in sensitive individuals. For more information, refer to the index.

IVY, ENGLISH IVY—*HEDERA HELIX*—ARALIACEAE

Children have been seriously poisoned from the berries and leaves. English ivy can cause contact dermatitis in sensitive individuals.

JAPANESE YEW—*PODOCARPUS MACROPHYLLA*—TAXACEAE

The blue or purple berries of the evergreen shrub can cause severe gastrointestinal distress. Leaves have caused death in horses. This plant is related to the red-fruited yew, *Taxus,* which has highly toxic seeds and leaves but is not usually planted in Texas.

JASMINE, CAROLINA JASMINE, YELLOW JESSAMINE, JAMÍN AMARILLO— *GELSEMIUM SEMPERVIRENS*—LOGANIACEAE
(See illustration, page 264.)

All parts of this plant are deadly poisonous, including the flowers, and honey from the flowers is toxic. The plant also can cause a skin rash in sensitive persons. For illustration and details on this native vine, refer to the index.

JERUSALEM-CHERRY—*SOLANUM PSEUDOCAPSICUM*—SOLANACEAE

The shrubby garden and pot plant contains highly toxic alkaloids in both the fruit and the leaves. The round yellow to red berries may be confused with those of chile pequín, which usually are not fully round (refer to the index for descriptions of both species). Jerusalem-cherry occasionally may be found in the wild in Southeast Texas.

JESSAMINE, JASMINE—*CESTRUM* SPECIES—SOLANACEAE

All parts of the shrubs are highly toxic. Poisoning usually involves the attractive white, black, or purple berries. Both ripe and unripe berries can cause serious poisoning, paralysis, and death in humans and pets. For details about the three ornamentals, sometimes found wild in South Texas, refer to the index.

JIMSONWEED—*DATURA* SPECIES—SOLANACEAE
(See illustration, page 272.)

All parts of the shrubby garden flower are highly toxic. Children have died from eating the seeds and leaves. The plant is well known for its hallucinogenic effects. A large percentage of attempts to get high from eating the seeds result in moderate to severe poisoning. The plant also can cause dermatitis in sensitive individuals. For further details on jimsonweed, see the index.

KENTUCKY COFFEE TREE—*GYMNOCLADUS DIOICA*—FABACEAE

The seeds and pods of this plant have caused severe poisoning. Though uncommon in North Texas landscapes, the tree may be confused with the honey locust (*Gleditsia triacanthos*), which has sweet pulp around its seeds. For descriptive information on both plants, see the index.

LANTANA—*LANTANA CAMARA*—VERBENACEAE
(See illustration, page 184.)
Unripe lantana fruit has caused deaths in children, pets, and livestock. The leaves and ripe fruit of the shrub are also toxic. Plant hairs can cause skin rash in sensitive individuals. For details, see the index.

LARKSPUR, DELPHINIUM—*DELPHINIUM* SPECIES—RANUNCULACEAE
All parts of the garden flower are deadly. The seeds, roots, and new growth contain the highest levels of toxic alkaloids. Severe poisoning and death can occur rapidly. Until recent years a lotion prepared from the seeds was used to treat head lice. The lotion was taken off the market because of human poisonings both from ingestion of the lotion and absorption through cuts in the skin. Wild species of larkspurs have caused much cattle loss in the West.

LAUREL CHERRY—*PRUNUS CAROLINIANA*—ROSACEAE
(See photograph, plate 15.)
The leaves, bark, and seeds of the evergreen shrub or tree are highly toxic. The fruit is very astringent and inedible. The seeds and foliage of the edible cherry trees also can cause poisoning (refer to the index).

LIGUSTRUM, PRIVET—*LIGUSTRUM* SPECIES—OLEACEAE
(See photograph, plate 13.)
The blue-black berries, leaves, and possibly other parts of these shrubs and trees are toxic to humans and livestock. Berries have caused fatalities in children. For a description of the plant, refer to the index.

LILY OF THE VALLEY—*CONVALLARIA MAJALIS*—LILIACEAE
All parts of the garden flower are deadly poisonous, and the poison acts rapidly. Part of one leaf can cause death. For further information on toxic and edible members of the lily family, see the index.

MESCAL BEAN, TEXAS MOUNTAIN LAUREL, FRIJOLILLO—*SOPHORA SECUNDIFLORA*—FABACEAE
(See photograph, plate 11.)
All parts of the shrub or tree are toxic to humans and livestock. A single seed can potentially kill an adult, though the hard seed coat usually pre-

vents poisoning. Though Warnock (1970) reports that flowers brought into the house can cause nausea, the Texas State Poison Center has had no reports of such problems. For further information on this native bean, see the index.

MISTLETOE—*PHORADENDRON* SPECIES—VISCACEAE

All parts of this Christmas ornament are highly toxic. Deaths have occurred in children and adults from eating the berries and drinking a tea of them. The plant can cause a skin rash in sensitive persons. For illustration and details about mistletoe, see the index.

MONKSHOOD—*ACONITUM* SPECIES—RANUNCULACEAE

All parts of the garden flower are highly toxic. Convulsions and death can occur in a few hours.

MORNING GLORY—*IPOMOEA VIOLACEA*—CONVOLVULACEAE

Seeds of the vine consumed accidentally by children or for hallucinogenic effects by adults can cause nausea and psychotic reactions. Packaged seeds are treated with toxic insecticides.

NANDINA—*NANDINA DOMESTICA*—BERBERIDACEAE

Cats have been poisoned by the red berries of the shrub. Michael Ellis (interview, January 1986) reports that in humans the only toxic symptom on record is a mildly upset stomach.

OLEANDER—*NERIUM OLEANDER*—APOCYNACEAE
(See illustration, page 276.)

All parts of the shrub are deadly, including the flowers. Honey from nectar may also be toxic. A single leaf is considered lethal to an adult. The plant contains cardiac glycosides. Near deaths occurred recently when two children made a tea of the leaves and flowers. Though one source (Kinghorn 1979) says that smoke from burning the shrubs may be toxic, the Texas State Poison Center has no reported cases.

PERIWINKLE—*VINCA* SPECIES—APOCYNACEAE

The dried leaves of this ground cover have been smoked for a hallucinogenic effect, but the plant contains toxic alkaloids and can cause kidney and liver damage if large amounts are consumed. Compounds derived from *Vinca* are used in medicines for treating childhood leukemia and Hodgkin's disease (Lewis and Elvin-Lewis 1977).

PIGEONBERRY, ADONIS MORADO—*DURANTA REPENS*—VERBENACEAE

The yellow fruit of this South Texas ornamental shrub has caused death in children.

PITTOSPORUM—*PITTOSPORUM* SPECIES—PITTOSPORACEAE

These plants contain toxic saponins. Poisoning usually involves the berries and can cause severe gastrointestinal distress.

POINCIANA, BIRD-OF-PARADISE—*CAESALPINIA GILLIESII*—FABACEAE

The green seeds and pods of this plant have caused gastrointestinal distress. The shrub occasionally grows wild in arid areas of Central and West Texas. Native *Caesalpinia* species may also be toxic. For information on recognizing members of the legume family, see the index.

POINSETTIA—*EUPHORBIA PULCHERRIMA*—EUPHORBIACEAE

All parts of the houseplant can cause gastrointestinal distress, but no reports of death in humans have been verified. The milky sap can irritate skin.

SANSEVIERIA, MOTHER-IN-LAW'S-TONGUE—*SANSEVIERIA* SPECIES—LILIACEAE

Though rarely causing toxicity in humans, the houseplant has caused deaths of dogs and is potentially toxic to humans.

SCHEFFLERA—*SCHEFFLERA* SPECIES—ARALIACEAE

Dogs have died from eating the houseplant. The 1982 NCPCC report indicates several cases of toxic ingestion by children.

SWEETPEA—*LATHYRUS LATIFOLIUS, LATHYRUS ODORATUS,* AND OTHER SPECIES—FABACEAE

Ingestion of a large number of the seeds of this garden vine can cause paralysis and convulsions. For details, see the index.

TALLOW TREE, CHINESE TALLOW TREE—*SAPIUM SEBIFERUM*—EUPHORBIACEAE

The green to blackish fruit of the tree has caused severe gastrointestinal distress, although there are no records of poisoning from the hard white seeds. The leaves and white milky sap are also toxic and irritant. See the index for a description of the plant.

TUNG OIL TREE—*ALEURITES FORDII*—EUPHORBIACEAE

All parts of the tree are toxic, but poisoning usually occurs from confusing the nut with a brazil nut. One to three seeds can produce severe illness. Fatalities are rare, though, and recovery is usually rapid. The plant can cause dermatitis in sensitive individuals. Tung oil trees have been planted in the southeastern part of the state.

WISTERIA—*WISTERIA* SPECIES—FABACEAE
(See photograph, plate 4.)

Pods, flowers, and seeds of the vine are toxic. One or two seeds can cause severe gastrointestinal distress in children. No human fatalities have been reported. See the index for a description of wisteria.

YESTERDAY-TODAY-AND-TOMORROW—*BRUNFELSIA* SPECIES—SOLANACEAE

Dogs have died from eating this houseplant. Consider it potentially toxic to humans.

Poisons in the Garden

Information on poisonous plants would be incomplete without mention of the potentially poisonous plants in our gardens and in our kitchens. We take for granted that the vegetables we eat daily can do us no harm. And yet, many people have an allergic reaction when they eat certain types of foods—peanuts, milk, eggs, wheat, and corn, to name a few. And some people develop an allergic dermatitis after handling certain fruits and vegetables. For example, cashews and mangoes, relatives of poison ivy, can induce a skin rash similar to that caused by the ubiquitous ivy.

Besides causing allergic reactions in some people, a number of our most commonly consumed vegetables can cause illness, even death, when eaten raw or consumed in large quantities. And whether you grow your own vegetables or pick them out at the grocery, it's useful to know that the plants on which some vegetables grow can cause poisoning. Most of us would not think of adding tomato leaves to a salad, for instance, but if your child asked you if she/he could eat the leaves, would you know what to say? As with so many other members of the nightshade family, the foliage of the tomato, *Lycopersicon esculentum,* is poisonous. Children drinking teas made of the leaves have become very ill (Hardin and Arena 1974), and livestock have died from eating the vines.

The chapter on toxic wild plants includes information on numerous toxic nightshades. The edible members of the family—tomatoes, potatoes, eggplant, and the peppers chile, jalapeño, and bell—all have toxic parts. Some persons have a strong allergic reaction to the edible nightshades, and research links the vegetables and fruits to certain types of arthritis. The foliage of all of these plants contains toxic alkaloids. While still green, the fruits of the eggplant (*Solanum melongena*) can cause poisoning. And though we do not think of peppers (*Capsicum*) as toxic, the irritants in the hot peppers can cause severe damage to internal tissues if they are eaten in quantity.

Never eat anything green on a potato, *Solanum tuberosum*. Potatoes allowed to sit out in the sun quickly develop a layer of green beneath the skin. Even ungreen potatoes contain low levels of the alkaloid solanine under the skin. At low levels of toxicity, boiling water will leach out the solanine. But don't eat potatoes raw, and always peel off any green spots and sprouts before cooking the spuds. Throw out any tubers that have a lot of green under the skin or have spoiled (Schmutz and Hamilton 1979). Livestock deaths from eating the raw peelings, sprouts, and vines of potatoes happen occasionally. Human poisonings from potatoes occur very rarely, usually when someone eats green or spoiled potatoes in quantity. For example, all four members of a family became ill after two days of eating cooked potatoes. The potatoes had been allowed to sit in the sun when the family picked them from the garden. Because they did not realize what was causing the illness, they continued to eat the potatoes daily for ten days. Two family members died (Hansen 1925).

We cannot leave our discussion of the nightshade family without mentioning that infamous toxic nightshade tobacco, *Nicotiana tabacum*. Tobacco contains the alkaloid nicotine, one of the most highly toxic alkaloids known. Forty milligrams, a fraction of an ounce, of pure nicotine constitutes a lethal dose for an adult. Eating tobacco or absorbing the toxin through the skin has proven fatal. Tobacco leaf enemas have caused deaths, and one man died in an attempt to avoid paying customs duty by smuggling tobacco leaves wrapped around his body (Kinghorn 1979). His sweat soaked the leaves, enabling the nicotine to become absorbed through his skin. As with most cases of accidental poisoning, the children suffer most often from our neglect. Children have died after swallowing moderate amounts of tobacco. We should not overlook this potential source of poisoning in our homes if we wish to keep our children and pets out of harm's way. Keep all forms of tobacco and pipes containing tobacco out of reach.

While the name "nightshade" bears with it a reputation for toxicity, the rose family, Rosaceae, with its many delicious fruits, would seem safe enough. Nonetheless, members of the genus *Prunus* have caused numerous livestock and human deaths worldwide. The genus includes the trees that bear peaches, plums, apricots, cherries, and nectarines. While the fleshy fruits of all of these provide sweet nutritious foods, other parts of the tree are deadly poisonous. The seeds, foliage, and bark contain high concentrations of cyanogenetic glycosides. When eaten, the glycosides hydrolyze into hydrocyanic acid, or cyanide.

Human cyanide poisoning most frequently occurs from ingestion of the seed kernels inside the stony pits. The classic poisoning story tells of a man who relished apple seeds also in the rose family. He saved up a large number, then ate them all at once. It was his final meal (Ricciuti 1978). In recent years health food enthusiasts have encouraged the eating of apricot seeds as a source of laetrile, allegedly to prevent cancer. Though a single apricot seed probably can be considered safe for an adult, a man who ate 28 died (Michael Ellis, letter to the author, August 1986). A small child reacts to a much lower dose of a toxin than does an adult. As few as two to five apricot or peach kernels can be fatal for a child (Ellis 1978). Cyanide has a very low lethal dose, and death can occur rapidly. Ingestion of a quantity of seeds or leaves of any of these fruit trees should be considered a medical emergency.

A few other vegetables and fruits should be treated with caution. As long as you eat lima beans in the United States, you need not worry, but if you travel outside the States, beware. Lima beans, *Phaseolus limensis* and *P. lunatus,* contain the cyanogenetic glycoside phaseolunatin, which also converts to cyanide in the body. Cyanide levels of lima beans sold in the United States have been monitored since World War I. Before that time, some varieties of the beans imported from India, Indonesia, and Puerto Rico caused human poisoning from the high levels of cyanide (Kingsbury 1964; Allen and Allen 1981). The vines have caused livestock poisoning.

My pet peeve is that produce workers often do not remove the green leafy part of the rhubarb, *Rheum rhaponticum,* before placing the red stalks out for sale. Malic acid, the same compound that makes apples taste sour, flavors the edible stalks, but toxic concentrations of oxalic acid develop in the green blades. Toxicity varies, but a single meal of the blades potentially yields a lethal dose. During World War I, British officials advocated eating rhubarb blades as part of the conservation effort. Several serious poisonings and deaths resulted before the poorly documented advice could be rescinded (Kingsbury 1964).

Surprisingly, the avocado (*Persea americana*), one of my favorite fruits, occasionally causes poisonings in animals. Cattle, goats, and horses have died from browsing on the foliage, branches, seeds, and even the ripe fruit, but I have found no reports of human poisonings. The fruit has caused the death of canaries. And avocado leaves that fell into a pond may have killed several fish.

The plants mentioned above all bear certain parts that are highly toxic, or in rare circumstances the normally edible fruits or vegetables become toxic. But few of us think about the edibility of our common kitchen spices. Spices cannot safely qualify as edible plants. Most contain volatile oils or other substances that could severely irritate soft tissue if eaten as we would a vegetable. Horseradish, a member of the mustard family, contains the strong irritant mustard oil. Horseradish can cause lesions in the gastrointestinal tract that may result in death. Fortunately, the irritants in spices normally would discourage children from swallowing toxic amounts. But relatively small amounts of some spices are deadly. Two nutmeg seeds are sufficient to kill an adult (Keeler, Van Kampen, and James 1978), and two level tablespoons of salt can kill a child. Consider all spices potentially hazardous, and keep them out of the reach of children.

A number of vegetables that cause no problems when eaten as an occasional part of the diet can cause illness if eaten on a daily basis over a period of time. Large servings of cabbage eaten daily, for instance, can suppress iodine intake, eventually causing goiter. Poisonings from cabbage and related vegetables in the mustard family (kale, broccoli, turnips, rape, rutabaga, mustards, and brussels sprouts) almost always happen with livestock that are fed large amounts of the plants. Humans rarely eat these vegetables in large enough amounts or often enough to cause problems. In areas of the world where iodine is low in the diet, however, eating cabbage or its cousins on a regular basis could result in goiter (Keeler, Van Kampen, and James 1978).

Moderation in all things seems to be the message. You cannot remain healthy on a diet consisting largely of a single vegetable. Even onions, if eaten in moderate to large amounts for several days, can cause severe anemia. One large onion a day could cause problems after a while. But again, this type of poisoning predominantly affects livestock who suddenly have access to very large quantities of onions.

I'll close this section with what strikes me as one of nature's strangest ironies, spinach. Although spinach has long been touted as a good source of calcium, researchers have discovered that though the leafy greens do contain calcium, that calcium may not do you any good. Beet tops, spinach, and Swiss chard all contain fairly high concentrations of oxalic acid, as much as 10 percent by dry weight. Oxalic acid tends to tie up calcium, keeping your body from properly absorbing it. Unless you eat other foods or supplements high in calcium, eating these vegetables on a daily basis can eventually deplete your body of that essential nutrient. In a study by E. F. Kohman (1939), rats fed a balanced diet that included spinach as the main source of calcium for 70 days failed to develop good bone structure, and several died. On the other hand, rats fed turnip greens, a vegetable high in calcium and low in oxalic acid, thrived. Other good vegetable sources of calcium are collards, mustard greens, broccoli, kale, and cabbage. Wild vegetables high in calcium and low in oxalic acid are dandelion and amaranth greens. So the next time your parents tell you, "Eat your spinach—it's good for you," just show them this book. Then volunteer to gather dandelion greens for the next meal.

Rashes and Sneezes

Contact Dermatitis

The term "contact dermatitis" refers to any inflammation of the skin caused by contact with a substance. As I reviewed a number of books on the subject of dermatitis, it became apparent that just about anything can bring on a dermatitis reaction in someone. Many manufactured products, such as detergents, petroleum products, and rubber, cause dermatitis. This section includes information on a number of plants that are responsible for skin rashes either because they cause an allergic reaction or because they contain caustic or irritating oils, juices, hairs, or spines.

The symptoms of dermatitis might include several or all of the following: itching, redness, swelling, the development of tiny pimples, blistering, oozing of fluid from the blisters, and the formation of a crust over the blistered skin. The inflammation may last just a couple of days or several weeks, depending on the irritant substance and your personal sensitivity to it. In treating a skin rash, be conservative. Compresses of cool water, applied as needed, may be sufficient to relieve itching while the rash runs its course. Excessive scratching can result in secondary infections, such as impetigo. To protect children from infection, trim their fingernails and keep their hands clean. Contact a doctor if the rash persists or becomes severe or infected.

ALLERGIC CONTACT DERMATITIS

Allergic contact dermatitis develops only in individuals who have become sensitized to certain allergens. The appearance of dermatitis symptoms is delayed, developing several hours or days after contact with the allergen. Though just about any plant can cause an allergic reaction in someone, some species are responsible for allergic reactions in a larger percentage of the population. Dr. Alexander Fisher (1973) reports that poison ivy and its relatives probably cause more allergic dermatitis than all other sensitizers (including nonplant allergens) combined. A full-

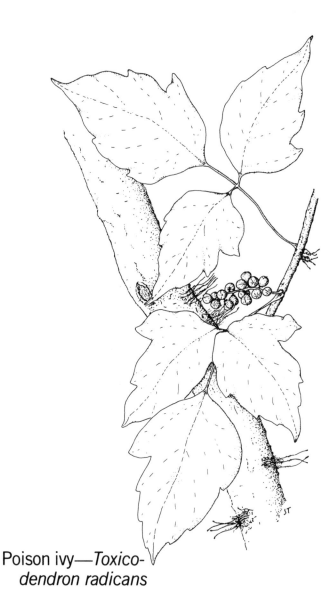

Poison ivy—*Toxico-
dendron radicans*

length discussion of the vine, including its plant characteristics and clues to prevention and treatment of poison ivy rash, begins on page 293.

General rules about allergic sensitivities are difficult to make. Each allergen has its own potential reactivity and so does each individual and each population of individuals. Your personal sensitivity to a certain plant may change at different stages of your life. You may never have had an allergic skin rash in your childhood but suddenly find yourself plagued with rashes in your twenties, thirties, or even in your seventies. You may lose your sensitivity to a particular substance as you age, or you may never lose it. Once you become sensitized to a plant, regular contact with the plant may increase your sensitivity, possibly resulting in more severe reactions over time. Sensitivity may become reduced or eliminated if you succeed in avoiding all contact with the plant for several months or several years. But you may go many years without contact with poison ivy, and then take a jaunt in the woods and develop a skin rash the next morning.

Some plants are more likely to cause an allergic reaction in particular populations than in others. For example, ragweed dermatitis (principally from *Ambrosia artemisiifolia* and *A. bidentata*) affects men 20 times more frequently than women. And false ragweed (*Parthenium hysterophorus*), a native of the United States that has recently become a weed in India, is causing an epidemic of allergic dermatitis among adult men in that part of the world.

Drs. Mitchell and Rook (1979) report that the initial sensitizing contact with a plant does not produce a dermatitis reaction. The body typically requires several days to develop full sensitivity by sending sensitized lymphocytes into the blood system. Once a person becomes sensitized, however, subsequent contacts with the plant result in the development of symptoms usually within two days (rarely sooner than eight hours and rarely as long as ten days later).

My first close encounter with poison ivy provides a typical example of the development of sensitivity. Over several years of frequent hikes through the woods, I had never developed a poison ivy rash. During a summertime hike at age 25, I answered the calls of a youth clinging to the rocks on a slope ten yards below my feet. While I crawled down through the vegetation to assist him, he made his way to safety in another direction. The boy suffered no harm, but I found myself entangled in a bed of poison ivy! With a few mild oaths in the direction of the wayward youth, I returned home.

To my surprise, I did not develop a rash as a result of my adventure. I breathed a sigh of relief, assuming that I was one of the lucky few with a true immunity to the treacherous vine. One week after my first excursion, I ventured out on another trek, throwing my backpack over my shoulder. That was my mistake. The backpack was the same one I had been wearing when I plunged through the brush a week before. Not realizing that urushiol, the allergenic oleoresin found in the sap of poison ivy, could cling to clothing indefinitely, I had not washed the pack. It takes a minimum of six days for the body to develop a sensitivity to urushiol. On the seventh day, all I had to do was to pick up the contaminated pack to re-expose myself to the allergen. The next morning, I woke up with my first full-scale, full-body poison ivy rash.

Certain allergenic substances may occur in several different species of plants. If you develop sensitivity to one of those plants, you may also have a cross sensitization to some or all of the other species containing the same or similar substance. For example, if you are allergic to one species of poison ivy, expect to have a similar reaction to the other species of poison ivy and to poison sumac—all members of the genus *Toxicodendron.* Sensitivity to poison ivy does not mean that you will also be allergic to other members of the sumac family, such as the cashew, mango, pistachio, and wild sumacs. If you belong to the small percentage of the population that has become sensitized to cashews, mangoes, or pistachios, however, stay away from the wild sumacs and the poison ivies.

Gardeners or florists working with chrysanthemums may develop an allergic reaction to the flowers. Once becoming sensitized to one member of the sunflower family, those persons may also react to any of a large number of other members of the family, such as daisies, asters, lettuce, chicory, or thistles (see the index for information on identifying members of the sunflower family).

Because we come in contact with ornamental plants more often than with wild plants, ornamentals frequently become sensitizers and cause skin rashes. Primroses (*Primula* species), geraniums, and the bulbs of many garden flowers such as daffodils, lilies, and tulips can also cause problems for florists and gardeners. See the section on toxic ornamental houseplants and yard plants in this chapter for information about additional ornamentals that commonly cause dermatitis. A large number of food plants also are responsible for skin irritations. Oranges, lemons, grapefruit, onions, garlic, artichokes, spinach, beets, asparagus, potatoes, tomatoes, and pineapple have caused dermatitis, as have many spices.

Wild plants noted for causing allergic reactions include ragweeds (*Ambrosia,* illustrated), sneezeweeds (*Helenium*), wormwood and mugwort (*Artemisia*), chamomile and mayweed (*Anthemis*), marsh elder (*Iva*), cocklebur (*Xanthium*), and *Gaillardia,* all members of the sunflower family. The trumpet creeper vine (*Campsis radicans*) and the inky juice in the husk of walnuts can cause dermatitis. Grasses and grains may produce dermatitis in harvesters. Foresters and tree cutters may develop allergies not only to the woods with which they work (particularly poplars, in the United States) but also to lichens growing on the trees.

Poison Ivy, Poison Oak, Poison Sumac—*TOXICODENDRON RADICANS* and Other Species—ANACARDIACEAE
(See illustration, page 290.)

About 50 percent of the people in the United States have had a run-in with poison ivy rash at least once. Probably less than half of the others have a true immunity to urushiol, the oleoresin found in the sap (Ellis 1978; Mitchell and Rook 1979). If you have not yet contracted the rash, chances are that previous circumstances have not been quite right for the sap to cause sensitivity in your body. If you maintain a cautious attitude toward the plant, you may avoid the rash indefinitely. But don't show off to the neighbors by pulling up the plant bare-handed.

Merely brushing against any part of the plant—the leaves, vines, or berries—releases the sap to do its damage. Even if you wear protective clothing, you may still be exposed to the sap indirectly. If you step on the ivy and then touch your boots, if you dig the plant out of the flower bed and then handle the blade of the shovel, or if you pet the family dog after a romp in the woods, the urushiol can be transferred to your skin. Burning the vines is also a no-no. The resin can become airborne, causing an all-over rash and possible respiratory complications.

Once you become sensitized to the plant, a process that requires a minimum of six days, subsequent contacts with the plant usually result in the development of the earliest symptoms—itching, redness, and bumps—within a day or two. The rash may not progress beyond that point. But frequently, oozing blisters develop that eventually form crusty sores. Contrary to popular belief, the fluid in the blisters does not contain any allergenic substance (Fisher 1973). If the rash spreads beyond the initial area of contact, it has not been spread by the oozing fluids. If you did not wash your body and clothing soon after contacting the plant, however, you may have spread the sap that remains on the surface of your skin to other areas of your body. Sometimes, old rash sites seem to be reactivated by the development of a new rash.

In rare cases, individuals become highly sensitized and the skin rash can progress into systemic complications, including vomiting, diarrhea, fever, convulsions, and kidney inflammation. A woman recently died from kidney shutdown resulting from a severe reaction to poison ivy (Michael Ellis, interview, January 1986). She had been exposed to the ivy sap every fall while washing her husband's hunting clothes.

Fortunately, most rashes are limited to a maddening itch and blisters that finally, thankfully, subside in their own good time. If protected from infection, the rash will run its course in about seven to fourteen days. With careful early treatment, the duration and severity of the rash can be reduced dramatically.

The trick to dealing with poison ivy rash is to catch it as early as possible. Even better, anticipate the skin eruption before it develops. Any time that you go out walking in areas infested with the ivy, bathe your skin well as soon as you get home. Plain soap and water may be sufficient. I use an astringent wash (either one of the teas mentioned below or a poison ivy wash from the drugstore) to be sure to remove the unbound urushiol from the surface of my skin. Research shows that urushiol can bind with the skin within ten minutes (Fisher 1973). Washing your skin may not prevent the itch from developing, but by removing any unbound urushiol from the surface of your skin, you protect other areas of your body from contamination. Also remove contaminated clothes as soon as possible, and wash them separately.

Start treating the pimplelike bumps as soon as they begin to itch. The longer you wait, the more severe the blistering can become. The first goal of treating poison ivy rash is to prevent scratching of the inflamed areas. The easiest way to prevent scratching is by relieving the itch. In the early stages of the rash, a simple cool-water or aloe vera compress, applied frequently throughout the day and night, may be sufficient.

While water provides the safest method of treatment, it often simply does not provide sufficient relief. A warning must preface any experimentation with home remedies or druggists' remedies, however. A number of poison ivy treatments available at drugstores contain ingredients, such as benzocaine, that are potent sensitizers themselves, causing dermatitis reactions in large numbers of people. Consult your doctor for recommendations on ointments that work well with the least likelihood of allergic reaction. Dr. Fisher recommends cold compresses of Burow's solution in the early stages of the rash, with cold compresses of boric acid for eyelids. Refer to his book *Contact Dermatitis* (1973) for suggested treatment of advanced cases.

I have found several home-prepared herbal remedies to be quite effective for relieving the itch. In fact, I often have had better luck with my fresh home brews than with drugstore remedies. A tea made with gumweed (*Grindelia squarrosa*, photographed), giant ragweed (*Ambrosia trifida*, illustrated), or dock (*Rumex*, illustrated) or a decoction of jewelweed (*Impatiens capensis*) produces an astringent liquid. To prepare the tea, pour boiling water over a bowlful of the *fresh* leaves of ragweed, gumweed, or dock. Let the tea steep until it cools. With jewelweed (unfortunately rare in Texas), boil the leaves and succulent stems for a few minutes, and use the cooking water as your astringent wash. Dabbed on your skin, the cooled liquid pacifies the itch temporarily and seems to help dry up the bumps. Of these herbal remedies, Scooter Cheatham (interview, March 1985) has had success with only jewelweed and gumweed. I have found the more common ragweed soothing, and I have had excellent results with aloe vera juice as well. Even a freshly made dilute solution of bleach (1 part bleach to 9 parts water) provides relief.

With any of these treatments, you can count on repeating the applications several times throughout the day, possibly for several days. Homemade teas have a short shelf life. Renew your supply every few days. Euell Gibbons (1966) sometimes froze his jewelweed concoctions to preserve them.

Warning

All of these plants can cause skin irritation themselves, so take your personal sensitivities into consideration before using them. Wear gloves while collecting the fresh plants, as the stiff hairs on gumweed and ragweed and the acids in jewelweed and dock may irritate your skin. Though some of the small ragweeds are themselves responsible for considerable allergic dermatitis, Drs. Mitchell and Rook (1979) report that giant ragweed rarely causes sensitization.

I have found that if I begin my treatments as soon as I become aware of the rash, the rash doesn't develop beyond those first few bumps, and it clears up completely in one to a few days. But if left to its own devices, the rash tends to spread and become more severe. At that stage, my home brews seem less effective, and nonsterile teas could contribute to infection.

Contact your doctor for his or her recommendations for treating the more severe inflammations. And resign yourself to a couple of weeks of agony. Once you've suffered through a turn with poison ivy, you'll agree wholeheartedly with the maxim "An ounce of prevention is worth a pound of cure."

A few individuals have touted the virtues of eating the young leaves of poison ivy with the hope of building up an immunity to urushiol. Besides being ineffective, this practice is dangerous (Lampe and Fagerström 1968). You'll find it much easier to tolerate the external skin rash than the swelling and painful itching that can erupt in the sensitive tissues of your mouth. And remember that what goes in must come out! Besides the dermatitis symptoms, other symptoms such as vomiting, diarrhea, and occasionally severe systemic problems can develop from ingestion of the leaves and berries.

In hundreds of years of experience with the plant, people have made little progress in producing treatments for the rash that can beat those used for centuries by native Americans across the continent. Members of the medical profession have come to the conclusion that no preventive or curative treatment works consistently, and I agree (Mitchell and Rook 1979). An interesting development in poison ivy treatments is an old idea made new, a combination of the red man's and the white man's ingenuity. Michael Ellis, of the Texas State Poison Center, recommends a product called Easy-Ivy (also marketed as Ex-Nolo-Thylene) as the best poison ivy treatment that his center has tried. On contacting Bethurum Research and Development in Texas City, I learned the history of the spray mist product. George Bethurum manufactures Easy-Ivy from a special extract of three wild plant roots. Members of a California Indian tribe prepare the extract for him. I have found several other ivy ointments manufactured from wild plants.

Plant Characteristics

A native of North America and eastern Asia, poison ivy has been accidentally transported and now grows like a weed in England, continental Europe, Australia, and South Africa. Several species of poison ivy or poison oak grow in the United States and Texas, as well as one species of poison sumac.

Recognizing the poison ivies, some of the most widespread wild plants in the country, is not as simple as you might think. The chameleonlike nature of the herbs makes them easy to overlook until you are smack-dab in the middle of a patch. Even the adage "Leaflets three, let it be" will not always save you. Though the plants almost always produce the familiar clusters of three leaflets, in a few areas of the state you may run across a vine with five (and more rarely seven) leaflets. The leaflets vary in size and shape, the more common varieties having smooth, glossy, bright green surfaces. Very young leaves may have a reddish tint. The margins of the leaflets may be smooth or lobed or bear irregular teeth. In some varieties the leaflets resemble the lobed leaves of an oak, thus the common name "poison oak." The leaves alternate on the stems, a characteristic that distinguishes them from the compound leaves of the box elder tree, which occur in pairs. In the fall the dying leaves turn beautiful shades of red and gold, tempting you to pick them up to add color to flower arrangements. But beware: even the dead leaves and vines are dangerous.

If you think you're looking at poison ivy, but you just aren't sure, look (but not too closely) for clusters of tiny white flowers in the spring, followed by cream-colored waxy berries in the summer. The white berries clearly distinguish the plant from other common vines, such as Virginia creeper.

The poison ivies take on a variety of growth habits. One may form a low-growing ground cover, almost buried amid a dozen other herbs beneath the shade of a tree. Another may resemble a shrub, or it may twine up a tree trunk or along a fence. If you think you've got the characteristics down pat, just travel to another part of the country. You may have to learn to recognize poison ivy all over again.

The most common species in the United States is *Toxicodendron radicans,* with numerous varieties found in Texas. This species grows from

Canada to Guatemala and in eastern Asia. *Toxicodendron toxicarium* grows on the Atlantic and Gulf coasts and has expanded its range west into East Texas and north into Oklahoma and Kansas *Toxicodendron rydbergii* extends south from Canada into the northeastern and the northwestern United States and into the Texas Panhandle and the Trans-Pecos. Western poison oak, *T. diversilobum,* grows only along the Pacific Coast of the United States, British Columbia, and Baja California (Gillis 1971). Deciding which species you have in your back yard hardly matters. The common names "poison ivy" and "poison oak" are used interchangeably, and even the scientific names have gone through a number of revisions. If you are sensitive to one species or variety, expect to be sensitive to all, including the shrubby cousin poison sumac, *T. vernix.*

Poison sumac bears pinnately compound leaves with five to thirteen elliptic leaflets that have entire margins. Like the vining species, it produces white, creamy, or greenish berries, which easily distinguish it from the nonpoisonous sumacs (refer to the index for information on those). Fortunately for us Texans, plagued with so many different species and varieties of poison ivy, poison sumac grows only in bogs and swamps and along streamsides in a limited area of deep East Texas, predominantly between Shelby and Hardin counties.

Pollen Dermatitis

The pollen of some plants causes an allergic contact dermatitis. Fortunately for us hay fever sufferers, we are no more susceptible to allergic dermatitis than are individuals who do not suffer from hay fever or asthma (Fisher 1973). The small ragweeds *Ambrosia artemisiifolia* and *A. bidentata* are among the most common causes of pollen dermatitis. An oleoresin in the pollen, as well as on the leaves and stems, causes the allergic reaction. Several other members of the sunflower family, such as chrysanthemums, cause pollen dermatitis. Some trees that produce abundant pollen (elm, maple, box elder, cottonwood, poplar, and ash, for example) also may be culprits. Surprisingly, and most fortunately, Drs. Lampe and Fagerström (1968) report that poison ivy does not have allergenic pollen.

Photodermatitis

After coming in contact with certain allergens, such as fig leaves, sensitized persons develop redness, itching, and other symptoms of dermatitis only when their skin is exposed to light (Lampe and Fagerström 1968). Other plants noted for causing photodermatitis include members of the carrot family (such as carrots, fennel, parsnips, dill, parsley, and celery—refer to "carrot family" in the index for a list of some of the wild members of the family), mustard, buttercup (*Ranunculus*), lamb's-quarters, and yarrow.

IRRITANT DERMATITIS

Chemical Irritants

Certain plants contain juices or needlelike crystal structures that irritate the skin and may result in temporary or permanent eye damage. These substances can cause immediate itching, redness, and sometimes blistering in anyone; thus the reaction is not an allergic one. As a treatment, washing the affected area in cool water often is sufficient to relieve pain. Contact a doctor in the event of any injury to the eyes or any severe reactions to the plants.

Quite a few of these plants also can produce an allergic skin rash in sensitive individuals. Because of the strong irritants, all of these plants are moderately to severely poisonous if consumed (the acidic wild grapes may be eaten when cooked). Many of these plants contain toxic alkaloids in addition to the irritants.

Narcissus and hyacinth bulbs and the bulbs and leaves of the elephant ear and other members of the arum family (refer to the index) contain compounds that irritate the skin of gardeners. The acid in some raw wild grapes chafes the skin. Most agaves have a caustic sap that can blister the skin of workers harvesting the plants for fibers. Guayule, a native source of rubber, also contains an irritant (Bungay 1981).

Several members of the buttercup family, Ranunculaceae, contain highly caustic, acrid juices, particularly buttercups (*Ranunculus*), clematis vines (*Clematis*), and pasqueflower (*Anemone patens*) (Kingsbury 1964; Ricciuti 1978; Mitchell and Rook 1979). The sap of many plants contains an irritant milky latex, such as the milky or colored sap of poppies (*Papaver* species) and prickly poppies (*Argemone* species), and the white sap of mulberries and lettuce plants.

Many members of the spurge family, Euphorbiaceae, irritate the skin, and some can severely blister it. Members of the spurge family have caused quite a bit of illness and death in livestock. African warriors have used the milky sap of some of the highly caustic species of *Euphorbia* as an arrow poison (Kinghorn 1979). Snow-on-the-mountain (*Euphorbia marginata*), snow-on-the-prairie (*E. bicolor,* photograph on plate 10), candelilla, poinsettia, bull nettle (*Cnidoscolus texanus*), and Chinese tallow tree have an irritant white milky sap. Some of the crotons (*Croton* species) contain a highly irritant oil. The oils of the castor bean and the tung oil tree can cause allergic dermatitis.

Many spices also can be irritants. United States postal carriers use a tear gas made from the oleoresin of cayenne peppers (*Capsicum*). Many members of the mustard family (listed in the chapter "Teas and Spices") contain strongly acrid mustard oil. Pure mustard oil can cause blindness. A mustard plaster left in place too long may have been responsible for the death of a child (Mitchell and Rook 1979). Smartweeds (*Polygonum*) also contain a peppery oil.

Mechanical Irritants

The spines, thorns, prickles, and stiff hairs found on many plants can cause immediate irritation simply from mechanical injury. In most cases, removing the spines and cleaning the affected area relieves the pain and prevents infection. The spiny parts sometimes contain a chemical irritant as well that prolongs the irritation and may cause allergic dermatitis. The tiny hairlike spines, called glochids, found at the base of the long spines on prickly pair cactus, are difficult to remove from the skin. Glochids can cause a skin rash resembling scabies (Lampe and Fagerström 1968), and both glochids and the larger spines of cacti can cause severe infection if they are not removed and the area is not well cleaned. Agaves, yuccas, mesquite trees, thistles, rosebushes, and horse nettle (*Solanum carolinense*) have irritating spines that can cause a skin rash. The stiff hairs on lantanas, jimsonweeds, figs, and elm leaves have been responsible for inflammations.

Stinging Nettles

Perhaps the most interesting examples of mechanical and chemical ir-ritants combined are found in the plants with stinging bristles, often collectively referred to as stinging nettles. The following wild Texas plants bear stinging hairs: the true stinging nettles (*Urtica* species), bull nettle (*Cnidoscolus texanus*), noseburns (*Tragia* species), and stinging cevallia (*Cevallia sinuata*). These plants come from different families: the bull nettle and noseburns from Euphorbiaceae, the true nettles from Urticaceae, and cevallia from Loasaceae.

In general, most stinging plants act like miniature hypodermic needles. Contact with the bristles breaks off the tip, enabling the sharp point to penetrate the skin. The bending hair puts pressure on a bulbous sac at its base, forcing the toxic fluids through the tubular bristle into the skin. The fluids cause an immediate stinging and itching and may produce redness and bumps. In most cases the pain subsides in a few minutes or an hour, but the redness and itching may persist for several days. For a mild sting, cool water may be sufficient to reduce the pain. Michael Ellis of the Texas State Poison Center recommends either a dilute solution of bleach (1 part bleach to 9 parts water) if you are near home when the sting occurs, or a product such as Easy-Ivy (formerly known as Ex-Nolo-Thylene) to carry along on hikes to relieve stings.

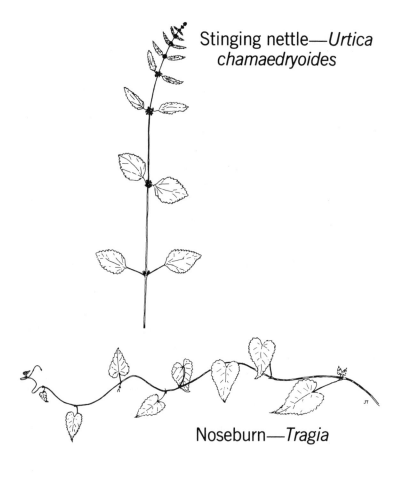

Stinging nettle—*Urtica chamaedryoides*

Noseburn—*Tragia*

Though severe reactions in humans are rare, if nausea, vomiting, or difficult breathing develops, call for medical help immediately. *Urtica* species have caused serious toxic reactions in dogs and livestock, but American species are mild compared with those in some other parts of the world. A New Zealand species has killed horses, and a species in New Guinea is attributed with at least one human death (Thurston and Lersten 1969).

Studies attempting to determine the factors involved in the sting have come up with inconclusive results. Various species of stinging plants were long thought to contain formic acid, which is similar to the acid that makes ant bites so painful. Recent work by Thurston (1974) shows no evidence of formic acid in the *Urtica* species he studied. The stinging principle in some species includes histamine, acetylcholine, 5-hydroxytryptamine, and some undetermined compounds. The bristle tips, made of silica, add a mechanical source of injury. At least one irritant factor in *Tragia* species is the presence of calcium oxalate crystals in the bristles.

The true stinging nettles vary considerably in their potency. I have had run-ins only with *Urtica chamaedryoides,* in Central and South Texas. The pain was more intense than with the fairly mild noseburns I've handled, and it lasted longer. Twenty-four hours after my encounter, I still experienced a mild pain and some redness. With noseburns, the irritation usually subsides in a few minutes, and all redness and bumps disappear within an hour or so. I have collected noseburns and the small nettles bare-handed. The tough skin on my fingertips has saved me from the sting. If the stinging hairs brush against my legs, arms, or the tops of my fingers, however, I know it immediately. For descriptions of *Urtica* and *Tragia* species, and information on how to cook the leaves for food, refer to the index. The true stinging nettles do not grow in abundance in Texas, but noseburns are common.

Stinging cevallia, a perennial herb to 2 feet (6 dm) tall, grows only in the western half of the state, particularly along the Rio Grande. The bristle-covered plant produces small yellow flowers.

Bull nettle (*Cnidoscolus texanus,* photograph on plate 9) is considered one of the most painful nettles in the United States and grows commonly throughout most of Texas. Unlike the relatively inconspicuous true nettles and noseburns, which usually introduce themselves by their sting, bull nettle is easier to spot. So far I have avoided an unplanned encounter with the plant. Its large white flowers distinguish it from the other plants with stinging hairs. In addition to its sting, bull nettle contains irritant white sap that is poisonous. You can eat the smooth seeds that develop inside the bristly capsules, though. Refer to the index for details.

Giant ragweed—
Ambrosia trifida

Short ragweed—
Ambrosia artemisiifolia

Hay Fever Plants

If you have recently left the bitter cold of the North to bask in the sunny climes of Texas, you may soon discover that you have traded a winter of shoveling snow for a winter of blowing your nose. Texas has the dubious distinction of being one of the few states in the Union where you can suffer from hay fever every month of the year.

Because Texas has such a long growing season, those extra months of green also mean extra months when trees, shrubs, herbs, and grasses can flower and produce pollen. A great deal of the state remains fairly humid much of the year, but especially in the fall and winter, encouraging the growth of molds. Wafted on gentle breezes and hard gales, pollen and mold spores make their way to your nose in the fall, winter, spring, and summer.

How can you tell if you are one of the 7 percent of Americans who suffer from hay fever? The symptoms may fool you into thinking you just have a cold. But rather than going away in a few days, the runny nose and frequent sneezes continue and may come and go for weeks. Additional symptoms may include itchy, watery eyes and an itchy throat, congested sinuses, headache, sore throat, cough, fatigue, and irritability. Your reaction may differ slightly with different allergens. Even if you never had hay fever before, you may develop allergies to the potent pollens in Texas several years after you move to the sunny state.

For some people, hay fever develops into something even more troublesome than a runny nose. Respiratory complications such as asthma, bronchitis, or pneumonia can occur. Unfortunately for the 15 million Americans who suffer from the malady each year, no cure exists for pollen allergies, and the wide variety of treatments have only limited success. As a result, Americans spend half a billion dollars annually in medical care and drugs for treating allergies, money that many of the same individuals will cough up (ahem) year after year (Newman 1984).

In spite of the problems that pollen and mold spores cause humans, they provide us with so many of the necessities of life that we could not survive without them. A fundamental ingredient in the sexual reproduction of plants, pollen bears the genetic material produced by the male organs of plants. That material is necessary for the fertilization of the female ovaries, which enclose the seeds that will develop into the next generation of plants. Mold spores differ from pollen in that they emerge from fruiting bodies of fungi. Microscopic spores carried by the breezes land randomly across the countryside, and where a suitable substrate exists, the spores grow into new fungi.

Flowering plants have a great variety of ways for transporting their pollen. Everyone has observed a bee or butterfly land on a beautifully colored flower, stealing inside to capture some of its sweet nectar. When the insect leaves, it carries with it a small load of pollen. The insect deposits its bundle on the next flower visited. If the plant's luck holds out, the next flower visited is the same species as the first, the ovaries become fertilized, and fruits develop.

The whole process of pollination has been intricately worked out over millions of years of plant evolution. It involves careful timing and the cooperation of an outsider—a risky business. The pollinator need not be an insect; birds and bats also can carry out that role. Wind pollination is a simple yet amazingly well orchestrated process. The male flowers, rather than producing showy, colorful petals, usually consist of little more than a cluster of stamens. The flowers may line an erect spike atop a ragweed plant or form drooping tassels hanging from a pecan tree. The wind carries the pollen randomly through the air, hopefully in large enough quantities and far enough to enable it to brush against a ripe female flower of the same species. Wind pollination is enormously successful in Texas, where vast open plains encourage strong winds to well up frequently throughout the year.

Not all types of pollen cause hay fever. For pollen to be a significant cause of hay fever, it must attach loosely to the plant and be buoyant, so that it will float a considerable distance in the wind. The pollen grains must actually irritate the sinuses, a rather poorly defined quality known as allergenic toxicity. And finally, the pollen must be produced in abundance (Wodehouse 1971).

Many insect-pollinated plants, particularly members of the sunflower family, yield allergenic pollen, but most insect-pollinated plants do not need to produce abundant pollen to ensure effective pollination, and usually the pollen is not very buoyant. Thus, few insect-pollinated plants are causes of hay fever. On the other hand, not all wind-pollinated plants bear allergenic pollen. Pines produce prodigious quantities of highly buoyant pollen that may travel more than a thousand miles before it comes to earth. I have seen cars in East Texas covered with a yellow film of pollen in the spring. Luckily for us, Dr. Wodehouse (1971) maintains that pine pollen is not particularly irritating and causes very little hay fever.

Let's examine the seasonal Texas plants that do produce abundant, buoyant, allergenic pollen. Data on pollen problems in Texas come from Wodehouse (1971), Newman (1984), Quel (1984), and pollen counts reported in San Antonio, Austin, and Dallas newspapers.

FALL

Autumn is one of the most pleasant times to be outdoors in Texas. The September rains furnish a welcome respite from the heat of summer. Fall wildflowers create beautiful sceneries across the countryside. Gentle breezes blow. But all summer long, even when many other plants die back in the worst part of the season, giant ragweed (*Ambrosia trifida,* illustrated) has been growing taller and taller, waiting only for the replenishing rains of late summer to provide the moisture for its last burst of growth before its 10- to 20-foot tall stalks burst into bloom.

Late summer to early fall is ragweed season throughout much of the United States, and that's when Texas' largest ragweed, giant ragweed, struts its stuff in the eastern and northern halves of the state. But in Texas, we have eight species of ragweed with which to wage battle, and some of the western species can begin blooming in the early summer. Ragweeds account for more hay fever in the United States than all the other pollen producers combined. Giant ragweed is the most conspicuous because of its impressive size and large leaves. The other species of *Ambrosia,* though small insignificant-looking weeds, nonetheless also produce an abundance of highly allergenic pollen.

Even giant ragweed, with its inconspicuous green spikes of flowers, generally goes unnoticed by the casual observer. Meanwhile goldenrod (*Solidago* species; see photograph), frequently blooming side by side with ragweed, yields showy spikes of yellow wildflowers. Goldenrod frequently takes the blame for many a September sneeze that is actually caused by ragweed. Although goldenrod pollen is allergenic, it usually is produced in fairly small quantities and is not as buoyant as that of ragweed. If you bring a large bouquet of goldenrod into your living room, it could indeed cause an allergic reaction, but its camouflaged cousin ragweed needs only to be within a few blocks of your home to cause runny noses, itchy eyes, and downright misery well into October. Another plant that may be unfairly blamed for hay fever is the sunflower. If you walk by a field full of sunflowers (*Helianthus annuus*) on a breezy day in late summer, you may catch enough of the fairly buoyant pollen to cause some sneezes, but sunflowers are significant factors in hay fever only where they grow in abundance. (Refer to the index for further information about and uses of goldenrod, sunflowers, and ragweeds.)

Although most trees bloom in the spring or summer, cedar elm (*Ulmus crassifolia*) blooms in the late summer and fall. Its allergenic pollen hangs on long tassels called catkins. Breezes toss the drooping catkins about, shaking the pollen loose and adding another dose of allergen to the already pollen-laden autumn air.

Ragweeds occur all over the state, but cedar elms grow mainly in Central and South Texas. Pelocote, or marsh elder (*Iva annua*), causes some hay fever in East Texas, and in West Texas you can count on the addition of tumbleweed (illustrated) pollen to your fall ragweed dose. Seeds of tumbleweed, *Salsola kali,* were accidentally introduced into the United States in 1873 in Eurasian flaxseed (Foster, Rawles, and Karpiscak 1980). The fast-spreading plant quickly became a nuisance weed and a major cause of hay fever in the Southwest.

Along with pollen, an outburst of mold spores is encouraged by the fall rains. In all seasons the dustlike spores can form a background of nasal irritants. Rather than allowing us a respite between ragweed fever in early fall and cedar fever (described below) in the winter, mold spores fill the gap, keeping us on our toes.

WINTER

In Texas, allergists stay the busiest in winter. From late December to February, mountain cedar, *Juniperus ashei* (see photograph), takes up where ragweed leaves off, testing your sinuses and your patience. Once the cedars get going, thick yellow masses of pollen can fill the air for as long as eight weeks. In some years the trees start producing pollen as early as October, and in others pollen production may stretch into April. The male trees turn golden brown when pollen production is at its peak. Mild winters provide us with warm sunny days but promote such high pollen yields that many of us cannot afford to enjoy the sunshine. Mountain cedar is one of the most abundant trees on the Edwards Plateau and extends somewhat to the north and south of the plateau. More appropriately called junipers, members of the genus *Juniperus* are not true cedars. Several species of junipers grow in Texas, all yielding allergenic pollen. Mountain cedar produces the most highly allergenic pollen of any juniper in the United States. In Central and West Texas, red-berry juniper (*J. pinchotii*) comes in as a close second. Most of the other species, including eastern red cedar (*J. virginiana*), bloom in the spring and cause fewer hay fever problems.

SPRING AND SUMMER

Now that you've survived the Texas winter, you look forward to a pleasant spring. While your Yankee cousins fight blizzards, you have started your spring garden. Soon wildflowers blanket the roadsides and fields throughout Texas, a spectacular sight that almost makes up for missing that autumn color change. But along with the colorful flowers come the not so colorful and not so welcome wind pollinators. For spring is the season of trees, when the majority of the wind-pollinated trees begin to bloom.

Wodehouse (1971) reports that the spring trees cause much less hay fever than ragweed and mountain cedar do. Nonetheless, some of the spring bloomers can cause some particularly severe cases of hay fever in susceptible individuals. The trees that cause the most problems include oaks (particularly the live oaks *Quercus virginiana* and *Q. fusiformis*), pecan, cottonwood, and mesquite (illustrated), which is both wind- and insect-pollinated. In the eastern part of the state, river birch (*Betula nigra*) causes problems, and in the Trans-Pecos, Arizona ash (*Fraxinus velutina*), which is also a common ornamental in Central Texas suburbs, can be a major factor. Four-wing saltbush (*Atriplex canescens*), a western shrub, is one of the most important contributors to hay fever in the Southwest and blooms from spring to fall.

The ornamentals paper mulberry (*Broussonetia papyrifera*), white mulberry (*Morus alba*), and privets (*Ligustrum* species), as well as the native red mulberry (*Morus rubra,* illustrated), can cause quite a lot of hay fever where they grow in large numbers. Other native trees often used ornamentally cause problems in localized areas: elms, box elder (*Acer negundo*) and other maples, hackberries (*Celtis* species), Osage orange (*Maclura pomifera*), sycamore (*Platanus occidentalis*), willows (*Salix*), acacias, and sweet gum (*Liquidambar styraciflua*). Two other Chinese imports, tree-of-heaven (*Ailanthus altissima*) and mimosa tree (*Albizia julibrissin*) also cause occasional problems.

But trees have not cornered the market on spring. A few weedy plants that go virtually unnoticed cause a lot of misery in localized areas where they grow in abundance. Several pigweeds (*Amaranthus*) and lamb's-quarters (*Chenopodium album,* illustrated) grow throughout the state and bloom practically all year, but they generally create a problem only in West Texas. Water hemp (*Acnida tamariscina*) seems to be a problem mainly in North Central Texas and Oklahoma.

Though Texas has more than five hundred species of native grasses, all of which are wind-pollinated, very few produce enough pollen to cause hay fever. Two nonnative species—Bermuda grass (*Cynodon dactylon*) and Johnson grass (*Sorghum halepense*)—have become major problems in the spring and summer and even into the fall. Indeed, it is from these two hay plants that the term "hay fever" was derived. The other cultivated sorghums and sugar beets also cause hay fever, as does Kentucky bluegrass (*Poa pratensis*), a lawn grass. Keeping your lawn mowed can eliminate a lot of problems for you and your neighbors by preventing the grasses from pollinating.

In reviewing the above list of hay fever plants, you may have noticed that many of the plants are used as ornamentals or agricultural crops. The rest of the list includes a number of native plants that were not nearly as common a hundred years ago as they are today. Human intervention has changed the Texas landscape drastically in the last century. Ranching and farming have obliterated native stands of grasses, and Mother Nature has replaced them with ragweed, pigweed, mesquite, and cedar, among others. The loss of the grasses meant the loss of much valuable topsoil. The herbs, shrubs, and trees that followed the grasses play an important role in salvaging what remains of our priceless soil. Many plants that are exceedingly abundant today were much more restricted in their range and abundance a few decades ago. It is thought that a hundred years ago giant ragweed, for example, was restricted mainly to stream bottoms.

This fast-growing species expanded its range as land was opened up by overgrazing, farming, and, now, urban sprawl. In addition to these native species, large numbers of introduced species also moved into the open areas, such as tumbleweed, Johnson grass, and Bermuda grass. In a sense then, our hay fever problems are closely related to the way we use the land, and many of the ornamentals we like to have near us exacerbate the dilemma. No longer are Easterners encouraged to send their sinuses to Arizona. Today Tucson has a pollen count three times higher than the national average (Newman 1984). The prevalence of ornamentals such as mulberries and lawns of Bermuda grass, along with the spread of tumbleweeds and other hay fever plants into the region, has turned paradise into hell.

In spite of being a nuisance, pollen furnishes modern humanity with some amazing resources. Oil well drillers use fossil pollen to assist in locating oil. Archeologists and geologists use it to identify plants and, indirectly, climatic conditions of ages past. Considered sacred by the Navahos, Apaches, and many other Indian tribes, corn and cattail pollen are used in religious ceremonies. In recent years pollen has gained a reputation as a health food, valued for its protein and vitamin B_{12} content (a "food," by the way, only for people without pollen allergies). And while the change of seasons brings with it the dread of another bout with hay fever, we cannot deny the importance that pollen has in our daily lives. Pollen and spores make it possible for humans to survive on the planet by providing us with plants that give us food, oxygen, fuel, shelter, and innumerable other products essential to life.

5 Colorful Dyes with Texas Plants

Vegetable Dyes: A Historical Perspective

In the fifteenth through the mid-nineteenth centuries, as Europeans expanded their influence around the world, among the products they sought and brought back home were new sources of brightly colored dyes. Today we have become so accustomed to brilliant colors in many hues that we find it difficult to imagine that before the mid-1800s, colorful clothing, rugs, and furnishings were rare commodities. In Europe most dyes from plants provided only yellows, tans, or browns. Fashion-conscious Europeans, not content with the limited variety of dyes they had at hand, put much effort into obtaining exotic red and blue dyes. Blue from the indigo plant of India, reds from the madder of Asia and the brazilwood tree of Brazil, and purple from the Central American logwood tree—all became an important part of the economics of world trade (Schery 1972; Allen and Allen 1981). To the list of exotic plant dyes, Europe added the red dye from the cochineal insect of Mexico and royal purples extracted from certain sea mollusks.

Europeans who settled in the New World relied almost exclusively on the dyes they, in turn, imported through trade with Europe. In some areas, such as isolated pockets of the Appalachians, women experimented with the native plants around them, but few Europeans bothered to learn about native dye materials from the native Americans. And yet, before the Spanish arrived in North America, the indigenous peoples had utilized many plant and mineral materials as dyes and stains. The Ojibwas dyed porcupine quills a reddish brown with the inner bark of the black oak. The Hopis used sunflower seeds to dye baskets a pale blue. The Zunis dyed deerskins black with iron minerals and the roots of Indian paintbrush (Bearfoot 1975). With the dye materials brought by the Spanish, Hopi men added cochineal red and indigo blue to their beautifully woven white cotton cloth.

The Spanish introduction of sheep into the American Southwest in the late 1500s brought about significant cultural changes among the Navaho and Pueblo tribes of the Southwest. Already highly skilled at weaving cotton, these peoples eventually became skilled wool weavers. Unfortunately, the beautiful cotton and wool cloth, blankets, and rugs produced by the native Americans became such popular items of trade that the Spanish forced the weavers into slavery to mass-produce these highly desirable objects.

The early Navaho wool blankets made use of the natural grays, browns, and cream colors of the wool, with only a few vegetable dyes. According to early reports from Anglos observing the Navahos at work, commonly used dyes included yellow from rabbitbrush or dock roots and reddish browns from the bark of an alder or the root of mountain mahogany. The naturally brown wool was dyed black with a combination of sumac leaves, the sap of the piñon, and yellow ochre, an iron mineral.

An interesting by-product of trade with the Spanish was the incorporation of the bayeta into Navaho weavings. Bayetas were woven cloths from Europe dyed with various bright colors. The Navahos would unravel the brightly colored yarns (red from cochineal being the favorite), and then use the yarns in their own weavings (Kent 1961; James 1937).

The history of the development of dye materials underwent a revolutionary change in direction in 1856. William Perkin, an English chemist, serendipitously discovered how to produce a lavender dye from aniline, a coal tar derivative. Perkin's mauve soon became the rage in Europe. By the end of the nineteenth century, synthetic dyes had taken over the market, and only a few natural dyes were still in common use (Grae 1974; Adrosko 1971; Schetky 1964).

Dyes Today: Synthetic Versus Vegetable Dyes

Why did synthetic dyes gain popularity so quickly? Synthetic dyes offer a number of commercial advantages over vegetable dyes. For one thing, the bright blues and reds so rare in nature now can be manufactured readily in the laboratory. Manufacturers can produce inexpensive synthetic dyes that are easy for the consumer to obtain and use. Synthetic dyes yield more predictable colors than dyes from plants. Many factors influence the color or shade of color that a particular plant will furnish, and the colors are difficult, if not impossible, to replicate. In addition, synthetic dyes often have more reliable colorfastness than vegetable dyes do. Mass production of clothing and other textiles demands a predictable product, and synthetic dyes fulfill that need.

Although mass-produced textiles seek duplication of colors, the artist looks for uniqueness. Natural dyes produce distinctive colors, in a great variety of hues. The pleasing colors can be soft and earthy or rich and vibrant. Though most modern weavers rely on the convenient and reliable colors available from petroleum dyes, artisans are finding that high-quality weavings can often be enhanced, and bring a higher price, if they are woven with natural colors. Thus, while synthetic dyes still dominate the world of mass-produced textiles, natural dyes have regained popularity in the world of the artisan and the artist. The high price tag on antique Persian carpets and Navaho rugs attests to the strong appeal that naturally dyed wools still have to modern eyes. After relying on aniline dyes for nearly a century, Navaho weavers have revived the use of vegetable dyes in the past few decades. Today, in several areas of the Navaho Indian Reservation, weavers rely exclusively on natural wool colors and plant dyes in their weavings (Kent 1961; Amsden 1934; Gilpin 1968).

Dyeing fibers with vegetable dyes is an art form that has existed for thousands of years. As early as 3000 B.C., the Chinese were conducting dye workshops, probably not so very different from the workshops that are conducted at colloquiums of handweavers and spinners in Texas today. Dyers have passed down their techniques through the generations and shared them with other cultures. You too can participate in this ancient art. Scores of Texas' native and naturalized plants lie at your disposal as sources of dyes for wool, cotton, and other fibers. You can obtain an astonishing diversity of colors and shades from Texas' wild dye plants, including warm golds and bright yellows from *Coreopsis* and goldenrod, deep browns from walnut hulls, red and blue from pokeberries, orange from the roots of the bois d'arc, and rich magenta from prickly pear cactus (see photograph, plate 7).

Mustang grape—*Vitis mustangensis*

This chapter includes all the basic information you will need to use Texas' native and naturalized plants as dyes. Refer to the books listed at the end of the chapter if you are interested in dyeing with some of the exotic dye plants such as indigo, madder, brazilwood, and logwood that yield bright blue, red, and purple dyes. You must order such dye materials from special suppliers. You can also order cochineal, but Texas has its own wild source of the red dye. The cochineal insect, appearing as a white ball of fuzz, lives on the pads of the prickly pear cactus. Because cochineal supplies one of the best dyes in the state, I have included it in the dye recipes at the end of the chapter.

Fibers for Dyeing

You can color a wide variety of textile fibers with vegetable dyes. Animal fibers take the colors best. Wool, mohair (from Angora goats), silk, and dog hair all supply interesting possibilities. The high tannic acid content of a number of plants makes then useful for both dyeing and tanning leather. And some of the dyes extracted from plants have been used for dyeing human hair (for more information, refer to "Kitchen and Garden Dyes," beginning on page 326.) Some very beautiful textiles and clothing are being produced today from raw silk that has been dyed naturally.

Texans raise both sheep and Angora goats, and you can purchase fleeces or unspun wool and mohair directly from local growers. A few specialty weaving shops supply undyed, untreated wool (commonly referred to as raw wool) spun into skeins. If you cannot obtain raw wool, try white wool yarn as a substitute.

Because of wool's receptivity to natural dyes and its warmth and durability in clothing, blankets, and rugs, it is probably the most commonly used fiber for natural dyeing. For that reason, the instructions below generally refer to dyeing wool. Mohair can be scoured, mordanted, and dyed in the same manner as wool. Except where noted otherwise, treat silk as you would wool. Most raw silk skeins come prescoured. If you need instructions for scouring silk, refer to Ida Grae's book, *Nature's Colors*.

You can also experiment with dyeing plant fibers, including cotton, linen, and basketry materials, such as raffia, grasses, jute, and sisal, but cellulose fibers do not accept most natural colors as easily as do animal fibers. Special scouring and mordanting techniques will help plant fibers accept plant dyes. The chapter "Fibers From Texas Plants" includes instructions for dyeing plant fibers. In general, synthetic fibers do not take natural dyes, although rayon and some forms of nylon are reported to respond reasonably well to natural colors.

Factors That Influence Dye Colors

In dyeing fibers with plants, a number of factors can affect what color or shade will result. The shades and tones of color vary with all the factors that influence the growth of the plant: the type of soil in which it grows, the season in which the plant is collected, the amount of moisture the plant has received, and the age of the plant. In addition, which plant parts you use, how soon after collection you process it, how you store it, and the quantity of plant material you place in the dyebath all affect the final outcome. Other factors include the acidity and mineral content of the water, the type of textile to be dyed, the mordant, the length of time the plant or textile is in the dyebath, the type of dye process, and the mineral composition of the dye pot.

Because of the complex interplay of all of these factors, the colors reported here, or in any other book on vegetable dyes, may not always be what you achieve from the plants. You may have disappointing results, or you may create new colors. Through your own experiments, you may discover plants not recorded here that also produce interesting colors. While the unpredictable nature of vegetable dyes can cause frustration, particularly if you try to match a wool you dyed last year with the wool you are dyeing today, the uniqueness of the colors adds to their fascination.

Pigments From Plants

The dye colors you can obtain from plants come in a diversity of shades and quality of colors. While nearly all the colors of the rainbow are possible, reds and blues are rare and bright greens practically nonexistent, and browns, yellows, and tans are the most common. The color range is due to the nature of plant pigmentation.

The colors that you see in a flower or leaf represent certain combinations of plant pigments, but often more than one color-producing pigment coexists in the same flower or leaf. For example, the color that you see may not be the same color that an insect sees. An infrared photograph of a white flower may reveal blue-green colors undetectable by the human eye.

For this and other reasons, the colors we see in the plant are not necessarily the colors that end up in the wool. The pigment itself is not a dye. In the dyebath, pigments are altered by heat, the pH of the water, and the presence of various additives (described in the section "Mordants") to form a dyebath. Some pigments are more soluble in water than others, and the mineral content of the plant also affects the color of the dye.

The pigments responsible for most dye colors are listed below (Williams 1983; Smith 1976; Meeuse and Morris 1984).

Green

Chlorophyll pigments furnish the green color in plants. The role of chlorophyll is to allow plant cells to carry out the intricate process of photosynthesis, manufacturing starches, proteins, and sugars for the growth of the plant. Unfortunately for the dyer, chlorophylls are relatively insoluble in water, and so, despite the abundance of green color in plants, strong green dyes are exceedingly rare. The greens that I have obtained from plants have been either very pale greens, from the flowers of bluebonnets and the roots of the Maximilian sunflower, or forest or khaki greens. To obtain bright colorfast greens, dyers rely on two basic processes. You can add a copper mordant to a yellow dyebath, or you can dye the fiber in two dyebaths, a yellow dye and a blue dye. Indigo produces the strongest blue dye, so it is most commonly used for this purpose.

In fall and winter much of the food production that occurs in plants comes to a halt because of the reduced availability of sunlight. The production of chlorophyll is decreased or stopped, and the green pigments break down. As the greens fade, the yellows, golds, and oranges, the tans, browns, and burgundies, of autumn appear at last. These colors represent both pigments that were present in the plant all along and pigments the leaves produce because of the onset of cold weather.

Brown

Tannic acid produces the tans and browns in autumn leaves. Tannic acid, or tannin, is concentrated in the leaves, bark, and wood of trees. In contrast to the elusive greens of chlorophyll, tannins form unusually strong dyes. Besides making good dyes, tannins have a variety of uses in tanning leather, mordanting fibers, and making ink. Tannic acid makes tea and coffee black. The hulls of walnuts and pecans, high in tannins, furnish rich deep-brown dyes. When exposed to light, colors produced by plants high in tannic acid tend to become darker rather than fade. For example, the shrub agarita produces a yellow dye that is strong enough to cover the tan color produced by tannic acid, but with exposure to light, the tan darkens, overpowering the yellow and altering the color to light brown.

Mullein—*Verbascum thapsus*

Yellow and Orange

The yellows, golds, and reddish oranges in autumn leaves are caused by a group of fat-soluble pigments called carotenoids, including carotin, the pigment responsible for the color of carrots. Carotenoids occur in leaves, flowers, fruits, and roots. Water-soluble flavonoids are another group of pigments that produce yellows and cream colors, particularly in flowers.

As anyone who has experimented much with plant dyes can tell you, almost everything seems to be able to produce some sort of a yellow dye. Many wildflowers and garden flowers in the sunflower family, the largest family of flowering plants in the world, produce yellow dyes. Yellow dyes vary from the pale yellow of sunflowers to the brilliant yellows and golds of goldenrod and marigolds to the rusty oranges of *Coreopsis*.

Despite their abundance, most yellow to orange dyes tend to fade with exposure to light or with repeated washings. They are said to have poor colorfastness. Marigolds are a favorite for achieving bright golden colors, but the colors fade with prolonged exposure to light. According to research by Crews (1981a), lightfast yellows can be obtained from peach and cherry leaves, yellow sweet clover, and mullein flowers. Unfortunately, with the exception of mullein, these plants produce fairly pale yellows. With these and with most plants that produce yellows and oranges, the addition of certain metallic salts or chemicals, known as mordants, is essential to obtaining reasonable fastness to light and washing.

Red and Blue

In autumn leaves, most reds are created by anthocyanins, which are part of the water-soluble flavonoid group of pigments. Anthocyanins produce most of the reds, blues, and violets in plants. Some reds and purples—for example, the red of beets—come from pigments called betacyanins. If you have ever tried dyeing wool with beets, you were probably excited by the bright color of the dyebath, only to be disappointed by the pale color it gave to the wool. Blues, reds, and purples are usually delicate dyes that fade considerably with washing and exposure to light. A number of fruits, such as grapes, prickly pears, and pokeberries, produce bright blue, purple, or red dyes that fade quickly. Proper mordanting and dyeing twice will help improve colorfastness, but will not completely prevent fading.

A few bright and colorfast red and blue dyes do occur in nature. Indigo produces brilliant blues that are extremely lightfast. The pigment indigotin is responsible for this strong blue dye. Madder root produces strong lightfast reds. Logwood, which produces lightfast purples, is also one of the best sources of a black dye. None of these excellent dyes grows wild in the United States. Cochineal produces a variety of lightfast reds, pinks, and violets, however, and can be found on prickly pear cactus in Texas.

Colorfastness

Obtaining colors that do not fade over time is perhaps the primary concern of those who choose to dye with plants. Prickly pear fruits produce fantastic magentas, but if the fruits are cooked, the purple disappears in the rinse water. Turmeric produces a bright yellow-orange color in wool that does not wash out but does fade considerably when exposed to light. On the other hand, the colors obtained from walnut hulls do not fade but grow darker with exposure to light. For those plants that do not yield colorfast dyes, techniques such as simmering a long time, using mordants properly, and dyeing twice can improve lightfastness and washfastness. When information on colorfastness is available, I have included it with the dye recipes.

Testing for Lightfastness

Set a small sample of the dyed wool in direct sunlight for two weeks. If the color does not fade after two weeks of bright sunlight, you have an excellent product that will endure years of interior lighting (Grae 1974). The wool will work well in a wall hanging or rug. If the color fades only slightly in two weeks, you can still consider it fairly lightfast. Slightly faded tones often develop into attractive pastels. If a fairly lightfast dye has good washfastness, the wool may work well in clothing, which is stored in a dark closet between wearings. If the color fades considerably in a few days, the lightfastness is poor. For dyes that darken with exposure to light, you may want to force the darkening effect before using the wool in a weaving. Dry the newly dyed wool in direct sunlight. The darkened color may then remain quite colorfast.

Testing for Washfastness

Before washing out the newly dyed wool, thoroughly wash a small sample. Does it fade considerably in the washing? Rinse the sample until the water runs clear, then lay it on a piece of white paper. Does the color bleed onto the paper as the sample dries? If the sample shows poor color-fastness, try drying the rest of the wool without washing it, then redye it in a few days. After-mordanting the wool in chrome improves wash-fastness but darkens the color. Once you have done all you can to improve the washfastness, wash and rinse the wool. If the wool is lightfast but not washfast, use it in a wall hanging or some other item that will not require further washing. Wools can be dry-cleaned to prevent fading caused by washing.

Any naturally dyed weaving or fabric should be protected from pro-longed exposure to the strong rays of the sun. With proper care many vegetable dyes will retain their unique earthy quality and beauty over the years. To prove the point, you have only to look at an antique Persian rug. The colors have been carefully selected to stand the test of time, and they retain their blues and reds with remarkable clarity (Grae 1974; Crews 1981a; Bliss 1976a).

Water

To improve consistency in your dye colors, most dyers recommend using distilled or deionized water or rainwater. Water that contains no minerals and has a neutral pH will not affect the colors produced by the plants. In Central and West Texas the tap water contains high concentra-tions of calcium and is known as hard water. In East Texas the water is high in iron and is called soft water. Both types of mineral-rich water will alter the colors of your dyes. Calcium-rich water is alkaline and sup-posedly hinders the ability of the dye to penetrate the fiber, although some dyers like to add lime (calcium) to the dyebath to bring out greens. I used calcium-rich water from the Edwards Aquifer for most of my dyes and obtained excellent results, including some particularly good greens. If you dye your fibers in water that is high in iron, the iron will dull or darken the colors, just as it will if you purposely add an iron mordant.

If you do not like the results you achieve with your local tap water, you have several alternatives to buying expensive distilled water. You can use rainwater collected in plastic buckets (unless you live in a smoggy area where the rain may be acidic). You can boil tap water to produce water containing fewer minerals. Some of the minerals precipitate and fall to the bottom of the pan, so scoop out the water from the top of the pan.

You also can modify the pH by adding vinegar to calcium-rich water or by adding baking soda to iron-rich water. You need a pH meter to determine when you have reached a neutral level, though, so this method is not practical for most dyers.

If you plan to do a lot of dyeing and are determined to use water that is free of minerals and has a neutral pH, a good alternative to buying distilled water is to purchase a deionization bottle from a water refining company, such as Culligan. Then you can deionize your own tap water at about a third the cost of buying distilled water. Do not use water-softening agents that contain sodium lauryl sulfate for dyeing purposes. Such agents are designed to block the calcium in the water from binding with soap. These products do not alter the pH of the water nor do they remove the minerals.

Dyeing Techniques

Later in this chapter are instructions for three basic techniques of extracting dyes from plants. The traditional method involves simmering the plants in water. The other two techniques rely on the slow process of fermentation and solution in unheated water to form the dyes. For ease in distinguishing between the two noncooking methods, I call them solar dyeing and cold-water fermentation. With cold-water fermentation, the plants are soaked in water in a dark container, such as an enamel pot. With solar dyeing, the plants are soaked in glass jars set in the sun. Both the warmth and light of the sun assist in the process of forming the dye.

Each technique has its advantages and disadvantages. If you want to dye your wool in a hurry, you will need to simmer it. The hot water extracts the dyes from the plants in a few minutes or hours by breaking down the plant cells.

Extracting dyes from woods, barks, and other hard plant materials generally requires boiling the plants in water. You can extract most other dyes quite effectively, however, with either solar dyeing or cold-water fermentation. With delicate plant parts, such as flowers and soft fruits, solar dyeing preserves the bright colors that cooking may dull or destroy. Cold-water fermentation is the only method to use for some plants, such as prickly pears, that do not yield a good dye if they are exposed to either sunlight or excessive heat. Fermentation also is used to extract the blue dye from the indigo plant from India.

I began solar dyeing simply because of its convenience. In running tests for this book, I needed to experiment with a number of different dye plants at a time. Kitchen space was limited, but I had a number of large jars stored at the back of cupboards waiting to be put to use (gallon jars are ideal, though quart and half-gallon sizes are fine for small wool samples). I found that with solar dyeing, I could experiment with as many plants as I wanted by setting out several jars at once on my back porch. And I found that though I had to wait several days for the results, I did not have to spend hours tending pots in a hot kitchen in the middle of the summer.

I was surprised to find that in a number of cases, the colors I obtained with solar dyeing and cold-water fermentation were richer than those achieved by cooking the plants. I also achieved some dramatically different colors by using various techniques with the same plant. For example, I obtained a blue-gray by cooking greenbriar berries, and a deep forest green from them with solar dyeing.

Recipes for vegetable dyes found in books and magazines rely almost exclusively on techniques involving cooking, but once you have tried solar dyeing, you may have trouble going back to the stove. With stove dyeing, the smell of many plants is so strong that you need to work in a well-ventilated area. It is almost essential that you be able to do your cooking outdoors. Your family will insist that you do after the first few experiments. Besides being malodorous, many dye plants are toxic, not the sort of thing you want to keep around the kitchen to be mistaken for dinner! When solar dyeing, you also have to contend with the odors of decaying plants, but you can hold the odor and mold to a minimum by keeping lids tight on the jars. You will probably want to do your preliminary wool washing outdoors.

Perhaps the biggest advantage of solar dyeing is that it lends itself to spontaneous experimentation. You do not have to plan ahead to have the time to dye your wool. If you find an interesting-looking plant growing in a back alley, you can collect it, chop it up, throw it in a jarful of water, and forget about it for a few days. I find the method so convenient in my busy schedule that I dye almost all of my wool using this method.

Solar dyeing was introduced to me by my friends in the Weavers and Spinners Society of Austin. Few articles have been written on it, and many questions about its usefulness are not yet answered. For example, how does the light of the sun assist in the dye process? I find that glass jars work better than the plastic milky-colored containers, but I don't know why.

Further research is needed to determine which plants work best with solar dyeing, which are better suited to cold-water fermentation, and which produce a stronger dye if simmered. In general, I find that flowers, leaves, and soft fruits produce stronger colors when the noncooking techniques are used. I was impressed with the number of colorfast dyes I obtained with solar dyeing, but no one has compared the colorfastness of solar-dyed versus simmer-dyed wools. More research is also needed on the effectiveness of solar mordanting. Anne Bliss (1975) has experimented with raising the temperature of the solar pot by using reflectors. It would be valuable to know how that alternative compares with stovetop dyeing.

In the recipes included below, I have indicated which dyeing technique was used with each plant. Unless the recipe indicates that the particular method used is the only way of obtaining a good color, feel free to experiment with any of the three methods. You also can combine two methods. For example, you can extract the dye by simmering the plants in water and then solar-dye the wool. You'll be astounded at the varied results.

Plants for Dyes

Warning

When collecting plants for dyes, remember that a number of wild plants in Texas can cause poisoning. Protect children and pets from your dye pot. Cook plants in a well-ventilated area, and do not use dye pots for cooking foods. In the dye recipes, I have indicated which plants have known toxicity, but do not assume that any plant is edible simply because I have not indicated that it is poisonous. Refer to the chapter "Poisonous and Harmful Plants" for further information.

How Much Should I Collect?

Today, in a world where forests are disappearing rapidly, and more and more plants are being added to the lists of endangered species, each one of us shares the responsibility to protect what remains of our natural vegetation. State and city laws protect plants on public lands. Collect plants on privately owned land only with the owner's permission. Keep your eye out for vacant lots about to go under the bulldozer. With the owner's permission, you can collect landscaping plants, wild foods, and natural dyes to your heart's content.

When using a friend's back yard or field for collecting, use the following guidelines to preserve nature's bounty for future visitors. Gather only plants that are growing in large numbers or that you know to be common in your area. Do not disturb plants known to be rare or endangered unless they are about to be destroyed. Where they are applicable, I have added notes to those dye plants that are considered rare in Texas.

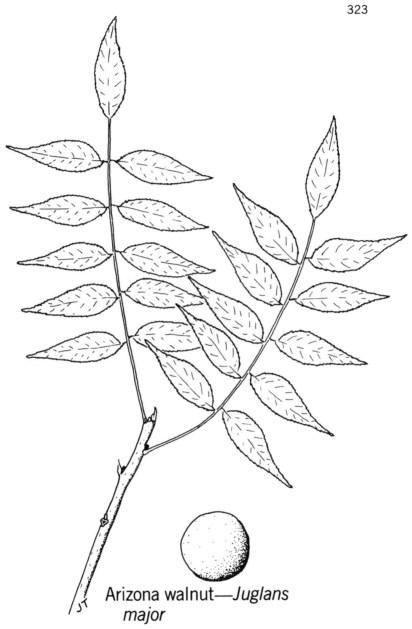

Arizona walnut—*Juglans major*

If a recipe calls for the whole herb of a perennial, cut it off above the ground, leaving the roots intact for next year's growth. When using wildflowers or berries, collect only a small percentage of the crop. Leave the rest for others to enjoy, for wildlife to eat, and for the plant to seed next year's harvest. Take a pair of clippers with you so that you can clip off the part of the plant you need without damaging the remainder of the plant.

Never destroy a mature tree or shrub in your pursuit for vegetable dyes. The plant you seek is probably older than you and, if left alone, may outlive you. Cutting into a tree opens it to possible fungal infection. Newly fallen branches or spring prunings usually work fine for recipes that call for bark, wood, or even roots. I have seen numerous recipes that call for a pound of tree bark or wood to dye a pound of wool. Rarely will you need to dye an entire pound of wool one color. If you need to dye only four ounces of wool, you will need only four ounces, and possibly less, of the wood.

Estimating how much plant material you need to dye a specific amount of wool presents a problem. With some plants, a small amount goes a long way. With others, you will require fairly large amounts of material for a strong dye. Several factors influence the strength of the dyes. Many dyers notice variations in the pigment concentrations of a plant population from year to year or season to season. Some dyers have noted that dyes are frequently stronger from plants collected in the drier times of the year. With synthetic dyes, it is possible to determine the exact amount of dye material needed to achieve the desired color. With plants, that achievement is always a matter of experimentation.

Several dyers recommend starting with a one-to-one ratio by weight of plant to textile. You can decrease or increase the amount as needed after experimenting with a small sample. In general, the more plant material you use, the deeper the color you can achieve. With plant parts that contain a lot of water, such as berries, you will probably need more plant by weight than wool.

In the days of the pioneers, wild plants were in great abundance. Old recipes often called for 1 peck (8 quarts) of plant material. A century ago, collecting a peck of flowers had no readily discernible effect on the plant population, but today, especially for those of us living in the ever-expanding urban areas of Texas, wild plants simply are not available in the quantities that our ancestors used them. In many cases relatively small amounts of plant material make a satisfactory dye. A peck may indeed yield a strong dyebath, but a quart may be plenty.

What Plant Parts Should I Use?

Because different pigments are concentrated in different parts of the plant, you will often obtain a good dye from one part of the plant and not from another. Here are some general guidelines on the collecting, storage, and use of various plant parts.

Plants almost always yield the best results when they are used fresh. If you must store your plants, protect them from molds.

FLOWERS

Though fresh flowers furnish stronger colors, you can obtain good results from cut flowers that have wilted (you may be able to pick up wilted flowers from florist shops for free). You can freeze fresh flowers for storage. Drying works well for some flowers and fails with others. In many cases the leaves and stems of herbaceous plants produce the same color as the flowers and can be added to the dye pot. Use mordants to bring out the colors and improve colorfastness. When extracting dyes, simmer most flowers for short periods of time (15 to 30 minutes) to preserve bright colors, such as yellows, reds, and blues. Longer cooking produces darker colors. Solar dyeing works well and usually takes three to seven days.

FRUIT

Pick berries and other soft fruits when they are fully ripe, and use them fresh. If you must store them, freezing is preferable to drying. In general, berries (elderberries and pokeberries, for example) can give a bright color to wool but have poor colorfastness. Mordanting and dyeing twice may help improve colorfastness. Mordanting is essential to intensify the colors. When extracting dyes, simmer the berries and soft fruits for short periods of time (15 to 30 minutes) to preserve the bright colors. Solar dyeing or cold-water fermentation provide good alternatives to the damaging effects of heat. Cold-water or solar dyeing usually takes three to seven days.

Pecan, hickory, and walnut hulls produce the deepest browns when they are used green. If stored, the hulls turn brown and produce lighter colors. Tannic acid in the hulls eliminates the need for mordanting and produces deep colors, but the colors tend to darken with exposure to light. To extract the dyes, boil (not simmer) the hulls for long periods of time, 30 to 60 minutes or even several hours. Solar dyeing also works well. The hulls can be left in the solar dye pot a few days or several weeks. Longer cooking or soaking yields darker colors.

WOOD, BARK, AND ROOTS

Most woods and woody roots yield the strongest dyes when they are collected in the fall from mature plants. Loose bark can be collected in the spring or fall from mature trees. Use newly fallen branches and twigs, and spring and fall prunings, rather than damaging a tree. Dry wood usually stores well. Dyes from woods generally are more potent and more color-fast than other dyes (Hearne 1978). Often a mordant is not required because of the presence of tannic acid in the wood. The tannic acid may cause the wool to darken with exposure to light, however. To extract wood dyes, the wood should be soaked for several days—in some cases, even weeks—before boiling it. Boil (not simmer) the wood in the soaking water for 30 to 60 minutes, two hours, or longer. With woods that require lengthy soaking times, solar dyeing is impractical and usually not as effective as simmering. A combination of simmering the wood to extract the dye and then solar dyeing the wool works well.

LEAVES

Collect leaves when they are young, green, and healthy, preferably before flowers appear on the plant. Use fresh leaves if possible. Tender leaves, such as spinach and wetland ferns, can be frozen, and tougher leaves sometimes will work when dried. Though tree leaves usually contain some tannic acid, in general you will need a mordant to bring out bright colors and improve colorfastness. Simmer very tender greens for only 10 to 30 minutes to extract the dye. Simmer tougher leaves, such as walnut leaves, 30 to 60 minutes or longer. Solar dyeing takes about three to ten days.

Kitchen and Garden Dyes

In addition to wild plant dyes, a number of garden vegetables and household spices produce bright colors. One evening after cooking a pot of collard greens, I noticed that the pot liquor was a golden yellow. I set the liquid in a jar with a bit of wool for a few days and came up with a lovely bright yellow. You can experiment with spinach and other vegetables simply by using the water in which you boiled the vegetables as the dyebath.

Nasturtium leaves (which are edible, by the way) make a yellow dye. Use red cabbage, canned beet juice, grape skins or concentrated grape juice, and fresh or frozen blueberries to obtain various red and blue shades. The spice turmeric makes a bright yellow to orange dye. Tea and coffee yield tans and browns. Onion skins are popular for dyeing because they produce a variety of rich golds and oranges. Banana leaves make a strong brown dye. Pomegranate skins furnish a variety of tans and browns.

When you use edible plants, kitchen dyes provide a safe and fun activity with children. Try dyeing some eggs with these kitchen dyes. Add to the safety of your dye experiments by using kitchen mordants such as salt, vinegar, and pickling alum.

If you use a part of the plant that is not normally eaten, you may be dealing with a poisonous substance. The leaves of tomatoes, for example, are toxic. Refer to Chapter 4 for more information.

If you do not suffer from allergic skin rashes, you might want to try some natural hair rinses. I haven't tried them out, but Robin Shepard (1982) recommends a number of hair colorants. Sage leaves darken brown hair, and chamomile and turmeric brighten blond hair. Prepare a simmer dyebath from one of these plants, then wash your hair and pour the cooled dyebath through your hair about a dozen times. Leave the concoction in your hair for 10 minutes, then rinse it out. Walnut and pecan hulls yield stronger brown dyes for hair, but be careful or you'll stain your skin as well. Use only nontoxic dyes in your hair.

A number of ornamental trees, shrubs, and flowers yield good dyes for wool, but many are also poisonous, so don't use them with children or on your skin. Marigolds are a favorite for yellow to gold colors. Chrysanthemum leaves also yield a yellow dye, and blues can be extracted from dark purple irises. In the dye plant recipes, I have included several ornamental trees and shrubs commonly found in Texas. Refer to Ida Grae's book, *Nature's Colors,* for more information on garden and kitchen dyes.

Mordants

Many vegetable dyes do not produce a strong color unless you treat the fiber that is being dyed with a mordant. A mordant is an additive that engages in one or both of two tasks: (1) it forms a chemical complex with the fiber to enable it to accept the dye more readily; (2) it reacts with the plant pigments, altering chemical bonds, to assist in the formation of the dyebath. Some people consider only the metallic salts, such as alum or potassium dichromate (chrome), as true mordants, but you may use a number of other substances in the formation and enrichment of dyes. I choose to call all these additives mordants. Nonmetallic mordants include synthetic chemicals, such as household ammonia, and natural substances with similar chemical reactions, such as urine.

The word "mordant" comes from the French "mordre," meaning "to bite or corrode," implying something about how people originally thought mordants worked—by corroding or biting into the surface of the fiber (Crowell and Majtenzi 1973). According to *Webster's,* a mordant is "any substance which, by combining with a dyestuff to form an insoluble compound, serves to produce a fixed color in a textile fiber." Contrary to common belief, however, few of the metallic salts are effective at significantly improving the lightfastness and washfastness of dyes. According to Patricia Crews (1981b), chrome and copper are the best mordants for improving lightfastness, and chrome works best for improving washfastness. Chrome yields fairly bright colors, though darker than those produced by alum and tin, and copper yields dark colors. Alum and tin, though not effective at improving colorfastness, produce such bright, pleasing colors that many dyers prefer to use them as mordants.

Though a dye plant usually will give some color to the fiber even if you do not use a mordant, often that base color is very pale. Mordants can make the base color richer, darker, or brighter, and in some cases they even alter the color drastically. A few plants produce strong colors without the use of a mordant. They include walnut and sumac, plants high in the natural mordant tannic acid. Even with these self-mordanting dyes, though, additional mordants will enrich the colors. Chrome and copper mordants can also help prevent the darkening that often occurs when wools dyed with tannic acid are exposed to light.

Warning

Most mordants are toxic. Protect yourself from toxic fumes by keeping the mordant pot covered and by working in a well-ventilated area, preferably outdoors. To prevent the release of toxic gases, always add the metallic salts to the water, rather than pouring water over the salts (particularly tin). Use rubber gloves to protect your skin from caustic chemicals. Store your mordants out of the reach of children. If you are working with children, the safest mordants to use are pickling alum (which is not quite as effective as the potassium alum preferred for dyeing), salt, and vinegar. You can also avoid using the toxic iron or copper chemicals altogether by using an iron or unlined copper dye pot. You can even experiment with the effects of brass and aluminum dye pots.

You can mordant wool before it is dyed (premordanting), while it is being dyed, or after it is dyed (after-mordanting). You can even combine two mordanting techniques. For example, if you premordant the wool with alum, then dye it in goldenrod flowers, you will get a yellow dye. If you then after-mordant the wool with iron, you will end up with a gray color.

Metallic Mordants

The following list includes the commonly used metallic salt mordants with their characteristics. After sifting through numerous books on natural dyes, most of which give different guidelines, I decided on what seemed the safest amount of each mordant to use without risking damage to the wool. Local water conditions can have an effect on the amount of mordant you need to achieve good colors. Calcium- or iron-rich waters both influence the colors of dyes. You may decide to adjust the amount of mordants you use as you gain experience with how the mordants affect colors under your local conditions. If you increase the amounts beyond those listed below, however, you do so at the risk of damaging the fiber or dulling the color (Grae 1974; Crowell and Majtenzi 1973; Lesch 1970; Robertson 1973; Davidson 1974; Krochmal and Krochmal 1974).

Amounts given are for use with one pound of wool, mohair, or silk and are dry-weight measurements. Volume measurements (in teaspoons and tablespoons) are approximations. Silk is more easily damaged by excess amounts of mordants, so you may find that you need to use less mordant than with wool. If mordanting less than a pound of wool, decrease the amount of the mordant proportionately. Refer to the section "Procedures for Dyeing Wool" for instructions on mordanting wool, mohair, and silk. For instructions on mordanting cotton and other plant fibers, refer to the chapter "Fibers From Texas Plants." Check with local spinners and weavers for local sources of mordants.

ALUM (POTASSIUM ALUMINUM SULFATE)

For premordanting or after-mordanting, use 2 to 4 ounces (4 to 8 tablespoons) alum with 1 ounce (2 tablespoons) cream of tartar. Alum brightens colors, but excess amounts of it make wool feel sticky and harsh and can cause streaking. Alum does not produce toxic fumes. The powder should not be eaten, however, as it can cause nausea and stomach pain. Alum is available at drugstores. Ammonium alum, or pickling alum, is available at grocery stores. It is not considered as effective but is a reasonable substitute. The Navahos collect raw alum, a mineral that is deposited by evaporation.

CHROME (POTASSIUM DICHROMATE)

For premordanting, use ¼ to ½ ounce (1 to 2 teaspoons) of chrome with ½ ounce (1 tablespoon) cream of tartar. As an after-mordant, use half as much of each. Chrome darkens colors slightly and is particularly effective in altering yellows and oranges to rich golds and browns. An excess amount of the mordant will darken or dull the color too much. Chrome is a good mordant for providing lightfastness, and the best for improving washfastness. Chrome is highly poisonous if eaten and is a skin irritant. Work in a well-ventilated area to avoid fumes, and use rubber gloves in handling. Because of the sensitivity of chrome to light, you must keep the mordant pot covered (and also the dye pot, though this is not as important) to prevent streaking. It is best to dye the wool immediately after mordanting. If you store the wool before dyeing, dry it away from strong light, and store it in a dark place. Potassium dichromate is available from chemical companies.

COPPER, BLUE VITRIOL (COPPER SULFATE)

For premordanting, use ½ to 1 ounce (about 1 tablespoon) copper. As an after-mordant, use ⅕ ounce (about 1 teaspoon) copper. If brighter colors are desired, add ½ ounce (1 tablespoon) cream of tartar. Copper is used to bring out greens and purples and to darken colors. Plants that produce yellows with alum or chrome will produce greens with copper. Copper is the best mordant for providing lightfastness. Excess will cause streaking of the wool. Copper is moderately toxic and is caustic to the skin. Work in a well-ventilated area to avoid fumes, and wear rubber gloves in handling. Copper is available from drugstores and farm supply stores. Dyeing the wool in an unlined copper pot can be used as a substitute for mordanting with the toxic chemical.

IRON, COPPERAS, GREEN VITRIOL (FERROUS SULFATE)

For premordanting, use ½ to 1 ounce (1 tablespoon or less) iron and 1 to 1½ ounces (2 to 3 tablespoons) cream of tartar. As an after-mordant, use slightly less. Iron darkens colors. Plants that produce yellow or brown with alum may be brown or olive green to black with iron. Use iron sparingly, as an excess amount or prolonged simmering will make wool brittle and harsh and cause streaking. The fumes are not toxic, but the powder is highly poisonous if eaten. Iron is available through drugstores and farm supply stores. Wool can be dyed in an iron pot as a substitute for the powder. You can even add some rusty nails to the pot, but try to keep the wool from touching the nails.

TIN (STANNOUS CHLORIDE)

For premordanting use ¼ to ⅔ ounce (2½ teaspoons or less) with ½ ounce (1 tablespoon) cream of tartar. As an after-mordant, use no more than ⅖ ounce (a pinch) tin. Tin produces beautiful bright colors and is often used to intensify yellows and reds. It is a poor mordant for improving lightfastness, though, so it is often used in conjunction with another mordant. Use tin sparingly, as it makes wool harsh to the touch, and the wool will become brittle if much tin is used or if it is cooked very long. Tin is toxic and is caustic to skin. Use it in a well-ventilated area to avoid fumes, and handle it with rubber gloves. Tin is expensive, and you may have to special-order it through a chemical company.

Other Mordants and Additives

AMMONIA—NONDETERGENT AND CLEAR (AMMONIUM HYDROXIDE)

As a mordant, amounts vary. As a rinse, add 1 teaspoon ammonia to 1 quart of water. Ammonia can be used as a mordant to assist in the formation of the dye. For example, lichens can be soaked in a strong ammonia bath to form purple dyes. Ammonia is more commonly used as a rinse to intensify yellows, reds, and blues. It may even alter the colors in the wool. For example, as a rinse after dyeing with brazilwood (a dye plant from Brazil), ammonia can change the red wool to a vibrant violet. Ammonia fumes are toxic. Ammonia is hard on wool, so it is best to expose the wool to it for only a few minutes, then rinse thoroughly. Ammonia is available at grocery stores.

CREAM OF TARTAR, TARTARIC ACID (POTASSIUM HYDROGEN TARTRATE)

Cream of tartar can be used with any of the metallic mordants to brighten colors and to help protect the wool from the damaging effects of the mordants, such as harshness, brittleness, and streaking. Cream of tartar is not toxic and is available in the baking section of grocery stores.

SALT (SODIUM CHLORIDE)

Common table salt can be added to the dyebath (use 4 tablespoons with a pound of wool), or add 2 teaspoons to a quart of warm water as a rinse. Use salt to intensify colors, particularly reds and blues, and to help the wool absorb the dye evenly, preventing streaking.

TANNIN, TANNIC ACID

As a premordant, use 2 ounces (10 tablespoons) of the powder. Tannin is the best mordant for cotton and other plant fibers. Tannins darken the colors of wool and help prevent fading. If exposed to light, however, colors may become darker over time. Tannic acid is a natural mordant found in many plants. Oak galls, sumac bark, and juniper leaf ashes are good natural sources. Powdered tannic acid should not be eaten, because of its acidity. It is available at chemical companies and can be special-ordered through drugstores. Tannin is expensive, but a few ounces go a long way.

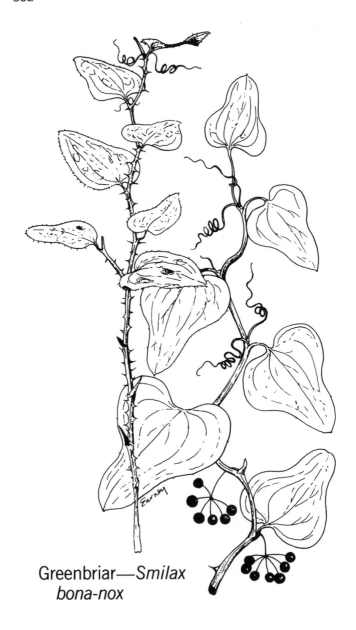

Greenbriar—*Smilax
bona-nox*

URINE

Urine has been used as a natural mordant for centuries for its salt and uric acid content (uric acid breaks down into ammonia).

VINEGAR (4% ACETIC ACID), LEMON JUICE

As a mordant, add 4 to 6 cups or more to the dyebath. As a rinse, add 2 tablespoons to 1 quart of water. Vinegar and lemon juice intensify yellows, reds, and blues. They are good to use in the dyebath with acidic fruits and are also used to alter the pH of calcium-rich water. Vinegar and lemon juice are not toxic and are available at grocery stores.

Procedures for Dyeing Wool and Other Fibers

Use the same procedures for dyeing wool and mohair and, with a few exceptions, silk. For instructions on dyeing plant fibers, such as cotton, linen, and raffia, refer to the chapter "Fibers From Texas Plants."

*Warning*_____

Most mordants and some plants are toxic. Do not use dye pots and dye utensils for any other purpose. Protect yourself from toxic fumes by keeping pots covered and by working in a well-ventilated area, preferably outdoors.

Equipment

EQUIPMENT FOR MORDANTING

Enamel or stainless steel pots, 8- to 12-quart size and/or 16-quart size (four ounces of wool requires at least a gallon of water, preferably more, for even mordanting. You need a 16-quart pot only if you want to mordant a full pound of wool in one pot. Galvanized steel, aluminum, iron, brass, or copper pots react with dyes, affecting the colors. Only use reactive pots if you intend to use the pot itself as a mordant.)
Mordants
Buckets for soaking and rinsing wool
Raw wool, in fleece or skeins
Stirring rods, glass or wooden (If wooden, use one for each mordant.)
Measuring spoons and cups

Cooking thermometer
Scales for weighing wool and mordants
Rubber gloves
Stove
Water (Deionized or distilled affects colors the least.)
Mild soap or detergent, such as dishwashing liquid or Woolite
String or yarn for tying skeins
Cheesecloth or nylon stockings to hold loose fleece
Scissors
Labels

EQUIPMENT FOR SIMMER DYEING

All of the same equipment used for mordanting, plus a sieve for straining out plant material (You may need to use different pots for mordanting and dyeing, as metallic mordants tend to cling to the mordant pots.)

EQUIPMENT FOR SOLAR DYEING AND COLD-WATER FERMENTATION

Large glass jars with lids for solar dyeing (A gallon jar will hold 3 to 4 ounces of wool.)
Enamel pots or crocks and lids for cold-water fermentation
Water (Deionized or distilled affects colors the least.)
Raw wool, in fleece or skeins
Scales for weighing wool and plants
Buckets for soaking and rinsing wool
Cheesecloth or nylon stockings to hold loose fleece or plant material
String or yarn for tying skeins
Rubber gloves
Stirring rods, glass or wooden
Mild soap or detergent, such as dishwashing liquid or Woolite
Sieve for straining out plant material
Scissors
Labels

Preparing the Plant Material for the Dye Pot

STEP 1: Review the information in the section titled "Plants for Dyes," beginning on page 322.

STEP 2: Speed up the release of the dye from the plant by one of the following methods: bruise flowers, tear or cut up leaves, mash fruit, cut or chop wood into tiny pieces or shavings.

STEP 3: Soak the plants in water for at least 24 hours prior to cooking them to assist in the extraction of the dyes. Some species of wood need to be soaked for several days, a week, or longer to achieve the best results. The soaking water, of course, should not be thrown out but becomes part of the dyebath.

Preparing the Wool

To protect wool, handle it gently at all stages of the dye process. To extract excess water from wool after washing or dyeing, gently squeeze the skeins. Wringing or twisting tends to cause felting (matting of wool fibers). Abrupt temperature changes can cause the wool to shrink, becoming harsh and matted. When heating wool, heat it slowly in the water, and do not transfer it directly from a hot bath to a cold one. Most books on dyeing warn against boiling wool, which causes shrinkage. Solar dyeing is an ideal way to prevent the adverse effects caused by cooking the wool and temperature shock.

When drying skeins of dyed wool, hang them away from direct sunlight to prevent excessive and uneven fading. To prevent the skeins from wrinkling as they dry, it is helpful to hang a small weight from the skeins. The slight tension will hold them taut as they dry.

SCOURING RAW WOOL

The purpose of scouring is to remove dirt and excessive amounts of lanolin, or grease, from the wool. Lanolin repels water and prevents dyes from penetrating the wool. Wool and silk skeins usually have been scoured. If you need to scour silk, refer to Ida Grae's book, *Nature's Colors,* for instructions.

STEP 1: If working with skeins, tie them loosely with string or yarn in at least three places.

STEP 2: Weigh the wool.

STEP 3: Soak the wook in warm water for at least an hour or, preferably, overnight.

STEP 4: Wash the wool in mild soap or washing soda and warm water, handling it as little as possible. If necessary, let the wool soak in the wash water several hours, or overnight, to release dirt and grease.

STEP 5: If the wool is excessively greasy, slowly heat it, submerged in the wash water, to a simmer for 30 minutes, gently moving it around in the water. Allow the water to cool before removing the wool.

STEP 6: Rinse the wool until the water runs clear.

STEP 7: Gently squeeze excess water out of wool.

STEP 8: If using fleece, you may want to pack the fleece loosely in nylon stockings or tie it in cheesecloth after it is scoured. Transferring the wool from one pot to another will then be much easier, and loose plant material will be prevented from becoming tangled in the wool.

MORDANTING THE WOOL

Review the section "Mordants" above. To prevent uneven dyeing and streaking, dissolve mordants thoroughly in the water before adding the wool. If the wool is already in the pot, remove it when you add mordants, until the additives are thoroughly dissolved in the water.

Premordanting

Mordanting the wool before it is dyed, or premordanting, yields stronger colors than mordanting in the dye pot. To save time, you can premordant a large quantity of wool (a pound or more) at one time, dry it, and store it to be used as needed.

STEP 1: If you have not already done so, weigh the wool, and tie the skeins loosely with string or yarn in at least three places.

STEP 2: Label the wool with something that will not melt or dissolve. I wrap a piece of masking tape around the string that holds the skeins and write the name of the mordant and dye plant on the tape in pencil. After I am through dyeing the wool, and it has dried, I replace the masking tape with a card label, giving the details of the dye procedure.

STEP 3: If wool is dry, soak it in water for at least an hour before mordanting. Wool is somewhat water-repellent and will not absorb the mordant evenly or as quickly if it is not thoroughly soaked beforehand.

STEP 4: If you are mordanting a pound of wool with one mordant, fill a 16-quart pot three-fourths full of water (at least 3 gallons of water). For mordanting 4 ounces of wool, use a container that will hold at least 1 gallon of water.

STEP 5: Weigh the mordant. Review the section titled "Mordants," beginning on page 327, for measurements and warnings on toxic mordants. If you are not mordanting a full pound of wool, remember to decrease the amount of mordant proportionately.

STEP 6: Stir the mordant into a cup of hot water to ensure that it is fully dissolved. To prevent toxic gases from forming, especially with tin, add the mordant to the water, rather than pouring water over the mordant. Add the dissolved mordant to the pot, and stir thoroughly.

STEP 7: Check the temperature of the wet wool to be sure that it is similar to that of the water in the mordant pot. Gently squeeze excess water from the wool.

STEP 8: Transfer the wool to the mordant pot.

STEP 9: Slowly heat the mordant pot. Simmer (180° to 200° F) for 45 to 60 minutes (20 to 40 minutes if using an iron mordant). To ensure even coverage of the mordant, stir the wool gently as it cooks, and keep it immersed in plenty of water. With silk, Ida Grae (1974) recommends keeping the water temperature below 160° F.

STEP 10: You now have several options:

(a) You can leave the wool sitting in the mordant pot until the water cools. This gives the mordant more time to soak into the wool and prevents rapid temperature changes. Some people recommend leaving the wool in the mordant overnight. With iron and tin, however, prolonged contact of the wool with the mordant bath can damage the wool. In those case, remove the wool from the mordant immediately.

(b) When you remove the wool from the mordant bath, you may then squeeze out excess water, hang the wool to dry in the shade, and store it in a dark place for future use. It is particularly important to dry chrome-mordanted wool away from direct light to prevent streaking. If you want to keep the wool wet so it will be ready for immediate dyeing later, you can store it in a plastic bag for a few days or, if refrigerated, for a week or two. If stored too long while wet, the wool will mold.

(c) If the dye pot is ready, you can squeeze out excess water from the wool and transfer the wool immediately to the dyebath. Before transferring the wool, check the temperatures of the mordant water and the dyebath to be sure the wool will not suffer temperature shock. If temperatures differ, cool down or heat up the dyebath to the same temperature as the mordant water before transferring the wool.

STEP 11 (OPTIONAL): Dyers differ on opinions of whether or not you should rinse the mordanted wool before dyeing it. Anne Bliss (1976a) believes that if you neglect to rinse the wool after mordanting it with the metallic salts, dyes that cling to the excess mordant on the wool may rub off when you wash the wool. I have not had any problems with dyeing unrinsed wool, though. To avoid temperature shock when rinsing, either let the wool cool before rinsing or transfer it to a hot-water rinse. If you plan to place several samples of wool that have been mordanted differently into the same dye pot, you will need to rinse them before they go into the dye pot so that the mordant on one skein will affect the colors in another skein as little as possible. I do not recommend mixing copper- or iron-mordanted wool and wool treated with other mordants. The copper or iron may darken all the skeins in the pot.

Mordanting in the Dyebath

To save time and energy, you can mordant the wool in the dyebath. Pre-mordanting usually gives stronger, brighter colors, though, probably because the mordant has more time to interact with both the fibers of the wool and the pigments of the dye plant. Use the same amounts of mordants in the dyebath as with premordanting.

To experiment with several mordants, separate the dyebath into several pots and add a different mordant to each. In most cases, you will dissolve the mordant in the dyebath just before adding the wool. If you simmer the wool in the dyebath for a while before adding the mordant, remove the wool while dissolving the mordant in the dyebath. Try to let the wool cook with the mordant for the full 45 to 60 minutes that you would use for premordanting. If using iron, add it to the dyebath for no longer than the last 20 to 40 minutes to prevent damaging the wool.

After-Mordanting (After-Bath)

You can mordant the wool after it has been dyed. This method is less effective than premordanting, but when you experiment with a new plant, you may want to see how it works with no mordant before deciding on which mordant, if any, would be best to darken, brighten, or set the colors you discover.

A more common method of after-mordanting involves using a second mordant on the wool after it has been mordanted and dyed. You may decide to after-mordant the wool in chrome to darken colors and improve colorfastness, or in tin to brighten colors. If you have obtained a yellow dye on alum-mordanted wool, you may want to try for a green color by after-mordanting with copper.

The after-mordant can be added directly to the dyebath. Remove the wool from the bath, add the mordant, and return the wool to the dyebath for 10 minutes or less. Lift the wool out of the bath every couple of minutes to check the color, removing it completely when you have achieved pleasing results. If you do not want to contaminate the dyebath with the mordant, dissolve the mordant in a separate hot bath of water, then transfer the dyed wool to the hot bath for up to 10 minutes. Once the wool has entered the after-mordant pot, you can turn off the heat. Refer to the section titled "Mordants," beginning on page 327, for amounts.

Solar Mordanting

I found little information on solar mordanting, and the few experiments I made with alum were unsatisfactory. Anne Bliss (1975) also reports that solar mordanting generally is not as effective as simmer mordanting. But if you want to get away from the hot stove completely, by all means try this simple method. If you are solar dyeing (see instructions below), simply dissolve the appropriate amount of mordant in the glass jar containing the dyebath just before adding the presoaked wool. Research is needed to determine ways to improve the effectiveness of solar mordanting. Since chrome is light-sensitive, you cannot use it with solar dyeing, but you can use chrome with cold-water fermentation.

Dyeing the Wool

SIMMER DYEING

STEP 1: Soak the wool in water for at least an hour before dyeing, or overnight if possible. If it is not thoroughly soaked, the wool may not absorb the dye evenly.

STEP 2: Pour the plant material and the water in which it soaked into a dye pot. Fill the pot about three-fourths full of water. The plants need to be fully covered with water. Adding more water to the pot will not reduce the amount of dye available from the plants. The size of the pot will depend on the volume of the plant material and the amount of wool you will be dyeing. Four ounces of wool needs at least a gallon of water for proper coverage and even dyeing—an 8-quart pot is a good size. A 16-quart pot is big enough for a pound of wool.

STEP 3: Slowly heat the pot to a simmer (180° to 200° F). Simmer gently for 10 to 60 minutes to extract the dye from the plant material (refer to the section "Plants for Dyes," beginning on page 322, for extraction times). In general, the longer you simmer the plants, the darker the colors. Add water as needed to compensate for evaporation.

STEP 4: Strain the plants out of the dyebath. If you want to leave the plants in the dyebath with the wool, protect the wool from becoming tangled with loose plant material by tying the plant material or the wool in nylon stockings, cheesecloth, or a muslin bag.

STEP 5: Before adding the wet wool, be sure that the wool and the dyebath are similar temperatures. You may need to heat or cool the dyebath, or the soaking water with the wool in it, to protect the wool from excessive shrinking and matting.

STEP 6: Lift the wool out of the soaking water. Gently squeeze out excess water, and place the wool in the dyebath.

STEP 7: Add more water to the dyebath to fill the pot three-fourths full. Slowly heat the dyebath to a simmer, stirring the wool as it heats. (If dyeing silk, maintain the water temperature below 160° F). Keep the wool in motion to ensure an even distribution of the dye. Add more water as needed to compensate for evaporation.

STEP 8: Check the color of the wool about every 10 minutes by lifting it out of the water. The color of the wet wool will be darker than that of the wool when it has dried. Ten to 30 minutes is usually long enough to dye the wool. Short simmering times preserve bright colors, but longer simmering (45 to 60 minutes) may improve colorfastness.

STEP 9: If you let the wool sit in the cooling dyebath overnight, the color achieved will be deeper and, some believe, faster. If you like the

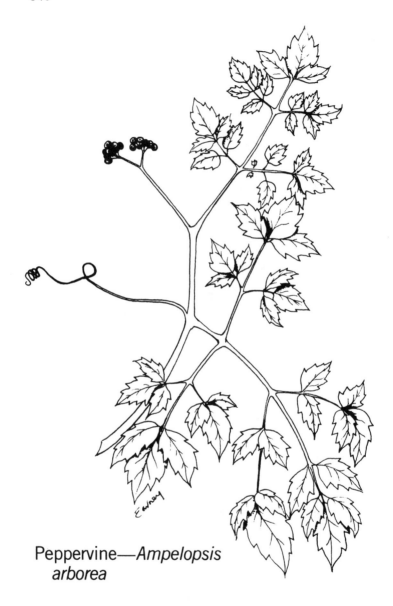

Peppervine—*Ampelopsis arborea*

color as it is, however, lift the wool out immediately, and place it in a hot water rinse to prevent temperature shock.

STEP 10: Rinse the wool until the water runs clear.

STEP 11: Wash the wool in warm water and mild soap. You may want to test the color for washfastness before washing it.

STEP 12: After washing, rinse the wool again until the water runs clear. Though washing and rinsing may cause the color to fade somewhat now, thorough washing at this stage may prevent loss of color in future washings. Gently squeeze out excess water, and hang the wool to dry in the shade.

STEP 13: Label the wool with the details of the dye procedure.

STEP 14: If you obtained a good color, do not throw out the dyebath. You can dye more wool in it if it is still strongly colored, though the next batch will be lighter in color.

Simultaneous Dyeing

If the pot is big enough to hold the wool and the plants together, you can place them both in the dye pot at the same time. This is a particularly good method if you are working with flowers, soft fruits, or delicate leaves that you want to simmer for just a few minutes. If you do not want to clean bits of plant material from the wool later, loosely wrap the plants or the wool in nylon stockings, cheesecloth, or a muslin bag.

SOLAR DYEING

STEP 1: Place the prepared plant material in a gallon glass jar. (A gallon jar will dye 3–4 ounces of wool.) Fill the jar with water, and set it outdoors in the sunlight. (If you plan to add the wool to the jar without removing the plant material, do not fill the jar completely with water.) Cover the jar tightly to keep down odors and mold.

STEP 2: Check the jar daily to see if the water is becoming colored. Solar extraction of dyes from flowers and soft fruits takes three to seven days; tougher plant parts may take a week or longer. Some woods take several weeks. Be patient.

STEP 3: Soak the wool in water for at least an hour, preferably overnight, before placing it in the dyebath. This step is not as important with solar dyeing as with simmering. If you plan to add any mordants to the dyebath (see "Solar Mordanting," page 338), the mordants will soak into the wool more readily and evenly if you presoak the wool.

STEP 4: When the dye water is a good, strong color, strain the plants out of the water, returning the water to the jar. If there is enough room in the jar for the wool and plant material together, you can add the wool to the dyebath at any time. To prevent the plant material from becoming entangled in the wool, wrap either the plant or the wool loosely in cheesecloth, nylon stockings, or a muslin bag.

STEP 5: Lift the wool out of the soaking water, and gently squeeze out excess water. Place the wool in the dyebath.

STEP 6: Check the odor of the wool daily. Add water if needed to keep the wool immersed. Gently shake the jars or stir the wool occasionally.

STEP 7: When the wool has taken on a satisfactory color, either lift the wool out of the jar or leave it in for another day to see if the color improves. If no improvement occurs, take the wool out of the jar. The colors may become duller instead of deeper if the wool is left in the dyebath too long.

STEP 8: Rinse the wool until the water runs clear.

STEP 9: Wash the wool in warm water and mild soap. The rotting plant material will make the wool smell bad. Soaking the wool in Woolite effectively removes the odor. You may want to test the color for washfastness (see page 319) before washing.

STEP 10: After washing, again rinse the wool until the water runs clear. Gently squeeze out excess water, and hang the wool to dry in the shade.

STEP 11: Label the wool with the details of the dye procedure.

STEP 12: If you obtained a good color, do not throw out the dyebath. You can dye more wool in it if it is still strongly colored. Subsequent batches will be lighter in color.

COLD-WATER FERMENTATION

Some dyes are destroyed by heat and by sunlight. Plants that produce purples and blues are often good candidates for cold-water fermentation. Follow all of the instructions given above for solar dyeing with one major difference. Rather than using a glass jar, use an enamel pot or a pottery jar, something that will keep out the light. Cover it tightly to keep down odors. Set the container outside in the warmth of the sun or indoors in a warm spot. The warmth will speed up the fermentation.

If you use a wooden pot for fermenting the dye, the tannic acid in the wood will act as a mordant, darkening the wool. I have not tried using an iron, copper, or brass container for cold-water fermentation. These containers should act as mordants, though the mordant may not react as strongly as it does when the wool is simmered in them.

Final Tips on Dyeing With Plants

When you end up with dull tans and beiges, don't despair. Add these dyed wools to a brightly colored dyebath later. You may come up with some unique shades of color. If all else fails, dye the wool brown.

TOP DYEING

If the wool you have dyed is a bright, pure color, particularly a yellow, red, or blue, you may want to try dyeing it in a second dyebath to get new colors. For example, bright yellow wools can be top-dyed in indigo to obtain bright greens.

RINSES

You can use an additive, such as salt, vinegar, ammonia, or washing soda as a rinse after dyeing. These additives often intensify yellows, blues, and reds or even alter the colors dramatically. Add 1 teaspoon ammonia, 2 tablespoons vinegar, or 2 teaspoons salt or washing soda to 1 quart water. Dip the dyed wool in the rinse for just a couple of minutes. Rinse in water afterwards.

LABELING

Get into the habit right away of labeling your dyed textiles. The more detail you put on your labels, the easier it will be to repeat the colors you like best. At the very least, list the name of the plant, the part used, the date the plant was collected, and the mordant and dye technique you used. For a comprehensive record, list the ratio of plant to wool by weight, and indicate whether the plant was used fresh or after storage, the type of water used, and the times for simmering and soaking.

STORING WOOL

To protect your dyed wool from moths, store it in a cedar chest. A number of wild Texas plants are reported to repel insects. You might try any of the following: cedar chips, mint leaves, sassafras wood, or wax myrtle leaves. I have not tried chemical moth repellents on naturally dyed wool, but I have heard that some natural dyes may change color when sprayed with the chemicals. If you have a wall hanging you want to protect, try the chemical repellents on samples of each color of wool before spraying the wall hanging.

Vegetable Dye Recipes

Because of the many factors that influence the colors that each dye plant may produce, books and articles on natural dyes may report different results with the same plants. I relied extensively on dye results obtained by other authors to locate dye plants initially. I have chosen to limit my reports, however, to colors obtained by Texas dyers, colors that I was able to verify either by doing my own dye experiments or by viewing the dyed wools of other dyers.

Lynn Marshall, assistant to Scooter Cheatham and Dr. Marshall Johnston, generously shared the results of their dye tests. The dye experiments of Eve Williams, Dona Price, Pat D. Crow, and Dorothy Matheson also provided me with invaluable information. In reviewing Elizabeth Coulter's master's thesis (1941), I was able to observe the effects of time on her samples.

The following list by no means includes all the Texas plants that furnish useful dyes. For further details, refer to the books and magazines listed in "Recommended Reading" at the end of this chapter and Chapter 6. In the recipes below, a color range, such as yellow to orange, indicates that the color will vary with the amount of plant material used and with the simmering time. In general, longer simmering produces a deeper or darker color. Different mordants produce slightly different colors or intensities of colors. The colors reported here were obtained with wool.

Symbol Code

(N)   No mordant is required to produce a strong color.

‼   This plant yields outstanding colors.

(P)   This plant is known to be poisonous.

These symbols found after the plant name provide information about the plant. The recipes indicate the colors achieved and the specific plant parts, the premordants, and the dye techniques used. I conducted light-fastness tests on a number of the dyed samples and have included these results in the recipes. In general, most of the plant dyes had good wash-fastness, but if the wool is used in clothing or other items that require repeated washings, I recommend dry cleaning to protect colors.

Plant Species Used for Dyes

ACACIA, HUISACHE—*ACACIA* SPECIES—FABACEAE

(N)   (See illustration, page 81.)

   TAN: Pods, bark, or prunings; no mordant, or use alum or chrome; simmer dye.

   GRAY: Same as above, with iron or copper after-mordant.

   ORANGE: Bark; tin; simmer dye.

Coulter (1941) reports good lightfastness only with the tan colors from *Acacia greggii.* Acacias contain high amounts of tannic acid, a natural mordant, and have been used in tanning and dyeing leather. The colors tend to darken with exposure to light. I obtained a lovely tan by solar dyeing with the prunings of *Acacia farnesiana.*

AGARITA—*BERBERIS TRIFOLIOLATA*—BERBERIDACEAE
(N) !! (See illustration, page 214.)

YELLOW TO ORANGE-YELLOW: Yellow roots and/or small branches (ratio 3 or more parts plant to 1 part wool, by weight); no mordant, or use alum, tin, or chrome; simmer dye.

YELLOW-GREEN: Same as above, with copper premordant or aftermordant.

Though the roots and branches initially produce a bright yellow, the tannic acid in the wood tends to darken the colors with exposure to light. Of Coulter's (1941) 45-year-old samples, those that retained a good yellow were the fabrics she had dyed by dipping the textiles in and out of the dyebath. Copper improves lightfastness quite well and yields an attractive shade of yellow-green.

The yellow wood is extremely hard. Chip it into small pieces and soak it for several days before simmering. Wahrmund suggests collecting wood in late summer for the strongest colors. Though most recipes call for the root, the small branches work fine and save the shrub from destruction. Solar dyeing produces pale colors. The combination of simmering and soaking works best. Though related species also have yellow wood, they are rare or limited in range in Texas and deserve protection. The red berries of agarita are edible.

AMARANTH, PIGWEED—*AMARANTHUS* SPECIES—AMARANTHACEAE
(See illustration, page 31.)

PALE YELLOW OR TAN: Whole plant; alum, chrome, or tin; simmer or solar dye.

The green plants produce poor colors. Red-flowered varieties reportedly yield red dyes that the Aztecs used in religious ceremonies. Amaranths furnish nutritious foods.

APPLE—*MALUS* SPECIES—ROSACEAE
(P)

TAN TO YELLOW: Leaves, bark; alum; simmer dye.
BROWN: Same as above, with copper mordant.
GRAY-BROWN: Same as above, with iron mordant.

Apple seeds, leaves, and bark are toxic.

ASH, TEXAS ASH—*FRAXINUS TEXENSIS*—OLEACEAE

PALE YELLOW: Bark, prunings; alum; simmer dye.

Related species may furnish similar colors.

ASTER—*ASTER* SPECIES—ASTERACEAE

YELLOW: Whole plant with white or purple flowers; alum or tin; simmer dye.

ORANGE: Same as above, with chrome mordant.

AZALEA—*RHODODENDRON* SPECIES—ERICACEAE
(P) !!

GOLD: Leaves; alum; solar dye.
BROWN: Same as above, with copper or iron mordant.

Please use only the ornamental varieties, as the native species are somewhat rare. All parts of the plant, including the flowers, are highly toxic.

BEDSTRAW—*GALIUM APARINE*—RUBIACEAE

TAN: Whole plant, excluding roots; chrome; solar dye.

Bedstraw is related to madder, the Asian red dye plant. The roots of some Texas species of *Galium* may yield red dyes. The roots are so tiny, though, that it hardly seems worth the effort of collecting them. Very young bedstraw leaves are edible.

BEE BALM, HORSEMINT, BERGAMOT—*MONARDA* SPECIES—LAMIACEAE
(See photograph, plate 12.)

YELLOW TO GOLD: Stems, leaves, and lavender flowers; alum; simmer or solar dye.
BROWN: Same as above, with chrome mordant.
OLIVE: Same as above, with copper mordant.
DARK GRAY: Same as above, with iron mordant.

BEGGAR'S-TICKS, WILD CARROT—*TORILIS ARVENSIS*—APIACEAE

YELLOW: Young leaves or older leaves and stems; alum; simmer or solar dye.
ORANGE: Young leaves; tin; solar dye.
GREEN: Young leaves; alum premordant; simmer dye; copper aftermordant.

A number of native Texas plants are called wild carrot. The true wild carrot is Queen Anne's lace (*Daucus carota*). Do not mistake these plants with their deadly poisonous cousins water hemlock and poison hemlock.

BINDWEED—*CONVOLVULUS ARVENSIS*—CONVOLVULACEAE
YELLOW: Whole vine with flowers; alum or tin; simmer dye.

BITTERWEED—*HYMENOXYS SCAPOSA*—ASTERACEAE
(P) !!
YELLOW: Yellow flowers; alum, chrome, or tin; simmer dye.
Coulter (1941) reports good lightfastness with all mordants.

BLACKBERRY—*RUBUS BIFRONS*—ROSACEAE
LIGHT BLUE TO PURPLE: Berries; alum; simmer dye.
GRAY: Young shoots; no mordant; solar dye.
OLIVE GREEN: Young shoots; alum or copper mordant; solar dye.
DARK BROWN: Young shoots; iron; solar dye.

Colorfastness is good with the shoots. Generally, the berries have poor washfastness and lightfastness, although Ida Grae (1974) describes techniques for producing strong, colorfast blues in her book *Nature's Colors*. You should get similar colors with other blackberries and dewberries.

BLUEBONNET—*LUPINUS TEXENSIS*—FABACEAE
(P) !!
LIGHT LIME GREEN: Flowers; alum; simmer flowers and wool together for 45 minutes.

Bluebonnets yield a lovely green but require a high ratio of flowers to wool. Poor lightfastness is achieved with alum; experiment with copper and chrome to improve lightfastness. Bluebonnets are the state flower and are protected on public lands. You can easily grow the flowers in your own garden, however.

BOX ELDER—*ACER NEGUNDO*—ACERACEAE
!!
YELLOW-GOLD: Leaves; alum; solar dye.
Lightfastness is very good.

BRACKEN FERN—*PTERIDIUM AQUILINUM* VAR. *PSEUDOCAUDATUM*— POLYPODIACEAE

YELLOW-GREEN: Young leaves or fiddleheads; alum; simmer dye.

Native American tribes in Northern California used this dye plant (Bearfoot 1975).

BRASIL, BLUEWOOD—*CONDALIA HOOKERI*—RHAMNACEAE

!! (See illustration, page 201.)

GREEN-GOLD: Berries; alum; cold-water fermentation.
RICH GRAY: Berries; copper or iron; cold-water fermentation.

Lightfastness is good. Use a high ratio of berries to wool. The dye technique and calcium-rich water I used may both have influenced the colors I obtained. You may be able to extract some blue tones with simmering. The reddish wood reportedly yields a blue dye, but this information is unverified. Coulter (1941) tried the red wood of lotebush (*Ziziphus obtusifolia*), a closely related species, and obtained browns with various mordants. Brasil berries are edible.

BROOMSEDGE—*ANDROPOGON VIRGINICUS*—POACEAE

TAN TO YELLOW: Young leaves and stalks; alum; simmer dye.

BROOMWEED—*XANTHOCEPHALUM TEXANUM, XANTHOCEPHALUM MICROCEPHALUM*—ASTERACEAE

(P) !!

BRIGHT YELLOW: Whole plant in bloom; alum or tin; simmer dye.
GREEN: Whole plant in bloom; alum premordant; simmer dye; copper after-mordant.
GOLD: Whole plant in bloom; alum; solar dye.
DARK BROWN: Whole plant in bloom; copper or iron; solar dye.

Colorfastness is very good with all mordants. *Xanthocephalum sarothrae* produces a yellow-green dye. Tin makes the yellows brighter and adds an orange tint.

CAROLINA BUCKTHORN—*RHAMNUS CAROLINIANA*—RHAMNACEAE

(P) !!

DARK BROWN: Berries; alum; solar dye.

Lightfastness is good. Use a high ratio of berries to wool to get a strong color. The cotton ties on my skein dyed gray. I found a report that the berries and bark of Carolina buckthorn also yield yellow dyes. Solar dyeing and calcium-rich water may both have influenced the color I obtained. Buckthorn berries may cause diarrhea if eaten.

CARRIZO, GEORGIA CANE—*ARUNDO DONAX*—POACEAE
(See photograph, plate 14.)
   YELLOW-GREEN: Leaves; alum; simmer dye.

CARROT, WILD CARROT—*DAUCUS CAROTA*—APIACEAE
   See "Queen Anne's lace."

CHERRY—*PRUNUS* SPECIES—ROSACEAE
(P)
   YELLOW: Leaves or bark; alum or chrome; simmer dye.

   Lightfastness is good with chrome. The leaves, seeds, and bark of cherries are highly toxic.

CHICORY—*CICHORIUM INTYBUS*—ASTERACEAE
   YELLOW TO GOLD: Whole plant in bloom; alum, tin, or chrome; simmer dye.

   The very young leaves are edible.

CLEMATIS, OLD-MAN'S-BEARD—*CLEMATIS DRUMMONDII*—RANUNCULACEAE
(P) !!
   GOLDEN BROWN: Leaves and vines; alum; solar dye.
   BROWN: Leaves and vines; copper or iron; solar dye.
   YELLOW: Leaves and vines; tin; simmer dye.

   Handle this plant carefully, as the sap is a skin irritant and may produce irritant fumes.

CLOVER—*TRIFOLIUM* AND *MELILOTUS* SPECIES—FABACEAE

RED CLOVER—*TRIFOLIUM PRATENSE*
   GOLDEN TANS: Whole plant in bloom; alum, tin, or chrome; simmer dye.
   GREEN: Whole plant in bloom; copper; simmer dye.

Sweet Clover—*MELILOTUS ALBUS, MELILOTUS OFFICINALIS*

PALE YELLOW OR TAN: All aboveground parts with flowers; alum or chrome; simmer dye.

Lightfastness is good with chrome.

COCHINEAL—*DACTYLOPIUS COCCUS*
(N) !! (See photograph, plate 7.)

PINK TO RED TO MAROON: Fresh or dried insect; no mordant, or use alum, tin, chrome, or vinegar mordants, which all yield slightly different shades; boil insects for a few minutes, let dyebath sit overnight, then simmer wool in dyebath until you get the shade you like. An alternate method is to pour boiling water over the insects to extract the dye, then solar-dye the wool.

Lightfastness and washfastness are good. Various rinses with vinegar, ammonia, salt, and oxalic acid will give different intensities of the colors, even producing some lavender shades.

Cochineal is a scale insect that lives in a white web on the pads of prickly pear cactus (*Opuntia engelmannii*). An ounce of the dried insect will dye a pound of wool. Though it is not a plant, I have included cochineal here because it yields the only wild source of a strong, colorfast red dye in Texas (Crews 1981a). No mordant is needed, but you can obtain a fascinating array of colors by experimenting with various mordants and rinses. For more information on cochineal, see Gerber and Gerber (1972b).

You can order the dried insects from dye supply houses, or collect your own from prickly pear pads. Use a stiff paintbrush to pick the webs off the cactus. To dry the insects for storage, place the webs in a pan in a hot oven until dry, then seal them in a jar.

COCKLEBUR—*XANTHIUM* SPECIES—ASTERACEAE
(P)

LIGHT YELLOW-GREEN: Leaves, stems, and burs; alum; simmer dye.
DARK GREEN: Same as above, with iron mordant.

COMA, GUM BUMELIA—*BUMELIA LANUGINOSA*—SAPOTACEAE
!! (See illustration, page 201.)

DARK BLUE: Crushed berries; tin; simmer dye.
BLUE-GREEN: Crushed berries; chrome or alum; simmer dye.
GRAY-GREEN: Berries; copper or iron; simmer dye.

Coulter (1941) reports fair to good lightfastness with her samples. After 45 years the samples still held a good blue color. My alum-mordanted sample only had fair lightfastness. Use a high ratio of berries to wool for a strong color. The ripe black berries are edible.

CONEFLOWER—*RUDBECKIA HIRTA*—ASTERACEAE

TAN TO YELLOW: Flowers; alum, chrome, or tin; simmer or solar dye.

GRAY: Flowers; copper or iron; solar dye.

Related species may also work, but they are rare or tend to be limited to their range in Texas.

COREOPSIS—*COREOPSIS TINCTORIA, COREOPSIS CARDAMINAEFOLIA*—ASTERACEAE

!!

YELLOW TO GOLD: Whole plant in bloom; alum or tin; short simmer dye.

RUSTY RED: Whole plant in bloom; alum; simmer plants 45 minutes, let sit overnight, then add wool and simmer an hour.

BRIGHT ORANGE: Whole plant in bloom; alum or tin; solar dye; ammonia rinse.

ORANGE TO REDDISH BROWN: Whole plant in bloom; chrome; simmer dye.

GREEN: Alum premordant; simmer dye; copper after-mordant, or copper alone as premordant.

Good lightfastness is achieved. Use an ammonia rinse to bring out reds. Related *Coreopsis* species also yield good dyes, but some are rare. The Zunis of New Mexico used *Coreopsis* as dye plants (Bearfoot 1975).

COTTONWOOD—*POPULUS DELTOIDES*—SALICACEAE

YELLOW: Leaves and buds (ratio 2 parts plant to 1 part wool, by weight); alum, tin, or chrome; simmer or solar dye.

KHAKI GREEN: Same plant parts as above; copper or iron; solar dye.

Colorfastness is good.

CRAPE MYRTLE—*LAGERSTROEMIA INDICA*—LYTHRACEAE

!!

KHAKI GREEN: Pink flowers; alum or copper; solar dye.

DARK BROWN: Same as above, with iron mordant.

CUDWEED—*GNAPHALIUM* SPECIES—ASTERACEAE
!!

    TAN: Whole plant in bloom; alum; simmer dye.
    YELLOW: Whole plant in bloom; tin mordant; simmer dye.
    BROWN: Whole plant in bloom; chrome or copper; simmer dye.

DANDELION—*TARAXACUM OFFICINALE*—ASTERACEAE
(See illustration, page 14.)

    PALE YELLOW OR TAN: Flowers or root; alum or tin; simmer or solar dye.

Though old dye books state that you can get magenta from dandelion roots, I found no valid reports that the roots produce anything better than a pale yellow. Young dandelion greens are edible.

DAY LILY—*HEMEROCALLIS FULVA*—LILIACEAE
(See illustration, page 112.)

    YELLOW: Flowers; alum; simmer dye.
    Day lilies are edible.

DOCK, CANAIGRE, CAÑAIGRÍA—*RUMEX* SPECIES—POLYGONACEAE
(N) !! (See illustration, page 136.)

Because of the tannic acid content of the plants, tans tend to darken to browns. If the wools are dried in bright sunlight, you can darken them before weaving with them. In contrast to the simmered materials, my solar-dyed gold wool showed very good lightfastness.

Docks are used by the Navahos for dyes and medicines (Bryan 1978). The Cheyennes obtained a blue dye from another *Rumex* species to color feathers and porcupine quills (Bearfoot 1975). Young dock leaves are edible.

CANAIGRE—*RUMEX HYMENOSEPALUS*

    TAN TO LIGHT BROWN: Roots; no mordant, or use alum, chrome, or tin; simmer dye.
    GREEN: Leaves; copper; simmer dye.

PALE DOCK —*RUMEX ALTISSIMUS*

    GOLD: Leaves; alum or copper; solar dye.
    MAUVE: Flowers; alum; solar dye.

DODDER—*CUSCUTA* SPECIES—CONVOLVULACEAE
!! (See photograph, plate 8.)
    YELLOW: Yellow vines; alum or chrome; simmer dye.
    ORANGE: Same as above, with tin mordant.

Colorfastness is good. The Pawnees are said to have used this dye to color feathers (Bearfoot 1975). The parasitic vine, resembling yellow or orange spaghetti, derives most of its nutrients from the herbs it entwines.

DOGWOOD, FLOWERING DOGWOOD—*CORNUS FLORIDA*—CORNACEAE
(N) !!
    RUSTY BROWN: Root, bark, or prunings; no mordant needed, but a variety of shades are produced with mordants; simmer dye.
    BRIGHT YELLOW: Leaves and twigs; alum; solar dye.

Good lightfastness is obtained. Various species of dogwood have been used by several native American tribes to dye baskets and porcupine quills.

ELDERBERRY—*SAMBUCUS CANADENSIS*—CAPRIFOLIACEAE
(P)   (See illustration, page 204.)
    BLUE TO PURPLE: Berries; tin; simmer dye.
    PALE LAVENDER TO BLUE-GREEN: Berries; chrome; simmer dye.
    GRAY: Berries; alum; simmer dye.
    BROWN: Berries; alum; solar dye.
    GRAY: Berries; iron or copper; solar dye.
    YELLOW-TAN: Leaves and twigs; alum; simmer or solar dye.
    BROWN: Leaves and twigs; iron or copper; solar dye.
    DEEP FOREST GREEN: Berries; alum or chrome; cold-water fermentation.

Colorfastness is poor to fair for blues but is somewhat improved with chrome mordant. The cold-water-fermented berries yielded fairly good lightfastness. Elderberries provide an excellent example of the varying results achieved by using the three different dye techniques. Calcium-rich water may have brought out the greens more.
    The Cahuillas dyed baskets with the leaves of *Sambucus mexicana* (Bearfoot 1975). The unripe berries and leaves and stems are poisonous.

ENGELMANN'S DAISY—*ENGELMANNIA PINNATIFIDA*—ASTERACEAE
    YELLOW: Whole plant in bloom; alum or chrome; simmer dye.

FIG—*FICUS* SPECIES—MORACEAE

YELLOW: Leaves; alum; simmer dye.

The sap of the plant irritates the skin. Wear rubber gloves when handling the plant.

FOUR-WING SALTBUSH, SHADSCALE, CHAMIZA—*ATRIPLEX CANESCENS*—CHENOPODIACEAE

YELLOW: Leaves, twigs, and flowers; alum; simmer dye.

The Navahos use this dye plant (Bryan 1978).

GOLDENROD—*SOLIDAGO* SPECIES—ASTERACEAE

!! (See photograph, plate 4.)

YELLOW TO GOLD: Flowers and buds; alum or chrome; simmer or solar dye.

ORANGE: Flowers and buds; tin; simmer dye.

TAN: Leaves; alum; solar dye.

OLIVE: Leaves; copper; solar dye.

GRAY: Leaves or flowers; iron; solar dye.

Lightfastness of the flowers is fair to good. Some species are rare, so collect flowers only when the plants are found in abundance.

GRAPE—*VITIS* SPECIES—VITACEAE

!! (See illustration, page 312.)

BRIGHT YELLOW: Leaves (ratio 2 parts leaves to 1 part wool, by weight); alum; simmer or solar dye; ammonia rinse.

GOLD: Leaves; copper; solar dye.

BROWN: Leaves, iron; solar dye.

DEEP BLUE: Grapes (high ratio of fruit to wool); tin; simmer wool and fruit together 20 minutes.

GRAY: Grapes; chrome; simmer dye.

DARK BROWN: Grape pulp remaining after grapes are boiled and the juice extracted for jelly; chrome; simmer dye.

BLUE-GREEN: Grape pulp remaining after grapes are boiled and the juice extracted for jelly; alum; cold-water fermentation.

OLIVE GREEN: Same as for blue-green, with copper mordant.

DARK GRAY: Same as for blue-green, with iron mordant.

Grape leaves were used for a yellow dye in antique Persian rugs because of their excellent lightfastness and washfastness (Grae 1974).

With the fruits, alum mordant usually produces blues and purples with very poor light- and washfastness. Chrome should improve the colorfastness if it doesn't alter the color too drastically. Coulter (1941) reported unexpectedly good lightfastness for her blue color with tin mordant. After 45 years her stored samples were still a rich blue.

GREENBRIAR—*SMILAX BONA-NOX* AND OTHER SPECIES—LILIACEAE
(N—roots only) !!   (See illustration, page 332.)

BLUE-GRAY: Berries; alum or tin; simmer dye.

YELLOW: Berries; no mordant; simmer dye.

FOREST GREEN: Berries; alum; solar dye.

GRAY-GREEN: Berries; iron; solar dye.

GRAY: Berries; no mordant; solar dye.

RUSTY RED: Root starch (chop roots into small pieces with a hatchet, pound them flat with a hammer, extract red starch by washing in water, and add both starch and bits of pounded root to the dyebath); no mordant, or use alum; simmer to extract the dye, then solar-dye the wool. Also a good dye for cotton.

TAN: Chopped root; alum; solar dye.

GRAY: Chopped root; iron; solar dye.

OLIVE GREEN: Chopped root; copper; solar dye.

The lovely reds produced by the root starch darken slightly with exposure to light. The forest green produced with solar dyeing had good lightfastness. A beautiful range of colors can be achieved from this common vine. My calcium-rich water may be partly responsible for the rich greens. The berries are not edible.

GREENTHREAD—*THELESPERMA FILIFOLIUM*—ASTERACEAE
(See photograph, plate 5.)

YELLOW TO ORANGE: Whole plant with blooms; alum; simmer dye.

RUSTY BROWN: Whole plant with blooms; chrome; simmer dye.

GROUNDSEL—*SENECIO* SPECIES—ASTERACEAE

YELLOW: Flowers; alum; simmer dye.

YELLOW-GREEN: Whole plant with flowers; alum, tin, or chrome; simmer dye.

Lightfastness is poor. Most *Senecio* species are rare or infrequent. Collect them only when they are found in abundance.

GUMWEED—*GRINDELIA SQUARROSA*—ASTERACEAE
(See photograph, plate 5.)

YELLOW TO GOLD: Flowers, or stalks and leaves (high ratio of plant to wool); alum, chrome, or tin; simmer dye; ammonia rinse.

Some related species are rare or infrequent. Use them only if they are growing in abundance.

HACKBERRY—*CELTIS* SPECIES—ULMACEAE
(N)

TAN: Leaves and twigs; alum; simmer or solar dye.

HICKORY—*CARYA* SPECIES—JUGLANDACEAE
(N) !!

BROWN: Bark; chrome or copper; simmer dye.
REDDISH BROWN TO DARK BROWN: Leaves; alum; simmer or solar dye.

HONEYSUCKLE, JAPANESE HONEYSUCKLE—*LONICERA JAPONICA*—CAPRIFOLIACEAE

YELLOW: Leaves; alum, tin, or chrome; simmer dye.
GRAY: Leaves; iron; simmer dye.
GOLDEN TAN: Leaves; alum; solar dye.

HOREHOUND—*MARRUBIUM VULGARE*—LAMIACEAE
(See illustration, page 161.)

GREENISH YELLOW: Stems and leaves; alum; simmer dye.
GREEN: Stems and leaves; copper; simmer dye.
TAN: Stems and leaves; alum; solar dye.

INDIAN BLANKET—*GAILLARDIA PULCHELLA*—ASTERACEAE

PALE GREEN: Flower heads; various greens with all mordants; simmer dye.
BRIGHT YELLOW: Flower heads; alum; solar dye.

Good lightfastness is achieved for yellow.

INDIAN PAINTBRUSH—*CASTILLEJA INDIVISA*—SCROPHULARIACEAE

GREENISH YELLOW: Stems, leaves, and flowers; alum; simmer dye.

Several native American tribes used various species of paintbrushes for tan to rust-colored dyes, but these beautiful wildflowers do not usually grow in abundance. If you find a large population, clip off the above-ground parts, leaving the roots for next year's growth.

INDIGO—*INDIGOFERA SUFFRUTICOSA*—FABACEAE
(P)

Indigofera suffruticosa is closely related to the indigo plant from India, *Indigofera tinctoria*. A native of tropical America, *Indigofera suffruticosa* is reported to have furnished an alternate commercial source for indigo blue dyes. Because it provides a bright blue color that has both good lightfastness and washfastness, *Indigofera tinctoria* has been in use as a dye for more than four thousand years (Allen and Allen 1981; Schery 1972). Dyers use special fermentation and oxidation processing to develop the blue color. Because of the difficulty in preparing the dye, I recommend ordering prepared indigo from dye supply houses rather than collecting wild plants. Refer to Ida Grae's *Nature's Colors* and Rachel Brown and Cheryl McGowan's *Weaving, Spinning, and Dyeing Book* for instructions on using prepared indigo. Grae also provides instructions for using the fresh leaves. Another native species, *Baptisia australis,* also is supposed to produce a light blue color.

JUNIPER, MOUNTAIN CEDAR—*JUNIPERUS ASHEI*—CUPRESSACEAE
EASTERN RED CEDAR—*JUNIPERUS VIRGINIANA*
(P) (N) !!   (See photograph, plate 8.)

LIGHT BROWN, TAN: Berries; no mordant; simmer or solar dye.
BROWN: Pollen-covered tips of branches; iron; simmer dye.
TAN TO RUSTY BROWN: Bark; no mordant, or use alum; simmer dye.
GOLD: Leaves; no mordant; solar dye.

Colorfastness is good. As with many trees, junipers contain a fair amount of tannic acid. The Yavapais reportedly have made a purple face paint from the berries of a juniper (Bearfoot 1975). The Navahos prepare a mordant from the green leaves by burning them to ashes (Bryan 1978).

KNOTWEED—*POLYGONUM AVICULARE*—POLYGONACEAE
!!

TAN TO YELLOW: Stems, leaves, and flowers (ratio of plant to wool, 3 to 1); alum, tin, or chrome; simmer or solar dye.

Lightfastness is good. This introduced species is now widespread in the United States. Most native Texas knotweed species are somewhat rare. The sap can irritate the skin.

LAMB'S-QUARTERS—*CHENOPODIUM ALBUM*—CHENOPODIACEAE
!! (See illustration, page 63.)
   BRIGHT YELLOW: Leaves (high ratio of plants to wool); alum or tin; simmer 10 minutes to extract color; solar-dye wool.

Lightfastness is good. The leaves provide an excellent vegetable. Serve the greens for dinner, and use the cooking water as your dyebath.

LARKSPUR—*DELPHINIUM* SPECIES—RANUNCULACEAE
(P)
   PASTEL ORANGE: Flowers; alum; cold-water fermentation.

Larkspurs are highly toxic plants. Do not use this or any other toxic dyebath as a hair rinse.

LETTUCE, WILD LETTUCE—*LACTUCA* SPECIES—ASTERACEAE
(See illustration, page 44.)
   YELLOW OR YELLOW-GREEN: Leaves, stalks, and blue or yellow flowers; alum, chrome, or tin; simmer or solar dye.

Lightfastness is poor to fair, fading to pale pastel yellow. Young wild lettuce leaves are edible.

LICHENS
(N) !!
   TAN TO ORANGE: Lichens, removed from tree bark (ratio of plants to wool, 2 to 1); no mordant; simmer dye.

Lightfastness is poor, the bright orange fading to tan. Lichens are peculiar plants formed by a symbiotic relationship between algae and fungi. They assist in breaking down rock and wood into soil. Use only the abundant tree lichens, as the rock lichens may be several hundred years old. You can collect lichens from fallen tree limbs and store them dry. In some areas of the country, fabulous pinks and magentas can be extracted from certain lichens using cold-water fermentation in an ammonia solution. Refer to Grae's *Nature's Colors* for details.

LIGUSTRUM, PRIVET—*LIGUSTRUM JAPONICUM*—OLEACEAE
(P) (N) (See photograph, plate 13.)

TAN TO LIGHT BROWN: Berries; various tans to browns with all mordants; simmer dye.

TAN TO LIGHT BROWN: Leaves or berries; various tans to browns with all mordants; solar dye.

Grae (1974) reports green and blue-gray with the berries. Ligustrum berries and leaves are toxic.

MESCAL BEAN, TEXAS MOUNTAIN LAUREL, FRIJOLILLO—*SOPHORA SECUNDIFLORA*—FABACEAE
(P) (See photograph, plate 11.)

DULL YELLOW-GREEN: Flowers; alum; solar dye.

I discourage using this plant as a dye. All parts are highly toxic. This solar dye experiment was the only one I conducted in which the dye pot fermented to an almost explosive state.

MESQUITE—*PROSOPIS* SPECIES—FABACEAE
(N) (See illustration, page 90.)

LIGHT BROWN: Bark; any mordant; simmer dye.

BROWN TO BLACK: Tree sap; no mordant; simmer dye.

Collect the sap as it oozes from the trunk in the spring. The Seri Indians used the sap as a face paint (Simpson 1977).

MEXICAN HAT—*RATIBIDA COLUMNARIS*—ASTERACEAE

BRIGHT YELLOW OR OLIVE GREEN: Flowers or whole plant in bloom; alum; simmer dye.

GREEN: Same as above, with copper mordant.

Lightfastness is good, washfastness fair.

MILKWEED—*ASCLEPIAS* SPECIES—ASCLEPIADACEAE
(P) !! (See illustration, page 248.)

YELLOW: Stems, leaves, and flowers; no mordant, or use alum or tin; simmer dye.

GREENISH YELLOW: Same as above, with chrome mordant.

Colorfastness is good. A number of Texas milkweed species produce good yellows. The milky sap is a skin irritant, and the plants are toxic.

MIMOSA TREE—*ALBIZIA JULIBRISSIN*—FABACEAE
!!
YELLOW: Pink flowers or leaves; alum; solar dye.
LIME GREEN: Same as above, top-dyed with indigo.

I obtained a beautiful golden yellow on mohair.

MISTLETOE—*PHORADENDRON TOMENTOSUM*—VISCACEAE
(P)   (See illustration, page 191.)
Though mistletoe is frequently included in dye books, the common Texas mistletoe found on broadleaf trees produces very pale tan, yellow, and green colors. The plant is highly toxic so you might just as well leave it alone. The mistletoes found on junipers and pines (*Phoradendron* and *Arceuthobium* species) in the Trans-Pecos might be worth experimentation, however. I have reports of brown dyes from juniper mistletoes with chrome mordants. Pat Crow (interview, June 1984) fermented a juniper mistletoe in New Mexico (species unknown) for four months, then simmered it. With copper and iron mordants, she obtained deep brown to black dyes. Such long fermentation time probably is not necessary.

MORNING GLORY, WILD MORNING GLORY—*IPOMOEA TRICHOCARPA*—CONVOLVULACEAE
SOFT YELLOW: Purple flowers; alum; solar dye.

MOUNTAIN MAHOGANY—*CERCOCARPUS MONTANUS*—ROSACEAE
(P) (N)
PINKISH TAN TO REDDISH BROWN: Reddish bark of root; no mordant; simmer dye.

The Navahos, Hopis, and Zunis all have used this dye plant, but the West Texas shrubs are not common (Bearfoot 1975; Bryan 1978). Please do not destroy a shrub to obtain the dye. Anne Bliss (1976b) reports tans and golds from simmer dyeing the leaves and twigs.

MULBERRY, RED MULBERRY—*MORUS RUBRA*—MORACEAE
(P)   (See illustration, page 209.)
TAN OR YELLOW-GREEN: Leaves and prunings (ratio of plant to wool, 4 to 1); alum; simmer or solar dye.

GRAY-LAVENDER TO PURPLE: Berries (ratio of plant to wool, 3 to 1); alum; simmer (a pinch of tin in the dyebath yields stronger blue).

Lightfastness and washfastness of berries is generally poor. The milky sap can cause dermatitis and is toxic. The ripe berries are edible.

MULLEIN—*VERBASCUM THAPSUS*—SCROPHULARIACEAE
(See illustration, page 316.)
YELLOW: Leaves or flowers (high ratio of plant to wool); alum, tin, or chrome; simmer dye.

Good lightfastness is obtained with chrome, though chrome makes the colors greener. Roman women used to dye their hair yellow with mullein flowers (Grae 1974).

NIGHTSHADE, SILVERLEAF NIGHTSHADE, TROMPILLO—*SOLANUM ELAEAGNIFOLIUM*—SOLANACEAE
(P)   (See illustration, page 274.)
TAN TO YELLOW: Green fruit (high ratio of fruit to wool); alum or tin; simmer dye.
GREENISH YELLOW: Same as above, with chrome mordant.
GREEN: Whole plant with purple flowers; copper; simmer dye.
GOLDEN TAN: Leaves; alum; solar dye.
GRAY-BROWN: Leaves; copper; solar dye.

The fruit and leaves of silverleaf nightshade are highly toxic.

OAK—*QUERCUS* SPECIES—FAGACEAE
(N) !!   (See illustration, page 101, and photograph, plate 11.)
Oak bark and galls are high in tannic acid, a natural mordant. Unless you use chrome or copper as a mordant, the colors will darken with exposure to light. Galls are swellings that form after insects lay their eggs inside the twigs of the tree. On live oaks, galls appear as hard balls that resemble fruits.
Various oaks yield yellows, oranges, browns, and greens with the bark, leaves, galls and various mordants. The Ojibwas are reported to have dyed porcupine quills reddish brown with the inner bark of black oak (Bearfoot 1975).

BLACK OAK—*QUERCUS VELUTINA*
YELLOW TO GOLD: Inner bark; no mordant, or use alum or chrome; simmer dye.

Plateau Live Oak—*QUERCUS FUSIFORMIS*

ROSY TAN: Pulverized galls (high ratio of plant to wool); alum; solar dye.

GREENS: Pollen tassels before they fall from the tree; pale green to dark khaki with no mordant or with alum and copper; simmer dye. The pollen of some oaks produces a yellow dye.

LIGHT BROWN: Pollen tassels that have fallen to the ground; no mordant; simmer dye.

Texas Oak—*QUERCUS TEXANA*

BROWN: Leaves; alum; solar dye.

ONION—*ALLIUM CEPA*—LILIACEAE
!!

YELLOW TO GOLD TO ORANGE: Yellow or red onion skins; no mordant, or use alum or tin; simmer or solar dye.

BROWNS: Yellow skins; copper or iron; simmer or solar dye.

GREEN: Yellow skins; copper; simmer dye.

BROWNS: Red skins; chrome; simmer dye.

SILVER-GRAY: Yellow skins; a pinch of both iron and copper in the dyebath; solar-dye on mohair.

Home dyers use onion skins frequently because the skins produce vibrant colors and good colorfastness. Salt in the dyebath or a vinegar rinse intensifies the colors.

OSAGE ORANGE, BOIS D'ARC—*MACLURA POMIFERA*—MORACEAE
(N) !!

YELLOW TO ORANGE: Orange root tips; no mordant, or use alum or tin; simmer dye.

GOLD TO GOLDEN BROWN: Same as above, with chrome mordant.

KHAKI GREEN TO DARK BROWN: Same as above, with copper or iron mordant.

Because the plant contains tannic acid, the colors tend to darken to browns. Mordant with chrome or copper to improve colorfastness. Solar dyeing does not work well with this wood.

A number of eastern native American tribes used Osage orange as a dye and as a bowwood. Modern tanners have used the bark of the trunk in tanning leather. The inedible green fruits are reported to repel roaches. The milky sap can cause dermatitis (Smith and Perino 1981).

PAPERFLOWER—*PSILOSTROPHE* SPECIES—ASTERACEAE

YELLOW: Leaves and flower heads; alum; simmer dye.
Colorfastness is fair to poor.

PARTRIDGE PEA—*CASSIA FASCICULATA*—FABACEAE
(P)

TAN: Stems, leaves, and blooms; alum; simmer dye.

PEACH—*PRUNUS PERSICA*—ROSACEAE
(P)

PALE YELLOW: Leaves and flowers; alum or chrome; simmer or solar dye.
PALE YELLOW TO PEACH: Bark or prunings; alum; simmer dye.

Lightfastness is good with chrome mordant. Peach leaves, seeds, and bark are toxic.

PECAN—*CARYA ILLINOINENSIS*—JUGLANDACEAE
(N) !!

TAN TO BROWN TO ALMOST BLACK: Green hulls or leaves; no mordant, or use various mordants to obtain deeper browns; simmer dye, solar dye, or cold-water fermentation.

The tannic acid content of pecans makes colors darken with exposure. If the wool is solar-dyed, the colors remain fast.
If you use many brown hulls, the dye will be a weak brown. You can let the solar or fermentation dye pot sit for weeks or months, adding leaves or hulls when they are available.

PEPPERGRASS—*LEPIDIUM VIRGINICUM*—BRASSICACEAE
(See illustration, page 174.)

BEIGE: Whole plant with flowers; alum; simmer dye.
PALE YELLOW: Same as above, with tin mordant.
GREEN: Same as above, with chrome mordant.

PEPPERVINE—*AMPELOPSIS ARBOREA*—VITACEAE
(N) !! (See illustration, page 340.)

GOLD: Vine tips and leaves; alum; solar dye.
RICH BROWNS: Vine tips and leaves; no mordant, or use copper or iron for progressively darker browns; solar dye.

Colorfastness is good. You do not need to use much plant material to get a strong color.

PERSIMMON, TEXAS PERSIMMON—*DIOSPYROS TEXANA*—EBENACEAE
(N) (See illustration, page 178.)
TAN: Black fruit; no mordant; simmer dye.

Further experiments are needed on this plant. Reportedly, you can get brown to purple-black from the fruits.

PINE—*PINUS* SPECIES—PINACEAE
(N) !!
TAN: Bark or pollen; alum; simmer dye.
YELLOW-GREEN: Bark; tin; simmer dye.
RUSTY BROWN: Bark; chrome; simmer dye.
OLIVE: Bark; copper; simmer dye.
GRAY-BROWN: Bark; iron, simmer dye.

LOBLOLLY PINE—*PINUS TAEDA*
GRAY: Needles; any mordant; simmer dye.

PIÑON, PINYON PINE—*PINUS EDULIS*
(See illustration, page 129.)
RUSTY BROWN: Pine cones; any mordant; simmer dye.

PLANTAIN—*PLANTAGO LANCEOLATA*—PLANTAGINACEAE
(See illustration, page 132.)
KHAKI TAN: Leaves, stems, and blossoms; alum; solar dye.

Colorfastness is good. Anne Bliss (1976b) reports yellow-green with a simmer dye. Young plantain leaves are edible.

PLUM, WILD PLUM—*PRUNUS* SPECIES—ROSACEAE
(P) (N) !! (See photograph, plate 15.)
PINK-TAN: Bark, prunings, or roots; no mordant, alum, tin, or chrome; simmer dye.
BROWN: Roots; alum or tin; simmer dye; chrome after-mordant.
GRAY: Roots; no mordant, or use alum or chrome; simmer dye; iron after-mordant.
YELLOW: Flowers and branch tips; alum; solar dye.
BROWN: Flowers and branch tips; copper or iron; solar dye.

Because of the tannic acid content of the plant, the colors darken with exposure to light. Wild plum leaves, seeds, and bark are toxic.

POKE, POKEWEED, ÑAMOLI—*PHYTOLACCA AMERICANA*—PHYTOLACCACEAE
(P) (N) !! (See illustration, page 267.)

PINK TO ORANGE TO RED: Berries (ratio of berries to wool, 3 to 1); no mordant, or use vinegar, alum, tin, or chrome; simmer with vinegar in the dyebath for a more intense color.

DARK BLUE: Berries; alum; cold-water fermentation in calcium-rich water.

BLACK: Berries; alum or chrome; cold-water fermentation in calcium-rich water; wool soaked in dyebath for three weeks.

Lightfastness and washfastness are poor for reds and blues, but the faded colors are attractive. Red fades to pastel peach, and blue fades to gray. The beautiful black fades only slightly. See Gerber and Gerber (1972a) for more recipes with pokeberries.

Pokeberries and prickly pear fruits are probably the only wild Texas plants that produce bright reds, but unfortunately those reds fade quickly. All parts of the poke are toxic. Protect your skin and eyes from the berry juice.

POMEGRANATE—*PUNICA GRANATUM*—PUNICACEAE
(N) !!

YELLOW TO BROWN: Skins of fruit; no mordant; simmer dye.

BROWN TO BLACK: Skins of fruit; iron; simmer dye.

BROWN: Red flowers; no mordant; simmer dye.

REDDISH BROWN: Red flowers; alum; solar dye.

YELLOW: Red flowers; alum; cold-water fermentation.

Colorfastness is good. By solar-dyeing the wool in a jar that was partly enclosed in foil, I got a variegated wool with yellow, reddish, and brown colors.

PRAIRIE TEA—*CROTON MONANTHOGYNUS*—EUPHORBIACEAE
(See illustration, plate 164.)

TAN: Whole plant; alum; simmer dye.

PRICKLY PEAR CACTUS—*OPUNTIA ENGELMANNII*—CACTACEAE
(N) !! (See photograph, plate 7.)

RED TO MAGENTA: Ripe red or purple fruits, mashed; no mordant, or use alum or chrome; cold-water fermentation.

TAN: Ripe fruits; no mordant; simmer or solar dye.

Prickly pears yield beautiful vibrant dyes that have poor lightfastness and washfastness. Dye twice and use chrome mordant to improve fastness. Cooking and sunlight destroy the purple dyebath. Collect the fruits with leather gloves and tongs. To remove the spines, singe them with a flame. Prickly pear fruits can be stored frozen. See Bryan (1978) for more recipes with prickly pears. Grae (1974) reports that the flowers also yield magenta. (See "cochineal" for dye recipes using the cochineal insect.)

PRICKLY POPPY, WHITE PRICKLY POPPY—*ARGEMONE ALBIFLORA*—PAPAVERACEAE
(P)

TAN: Whole plant with flowers; alum; simmer or solar dye.

PYRACANTHA—*PYRACANTHA COCCINEA*—ROSACEAE

PINKISH TAN: Branch tip prunings; alum; solar dye.

QUEEN ANNE'S LACE, WILD CARROT—*DAUCUS CAROTA*—APIACEAE

YELLOW: Leaves; alum; simmer dye.

Other species of plants that resemble wild carrots give similar colors, but be sure to distinguish wild carrots from poison hemlock (refer to the index).

RABBITBRUSH—*CHRYSOTHAMNUS NAUSEOSUS*—ASTERACEAE
!!

YELLOW TO GOLD: Flowering tops; alum or chrome; simmer dye.
ORANGE: Same as above, with tin mordant.

Lightfastness is good with chrome. The Zunis, Tewas, and Navahos all use this bright yellow dye for their wool weavings (Bearfoot 1975; Bryan 1978). Other rabbitbrush species are also reported to yield yellows.

RAGWEED, GIANT RAGWEED—*AMBROSIA TRIFIDA*—ASTERACEAE
(See illustration, page 302.)

YELLOW GREEN TO YELLOW: Leaves (ratio of plants to wool, 2 to 1); alum, tin, or chrome; simmer dye.

PALE GREEN: Leaves; alum; pour boiling water over leaves, let steep, then solar-dye the wool.

!! FOREST GREEN: Leaves; copper; same technique as for pale green.

Lightfastness is fair but can be improved with chrome. I conducted these experiments in calcium-rich water, which may have brought out the greens. I had poor results with one of the small ragweeds, *Ambrosia artemisiifolia*. Ragweeds can cause allergic dermatitis and are a major cause of hay fever in the United States.

RATTAN VINE—*BERCHEMIA SCANDENS*—RHAMNACEAE
(P) !!

BRIGHT YELLOW: Leaves and stems; alum; solar dye.

REDBUD—*CERCIS CANADENSIS*—FABACEAE
!! (See photograph, plate 11.)

BRIGHT YELLOW: Flowers; alum; solar dye.

Lightfastness is only fair.

REED, COMMON REED—*PHRAGMITES COMMUNIS*—POACEAE

The flower heads of this plant reportedly yield light green when boiled two hours with alum mordant. I have not communicated with anyone who has tested it out, however.

RETAMA, JERUSALEM THORN—*PARKINSONIA ACULEATA*—FABACEAE
(See illustration, page 98.)

YELLOW: Flowers; alum; simmer dye.

I obtained a pale yellow by solar-dyeing flowers and leaves together.

ROOSEVELT WEED, POVERTYWEED—*BACCHARIS NEGLECTA*—ASTERACEAE

YELLOW: Leaves and flowers; alum; simmer dye.

ROSE—*ROSA* SPECIES—ROSACEAE

YELLOW-GREEN TO YELLOW: Leaves, stems, and red flowers; alum or tin; simmer dye.

KHAKI TAN: Same plant parts as above; alum; solar dye.

KHAKI BROWN: Same plant parts as above; copper; solar dye.

GRAY-BROWN: Same plant parts as above, iron; solar dye.

I used ornamental roses. Rose hips are reported to yield a light pink dye.

SABAL PALM—*SABAL TEXANA*—ARECACEAE

YELLOW-GOLD: Black fruit; alum; solar dye.

Lightfastness is good. The sweet pulp of the fruit is edible, but do not confuse it with other inedible palms.

SAGEBRUSH, SAND SAGE, SILVERY WORMWOOD—*ARTEMISIA FILIFOLIA*—ASTERACEAE

YELLOW TO BROWN: Leaves and stems; alum, tin, or chrome; simmer dye.

DARK BROWN: Same as above, with copper mordant.

DARK GRAY: Same as above, with no mordant.

Colorfastness is fair. Related species may yield similar colors. Tin brings out a reddish tint.

SAINT JOHNSWORT—*HYPERICUM PERFOLIATA*—HYPERICACEAE
(N) !!

RUSTY BROWNS: Aboveground parts with flowers; no mordant, or get various browns and reddish browns with all mordants; simmer dye.

Use this species and its cousins only when they are found in quantity. Clip off a few branches from the shrub to minimize damage to the plant.

SHOWY EVENING PRIMROSE—*OENOTHERA SPECIOSA*—ONAGRACEAE
!! (See photograph, plate 13.)

YELLOW: Flower petals; alum; cold-water fermentation.

SILK TASSEL—*GARRYA* SPECIES—CORNACEAE

TAN: Leaves and flowers; alum; solar dye.

Grae (1974) reports some interesting colors, including maroon, with the green fruit of a California species. Experimentation is needed with the fruit of Texas species.

SNOW-ON-THE-PRAIRIE—*EUPHORBIA BICOLOR*—EUPHORBIACEAE
(P) (See photograph, plate 10.)

YELLOW: Stems, leaves, and flowers; alum or tin; simmer dye.

You might try other species of *Euphorbia*. With one of the small weedy spurges, *Euphorbia prostrata,* I obtained a khaki tan with solar dyeing.

Wear rubber gloves to protect your hands from the caustic sap throughout the dye process. Also beware of caustic fumes. Wash the wool thoroughly after dyeing.

SOAPBERRY—*SAPINDUS SAPONARIA* VAR. *DRUMMONDII*—SAPINDACEAE
(P) (N) !!   (See illustration, page 395.)
YELLOW: Berries; no mordant, or use alum, tin, or chrome; simmer or solar dye.
KHAKI TAN: Berries; copper or iron; solar dye.

I obtained a particularly bright yellow with solar dyeing and alum. An ammonia rinse intensified the color. Lightfastness is only fair, but the faded color is an attractive pastel yellow. The berries produce a good lather for washing clothes but are toxic if eaten.

SOW THISTLE—*SONCHUS OLERACEUS, SONCHUS ASPER*—ASTERACEAE
(See illustration, page 44.)
YELLOW: Leaves, stems, and flowers; alum or tin; simmer dye.

Young sow thistle leaves are edible.

SUMAC, PRAIRIE FLAMELEAF SUMAC—*RHUS LANCEOLATA* AND OTHER SPECIES—ANACARDIACEAE
(N) !!   (See illustration, page 36.)
REDDISH BROWN: Red fruit; no mordant, or use alum, chrome, or vinegar; simmer or solar dye. Various mordants provide varying intensities of color.
GRAY: Red fruit; no premordant; simmer dye; copper or iron after-mordant.
DARK GRAY TO ALMOST BLACK: Red fruit; chrome premordant; simmer dye; iron after-mordant.
PURPLE: Red fruit; tin; cold-water fermentation.
GOLD: Leaves; no mordant; solar dye.
DARK BROWN: Leaves; iron or copper; solar dye.
GRAY: Twigs; no mordant, or use copper and iron premordants to produce shades from light gray-brown to rich gray; solar dye.

Sumacs are high in tannic acid, a natural mordant. I was particularly pleased with the deep, rich colors and very good colorfastness I obtained with solar dyeing. Several native American tribes use these excellent dyes and mordants. Besides being used to dye wools, sumacs have been used to dye porcupine quills and basketry fibers and to tan skins (Bryan 1978; Bearfoot 1975).
Some individuals have an allergic dermatitis reaction to sumacs. Refer to the index for further information on uses of sumacs.

SUNFLOWER—*HELIANTHUS* SPECIES—ASTERACEAE

COMMON SUNFLOWER, MIRASOL—*HELIANTHUS ANNUUS*
PALE YELLOW: Flowers (ratio of flowers to wool, 4 to 1); alum or chrome; simmer dye.
PALE ORANGE: Flowers; tin; simmer dye.
PALE YELLOW-GREEN: Flower buds; alum; simmer dye.
KHAKI GREEN: Flower buds; copper; simmer dye.

Lightfastness is fair to poor. Sunflowers yield a weak dye, so use a large quantity of the flowers. The leaves produce even paler colors. I had poor results with solar dyeing. The Hopis are reported to have obtained a blue dye for baskets from the seeds (Bearfoot 1975). Refer to the index for further uses of sunflowers.

MAXIMILIAN SUNFLOWER—*HELIANTHUS MAXIMILIANI*
(See photograph, plate 5.)
YELLOW: Flowers; alum; simmer dye.
PALE GREEN: Root (ratio of root to wool, 3 to 1); alum; solar dye.
GRAY-GREEN: Root; copper; solar dye.
DARK GRAY: Root; iron; solar dye.

Lightfastness is fair to poor, and the greens fade to gray. I had poor results from solar-dyeing the flowers, and I obtained a stronger green by solar-dyeing the root than by boiling it. This beautiful sunflower has a variety of uses. Refer to the index for further information.

SYCAMORE—*PLATANUS OCCIDENTALIS*—PLATANACEAE
LIGHT YELLOW: Loose bark; alum; simmer dye.
!! GOLD: Leaves; alum; solar dye.

TALLOW TREE, CHINESE TALLOW TREE—*SAPIUM SEBIFERUM*—EUPHORBIACEAE
(P)
YELLOW-GREEN: Leaves; alum; solar dye.

The milky sap can cause dermatitis, and the leaves and fruit are toxic.

TEXAS DANDELION—*PYRRHOPAPPUS MULTICAULIS*—ASTERACEAE
!!
YELLOW-ORANGE: Flowers; alum; simmer dye.

Pat Crow (interview, June 1984) obtained this strong color with flowers that she had frozen before use. With solar dyeing, I got a pale orange that faded.

TEXAS THISTLE—*CIRSIUM TEXANUM*—ASTERACEAE
(See illustration, page 51.)
YELLOW: Whole plant with purple flower; alum; solar dye.

TRUMPET CREEPER—*CAMPSIS RADICANS*—BIGNONIACEAE
YELLOW: Flowers; alum; solar dye.

The vine can cause allergic dermatitis.

TURK'S CAP—*MALVAVISCUS ARBOREUS* VAR. *DRUMMONDII*—MALVACEAE
!! (See illustration, page 120.)
PALE PEACH: Red flowers; alum; solar dye.
DEEP PEACH: Leaves; alum; simmer extraction; solar dye.
MAUVE: Leaves; iron; simmer extraction; solar dye.
GOLDEN TAN: Leaves; alum; solar dye.

Lightfastness is only fair with alum, the peach color tending to fade to golden tan. You might try a chrome mordant to see if you can make the beautiful tones more colorfast. I'd like to experiment some more with this one. My best results involved simmering the leaves for about 10 minutes, then pouring the liquid into a jar and solar-dyeing the wool. I don't know if the leaves had a stronger concentration of orange pigments than the flowers, or if the leaves produced a deeper color because they had been simmered first. All the colors were lovely. By the way, Turk's cap flowers, fruit, and leaves are edible.

VERBENA, PRAIRIE VERBENA—*VERBENA BIPINNATIFIDA*—VERBENACEAE
(P) !!
BRIGHT YELLOW: Whole plant with flowers; alum; solar dye; ammonia rinse.

WALNUT—*JUGLANS* SPECIES—JUGLANDACEAE
(N) !! (See illustration, page 323.)
TAN TO DARK BROWN: Green hulls and nutshells (ratio of plant to wool, 2 to 1), or leaves and twigs (green or as they fall off the tree in autumn); no mordant, or use mordants to produce darker tones; simmer dye, solar dye, or cold-water fermentation.

GRAY TO BLACK: Same as above, with iron mordant or after-mordant.
ORANGE TO LIGHT BROWN: Pollen-bearing catkins; no mordant, or use alum, tin, or chrome; simmer dye.

Walnuts are high in tannic acid, a natural mordant. Browns may darken with exposure to light. Brown hulls yield lighter browns than green hulls. You can leave the hulls or leaves soaking for days, weeks, or months, and the dyebath can be stored and reused over and over again as more plant material is added. The longer the plants soak, the stronger the dye. Various native American tribes utilized this excellent dye.

WAX MYRTLE—*MYRICA CERIFERA*—MYRICACEAE

LIGHT BROWN: Berries; no mordant, or use alum; simmer dye.
DARKER BROWN: Berries; chrome or copper; simmer dye.
TAN: Leaves (ratio of leaves to wool, 3 to 1); alum; solar dye.
GRAY: Leaves; copper or iron; solar dye.

The berries are reported to produce blue or purple dyes—no luck here. You can use the wax coating on the berries to make candles, and the leaves serve as a spice and an insect repellent.

WILLOW, BLACK WILLOW—*SALIX NIGRA*—SALICACEAE

!! (See illustration, page 381.)

GOLD: Leaves (ratio of leaves to wool, 3 to 1); alum; solar dye.
ROSY TAN: Bark or prunings; alum; simmer dye.

Lightfastness for solar-dyed leaves was good. The Potawatomis reportedly have obtained a red dye from the roots that was used for ceremonial dress (Bearfoot 1975). I imagine the color was probably a reddish or rosy tan. Willow branches provide excellent basketry materials.

WINE-CUP—*CALLIRHOË* SPECIES—MALVACEAE

!! ORANGE: Flowers; alum; solar dye or cold-water fermentation; ammonia rinse brings out the red.
GRAY: Same as above, with iron or copper mordant.

Lightfastness is fair, the orange fading to a pastel peach. The leaves of wine-cups may produce the same color as the flowers. Collect the purple petals only when you find the plants to be fairly abundant. Try to remove petals from the flowers without disturbing the already fertilized ovary, thus protecting next year's crop. One *Callirhoë* species in Runnels County is very rare.

WOOD SORREL—*OXALIS* SPECIES—OXALIDACEAE

(See illustration, page 127.)

YELLOW: Whole plant in bloom; alum, tin, or chrome; simmer dye.

Coulter (1941) and Grae (1974) obtained good, lightfast yellows with various species. I tried solar-dyeing with yellow wood sorrel, *Oxalis dillenii*, and had no success whatsoever. Further experiments with solar and simmer dyeing are needed.

YARROW—*ACHILLEA MILLEFOLIUM*—ASTERACEAE
(P) !! (See illustration, page 5.)

YELLOW TO GOLD: Flowers (ratio of flowers to wool, 3 to 1) or whole plant in bloom; alum, tin, or chrome; simmer dye.

Good lightfastness is obtained. If you use the whole plant, the color will not be as bright as with flowers alone. A yarrow dyebath also works as a hair rinse to brighten blond hair. Yarrow can cause dermatitis. A tea of the leaves has medicinal value, but the leaves are toxic if eaten.

YAUPON—*ILEX VOMITORIA*—AQUIFOLIACEAE
(P) (See illustration, page 168.)

TAN: Leaves (ratio of leaves to wool, 3 to 1); alum; solar dye.
GRAYS: Leaves; no mordant, or use iron or copper; solar dye.
SOFT YELLOW: Red berries; alum; solar dye.

The red berries of yaupon are toxic.

Recommended Reading

Bliss, Anne. 1976. *Rocky Mountain Dye Plants.* Boulder, Colo.: Juniper House Press.

Brown, Rachel, and Cheryl McGowen. 1978. *The Weaving, Spinning, and Dyeing Book.* New York: Alfred A. Knopf.

Bryan, Nonabah G. 1978. *Navajo Native Dyes.* Palmer Lake, Colo.: Filter Press.

Grae. Ida. 1974. *Nature's Colors.* New York: Macmillan.

Rice, Miriam C., and Dorothy Beebee. 1980. *Mushrooms for Color.* Eureka, Calif.: Mad River Press.

Robertson, Seonaid. 1973. *Dyes From Plants.* New York: Von Nostrand Reinhold.

PERIODICALS

Shuttle, Spindle, and Dyepot. (Handweavers Guild of America, 65 La Salle Road, West Hartford, Connecticut 06107.)

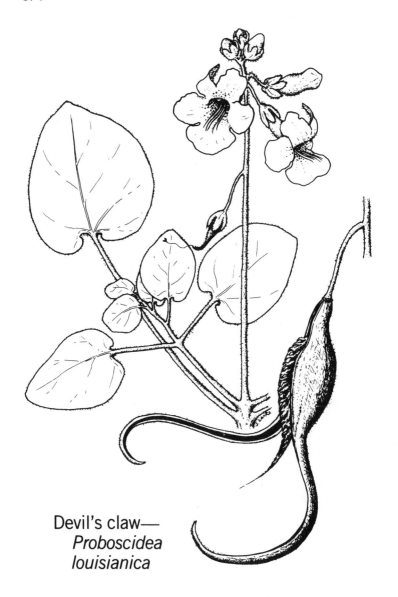

Devil's claw—
*Proboscidea
louisianica*

6 Fibers from Texas Plants

Today petrochemicals furnish many of our fibers, with natural fibers appearing in our clothing, upholstery, rugs, and curtains less and less often. Yet thousands of plants worldwide have been used for weaving cloth and making baskets over the centuries. Texas' native and naturalized plants yield a vast storehouse of useful fibers. You can collect vines, leaves, and branches to coil and twine into a basket. You can extract threads and cords from dozens of wild plants to use in weaving textiles. This chapter includes instructions for preparing both types of plant fibers. Also included are recipes for dyeing plant fibers and for papermaking. At the end of the chapter are listed several books and magazines that provide instructions on basketmaking and textile weaving. In addition to those resources and the references cited in the text, I relied on the following for information on plant fibers: Bearfoot (1975); Roberts (1972); Sue Smith (1983) and interview, May 1985; Amsden (1934); Kent (1961); Grummer (1980); James (1937); Gilpin (1968); Brumgardt and Bowles (1981).

Many of the plants mentioned in this chapter are illustrated or described elsewhere in the book. For further information on a particular species, look it up in the index.

Plants for Basketmaking

For millennia, people have made baskets and put them to a multitude of practical and decorative uses. Archeologists have discovered baskets in North America dating from 5000 B.C. (MacNeish 1971) and mats woven with cattail leaves that are more than 10,000 years old. Baskets furnish clues to the way of life of the people who constructed them. The style and size of the vessel often indicate its use. Baskets have been used for carrying food and supplies on the backs of donkeys, on the heads of women, and on the shoulders of men. Native Americans stored grains, acorns, and mesquite beans in large wicker containers, then sealed them with a lacquer extracted from the bodies of insects. Fishermen caught minnows in baskets, and food preparers winnowed grains in baskets. Baskets have been employed in wedding ceremonies, healing rituals, and burials.

The ancient art of basketmaking, at one time a basic skill shared by all, is known by few members of our modern societies. Despite the decline in the number of artisans, all baskets still are constructed by hand, with the exception of a few mass-produced items such as bushel baskets for fruit. You can explore any number of shops in America today and find dozens of small and large baskets on sale, often at remarkably low prices. And yet someone—probably on the other side of the world, in China, Hong Kong, or Taiwan—painstakingly handcrafted each item, using techniques that are hundreds of years old.

The same weaving techniques that are applied in basketmaking may be used to manufacture a variety of other items. Archeological digs in West Texas have uncovered sandals woven from sotol leaves. The Japanese weave beds, the Filipinos weave hats, the Chinese weave window coverings, wall hangings, and mats, and the Zulus weave houses.

In the United States a revival of interest in the craft has inspired some individuals to duplicate the centuries-old basketry techniques used in the Appalachians. Even the beautiful ash splint baskets of the Shakers recently have been duplicated by Martha Wetherbee in New Hampshire (Smith 1985). Others, such as Texas artisan Sue Smith (see Smith 1983), have developed their own styles, creating exquisite original works of art (see photographs, plate 2). In the Southwest the Papagos and weavers from other native American tribes produce fine-quality baskets sought after by an appreciative clientele. And a small company in North Carolina still constructs by hand the large baskets attached to hot-air balloons (Sue Smith, interview, May 1985).

Preparation of Plants

You will find plants suitable for basketmaking just about anywhere that you look for them. Look for plant parts that are flexible, long, slender, and of fairly uniform width (though you can compensate for tapering leaves by splitting them). The diversity of textures, colors, and sources of basketry materials will astound you. You can use leaves, branches, tree trunks, bark, roots, flowering stalks, seed pods, and vines. Some plant parts maintain their suppleness better than others, and some become too brittle when they dry. But even the brittle ones may have threadlike fibers that you can extract and use for stitching and weaving.

Many fiber plants are available year-round, but the best time to collect them is from fall to early spring. Ornamentals are pruned after they have completed flowering and producing fruit, and before the new spring growth emerges. Follow the same guidelines for collecting wild fibers as you would in pruning ornamentals to avoid disrupting the reproductive cycle. With care in pruning, you will not damage the remaining plant parts or inhibit next season's growth. If you are collecting parts from a perennial herb, clip off aboveground parts late in the year, and leave the roots intact for the spring growth. Though a number of plants produce long roots that are suitable for weaving, in most cases an interest in collecting a root does not justify destroying the whole plant.

A basket woven with green plants may become distorted and loose as it dries and the plants shrink. Thus, you will want to dry most plants before weaving with them (exceptions are listed below). Dry and store the plants in a cool, dry, well-ventilated spot away from direct sunlight. If you wish to sun-bleach your plants, keep in mind that plants dried in the sun may become brittle. When the plants are dry, you can enclose them in paper bags or wrap them in newspaper, but avoid using plastic bags, which may promote molds.

When you are ready to weave your basket, the plant fibers must be wetted to return them to a pliable state. Most fibers need to soak only 15 to 30 minutes before use, but some tough fibers require long soaking, an hour or a day, to render them pliable. Heavy vines, such as wisteria, require boiling to make them supple but do not need to be dried.

To avoid soaking the plants too long, which may weaken the fibers, soak them just until they are pliable. Wet only as much plant material as you think you can use in two or three days. Then keep the fibers wrapped in a damp cloth. Plants may be kept moist for a couple of days but may mold or disintegrate if dampened for too long. If you are delayed in completing the weaving, let the plant materials dry out, and resoak them when you are ready to continue. If the plant fibers become moldy, Sue Smith (1983) recommends adding a bit of vinegar to the water. Then dry the fibers thoroughly to verify that the mold hasn't damaged the material.

As you work the basket, keep it moist so that the fibers won't become brittle as you weave. A spray bottle filled with water is a handy item. Occasionally mist the basket to keep it pliable. If a basket takes you several days to complete, as most will, let it dry overnight, then resoak the whole basket for 20 to 30 minutes before working on it again.

Sue Smith (interview, May 1985) suggests freezing the completed basket to kill any insects that may be hiding in the plant material. Every few months, brush the basket with a mixture of one teaspoon glycerin in one quart water. The glycerin helps keep the fibers from becoming brittle with age.

Listed below are plants that are well known for their use in basketry. By no means should you feel restricted to just these plants in your baskets. The plants are divided into three groups: plants that must be dried before use, those that must be boiled, and those that do not need to be dried or boiled.

PLANTS TO DRY

Collect the following plant materials while they are green, and dry them before use.

Leaves and Flower Stalks

Feel free to experiment with the long, slender leaves and flower stalks of many different plants. Several of the basketry fibers commonly imported from Asia and sold in craft shops in the United States also grow wild in Texas. Ramie (*Boehmeria nivea*) and Japanese mat rush (*Juncus effusus*) both are naturalized in Southeast Texas (Correll and Johnston 1970).

To dry the green leaves of palms, Georgia cane (*Arundo donax*), pine needles, cattails, and other long, slender leaves, spread them out or wrap them in newspaper. Some will retain a pale green color if dried in the shade and will be lighter in color if sun-dried. Split broad leaves to the desired width before weaving. Brown pine needles that have fallen from the trees and dead leaves and flower stalks can be used without further drying.

Collect the leaves and flower stalks of grasses, sedges, and rushes with their seed heads intact. Seed heads often add an attractive effect to weavings. Tie the stalks in bundles, and hang them upside down or stand them upright in paper bags to dry. Preserve seeds by spraying them with hair spray or satin varnish.

Mature green stalks of bamboo and other large canes need drying, but the slender side twigs do not. Soak bamboo stalks four hours or longer, and split them to the desired width before use.

Tie the fresh leaves of beargrass (*Nolina*) in coils for drying. Watch out for the sharp, cutting teeth on the leaf margins. When you gather yucca leaves, trim off one edge of each leaf as soon as you collect them. Sue Smith (1983) maintains this will enable the leaf to soak up water more quickly when you are ready to weave. To harvest the leaves without damaging the rest of the shrub, grab a leaf near its base, twist, and pull it loose. Collect just a few from each plant, preferably after it has flowered. Split the leaves to the desired width when you are ready to weave. You can use red yucca (*Hesperaloë parviflora*) and sotol leaves in the same manner.

Warning

Agave leaves contain substances that will blister your hands if you harvest them bare-handed. Refer to page 384 for instructions on extracting agave fibers from the caustic pulp.

Branches

Collect the slender flexible branches of aromatic sumac (*Rhus aromatica*), hackberries (*Celtis*), cottonwoods (*Populus*), mulberries (*Morus*), and the shrubby dogwoods (*Cornus*). The Comanches favored the straight branches of the dogwoods for arrows. For a smoother texture, soak or boil branches to loosen the bark for stripping. You can split thick branches in half.

Wood and Bark

The inner bark of a number of trees has been used extensively in the past to make slats and splints for baskets. Please don't destroy any trees for this purpose, but should you come across a felled tree, you might want to use it, if you are very diligent. First you must remove the outer bark (soaking the log may help), and then pound out the growth rings in layers to form splints, a much more difficult task than can be imagined. The functional and beautiful Shaker baskets were made from splints of ash. Willow, cottonwood, basswood, oak, maple, box elder, elm, pine, hickory, and mesquite woods also furnish slats for baskets. The outer bark of the paper birch has been used to cover canoes and dwellings. Only the river birch (*Betula nigra*) grows in Texas. The shaggy bark of this birch peels off in weak, thin strips, but the strips can be added to weavings.

Seed Pods

One of the most unusual plant materials used in baskets is the seed pod of devil's claw (*Proboscidea* species, illustrated). When ripe, the coiled pod turns black and splits open to form two sharp-pointed claws. The Papago Indians of southern Arizona use them in their baskets and have developed cultivated varieties with extralong claws. Soak the woody pods in water until pliable, and split them into desired widths. You can use the sinewy fibers as threads.

COIL AND BOIL: VINES AND ROOTS

Most vines and roots do not shrink much and so do not require drying before use. They usually require boiling to render them pliable, though.

Exceptions are succulent or very slender vines, which may shrink considerably and should be dried and then soaked for one to several hours before weaving.

Clip long, straight sections of vines. Strip off the leaves and side branches. (Dewberry spines can be stripped off by pulling them through a gloved hand.) Split thick roots and vines in half before boiling them. Coil the vines, and tie them loosely together. Cover them with water, and boil 2 to 6 hours, depending on the rigidity of the vines. Let the vines soak in the water overnight. To obtain a smoother weaving material, rub or strip off the loosened bark. Use the vines immediately, or hang the coils to dry. When you are ready to use dry vines, soak them for 20 to 60 minutes.

Honeysuckle, wisteria, jasmine, trumpet creeper, kudzu, rattan vine (*Berchemia scandens*), dewberry, English ivy, periwinkle, morning glory, and Virginia creeper all are useful. Use clematis vines with caution, as they can blister the skin.

The shaggy bark on some grapevines is suitable for weaving. Boil the loose strips and slender vines for an hour. Strip the bark off the vines, and split them to the desired width. The vines themselves usually are too crooked for weaving, but a slender vine with tendrils makes an attractive basket handle.

NO FUSS, NO BOTHER

The following plants shrink very little after collection and so do not need to be dried. You can use them for weaving the same day they are collected. Simply soak them in water until they are wetted and supple (15 to 30 minutes), and proceed with your weaving. They can also be stored for later use.

Leaves and Flower Stalks

The leaves of iris and day lilies turn lovely shades of yellow and orange as they wilt, and they actually furnish better weaving materials when picked after the green colors fade. Use brown pine needles, the fallen leaf stems of walnuts, pecans, and hickories, the thin side branches of bamboo, and the brown leaves of cattails and palm fronds. After the seed head forms, cattail flower stalks may be split and dampened slightly for use. The smooth black stems of the leaves of the maidenhair fern (*Adiantum capillus-veneris*) and the stems and rhizomes of the bracken fern (*Pteridium aquilinum*) furnish strong stitching materials.

Branches

Green willow branches furnish excellent basketmaking materials that you can use immediately. Strip off the bark for a satiny smooth texture (boiling helps loosen the bark). Soak the green branches for about 30

Black willow—*Salix nigra*

minutes, and keep them wet as you use them. If you must store them for later use, they will require several hours of soaking to prevent brittleness. The ornamental weeping willow has the longest branches and turns nearly black when dry. The native black willow (*Salix nigra*) dries to a rich brown. Willow branches and saplings can be used to make rustic chairs and other furniture. Limbs ½ to 2 inches in diameter are flexible enough to bend into the desired shapes. Native Americans chewed willow twigs as a painkiller. The plant contains salicylic acid, the same compound from which aspirin is derived.

Bark

Use the loose threadlike fibers on the trunks of some junipers and on the trunks and leaf stalks of the sabal palm as weaving and stitching material.

Seed Pods

The long, straight seed pods of catalpa trees provide black basketry materials. Scoop them off the ground in summer, fall, and winter. If well aged, the pods can be used without additional drying. Soak them for about an hour, and split the halves in two with your fingernail or an awl.

Textile Fibers

Cotton and linen exemplify two types of plant fibers used to weave textiles. Flax (*Linum usitatissimum*), a native of Europe, contains long fibers in the outer layers of the stem. The fibers are extracted from the stem by processes called retting and scutching (Hill 1952). Then the fibers are spun together and woven into the cloth known as linen. Archeologists have found evidence that the Swiss Lake Dwellers cultivated and wove with flax fibers 10,000 years ago (Schery 1972). Native Americans used the fibers of *Linum lewisii* for weaving and making fishing line. Linseed oil, extracted from the seeds of *Linum usitatissimum,* is used in paints, varnishes, and linoleum, and flaxseeds are used as a laxative.

Cotton occurs as fluff attached to cottonseeds. The cotton is separated from the seeds, spun into threads, and then woven into cloth. When the Spanish first arrived in the New World, cotton (*Gossypium* species) was already in cultivation in Mexico and throughout the Southwest. The Pueblo Indians had been weaving cotton on frame looms since A.D. 700, if not earlier (Dockstader 1984). And archeologists have discovered loom-woven cotton textiles in Mexico possibly dating from 1500 B.C. (MacNeish 1971).

Though cotton and linen furnish the main vegetable fibers used for textiles today, previous generations relied on a much greater variety of plant fibers. Let's take a look at some examples of two types of textile fibers, those that must be extracted from the plant pulp and those that are attached to seeds.

Extracted Fibers: Retting and Scutching

The following plants contain threadlike fibers that require extraction from the plant pulp. To remove these fibers from the plant stems, leaves, bark, or roots, you can ret or scutch them or both. Retting involves simply soaking the plant in water until the fibers work loose from the pulp. The process usually takes several days. Take care not to ret the fibers so long that they become brittle. Scutching refers to scraping the fibers out of the pulp. Most fibers can be scutched without retting, but retting helps loosen the threads.

A number of economically important fiber plants, including cotton and jute, belong to the mallow family. Most bear their fibers in the bark of the stems. To remove the fibers, cut long stem sections and ret them for a few days. Gently tug the wet fibers apart by hand, scraping out the pulp as you separate the threads. Orinoco jute (*Corchorus hirtus*) is a Texas species in the same genus as the Old World jute. The colonists introduced chingma, or China jute (*Abutilon theophrasti*), into the United States in the 1700s as a fiber crop (Spencer 1984). Because chingma could not compete economically with hemp, attempts at cultivation soon were discontinued. Now considered a noxious weed, chingma costs American farmers more than $300 million in lost food crops annually. The Chinese still grow chingma for use in rugs and papermaking, however. The Mexican Kickapoos formerly used the stem fibers of Indian mallow (*Abutilon incanum*) for cordage (Latorre and Latorre 1977). A number of Old World species of *Hibiscus* and *Sida* contain strong stem fibers (Mitchell 1982). Our native mallows may be worthy of experimentation.

The bark of the stems of stinging nettles (*Urtica*), bequilla (*Sesbania macrocarpa*), common reed (*Phragmites communis*), milkweeds (*Asclepias*), Indian hemp (*Apocynum cannabinum*), kudzu (*Pueraria lobata*), and sunflowers (*Helianthus*) all contain usable fibers. Both ancient and modern peoples have used these fibers extensively. Nettle fibers have been used in recent times in Europe, and species of *Apocynum* in the USSR, as substitutes for flax (Hill 1952; Schery 1972). The Japanese weave kudzu fibers into kimonos (Tanner et al. 1979). Cattail leaves and stems also yield good fibers. The Russians have used the buoyant pith of sunflower stems as a flotation material for life preservers (Heiser 1976). Spanish moss (*Tillandsia usneoides*, photograph on plate 6) contains black wiry fibers throughout. Until plastics replaced these elastic fibers, American automobile manufacturers and furniture makers used the retted fibers to stuff automobile cushions and couches.

The leaves of agaves, red yucca (Hesperaloë parviflora), and sotol (*Dasylirion*), and the leaves and roots of yuccas, contain excellent fibers. The economically valuable fibers sisal and henequen are extracted from cultivated species of *Agave* in Mexico. Rope, twine, nets, blankets, rugs, and cloth are produced from these fibers. The Mexicans collect lechuguilla (*Agave lecheguilla*) leaves from the wild and extract the fibers by hand for brush manufacturers in the United States. The leaves of most agaves contain chemicals that can severely blister your skin. For that reason, the plants must be handled with great care. Protect your hands, arms, legs, and eyes from the caustic juices as you cut the thick leaves. Ret the leaves until the pulp is completely disintegrated, and wear gloves to scutch the fibers. Once you have eliminated the pulp, the fibers are safe to handle.

Fibers Attached to Seeds

Cattails produce brown spikes of seeds. Each seed clings to silky fibers that provide good insulation and are buoyant and water-resistant. During World War II the Navy used cattail floss as a substitute for kapok in life jackets. Also during the war, the Germans employed the fluff in the construction of boards for sound- and heat-insulating. You too can take advantage of these qualities of the cattail. Collect the seed heads in summer and fall, while they are still firm. Gently pull the fluff from the stalks. You don't have to remove the seeds to use the fluff. Loosen the fibers until the mass is fluffy, then use them to stuff pillows, jackets, and comforters.

The fluff in milkweed pods also provides insulation and buoyant waterproofing. You can spin cattail and milkweed fibers into threads. Formerly, milkweed threads were used for candlewicking. The two Texas species known to produce the best fibers are the swamp milkweeds *Asclepias incarnata* and *Asclepias curassavica*. The fluffy fibers produced by thistles (*Cirsium*) and some other wildflowers are too short to spin but may be used as tinder for starting fires or as an insulation for shoes.

Dyeing Plant Fibers

In many baskets and textiles the natural color and texture of the plant materials combine with the weave to form the only decoration. It is not uncommon, however, to see natural fiber baskets and woven textiles that have been painted or dyed. You can dye your own basketry or textile fibers in much the same way that you can dye wool. Unfortunately, plant fibers do not respond as well to vegetable dyes as do animal fibers such as wool, silk, and mohair. You may have to use synthetic dyes if you want strong colors, but a number of natural dyes work well on plant fibers. The colors listed in the chapter "Colorful Dyes From Texas Plants" are obtained on wool. Expect to get lighter, more muted colors on plant fibers. Some vegetable dyes won't work at all on plants. Start with dyes that you know produce strong, durable colors on wool. Onion skins, oak, walnut, hickory, pecan, sumac, cochineal, and indigo work well on cotton and other plant fibers. Though mordanting is not necessary with these particular dyes (except onions), mordants will produce stronger colors.

To prepare plant fibers for dyeing, scour them first. Tie the plant fibers in coils or bundles. If possible, soak the fibers in water overnight. Then scour cotton, linen, jute, reed, and other strong fibers by boiling them in water with mild soap and a bit of washing soda for 1 to 2 hours. With plant fibers, you do not have to worry about abrupt changes in water temperature as you do with wool. As an alternative scouring technique for raffia and other weak or brittle fibers, presoak the fibers for just a few minutes, then wash them gently in warm soapy water for a few minutes more. Rinse the scoured fibers, and mordant them using one of the following mordanting techniques.

Premordant the fibers using the same materials and techniques as for wool (see "Mordants," beginning on page 327, and "Mordanting the Wool," beginning on page 336). To prevent excessive wetting of weak or brittle fibers, mordant them in the dyebath.

As an alternative, Ida Grae (1974) recommends a three-step method for mordanting plant fibers: mordant them in tannic acid at 150° F, then mordant them in alum, then in tannic acid again.

After mordanting the fibers, you may want to leave them in the mordant bath overnight. Rinse the fibers briefly when you remove them from the mordant. You can then dye the fibers immediately or dry and store them for later dyeing. If they are dried, wet the fibers thoroughly before dyeing. For strong fibers that will not deteriorate with long soaking, an overnight soak is recommended.

Prepare a vegetable dye by choosing one of the plants listed in the dye chapter. Soak the dye plants in water for at least 24 hours. Follow the instructions for simmer dyeing, steps 2 and 3, on page 339. Then strain the vegetable matter from the dyebath.

Next, add your wet plant fibers to the dyebath. Add enough water to fill the pot three-fourths full. Bring the bath to a boil, and simmer for 10 minutes to 1 hour. Check the color periodically. Remove the fibers when the color is slightly darker than you want it. Wash and rinse the fibers. They are now ready for weaving or may be dried and stored for later use.

Papermaking

Before the invention of paper, people used whatever they had on hand for writing and drawing—stone, bone, wood, leaves, bark, mushrooms, leather, clay, and metal. Parchment and vellum were made from the skins of sheep or calves (in the old days, college students really did receive a sheepskin at graduation). Papyrus, while not truly paper, involved a higher degree of manufacture than most other writing surfaces. The earliest Egyptian papyrus book, the Prisse Papyrus, dates from 2200 B.C. and was made with the stalks of a sedge, *Cyperus papyrus.* Strips of the split stalks were placed crosswise on top of each other and pressed into a thin laminated sheet (Hunter 1967).

People in other areas of the world have constructed papyruslike material from other plants. The Samoans still use the inner bark of the paper mulberry tree (*Broussonetia papyrifera*) to make tapa cloth. Tapa provided the principal clothing material of many Polynesian peoples until the early twentieth century (Hill 1952). The South Pacific islanders scrape thin layers of wood from the tree trunk, soak them in water, and pound several layers together to form thin sheets. Today Samoans use tapa mainly as a surface for artwork. Introduced to the United States as an ornamental small tree, the paper mulberry now grows like a weed in Texas. Tonkawa Indians in Central Texas used the inner bark of our native mulberries (*Morus*) in a similar manner for cloth.

A Chinese man, Ts'ai Lun, is the earliest papermaker on record, about A.D. 105, though paper may have already been in use in China 250 years earlier. To make true paper, plants are chopped, retted, and pounded into minute fibers. Sheets of paper are molded from a slurry of the pulp fiber and water. For an excellent history of papermaking, read Dard Hunter's book, listed below.

From the time of Ts'ai Lun until about 180 years ago, all paper was made by hand. The invention of papermaking machinery rapidly shut down hand papermaking mills in the nineteenth century, but a few handmade paper organizations have kept the craft alive. Hand papermaking is an exciting art form. While certain plants work better for commercial paper production, there is practically no limit to the number of different plants that you can use to make your own paper at home. Every plant mentioned above as a fiber plant may be used for papermaking. The stalks and leaves of sedges, rushes, and grasses, cattail leaves and stalks, wisteria vines, dandelions, the inner bark of tree branches—all provide materials for experimentation.

How to Make Paper

The instructions below furnish the basic information for making paper with a minimum of equipment in your own kitchen or as an activity with schoolchildren. For details on sizing and dyeing paper, making watermarks, and building a mold and a paper press, refer to Weidenmüller's (1980) and Mason's (1963) books, listed below. For additional artistic hints for decorative papermaking, refer to Mason's and Hunter's (1967) books and other books on the topic.

EQUIPMENT

Papermaking mold (You can buy one already made, or make your own. For a simple mold for school or home experiments, I have used an embroidery hoop with bridal veil stretched across it. This device works reasonably well, but the round pieces of paper have the unfortunate quality of resembling a Texas cow patty, especially when they are made of unbleached plant fibers!)
Bleach
Caustic soda
Rubber gloves
Assorted pots, pans, washbasins, jars
Large wire sieves, coarse- and fine-wire mesh
Boards larger than your mold
Several dozen pieces of felt, slightly larger than the mold
An electric blender (optional but helpful)

PREPARING THE PULP

You can buy prepackaged pulp for papermaking at craft stores, but you miss out on half the fun. To prepare your own pulp from wild plants, follow these steps.

STEP 1: In your first experiments use one or two plants with soft parts, such as dandelion and sow thistle leaves, stalks, and flowers. As you become more skilled, you can try out some tougher materials, such as barks. Gather a large bagful of plant material. Cut the plants into small pieces, about ½ inch long or shorter. You may want to ret the plants slightly to loosen the fibers before proceeding. If so, put them in a container, add water, and let the mixture sit for a couple of days.

STEP 2: After retting, strain the plants through a coarse sieve, and throw out the water. Place the plants in a fresh pot of water. Bring the water to a boil, and simmer the plants until they are soft and mushy. (John Mason (1963) recommends adding a bit of caustic soda to the pot to help separate the fibers. Use very little soda, about 2 teaspoons or less per quart of liquid. Be sure to protect your hands from the soda by wearing plastic gloves. If working with children, do not use caustic soda.)

STEP 3: Strain the plants through a coarse sieve. While holding the plants under a faucet, work them with your hands to wash out the fleshy, nonfibrous plant material. Plunge the sieve in and out of a basin of water a few times. The suction will pull out some of the small pieces of flesh. Don't overdo this, however, or you'll start losing valuable fiber.

STEP 4: Ret the plants for a couple of days to further loosen the fibers. If you do not want your paper to be the color of the plant material, you can bleach it while you ret it. Place the plant fiber in a jar filled with water, and add about a cup of bleach per gallon of liquid. Add more bleach if needed, but be careful not to overdo it. Bleach can weaken the final product.

STEP 5: After retting the plants, strain them through a fine-mesh sieve. Run water through the sieve to remove all the bleach from the fibers.

STEP 6: Now you are ready to "beat it to a pulp." The fibers still form large clumps that need to be separated. The smaller the fibers, the smoother the paper. An electric blender will assist with this phase of pulp production. Run the pulp through the blender, then pound it out by hand with a mortar and pestle, a meat grinder, or anything you can find. Pound and blend the pulp until the fibers no longer form clumps when a teaspoon of pulp is stirred in a glass of water.

FORMING THE PAPER

STEP 1: Lay out a wooden or plastic board on which to set your paper sheets as you form them. Dampen the pieces of felt. Lay one piece of felt on the board.

STEP 2: Add a portion of the pulp to a large tub of water and stir. Add enough pulp to make a thick slurry. As you make pieces of paper, you will need to occasionally add more pulp to thicken up the slurry.

STEP 3: Now grasp your mold by the edges with both hands. Hold the mold vertical, and lower it into the tub. When the mold touches the bottom of the tub, turn the mold so that it is horizontal. Slowly raise the mold to the surface. When the edges of the mold break the water surface, gently shake the mold back and forth to distribute the fibers more evenly. Now lift the mold out of the water, and let the water drain out.

STEP 4: Carefully turn the mold facedown onto the dampened felt. Press the mold firmly onto the felt (if you use an embroidery hoop mold, you will need to remove the cloth from the hoop before pressing the cloth and paper onto the felt). As you carefully lift the mold, your first sheet of paper will cling to the felt. Lay another piece of damp felt over the paper. As you make more sheets of paper, lay them on top of the previous sheets with one or several pieces of felt between them.

STEP 5: When you finish making your paper, you will need to press the water out of the paper. You can press three or four sheets of paper at a time (still separated with felt) by placing the sheets on top of a wooden board and putting another board on top. Stand on the boards to press out the water.

STEP 6: Carefully pull the sheets of paper off the felt. You can dry them by hanging them on a line, laying them out on sheets of plastic, or ironing them between two cotton towels. Voilà! You have your own home-made paper.

Though today American paper manufacturers rely on only a few species of plants, predominantly pines, for commercial production of paper pulp, many other plants produce superior paper. Papermakers have utilized a number of the textile fiber plants listed above. The Romanians rely on common reed (*Phragmites communis*) for their paper pulp. Other large cane-producing grasses, such as *Arundo donax,* have commercial potential as substitutes for pine pulp. The Koreans make wallpaper from the kudzu vine. An American firm has reproduced an oriental process of papermaking and markets kudzu paper as a high-quality, special-purpose artists' paper. During World War II the Navy used leaf fibers of *Yucca glauca* to make a heavy paper. Other plants with potential for pulp production include water hyacinths, cattails, sunflowers, retama, alfalfa, and white sweet clover. As our forests diminish, we will be forced to look more closely at faster-growing alternatives to pines as commercial sources of pulp. Meanwhile, the hand papermaker need only turn to her or his back yard or alleyway to find an abundance of materials for making paper.

Recommended Reading

PAPERMAKING

Hunter, Dard. 1967. *Paper-making: The History and Technique of an Ancient Craft.* New York: Alfred A. Knopf.

Mason, John. 1963. *Paper Making as an Artistic Craft.* Leicester, England: Twelve by Eight Press.

Weidenmüller, Ralf. 1980. *Papermaking.* San Diego: Thorfinn International.

WEAVING AND BASKETMAKING

Black, Mary E. 1980. *Key to Weaving: A Textbook of Hand Weaving for the Beginning Weaver.* New York: MacMillan. (An essential book for any weaver.)

Brown, Rachel, and Cheryl McGowen. 1978. *The Weaving, Spinning, and Dyeing Book.* New York: Alfred A. Knopf.

Hart, Carol, and Dan Hart. 1976. *Natural Basketry.* New York: Watson-Guptill.

Held, Shirley E. 1973. *Weaving: A Handbook for Fiber Craftsmen.* New York: Holt, Rinehart and Winston.

Meilach, Dona Z. 1974. *A Modern Approach to Basketry With Fibers and Grasses.* New York: Crown.

Redding, Deborah. 1985. *Learning to Weave With Debbie Redding.* Loveland, Colo.: Interweave Press.

Smith, Sue M. 1983. *Natural Fiber Basketry.* Fort Worth, Tex.: Willow Bend Press.

PERIODICALS

Handwoven. (Interweave Press, 306 N. Washington Avenue, Loveland, Colorado 80537.)

Shuttle, Spindle, and Dyepot. (Handweavers Guild of America, 65 La Salle Road, West Hartford, Connecticut 06107.)

Spin-off. (Interweave Press, 306 N. Washington Avenue, Loveland, Colorado 80537.)

Threads. (Taunton Press, Newton, Connecticut 06470.)

Weaver's Journal. (Araña Press, 2304 University Avenue, P.O. Box 14238, St. Paul, Minnesota 55114.)

7 Rubber, Wax, Oil, and Soap

NOTE: Many of the plants in this chapter are illustrated or described elsewhere in the book. For more information about a particular plant, refer to the index.

Have you ever chewed candelilla gum? Or traveled on a guayule tire? No, candelilla and guayule are not brand names for new products. They are plants that grow in the Chihuahuan Desert of West Texas and northern Mexico. In the not so distant past, these plants played an important part in the economy of the Southwest. In the future, they may once again be elevated to a role of great importance.

Candelilla, *Euphorbia antisyphilitica* (see photograph, plate 9), consists of a cluster of leafless strawlike vertical stems, forming an elaborate candelabra growing close to the ground. A white wax coats the gray-green stems. Wax from the candelilla has provided a source of income for laborers on both sides of the Rio Grande since the early 1900s. The wax was in high demand during both world wars, when imported vegetable wax could not be obtained (Hodge and Sineath 1956; Maxwell 1968). Candelilla wax has been used in sealing wax and candles, in phonograph records, in waterproofing, in polishes for automobiles, floors, and shoes, in electrical wire insulation, and in cosmetics.

After World War II, production of wax from petroleum forced a drastic drop in the selling price of vegetable wax. The decimation of many wild stands of candelilla added to the impetus to shut down United States production of candelilla wax. But candelilla wax production continues today in Mexico, and it continues in much the same manner as it did seventy

Guayule—*Parthenium argentatum*

years ago. The shrubby plants are harvested from the wild and heated in a mixture of water and sulfuric acid. The wax floats to the top of the vat and is scooped off and placed in barrels to solidify. To prevent depletion of native stands of candelilla, the Mexican government has placed quotas on, and at times has prohibited, wax production and export. To circumvent government quotas, some wax producers have resorted to smuggling their wax across the border (Wauer 1973). Despite the availability of petroleum substitutes, a small market still remains for vegetable wax. Today manufacturers in the United States, the principal buyers of Mexican candelilla, use the wax mainly in chewing gum and cosmetics. Though cultivation of candelilla may soon become necessary to preserve native stands, currently cultivation in the United States is uneconomical while wild candelilla remains available.

Another southwestern industry followed a path similar to that of the candelilla. In 1888 researchers in England verified what American Indians had known for centuries. The stems and roots of guayule, *Parthenium argentatum* (illustrated), contain a gummy substance that can be used to make rubber. Guayule is a small shrub with narrow silvery-gray leaves. The flowers of this member of the sunflower family form tiny cream-colored heads on long, slender stalks. Archeologists have found small rubber balls in sites in Mexico. They believe that native Americans made the toy balls by chewing the bark of the guayule (Hill 1952). Guayule rubber does not flow in latex canals, as latex does in milkweed and other plants with milky sap (Schery 1972). In guayule the latex is trapped in the cells of the plant. It can be extracted by macerating the whole shrub and then separated by flotation.

The plants analyzed by the British researchers in 1888 contained 10 percent rubber by dry weight (Lloyd 1911). Later studies found that the plants vary in rubber content, with some individuals containing as much as 26 percent rubber. Financiers from the United States and Germany soon built rubber extraction companies in Mexico, and a rubber processing facility was constructed in the United States. By 1910 fourteen extraction facilities were in operation in Mexico and one in Marathon, Texas, in the Trans-Pecos. By that time 50 percent of the rubber used in the United States was produced from guayule.

But the first guayule boom was short-lived. Depletion of wild stands and the depredations of Pancho Villa forced rubber production out of Mexico in 1912. Using seeds smuggled out of Mexico, a company set up operations in Salinas, California, and continued to produce small amounts of rubber. The Texas factory thrived through World War I, but production there slowed after the war, as native stands were further depleted. Imported rubber again became the main source for the United States.

The para rubber tree, *Hevea brasiliensis,* is native to South America, but more than 90 percent of the world's natural rubber is grown on plantations in Southeast Asia (Holm et al. 1977; Baker 1965). During World War II the Japanese gained control of rubber production, and the United States lost practically all of its rubber supply. And so guayule production gained a second period of popularity. Mexican production was rejuvenated. The United States government purchased the California operation and began a massive guayule project, which included planting 30,000 acres of the shrubs, but the war ended before the planted crops reached maturity. At the end of the war Southeast Asian rubber again became available, and synthetic rubber from petroleum caught the interest of the American government. Guayule rubber, with its high resin content and depleted wild stands, was considered an unnecessary and undesirable third to para and synthetic rubbers. The crop planted in California was destroyed, and guayule rubber production in the United States and Mexico came to a dead stop within a few years (Ritchie 1979; Broad 1978).

Between 1945 and today, petroleum products have cornered much of the rubber market. Yet there still exists a demand for high-quality natural rubber. In the past few years the demand for natural rubber has increased as synthetic rubber has been found to be inferior to natural rubber, especially for use in tires. Today radial tires contain as much as 40 percent natural rubber, and tires for aircraft and heavy machinery nearly 100 percent. Rather than being less dependent, today the United States is even more dependent on imported natural rubber than it was before 1945, importing more than half a billion dollars' worth of natural rubber annually. It is estimated that world demand for natural rubber will soon exceed the supply.

These changes in the rubber market have prompted the United States and Mexican governments and private industries to take another look at guayule. The high resin content in the shrub, at one time considered an impediment to production of high-quality rubber, no longer poses a problem. Modern methods of solvent extraction enable separation of the resins, which themselves have value in industry. With its resins removed, guayule rubber is equivalent in quality to para rubber.

A pilot project in Saltillo, Mexico, funded by the Mexican government, has produced radial tires that pass United States high-speed endurance tests (Bungay 1981). In 1978 President Carter signed into law the Native Latex Commercialization Act, which provided funding for research and development of guayule rubber production. Firestone and Goodyear tire and rubber companies have both begun research on modern methods of extraction and have started plantings of guayule. The success of these latest guayule ventures depends on determined efforts at large-scale cultivation. The days of wild harvest of guayule will soon end. Only through the cultivation of these extraordinary desert plants can we produce a large volume of inexpensive rubber and assure the preservation of our remaining wild stands (Campos-López and Neavez-Camacho 1979).

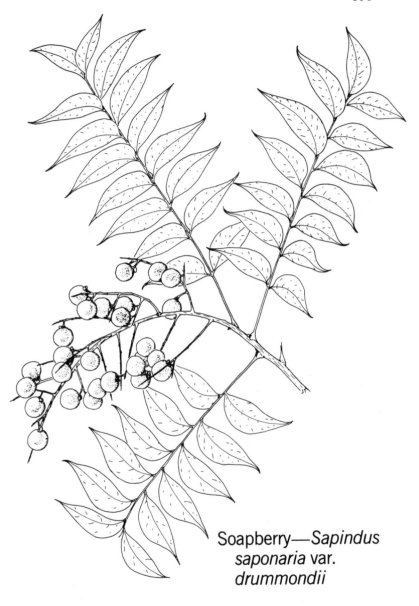

Soapberry—*Sapindus saponaria* var. *drummondii*

Candelilla and guayule are by no means the only plants that have the potential to provide us with wax, rubber, and other industrially valuable products. Thomas Edison promoted the use of several species of goldenrod as sources of rubber (Hill 1952; Schery 1972). Recent studies by the U.S. Department of Agriculture and several American universities have evaluated the chemical makeup of hundreds of native and naturalized North American plants (Carr, Phillips, and Bagby 1985; Carr 1985; Wang and Huffman 1981; Thompson 1985; Buchanan et al. 1978; McLaughlin and Hoffmann 1982). Dozens of the plants studied have been shown to contain latex that is high in hydrocarbons, the compounds that go into making fuels, rubber, plastics, organic chemicals, and textiles, all items that we derive from petroleum today. Waxes, vegetable oils, essential oils, resins, gums, tannins, and soaps are other industrially valuable products that may be obtained from these plants.

Today, much more than before World War II, we depend on foreign resources for many of these products. Although we manufacture petroleum products at home, most of our oil comes from the Middle East. Political instabilities abroad and the rapid depletion of world petroleum resources may soon force us to find alternatives to these foreign resources. Some of our native plants, if put into wide-scale cultivation, may provide us with those alternatives. Although nearly all of the major world industrial and food crops require large amounts of water for growth, many plants from the southwestern United States are suited to arid land cultivation. In fact, plants such as candelilla and guayule produce higher levels of wax and rubber in low-water situations. If agriculture in the arid Southwest continues at present water use rates, by the year 2000 the available water will supply only half of what is needed. Texas has already begun to feel the water crunch. Future agriculture will necessitate the cultivation of industrial and food crops that are low-water consumers. The time to start putting these plants into production is now, not later, when water and foreign resources are no longer so readily available to us.

Besides guayule, a large number of other species from the sunflower family contain potentially valuable hydrocarbons: gumweed (*Grindelia squarrosa*), rabbitbrush (*Chrysothamnus nauseosus*), giant ragweed (*Ambrosia trifida*), tall goldenrod (*Solidago altissima*), sow thistle (*Sonchus arvensis*), tall boneset (*Eupatorium altissimum*), compass plant (*Silphium laciniatum*), broomweed (*Xanthocephalum gymnospermoides*), and seepwillow (*Baccharis glutinosa*). Other Texas plants high in hydrocarbons include the spurges (*Euphorbia*), milkweeds (*Asclepias*), bergamot (*Monarda fistulosa*), Indian hemp (*Apocynum cannabinum*), *Amsonia*, wild-rye (*Elymus virginicus*), *Ruellia strepens, Pycnanthemum tenuifolium,* elderberry (*Sambucus canadensis*), and pines (*Pinus*).

Many of these plants also contain good amounts of oils and waxes. Some furnish fibers, protein, or carbohydrates. These multiple-use plants offer possible alternatives to the single-use crops we tend to emphasize in agriculture today.

When sisal and henequen fibers are extracted from agaves in Mexico, the residue yields a commercially valuable wax. Other local sources of wax include ocotillo, soapberry (*Sapindus saponaria*), and Chinese tallow tree (*Sapium sebiferum*). Native Americans and European pioneers put a number of plants to use as soaps. The coating on wax myrtle berries has been used to make candles and soaps. A high content of saponin (a toxic alkaloid) yields a cleansing lather in the following: soapberries, the leaves and roots of bouncing bet (*Saponaria officinalis*), and the roots of buffalo gourd, yuccas, and agaves. Soap made from bouncing bet, a Texas wildflower, is used in museums to clean antique draperies and textiles.

Besides having traditional uses in cooking, vegetable oils have industrial value as lubricants, as coatings (such as linseed oil on linoleum), and as ingredients in paints, pharmaceuticals, plastics, adhesives, and soaps. Some oils will burn in diesel engines. Sunflower seed oil is blended with linseed oil in paints and is used as a lubricant and an illuminant. Other species of sunflowers also furnish good sources of oils. The castor bean, a native of the Orient, produces highly toxic seeds, but the oil from the seeds provides one of the world's most valuable industrial oils. Castor oil is used in the making of pharmaceuticals, nylon, synthetic rubber, imitation leather, typewriter ink, a lubricant, and a score of other products. The United States currently imports about $40 million worth of the oil yearly (Thompson 1985). The seeds of our native bladderpods (*Lesquerella* species) contain an oil that may provide a good substitute for castor oil, and the plants can be grown in the United States with little water usage. Other Texas plants with seeds high in oils include milkweeds, soapberry, oaks, evening primrose (*Oenothera biennis, O. hookeri*), alfalfa, pines, grapes, buffalo gourd, mustards, spicebush, pokeweed, evergreen sumac (*Rhus virens* subsp. *choriophylla*), silk tassel (*Garrya wrightii*), cowpen daisy (*Verbesina enceloides*), devil's claw (*Proboscidea* species), and clammyweed (*Polanisia dodecandra*). Many of these oil plants also may be used in soapmaking (Jamieson 1943; Horrobin 1981; Schery 1972).

Aromatic essential oils, traditionally used in perfumes and as flavorings, can also be converted into organic chemicals for industry, and some of those oils, such as eucalyptus oil, have potential value as engine fuels. The essential oils in lemon mint (*Monarda citriodora*) yield citronellol, used as a perfume and insect repellent. Resins can be used to produce organic chemicals for various industrial purposes, including waterproofing, pharmaceuticals, varnishes, and paints. Pine resin, or turpentine, is combustible and may prove to be useful as a component in gasohol. Gums are valued as adhesives, sizings, thickeners, and stabilizers. Gum arabic, made from the sap of various Middle Eastern species of *Acacia,* is widely used in adhesives, confections, inks, cosmetics, medicinals, and a variety of other products. Huisache (*Acacia farnesiana*) and mesquite gum have potential as substitutes for gum arabic. Many species mentioned for hydrocarbon value are also sources of resins, gums, and essential oils. Other potential local sources include creosote bush (*Larrea tridentata*), sweet gum (*Liquidambar styraciflua*), and ocotillo.

Other usable plant resources are the tannins and phenolic compounds, collectively known as polyphenols. While vegetable tannins have limited value in the textile and leather industries of today, they have uses in other industries, such as in muds for oil well drilling. Polyphenols hold promise as sources of adhesives. Polyphenols may be obtained from sumac (*Rhus glabra, Rhus virens* subsp. *choriophylla*), retama (*Parkinsonia aculeata*), mistletoe (*Phoradendron villosum*), desert willow (*Chilopsis linearis*), wormwood (*Artemisia ludoviciana*), and *Aster ericoides*.

Several wild Texas plants have excellent potential as sources of starch, which has numerous industrial applications. Hydrolyzed, it can be converted into the sugars dextrin, maltose, and glucose, which are used in human and livestock foods and beverages as well as in fermentation processes. Hydrogen also can be produced from starch. The roots of buffalo gourd and cattails both have good economic potential for starch production.

These are but a few of the possible industrial and commercial uses for our native and naturalized plants. Many other local plants have yet to be investigated for their potential useful components. If you are interested in learning more about research in this area, see the references cited in this chapter.

Glossary

Achene—A small dry fruit containing a single seed (example: sunflower seed).

Aggregate fruit—A dense cluster of berries, such as a dewberry or blackberry.

Alternate—An arrangement of plant parts, such as leaves, that is neither opposite nor whorled (see black willow illustration on page 381).

Anther—The tip of the stamen, holding the pollen.

Areole—A small protrusion or depression, such as those scattered across the surface of cacti stems.

Axil—The juncture of a leaf or flower with a stalk.

Berry—A fleshy fruit without a hard stone (example: tomato).

Bilateral symmetry—Said of an object, such as a flower, that will form mirror-image halves when cut along only one plane (see devil's claw illustration on page 374; compare with "radial symmetry").

Bipinnately compound leaf—In this text, refers to a leaf composed of two or more pinnately compound sections joined at their bases (see honey mesquite illustration on page 90).

Blade—The broad, flat portion of a leaf or petal.

Bloom—A white waxy coating, such as that found on the surface of some fruits; also, a flower or blossom.

Bract—A structure occurring below the petals and sepals of a flower. Bracts are usually small and leaflike, but on some species they are colorful and showy, like petals.

Capsule—A dry fruit composed of more than one ovary (example: yucca fruit).

Catkin—A flower spike, often pendent in a tree or shrub. The tiny flowers usually lack petals and bear only male or only female parts (example: pecan or willow catkins).

Compound leaf—A leaf divided into two or more units, with each unit, or leaflet, resembling a separate leaf (see walnut illustration on page 323; compare with "simple leaf").

Disk flowers—The tubelike flowers found on the heads of members of Asteraceae (refer to page 38 for details).

Dissected leaf—A leaf blade that is cut into many small sections, such as a yarrow leaf (see illustration on page 5) or carrot leaf.

Drupe—A fleshy fruit with a single hard stone, such as in a cherry. The stone may contain several seeds.

Entire margin—A leaf edge that has no teeth or lobes (see illustration of poke on page 267).

Gall—A swelling on a plant, such as those resulting when an insect or mite lays eggs in a twig, leaf, or branch.

Glochid—A small barbed hairlike spine (see photograph of prickly pear cactus on plate 7).

Head—A cluster of flowers densely packed on a single receptacle. The cluster may resemble a single flower (see photograph of Maximilian sunflower on plate 5 and illustration of huisache on page 81).

Indehiscent—Describes a fruit that does not split open at maturity.

Inflorescence—A flower cluster.

Involucre—A whorl of bracts below an inflorescence (such as found on a sunflower).

Lanceolate—Lance-shaped; long and narrow, diminishing to a point at the tip (see leaves of green milkweed, illustrated on page 248).

Leaflet—One of the units of a compound leaf.

Lobe—A large indentation on the margin of a leaf (see castor bean illustration on page 276).

Margin—The edge of a leaf.

Oblanceolate—Lance-shaped; long and narrow, with the fatter end at the tip (see leaves of plantain, illustrated on page 132).

Obovate—Egg-shaped, with the broader end at the tip (see leaves on brasil illustration, page 201).

Opposite—An arrangement of plant parts, such as leaves, in which two occur at one point on the stalk (see horehound illustration on page 161; compare with "whorl" and "alternate").

Oval—A broad ellipse, with both ends the same width (see leaves on Texas persimmon illustration, page 178; compare with "ovate").

Ovary—The base of the pistil (the female organ of a flower), containing the embryos that develop into seeds.

Ovate—Egg-shaped, with the broader end at the base (see leaves on chile pequín illustration, page 217).

Palmately compound leaf—A compound leaf in which all the leaflets are united at a single point (see red buckeye illustration on page 263; compare with "pinnately compound leaf").

Palmately lobed—Having large indentations diverging from a single point (see leaves on castor bean illustration, page 276; compare with "pinnately lobed").

Panicle—A type of flower cluster. The flowers, each on a short stem, are arranged along a stalk that branches off a central stalk (see arrangement of fruits on prairie flameleaf sumac illustration, page 36).

Papilionaceous flower—A particular type of flower of the legume family with bilateral symmetry, such as a bluebonnet. The top petal is called the banner, the two side petals are the wings, and the bottom two petals form a tiny boatlike keel (see mescal bean photograph, plate 11).

Pedicel—The stem of a single flower.

Petals—The leaflike parts of a flower that are usually brightly colored and enclose the reproductive organs (compare with "sepals" and "tepals").

Petiole—The stem of a leaf.

Pinnately compound leaf—A compound leaf composed of numerous leaflets attached to each side of a central stem. The leaflets may be alternate or opposite on the stem (see soapberry and walnut illustration on pages 395 and 323; compare with "palmately compound leaf").
Twice pinnately compound leaf—A compound leaf in which the pri-

mary units are again divided into pinnately compound sections (see huisache and peppervine illustrations on pages 81 and 340).

Pinnately lobed—Large indentations along two sides of a central axis (see leaves on bur oak illustration, page 101; compare with "palmately lobed").

Pistil—The egg-bearing (female) part of a flower, which includes the ovary, style, and stigma.

Raceme—A type of flower cluster. Each flower has a short stem and is arranged along a central axis (see coral bean illustration on page 255).

Radial symmetry—Said of an object, such as a flower or pie, that will form mirror-image halves when cut along more than one plane (see buffalo gourd photograph on plate 8; compare with "bilateral symmetry").

Ray flower—The straplike flowers found on the heads of members of Asteraceae (see page 38 for details).

Rosette, basal rosette—A circular cluster of leaves at ground level (see shepherd's purse illustration, page 174).

Sepals—Leaflike structures, usually green, arranged in a whorl below the petals of a flower. Some sepals are colorful and indistinguishable from petals (see "tepals" and "bract").

Serrate—Lined with small notches, like a saw blade (see red mulberry leaf illustration on page 209).

Silique—The many-seeded capsule of members of Brassicaceae. Siliques occur in a variety of shapes (see shepherd's purse and peppergrass illustrations on page 174).

Simple leaf—A leaf that is not compound but has a single blade (see poke illustration on page 267; compare with "compound leaf").

Spike—A type of flower cluster. The individual flowers lack stems and are attached directly to the long central stalk (see mullein illustration on page 316).

Stamen—The male part of a flower, usually composed of a long slender stem (the filament) and an enlarged tip that holds the pollen (the anther).

Stigma—The tip of the pistil (the female organ of the flower).

Style—The stem of the pistil.

Teeth—Small notches on the leaf margin (see yaupon and red mulberry illustrations on pages 168 and 209).

Tepals—Refers to both petals and sepals when they are indistinguishable from each other.

Umbel—A type of flower cluster. The individual flowers occur on stems of nearly equal length; the stems unite at one point, at the top of the flower stalk (see green milkweed illustration on page 248).

Whorl—More than two plant parts, such as leaves or flowers, attached in a circle around one point on a stalk.

Bibliography

Abbott, Carroll. 1982. "Poke." *Texas Gardener* (January—February): 23—24.

Adovasio, J. M., and G. F. Fry. 1976. "Prehistoric Psychotrophic Drug Use in Northeastern Mexico and Trans-Pecos Texas." *Economic Botany* 30 (1): 94—96.

Adrosko, Rita J. 1971. *Natural Dyes and Home Dyeing.* New York: Dover.

Ajilvsgi, Geyata. 1979. *Wildflowers of the Big Thicket and East Texas.* College Station: Texas A&M University Press.

———. 1984. *Wildflowers of Texas.* Bryan, Tex.: Shearer.

Allan, Melinda. 1980. "Cattails Against the Cold." *Mother Earth News,* no. 64: 78.

Allen, O. N., and Ethel K. Allen. 1981. *The Leguminosae.* Madison: University of Wisconsin Press.

Amsden, Charles A. 1934. *Navaho Weaving.* Santa Ana, Calif.: Fine Arts Press.

Arnott, Margaret, L., ed. 1975. *Gastronomy: The Anthropology of Food and Food Habits.* The Hague: Mouton.

Baker, Herbert G. 1965. *Plants and Civilization.* Belmont, Calif.: Wadsworth.

Barker, B. E., P. Farnes, and P. H. LaMarche. 1966. "Peripheral Blood Plasmacytosis Following Systemic Exposure to *Phytolacca americana.*" *Pediatrics* 38 (3): 490—93.

Basehart, Harry W. 1974. *American Indian Ethnology*. Vol. 12 of *Indians of the Southwest: Apache Indians*. New York: Garland.

Bearfoot, Will. 1975. *Mother Nature's Dyes and Fibers*. Willits, Calif.: Oliver Press.

Becker, Robert, and Ok-koo K. Grosjean. 1980. "A Compositional Study of Pods of Two Varieties of Mesquite." *Journal of Agricultural Food Chemistry* 28 (1): 22–26.

Bennett, Wendell C., and Robert M. Zingg. 1935. *The Tarahumara*. Chicago: University of Chicago Press.

Berkman, Boris. 1949. "Milkweed: A War Strategic Material." *Economic Botany* 3 (3): 223–39.

Berry, J., P. K. Bretting, G. P. Nabhan, and C. Weber. 1981. "Domesticated *Proboscidea parviflora:* A Potential Oilseed Crop for Arid Lands." *Journal of Arid Environments* 4 (2): 147–60.

Beverley, Robert. 1947. *The History and Present State of Virginia*. Chapel Hill: University of North Carolina Press.

Biesboer, David D. 1984. "Nitrogen Fixation Associated With Natural and Cultivated Stands of *Typha latifolia*." *American Journal of Botany* 71 (4): 505–11.

Bingham, Robert, M.D., Bernard A. Bellew, M.D., and Joeva G. Bellew. 1975. "Yucca Plant Saponin in the Management of Arthritis." *Journal of Applied Nutrition* 27 (2): 45–51.

Blanchard, Florence. 1977. "Piñon." *Mother Earth News,* no. 46: 84.

Bliss, Anne. 1975. "Solar Dyeing." *Interweave* (Fall).

———. 1976a. "Dyeing in the Rockies." *Shuttle, Spindle, and Dyepot* 13 (1): 15–17.
———. 1976b. *Rocky Mountain Dye Plants*. Boulder, Colo.: Juniper House Press.

Borland, Hal, and Les Line. 1981. *A Countryman's Flowers*. New York: Alfred A. Knopf.

Boyd, J. W., D. S. Murray, and R. J. Tyrl. 1984. "Silverleaf Nightshade." *Economic Botany* 38 (2): 210–17.

Bretting, P. K. 1984. "Folk Names and Uses for Martyniaceous Plants." *Economic Botany* 38 (4): 452–63.

Broad, William J. 1978. "Boon or Boondoggle: Bygone U.S. Rubber Shrub Is Bouncing Back." *Science* 202: 410–11.

Brown, Rachel, and Cheryl McGowen. 1978. *The Weaving, Spinning, and Dyeing Book.* New York: Alfred A. Knopf.

Brumgardt, John R., and Larry L. Bowles. 1981. *People of the Magic Waters.* Palm Springs, Calif.: ETC.

Bryan, Nonabah G. 1978. *Navajo Native Dyes.* Palmer Lake, Colo.: Filter Press.

Buchanan, R. A., I. M. Cull, F. H. Otey, and C. R. Russell. 1978. "Hydrocarbon- and Rubber-Producing Crops." *Economic Botany* 32 (2): 131–53.

Bulfinch, Thomas. 1959. *Mythology.* New York: Dell.

Bungay, Henry R. 1981. *Energy: The Biomass Options.* New York: John Wiley and Sons.

Burlage, Henry M. 1968. *Index of Plants of Texas With Reputed Medicinal and Poisonous Properties.* Austin, Tex.

Busch, Phyllis S., and Anne Ophelia Dowden. 1977. *Wildflowers and the Stories Behind Their Names.* New York: Charles Scribner's Sons.

Campos-López, E., and E. Neavez-Camacho. 1979. "The Rubber Shrub." *Chemtech* 9 (January): 50–57.

Carr, M. E. 1985. "Plant Species Evaluated for New Crop Potential." *Economic Botany* 39 (3): 336–45.

Carr, M. E., B. S. Phillips, and M. O. Bagby. 1985. "Xerophytic Species Evaluated for Renewable Energy Resources." *Economic Botany* 39 (4): 505–13.

Chandler, R. F., S. N. Hooper, and M. J. Harvey. 1982. "Ethnobotany and Phytochemistry of Yarrow." *Economic Botany* 36 (2): 203–23.

Correll, Donovan S., and Marshall C. Johnston. 1970. *Manual of the Vascular Plants of Texas.* Renner, Tex.: Texas Research Foundation.

Coulter, Elizabeth L. 1941. "Some Dye Plants of the Texas Plains Region." Master's thesis, North Texas State University.

Craighead, John J., Frank C. Craighead, Jr., and Ray J. Davis. 1963. *A Field Guide to Rocky Mountain Wildflowers.* Boston: Houghton Mifflin.

Crews, Patricia. 1981a. "Considerations in the Selection and Application of Natural Dyes: Dye Plant Selection." *Shuttle, Spindle, and Dyepot* 12 (3): 52–53.

408

——. 1981b. "Considerations in the Selection and Application of Natural Dyes: Mordant Selection." *Shuttle, Spindle, and Dyepot* 12 (2): 15–16.

Crockett, Lawrence J. 1977. *Wildly Successful Plants.* New York: Macmillan.

Croom, Edward M., Jr. 1983. "Documenting and Evaluating Herbal Remedies." *Economic Botany* 37 (1): 13–27.

Crowell, Carolyn, and Joan M. Majtenzi. 1973. "Color From the Fields." *Chemistry* 46 (9): 14–17.

Crowhurst, Adrienne. 1972. *The Weed Cookbook.* New York: Lancer Books.

Davidson, Mary Frances, 1974. *The Dye-Pot.* Gatlinburg, Tenn.

DeVeaux, Jennie S., and Eugene B. Schultz, Jr. 1985. "Development of Buffalo Gourd as a Semiaridland Starch and Oil Crop." *Economic Botany* 39 (4): 454–72.

DiPalma, Joseph R., M.D. 1981. "Mushroom Poisoning." *Afp—Clinical Pharmacology* 23 (5): 169–72.

Dockstader, Frederick J. 1984. *Weaving Arts of the North American Indian.* New York: Thomas Y. Crowell.

Doebley, John F. 1984. "Seeds of Wild Grasses: A Major Food of Southwestern Indians." *Economic Botany* 38 (1): 52–64.

Duke, James A. 1981. *Handbook of Legumes of World Economic Importance.* New York: Plenum Press.

Dyer, Anne. 1976. *Dyes From Natural Sources.* Newton, Mass.: Charles I. Branford.

Elias, Thomas S., and Peter A. Dykeman. 1982. *Field Guide to North American Edible Wild Plants.* New York: Outdoor Life Book.

Elliott, Douglas B. 1976. *Roots: An Underground Botany and Forager's Guide.* Old Greenwich, Conn.: Chatham Press.

Ellis, Jennie Faye. 1973. "Poisonous Dye Plants." *Shuttle, Spindle, and Dyepot* 4 (2): 46–47.

Ellis, Michael D., ed. 1978. *Dangerous Plants, Snakes, Arthropods, and Marine Life.* Hamilton, Ill.: Drug Intelligence.

Emboden, William. 1979. *Narcotic Plants.* New York: Macmillan.

Erickson, David W., and James S. Lindzey. 1983. "Lead and Cadmium in Muskrat and Cattail Tissues." *Journal of Wildlife Management* 47 (2): 550–55.

Fernald, Merritt L., Alfred C. Kinsey, and Reed C. Rollins. 1958. *Edible Wild Plants of Eastern North America.* New York: Harper and Row.

Fisher, Alexander A., M.D. 1973. *Contact Dermatitis.* Philadelphia: Lea and Febiger.

Fleming, Gary. 1975. *A Guide to Plants of Central Texas With Edible, Medicinal, and Ecological Value.* Unpublished manuscript.

Foster, Kenneth E., R. Leslie Rawles, and Martin M. Karpiscak. 1980. "Biomass Potential in Arizona." *Desert Plants* 2 (3): 197–200.

Gaertner, Erika E. 1979. "The History and Use of Milkweed." *Economic Botany* 33 (2): 119–23.

Gentry, Howard Scott. 1982. *Agaves of Continental North America.* Tucson: University of Arizona Press.

Gerber, Fred, and Willi Gerber. 1972a. "Notes on Vegetable Dyeing." *Handweaver and Craftsman* 23 (3): 28–32.

———. 1972b. "Cochineal as a Domestic Dyestuff." *Handweaver and Craftsman* 23 (6): 16–21.

Gibbons, Euell. 1962. *Stalking the Wild Asparagus.* New York: David McKay.

———. 1964. *Stalking the Blue-eyed Scallop.* New York: David McKay.

———. 1966. *Stalking the Healthful Herbs.* New York: David McKay.

Gibbons, Euell, and Gordon Tucker. 1979. *Euell Gibbons' Handbook of Edible Wild Plants.* Virginia Beach, Va.: Donning.

Gilbert, Lawrence. 1984. Interview in *On Campus* (University of Texas at Austin publication), March 5.

Gillis, William T. 1971. "The Systematics and Ecology of Poison-Ivy and the Poison-Oaks." *Rhodora* 73: 72–237, 370–443, 465–540.

Gilpin, Laura. 1968. *The Enduring Navaho.* Austin: University of Texas Press.

Grae, Ida. 1974. *Nature's Colors.* New York: Macmillan.

Grummer, Arnold E. 1980. *Paper by Kids.* Minneapolis: Dillon Press.

Hackett, Clive, and Julie Carolane, eds. 1982. *Edible Horticultural Crops.* Sydney: Academic Press.

Hansen, Albert A. 1925. "Two Fatal Cases of Potato Poisoning." *Science* 61: 340.

Hanson, C. H., ed. 1972. *Alfalfa Science and Technology.* Madison, Wis.: American Society of Agronomy.

Hardin, James W., and Jay M. Arena, M.D. 1974. *Human Poisoning From Native and Cultivated Plants.* Durham, N.C.: Duke University Press.

Harlan, Jack R. 1975. *Crops and Man.* Madison, Wis.: American Society of Agronomy, Crop Science Society of America.

Harrington, H. D. 1972. *Western Edible Wild Plants.* Albuquerque: University of New Mexico Press.

Hart, Carol, and Dan Hart. 1976. *Natural Basketry.* New York: Watson-Guptill.

Hearne, Gladys. 1978. "Adventures in Dyeing Wood and Bark." *Shuttle, Spindle, and Dyepot* 9 (3): 20–22.

Heiser, Charles B., Jr. 1969. *Nightshades: The Paradoxical Plants.* San Francisco: W. H. Freeman and Co.

———. 1976. *The Sunflower.* Norman: University of Oklahoma Press.

Held, Shirley E. 1977. "Dyeing With Tree Blossoms." *Shuttle, Spindle, and Dyepot* 8 (4): 41–44.

Hill, Albert F. 1952. *Economic Botany.* New York: McGraw-Hill.

Hodge, W. H., and H. H. Sineath. 1956. "The Mexican Candelilla Plant and Its Wax." *Economic Botany* 10 (2): 134–54.

Holm, LeRoy G., Donald L. Plucknett, Juan V. Pancho, and James P. Herberger, 1977. *The World's Worst Weeds.* Honolulu: University Press of Hawaii.

Hope, Paul. 1985. "Mesquite." *Texas Parks and Wildlife* 43 (9): 11–16.

Horrobin, David. 1981. "Evening Primrose Oil: Miracle Worker of the Eighties." *Health Quarterly* (September–October).

Hunter, Dard. 1967. *Paper-making: The History and Technique of an Ancient Craft.* New York: Alfred A. Knopf.

Irwin, Howard S. 1975. *Roadside Flowers of Texas.* Austin: University of Texas Press.

James, George W. 1937. *Indian Blankets and Their Makers.* New York: Tudor.

James, Wilma Roberts. 1973. *Know Your Poisonous Plants.* Healdsburg, Calif.: Naturegraph.

Jamieson, George S. 1943. *Vegetable Fats and Oils.* New York: Reinhold.

Keeler, Richard F., Kent R. Van Kampen, and Lynn F. James, eds. 1978. *Effects of Poisonous Plants on Livestock.* New York: Academic Press.

Kent, Kate. 1961. *The Story of Navaho Weaving*. Phoenix: McGrew Printing.

Kinghorn, A. Douglas, ed. 1979. *Toxic Plants*. New York: Columbia University Press.

Kingsbury, John M. 1964. *Poisonous Plants of the United States and Canada*. Englewood Cliffs, N.J.: Prentice-Hall.

———. 1965. *Deadly Harvest*. New York: Holt, Rinehart and Winston.

Kirk, Donald R. 1975. *Wild Edible Plants of the Western United States*. Healdsburg, Calif.: Naturegraph.

Kohman, E. F. 1939. "Oxalic Acid in Foods and Its Behavior and Fate in the Diet." *Journal of Nutrition* 18 (3): 233–46.

Kreig, Margaret B. 1964. *Green Medicine*. Chicago: Rand McNally.

Krochmal, Arnold, and Connie Krochmal. 1974. *The Complete Illustrated Book of Dyes From Natural Sources*. Garden City, N.Y.: Doubleday.

Lampe, Kenneth F., and Rune Fagerström. 1968. *Plant Toxicity and Dermatitis*. Baltimore: Williams and Wilkins.

Lancaster, Mark, Richard Storey, and Nathan Bower. 1983. "Nutritional Evaluation of Buffalo Gourd: Elemental Analysis of Seed." *Economic Botany* 37 (3): 306–9.

Larkin, Tim., 1983. "Herbs Are Often More Toxic Than Magical." *FDA Consumer* 17 (8): 4–11.

Latorre, Dolores L., and Felippe A. Latorre. 1977. "Plants Used by the Mexican Kickapoo Indians." *Economic Botany* 31 (3): 340–57.

Lesch, Alma. 1970. *Vegetable Dyeing*. New York: Watson-Guptill.

LeStrange, Richard. 1977. *A History of Herbal Plants*. New York: Arco.

Lewis, Walter H., and Memory P. F. Elvin-Lewis. 1977. *Medical Botany*. New York: John Wiley and Sons.

Lloyd, Francis E. 1911. *Guayule: A Rubber Plant of the Chihuahuan Desert*. Washington, D.C.: Carnegie Institute.

Loughmiller, Campbell, and Lynn Loughmiller. 1984. *Texas Wildflowers*. Austin: University of Texas Press.

Lust, John. 1974. *The Herb Book*. New York: Benedict Lust.

Luther, George. 1979. "Down Home Country Lore." *Mother Earth News*, no. 59: 52.

Lynch, Daniel. 1981. *Native and Naturalized Woody Plants of Austin and the Hill Country*. Austin, Tex.: St. Edward's University.

MacNeish, Richard S. 1971. "Speculation About How and Why Food Production and Village Life Developed in the Tehuacán Valley, Mexico." *Archeology* 24 (4): 307–15.

Martin, Franklin W., and Henry Y. Nakasone. 1970. "The Edible Species of *Passiflora*." *Economic Botany* 24 (3): 333–43.

Martinez, Maximino. 1959. *Plantas Utiles de la Flora Mexicana*. Mexico: Andres Botas.

Mason, C. F., and R. J. Bryant. 1975. "Production, Nutrient Content, and Decomposition of *Phragmites communis* and *Typha angustifolia*." *Journal of Ecology* 63 (1): 71–95.

Mason, John. 1963. *Paper Making as an Artistic Craft*. Leicester, England: Twelve by Eight Press.

Maxwell, Ross A. 1968. *The Big Bend of the Rio Grande*. Guidebook no. 7. Austin: University of Texas Bureau of Economic Geology.

McClure, F. A. 1966. *The Bamboos*. Cambridge: Harvard University Press.

McDonald, Rebecca C., and B. C. Wolverton. 1980. "Comparative Study of Wastewater Lagoon With and Without Water Hyacinth." *Economic Botany* 34 (2): 101–10.

McLaughlin, Steven P., and Joseph J. Hoffman. 1982. "Survey of Bio-crude-Producing Plants from the Southwest." *Economic Botany* 36 (3): 323–39.

Medsger, Oliver Perry. 1966. *Edible Wild Plants*. New York: Macmillan, Collier.

Meeuse, Bastiaan, and Sean Morris. 1984. *The Sex Life of Flowers*. New York: Facts on File.

Meijer, Willem. 1974. "May Apple: A Potential New Cash-Crop Plant of Eastern North America." *Economic Botany* 28 (1): 68–72.

Meilach, Dona Z. 1974. *A Modern Approach to Basketry With Fibers and Grasses*. New York: Crown.

Mitchell, Andrew S. 1982. "Economic Aspects of the Malvaceae in Australia." *Economic Botany* 36 (3): 313–22.

Mitchell, John, M.D., and Arthur Rook, M.D. 1979. *Botanical Dermatology*. Vancouver: Greengrass.

Monsod, Godofredo G., Jr. 1979. *Man and the Water Hyacinth*. New York: Vantage Press.

Morton, Julia F. 1975. "Cattails: Weed Problem or Potential Crop?" *Economic Botany* 29 (1): 7–29.

National Academy of Sciences, 1975. *Herbal Pharmacology in the People's Republic of China.* Washington, D.C.

National Clearinghouse for Poison Control Centers. 1981. *NCPCC Bulletin* 25 (6).

Newcomb, W. W., Jr. 1961. *The Indians of Texas.* Austin: University of Texas Press.

Newman, Cathy. 1984. "Pollen: Breath of Life and Sneezes." *National Geographic* 166 (4): 490–521.

Niethammer, Carolyn. 1974. *American Indian Food and Lore.* New York: Macmillan.

———. 1983. "Tepary Cuisine." *Desert Plants* 5 (1): 8–10.

Orr, Robert T., and Margaret C. Orr. 1974. *Wildflowers of Western America.* New York: Alfred A. Knopf.

Peterson, Lee. 1977. *A Field Guide to Edible Wild Plants of Eastern and Central North America.* Boston: Houghton Mifflin.

Quel, J. A., M.D., ed. 1984. *Statistical Report of the Pollen and Mold Committee, 1984.* Milwaukee: American Academy of Allergy and Immunology.

Ricciuti, Edward R. 1978. *The Devil's Garden.* New York: Walker and Co.

Rickett, H. W. 1969. *Texas.* Vol. 3 of *Wildflowers of the United States.* New York: McGraw-Hill.

Ritchie, Gary A., ed. 1979. *New Agricultural Crops.* Boulder, Colo.: Westview Press.

Roberts, Helen H. 1972. *Basketry of the San Carlos Apache Indians.* Glorieta, N.Mex.: Rio Grande Press.

Robertson, Seonaid. 1973. *Dyes From Plants.* New York: Von Nostrand Reinhold.

Rodriguez, Barbara. 1985. Unpublished manuscript.

Russell, Sharman. 1983. "Tepary." *Mother Earth News,* no. 82: 70–71.

Samuel, Cheryl, and Carol Higgins. 1976. *Gentle Dyes.* (4727 Lake Washington Blvd. South, Seattle, Washington 98118.)

Sayre, Roxanna. 1986. "Creatures." *Audubon* 88 (2): 42.

Schery, Robert W. 1972. *Plants for Man.* Englewood Cliffs, N.J.: Prentice-Hall.

414

Schetky, Ethel Jane M., ed. 1964. *Dye Plants and Dyeing.* Brooklyn: Brooklyn Botanic Garden.

Schmutz, Ervin M., and Lucretia B. Hamilton. 1979. *Plants That Poison.* Flagstaff, Ariz.: Northland Press.

Seigler, D., F. Seaman, and Tom J. Mabry. 1971. "New Cyanogenetic Lipids from *Ungnadia speciosa.*" *Phytochemistry* 10 (2): 485–87.

Sheldon, Sam. 1980. "Ethnobotany of *Agave lecheguilla* and *Yucca carnerosana* in Mexico's Zona Ixtlera." *Economic Botany* 34 (4): 376–90.

Shepard, Robin. 1982. "Color Your Hair . . . Naturally." *Mother Earth News,* no. 74: 52–53.

Shurtleff, William, and Akiko Aoyagi. 1977. *The Book of Kudzu: A Culinary and Healing Guide.* Brookline, Mass.: Autumn Press.

Silverman, Maida. 1977. *A City Herbal.* New York: Alfred A. Knopf.

Simmonds, N. W., ed. 1976. *Evolution of Crop Plants.* London: Longman.

Simpson, B. B., ed. 1977. *Mesquite: Its Biology in Two Desert Ecosystems.* Stroudsburg, Pa.: Dowden, Hutchinson, and Ross.

Simpson, Benny. 1982. "Native Fruits of Texas." *Texas Wildflower Newsletter* 6 (3): 5–8; 6 (4): 3–7.

Smith, Jeffrey L., and Janice V. Perino. 1981. "Osage Orange: History and Economic Uses." *Economic Botany* 35 (1): 24–41.

Smith, Linda Joan. 1985. "The Shaker Basket." *Country Home* (August): 75–80.

Smith, Philip M. 1976. *The Chemotaxonomy of Plants.* London: Edward Arnold.

Smith, Sue M. 1983. *Natural Fiber Basketry.* Fort Worth, Tex.: Willow Bend Press.

Spencer, Neal R. 1984. "Velvetleaf, *Abutilon theophrasti:* History and Economic Importance in the United States." *Economic Botany* 38 (4): 407–16.

Sperry, Neil. 1982. *Complete Guide to Texas Gardening.* Dallas: Taylor.

Sperry, O. E., J. W. Dollahite, G. O. Hoffman, and B. J. Camp. 1964. *Texas Plants Poisonous to Livestock.* College Station: Texas Agricultural Extension Service, Texas A&M University.

Stahl, Carmine A. 1974. *Papa Stahl's Wild Stuff Cookbook.* Houston: Grass Root Enterprises.

Stanford, Jack W. 1976. *Keys to the Vascular Plants of the Texas Edwards Plateau and Adjacent Areas.* Brownwood, Tex.: Howard Payne University.

Starry, Roberta M. 1981. "North America's Wild Chokecherry." *Mother Earth News,* no. 70: 80—82.

Stephens, H. A. 1980. *Poisonous Plants of the Central United States.* Lawrence: Regents Press of Kansas.

Stroud, Robert. 1964. *Stroud's Digest on the Diseases of Birds.* Jersey City, N.J.: T.F.H.

Struever, Stuart, ed. 1971. *Prehistoric Agriculture.* Garden City, N.Y.: Natural History Press.

Summerfield, R. J., and A. H. Bunting, eds. 1978. *Advances in Legume Science.* Kew, Australia: Royal Botanic Gardens.

Swain, Tony, ed. 1972. *Plants in the Development of Modern Medicine.* Cambridge: Harvard University Press.

Tanner, Robert D., S. Shahid Hussain, Lindsey A. Hamilton, and Frederick T. Wolf. 1979. "Kudzu: Potential Agricultural and Industrial Resource." *Economic Botany* 33 (4): 400—12.

Tate, Joyce L., ed. 1972. *Cactus Cook Book,* Riverside, Calif.: Cactus and Succulent Society of America.

Thompson, Anson E. 1985. "New Native Crops for the Arid Southwest." *Economic Botany* 39 (4): 436—53.

Thurstan, Violetta. 1968. *The Use of Vegetable Dyes.* Leicester, England: Dryad Press.

Thurston, E. Laurence. 1974. "Morphology, Fine Structure, and Ontogeny of the Stinging Emergence of *Urtica dioica.*" *American Journal of Botany* 61 (8): 809—17.

Thurston, E. Laurence, and Nels R. Lersten. 1969. "The Morphology and Toxicology of Plant Stinging Hairs." *Botanical Review* 35 (4): 393—405.

Turner, B. L. 1959. *The Legumes of Texas.* Austin: University of Texas Press.

University of Texas Rare Plant Study Center. 1974. *Rare and Endangered Plants Native to Texas.* Austin.

Van Emon, Jeanette, and James N. Seiber. 1985. "Chemical Constituents and Energy Content of Two Milkweeds." *Economic Botany* 39 (1): 47—55.

416

Vines, Robert A. 1960. *Trees, Shrubs, and Woody Vines of the South-west.* Austin: University of Texas Press.

Wahrmund, Peggy Stieler. n.d. *Natural Dyes of the Texas Hill Country.* Austin: Texas Tourist Development Agency.

Wang, Shih-chi, and J. B. Huffman. 1981. "Botanochemicals: Supplements to Petrochemicals." *Economic Botany* 35 (4): 369–82.

Warnock, Barton H. 1970. *Wildflowers of the Big Bend Country, Texas.* Alpine, Tex.: Sul Ross State University.

―――. 1974. *Wildflowers of the Guadalupe Mountains and the Sand Dune Country, Texas.* Alpine, Tex.: Sul Ross State University.

Watt, John M., and Maria G. Breyer-Brandwijk. 1962. *The Medicinal and Poisonous Plants of Southern and Eastern Africa.* Edinburgh, Scotland: E. and S. Livingstone.

Wauer, Ronald H. 1973. *Naturalist's Big Bend.* Sante Fe, N.Mex.: Peregrine Productions.

Weddle, Ferris. 1980. "The Delicious Lilies." *Mother Earth News,* no. 64: 146.

Weidenmüller, Ralf. 1980. *Papermaking.* San Diego: Thorfinn International.

Weishuhn, Larry L. 1980. "Munching on Prickly Pear." *Texas Parks and Wildlife* 38 (2): 14–15.

Wells, Larry J. 1982. "The Sego Lily and the Death Camas." *Mother Earth News,* no. 76: 76–77.

Weniger, Del. 1970. *Cacti of the Southwest.* Austin: University of Texas Press.

―――. 1984. *Cacti of Texas and Neighboring States.* Austin: University of Texas Press.

Wickler, Wolfgang. 1968. *Mimicry in Plants and Animals.* New York: McGraw-Hill.

Williams, Sharon Flynn. 1983. "Plant Pigments and Natural Dyeing." *Shuttle, Spindle, and Dyepot* 14 (2): 32–33.

Wills, Mary Motz, and Howard S. Irwin. 1961. *Roadside Flowers of Texas.* Austin: University of Texas Press.

Wodehouse, Roger P. 1971. *Hayfever Plants.* New York: Hafner.

Wolverton, B. C. 1982. "Hybrid Wastewater Treatment System Using Anaerobic Microorganisms and Reed." *Economic Botany* 36 (4): 373–80.

Wolverton, B. C., and Rebecca C. McDonald. 1981. "Energy From Vascular Plant Wastewater Treatment Systems." *Economic Botany* 35 (2): 224–32.

Zennie, Thomas M., and C. Dwayne Ogzewella. 1977. "Ascorbic Acid and Vitamin A Content of Edible Wild Plants of Ohio and Kentucky." *Economic Botany* 31 (1): 76–79.

Index

449